THE CRITICISM OF HENRY FIELDING

Edited by

IOAN WILLIAMS

Lecturer in English Literature
University of Warwick

NEW YORK

BARNES & NOBLE, INC.

First published in Great Britain 1970

Published in the United States of America 1970
by Barnes & Noble Inc., New York, N.Y. 10003

SBN 389 01084 7

Printed in Great Britain

Contents

PART NINE: THE 'NEW PROVINCE' OF WRITING

Preface

The material in this volume has been selected from the whole range of Fielding's work in order to represent, with the minimum of repetition, every aspect of his social and literary criticism. In choosing from among the many possible items, precedence has been given to those which have not been republished or which are difficult for the ordinary reader to obtain. The seventy-two items have been arranged in nine sections which correspond to rough divisions of the subject-matter. Chronological order has been preserved within each section. The three Appendices contain material to which, for different reasons, the reader may find it convenient to refer. Editorial notes have been placed at the end of the volume, but those provided by Fielding have been put at the foot of the page.

As a general rule, the texts have been reproduced from first or second editions. The exceptions are: *The Champion*, up to June 19, 1740, for which the two-volume reprint of 1741 was used; *Tom Jones*, which was taken from the Henley edition (1903); *Covent Garden Journal*, which was based on G. E. Jensen's edition (1915, reprinted 1964). All the texts have been subjected to minor correction with regard to spelling and italicization of titles.

Acknowledgements

In preparing this edition I have benefited greatly from being able to use the work of W. L. Cross and G. E. Jensen and found reason to be grateful for that of J. T. Hillhouse, M. C. Battestin, M. Locke and R. P. C. Mutter, and I would like to acknowledge my debt to them. I am grateful also to Professor G. K. Hunter and Mr. C. Rawson, to Mr. K. Stubbs and Mr. Harold Beaver for the help which they have so willingly given me, and to the staff of the Library of the University of Warwick. I should like to thank the Library of the British Museum and the Bodleian Library for permission to reproduce material in their possession. I should also like to thank the editors of the *Yale Review* and Mr. E. L. McAdam, Jr., for permission to reproduce Fielding's letter to Richardson.

Introduction

Henry Fielding began his literary career in 1728 at the age of twenty-one; he continued writing until 1754, when he died in Lisbon at the age of forty-seven. This relatively short period of twenty-six years was one of ceaseless activity and incredible diversity. Fielding was dramatist, poet, translator, essayist, political journalist, pamphleteer, novelist, theatre-manager, lawyer and magistrate. In the first nine years of his career he produced twenty-five burlesques, farces, political satires and comedies, until his activity was brought to a sudden end by the Stage Licensing Act of 1737. He then turned to more general activities, became a lawyer and a political journalist. In his first newspaper, *The Champion*, which he ran from November 1739 to June 1741, he attacked the Walpole Government and defined his position as moralist and social critic. In 1741 he published *Shamela*, his burlesque of Samuel Richardson's *Pamela* (1740), following it in 1742 with his own first novel, *Joseph Andrews*. His next major publication was the three-volume *Miscellanies* (1743), in which he published the first version of his *Jonathan Wild*, his Essays, *On Conversation* and *On the Knowledge of the Characters of Men*, together with poems on good nature and true greatness.

Between 1743 and 1749 Fielding was again concerned with political journalism, this time in support of an Administration of which he approved. In defence of the Government of the Pelhams he conducted *The True Patriot* from November 1745 to June 1746. After the Jacobite Rebellion was over, he defended the 'Patriot' Administration against the attacks of the Jacobites and malcontents in the columns of *The Jacobite's Journal* between December 1747 and November 1748. Only six months later he published *Tom Jones*, and at about the same time became Justice of the Peace for Westminster and Middlesex. In spite of the enormous exertions which his duties as magistrate involved, he followed *Tom Jones* with *Amelia* in December 1751 and began his last newspaper, *The Covent Garden Journal*, which he kept up almost single-handed from January to November 1752. His last finished work, *The Journal of A Voyage to Lisbon*, was published posthumously in 1755.

A selection of Fielding's criticism must draw on the whole range of his work, including material from plays, novels and newspapers. W. L. Cross rightly said of him: 'His works, though they all unroll in different patterns, were really all of a piece. No writer was ever more uniformly himself.'[1] Whatever type of literature he was writing, his attitude was the same: 'the Covetous, the Prodigal, the Ambitious, the Voluptuous, the Bully, the Vain, the Hypocrite, the Flatterer, the Slanderer' called aloud for his vengeance. Everything he wrote proceeded from a conviction that 'whatever is wicked, hateful, absurd, or ridiculous, must be exposed and punished before this Nation is brought to that Height of Purity and good Manners to which I wish to see it exalted'.[2] For him social converse, political behaviour, the conduct of the theatre, acting and writing, were all subject to the laws which governed human life and thought. He considered it his function to bring the powers of judgement and intelligence to bear on human behaviour, and though far from reactionary, he saw himself as a guardian of intellectual and moral standards in a world which seemed increasingly to ignore or distort them.

This conviction Fielding shared with many of the best among his contemporaries and predecessors, and he drew immediate inspiration from their works. He held many opinions in common with Addison, Steele, Shaftesbury, Swift and Pope, borrowed many of the devices which he used most frequently from the *Spectator*, the *Tatler*, *The Tale of a Tub* (1704), *The Art of Sinking* (1728) and *The Dunciad* (1729 and 1742), and associated himself with the authors of the Scriblerus papers by direct quotation and the pseudonym Scriblerus Secundus.[3] Behind *Jonathan Wild* (1743) *The Beggar's Opera* (1728) is clearly visible, behind *The Tragedy of Tragedies* (1731) the Duke of Buckingham's *The Rehearsal* (1672). His earliest work and his latest, his farces, his essays in *The Champion* and *The Covent Garden Journal*, his attacks on confusion, false criticism, pedantry, pertness, the debasement of the stage, the unscrupulous tricks of booksellers, the grotesque self-seeking of politicians are closely related to the work of the English satirists from Samuel Butler to Alexander Pope.

Moreover, Fielding's relationship with other English writers of Restoration and early eighteenth-century England was closer than superficial resemblances of style and subject would indicate. His whole mental outlook was deeply affected by the events in recent history and the related developments in religious thought and literary taste. His mind took shape under the influence of the philosophers, moralists, historians and divines who preceded him. An early reading of Hobbes, Locke, Shaftesbury, Clarendon and the Restoration divines had given him, in common with many of his contemporaries, a tendency to value most highly those political, intellectual and social qualities which seemed able to ensure stability of government and freedom and security in social life. Repugnance for enthusiasm, excess and distortion of any kind was deep in Fielding's mind. His idea of political rectitude was founded on the principles of the Whig Revolution of 1688 and his concept of healthy religious devotion on a feeling that it was necessary to adapt the demands of Christianity to fit the context of civilized life.

In spite of the trouble he often took to define terms and outline principles, Fielding was not primarily interested in theory. He touched on theory in order to establish a standard by which practice in literature and life might be assessed. He defined comedy in order to explain his own practice in *Joseph Andrews*; he defined humour in order to undermine the prevailing taste for crude and malicious raillery, slander and indecency, which he felt was the cause of the public rejection of *Amelia*; he discussed good breeding only in order to justify his statements about the standards of proper behaviour in political and social converse. His prevailing purpose was the dual one of establishing moral standards and providing his society with a procedure for distinguishing truth from falsehood. As a critic of society and as an ironist, he had a great deal in common with Swift and Pope, but he differed from them both in temperament and outlook. He took the stance of the satirist for a purpose, and was ready to change it for that of the moralist as circumstances demanded, to shift from seriousness to wit, from irony to direct statement, not only within the essay, but even within the paragraph and the sentence. He borrowed Swift's techniques and used them without severity: like Pope, he maintained a distance between himself and his subject, but he did not care to maintain it as a principle of art. Like Pope, again, he attacked Colley Cibber and praised Ralph Allen, but, though he promised his prose *Dunciad*, he never wrote it.

At the basis of Fielding's attitude to life and art was the firm and constant religious conviction which led one modern critic to call him 'the most important Christian moralist of his generation',[4] and which allowed him to avoid the Deistic and materialistic tendencies of several of the writers whom he most admired. The unique quality of his work rests upon his consistent attempt to relate this faith to the other convictions which he had derived from his thorough classical reading and his keen awareness of the lessons taught by recent political and religious history. He insisted that life should be governed by the 'only Laws which have corresponded throughout with Truth and common Sense, those Laws I mean which come from the Voice of God himself',[5] but he interpreted them according to his idea of the needs of his own day, rejecting poverty as a mode of life and urging temperate devotion, self-knowledge and the practical exercise of virtue. In his determination to project an idea of virtue in which reason and moderation were clearly evident, and at the same time to defend it against the attacks of the materialists, he ran the risk of undermining his own position. His justification of self-restraint, on the grounds that it permitted the only true enjoyment of pleasure, came perilously close to confusing the idea of virtue with that of vice itself:

> The temperate Man tastes and relishes Pleasure in a Degree infinitely superior to that of the voluptuous. . . . The virtuous and temperate Man only hath Inclination, hath Strength; and, (if I may be indulged in the Expression) hath Opportunity to enjoy all his Passions.[6]

More frequently, however, Fielding's fear of intolerance and repugnance for materialism caused him to assert the principle of charity as the basis of all religion and virtue. Without charity, he said, a Christian is unworthy of the name:

> Upon the whole, I hope, it appears, that a Person void of Charity, is unworthy the Appellation of a Christian; that he hath no Pretence to either Goodness or Justice, or even to the Character of Humanity; that he is in honest Truth, an Infidel, a Rogue, and a Monster, and ought to be expelled not only from the Society of Christians, but of Men.[7]

Christianity, Fielding argued, 'hath taught us something beyond what the Religion of Nature and Philosophy could arrive at' and is infinitely higher than Nature.[8] Yet a prerequisite for Christianity, he continued, was mere good nature, the 'aimiable Quality, which, like the Sun, gilds over all our other Virtues'.

> Good-nature is a Delight in the Happiness of Mankind, and a Concern at their Misery, with a Desire, as much as possible, to procure the former, and avert the latter; and this, with a constant Regard to Desert.
>
> . . . This only makes the dutiful Son, the affectionate Brother, the

> tender Husband, the indulgent Father, the kind Master, the faithful Friend, and the firm Patriot. This makes us gentle without Fear, humble without Hopes, and charitable without Ostentation, and extends the Power, Knowledge, Strength, and Riches of Individuals to the Good of the Whole. It is (as *Shakespeare* calls it) the Milk, or rather the Cream of Human Nature, and whoever is possessed of this Perfection should be pitied, not hated for the Want of any other. Whereas all other Virtues without some Tincture of this, may be well called *Splendida Peccata*. . . .[9]

Good nature so defined, Fielding believed, would be manifested in good breeding, which itself 'may be reduced to that concise, comprehensive rule in scripture—Do unto all men as you would they should do unto you'.[10]

By good breeding, or, as he sometimes called it, good manners, Fielding meant far more than the term usually included. He referred to a state of mind rather than to superficial behaviour, so that he would not 'have scrupled to call Socrates a well-bred man . . .'.[11] In a footnote to his translation of Aristophanes' *Plutus* (1742), he explained it as the opposite to a state of mind 'distracted with Passions, and polluted with Vices . . . in a maimed and distorted condition', 'the Good Order of the Mind' which 'When we translate . . . *Good-manners*, we must be understood in the true and genuine, and not the corrupted use of the Word'.[12] Good breeding, or 'artificial good-nature', was a mental condition which corresponded to the moral condition designated by charity. It showed itself in words, actions and writings and was outraged not merely by impoliteness, but by corruption in politics, rowdyism in the theatre, servility and falsehood in the world of letters, and by slander, cruelty and indecency of all kinds.

Good order within the individual and good order in the State both consisted in the preservation of a harmony of parts, and for this it was necessary that some means should exist for determining the true nature and relationships of things. This means, Fielding thought, was provided by the 'distinguishing faculty' in man, which enabled him to perceive truth and detect falsehood. At different times he spoke of this faculty as sense, wisdom, or discernment, but most frequently he followed Hobbes and Locke in calling it judgement. He considered it the dominant faculty of the mind, which was antipathetic to error, falsehood, impropriety and excess. It was required even for the exercise of good nature:

> . . . Good-nature requires a distinguishing Faculty, which is another Word for Judgement, and is perhaps the sole Boundary between Wisdom and Folly; it is impossible for a Fool, who hath no distinguishing Faculty, to be good-natured.[13]

Judgement was, likewise, a condition of good breeding. It was the one essential mental quality without which the good order of the mind or of society would be impossible.

Genius itself, Fielding argued, consisted in the possession of a certain degree and kind of judgement. Genius lies, he stated in *Tom Jones,* in 'those powers of the mind, which are capable of penetrating into all things within our reach and knowledge, and of distinguishing their essential differences'. These powers are 'no other than invention and judgement' (No. 68). Similarly, Fielding defined 'real Taste' as a 'nice Harmony between the Imagination and the Judgement' (No. 33), because the reader and the critic require some measure of the qualities of genius in order to appreciate its productions. Several times he pointed out, with varying degrees of seriousness, that 'This word critic is of Greek derivation, and signifies judgement' (No. 69). In Longinus he found judgement and imagination to such a degree that the reader would be puzzled to decide which 'shone the brighter in that inimitable Critic' (No. 69). Another such writer was Lucian, whose invention and perception Fielding praised most highly and whose style he confessed to using as a model for his own. In contrast, he scorned the critical tribe of his own day, from whom the distinguishing faculty was absent and whose activities served as a dramatic reminder of the process of degeneration which appeared to be going on around him.

In Fielding's mind the function of judgement was intimately connected with a sense of the need to distinguish the true nature and meanings of words. Whenever he was involved in the process of criticism, in constructing an argument, or establishing standards of appreciation, he turned for illustration to the chapter of Locke's *Essay Concerning the Human Understanding* where the dangers arising from the abuse of words were discussed. Locke said:

> . . . language being the great conduit, whereby men convey their discoveries, reasonings, and knowledge, from one to another; he that makes an ill use of it, though he does not corrupt the fountains of knowledge, which are things in themselves; yet he does, as much as in him lies, break or stop the pipes, whereby it is distributed to the public use and advantage of mankind.[14]

The detection of such 'ill use' was the function of the critic, and the frequency with which Fielding refers to Locke's discussion indicates the extent to which he felt that it was his own function. It was from this standpoint that he attacked Colley Cibber, whose misuse of words he thought was connected with devious attempts to defend the reputation of Sir Robert Walpole. Similarly, when he was defining good breeding, justifying his parody of the modern preface, describing good nature, introducing his Modern Glossary, or whenever, in short, he was trying to establish truth or attacking perversion, he recurred to the same illustration. Whether in jest or in earnest, he approached his victims in the same way and attempted to clarify the distinctions which had been blurred by dullness and vice.

Lord Shaftesbury had suggested that the natural tool of such a critic was wit:

> Truth, 'tis supposed, may bear all lights; and one of those principal lights, or natural mediums, by which things are to be viewed, in order to a thorough recognition, is ridicule itself, or that manner of proof, by which we discern whatever is liable to just raillery in any subject.[15]

Fielding followed Shaftesbury, and many of the other authors whom he most admired, in calling wit 'a Fiery test of Truth' (No. 5), and he would have agreed with his contemporary, Anthony Collins, who spoke of it as 'the True Method to bring things to a Standard':

> . . . to fix the Decency and Propriety of Writing, to teach Men how to write to the Satisfaction of the ingenious polite, and sensible Part of Mankind: for Decency and Propriety will stand the Test of Ridicule, and triumph over all the false Pretences to Wit; and Indecency and Impropriety will sink under the Trial of Ridicule, as being capable of being baffled by Reason, and fitly ridicul'd.[16]

On the other hand, Fielding was not as optimistic as Collins about the inevitability of the victory of truth and wisdom. The particular vice of his own age, as he explained in his defence of *Amelia* (No. 72), was the irresponsible encouragement of humour for its own sake and the substitution for true wit of slander, indecency, 'Blasphemy, Treason, Bawdry and Scandal'. Consequently, he felt it necessary to stress the subordination of wit to morality.

The writers whom Fielding most frequently praised were those who used wit in order to reveal the true nature of things. Rather than give an unqualified approval to wit or humour, he insisted that they be used, as they had been by Jonathan Swift, 'to the noblest Purposes', in conjunction with judgement, charity and good nature. His obituary notice of Swift in *The True Patriot* emphasizes the Dean's practical charity as well as his intellectual qualities, and mentions the latter only as they were used in the service of Truth:

> A few days since died in Ireland, Dr. Jonathan Swift, Dean of St. Patrick's in Dublin. A Genius who deserves to be ranked among the first whom the World ever saw. He possessed the Talents of a Lucian, a Rabelais, and a Cervantes, and in his Works exceeded them all. He employed his Wit to the noblest Purposes, in ridiculing as well Superstition in Religion as Infidelity, and the several Errors and Immoralities which sprung up from time to time in his Age; and lastly, in the Defence of his Country, against several pernicious Schemes of wicked Polititians. Nor was he only a Genius and a Patriot; he was in private life a good and charitable Man, and frequently lent Sums of Money without Interest to the Poor and Industrious.[17]

In the last analysis, Fielding was always prepared to put moral above intellectual qualities, and this was the basis of his distinction between Rabelais and Aristophanes on the one hand and Lucian, Cervantes, Molière, Shakespeare and Swift on the other (No. 33).

Laughter itself, Fielding thought, was potentially dangerous. Hobbes had described it as arising from a sudden discovery of superiority:

> *Sudden glory*, is the passion which maketh those *grimaces* called LAUGHTER; and is caused either by some sudden act of their own, that pleaseth them; or by the apprehension of some deformed thing in another, by comparison whereof, they suddenly applaud themselves.[18]

Laughter so conceived is antipathetic to good nature, and it was in this light that Fielding considered it in his *Essay on the Knowledge of the Characters of Men*:

> Mr. *Hobbes* tells us, that Laughter arises from Pride, which is far from being a good-natured Passion. And though I would not severely discountenance all Indulgence of it, since Laughter, while confined to Vice and Folly is no very cruel Punishment on the Object, and may be attended with good Consequences to him; yet we shall, I believe,

find, on a careful Examination into its Motive, that it is not produced from Good-nature.[19]

The strength of Fielding's antipathy to the cruder forms of wit is indicated by the fact that he chose to describe the personal form of raillery known as 'roasting' as the opposite to good nature:

> If we consider this Diversion in the worst Light, it will appear to be no other than a Delight in seeing the Miseries, Misfortunes, and Frailties of Mankind display'd; and a Pleasure and Joy conceiv'd in their Sufferings therein. A Pleasure, perhaps, as inhuman, and which must arise from a Nature as thoroughly corrupt and diabolical, as can possibly pollute the Mind of Man (No. 31; cf. above, p. xiv).

In the wrong hands, wit and humour were dangerous weapons, subversive of all civilized values:

> When Religion, Virtue, Honour, Modesty, or Innocence, are attack'd by this Weapon, it becomes a Sword in a Madman's Hand, and, instead of deserving our Praise, is really an Object of utter Detestation and Horror.[20]

Yet the potential of wit in the hands of the true critic remained, and rather than accept wholeheartedly the Hobbesian description of laughter, Fielding tried to develop ideas of comedy and humour which were not antagonistic to good nature and which preserved the distinction between virtue and vice.

In the Preface to *Joseph Andrews*, Fielding substituted for Hobbes's 'sudden glory' the statement that laughter arises from the discovery of a disparity between appearance and reality. The only true sense of the ridiculous, he argues here, is affectation, in either of its two main branches of vanity and hypocrisy, the latter of which causes a more intense feeling of ridicule because it is farther from the truth (No. 59). Laughter arising from the discovery of falsehood, unlike that which is produced by a sense of superiority, is easily reconcilable with good nature and good breeding, both of which rest on the capacity to discern the nature of things. Fielding qualifies his idea further by making an absolute distinction between affectation which involves the ridiculous and that which merely shocks. Neither the discovery of vice nor the revelation of virtuous poverty, he argues, can produce a sense of the ridiculous (No. 59). A similar point is made ironically in the course of one of Fielding's discussions of humour in the *Covent Garden Journal.*

'Nothing', he says, is 'so insettled and incertain, as our Notion of Humour in general', and begins a catalogue of some types of crude and malicious behaviour to which the name is usually given (No. 35). The source of real humour, Fielding explains in another paper (No. 36), is the tendency in individuals to give rein to their own desires and passions at the expense of those rules and conventions which have been created to facilitate and improve the social converse of mankind. Following Sir William Temple, William Congreve and Ben Jonson, he defines humour as proceeding from 'a Violent Bent or Disposition of the Mind to some particular point', which may alternatively be described as the excessive development of some parts of the mind at the expense of others. Independently of these authorities, he attributes it either to a lack of education among the refined classes, which permits in the individual a pampering of 'those inordinate Desires, which . . . are the true Seeds of Humour in the Human Mind', or to the rise of people from the lower classes who have not had time to acquire good breeding.

To the basic definition of humour which he derived from his predecessors, Fielding then adds a clause which ensures that the distinction between vice and virtue is kept in mind. Excess in itself, he says, is absolutely bad, and those who give themselves to it are likely to become ridiculous. In this category, presumably, he would put his own Parson Adams, whose case is covered only in part by the definition of comedy which he gives in the Preface to *Joseph Andrews*. Adams's animadversions against vanity, his claims to knowledge of the world and his sermonizing on the subject of immoderate grief are all comic by virtue of our realization that they do not correspond to the reality of his own character and behaviour. His character as a whole, which also causes a sense of the ridiculous, only does so by means of his excessive virtue, simplicity and innocence, which are often demonstrated inappropriately:

> Excess, says Horace, even in the pursuit of Virtue, will lead a wise and good Man into Folly and Vice. So will it subject him to Ridicule; for into this, says the judicious Abbé Bellegarde, a man may tumble headlong with an excellent Understanding, and with the most laudable Qualities. Piety, Patriotism, Loyalty, Parental Affection, &c., have all afforded Characters of Humour for the Stage (No. 36).

Mere excess, however, may produce viciousness rather than humour, and Fielding takes care to introduce a qualifying clause concerning the manner as opposed to the degree of selfishness involved. According to the way it operates, the excessive 'Passion or Humour of the Mind' becomes either ridiculous or detestable. 'It is the same ambition which raises our Horror in *Macbeth* and our Laughter at the drunken sailors in the *Tempest*'; 'Nero had the art of making Vanity the Object of Horror, and Domitian, in one instance at least, made Cruelty ridiculous'.

> By Humour, then I suppose, is generally intended a violent Impulse of the Mind, determining it to some one peculiar Point, by which a Man becomes ridiculously distinguished from all other Men (No. 36).

The reasoning behind this definition is closely related to that which characterizes Fielding's discussion of literary matters. Common to his thought on both subjects—indeed, on all subjects—there is a strong distaste for excess and disproportion of any kind. The quality which he seems to have appreciated most highly was the order and design which Parson Adams describes in his apostrophe to Homer (No. 38). Even Homer, however, was open to criticism on the grounds of what Rapin called 'an Intemperance of Words', and Cervantes, for some of whose qualities Fielding had the highest admiration, was to be compared unfavourably with Charlotte Lennox, because 'the Adventures are much less extravagant and incredible in the English than in the Spanish Performance' (No. 40).

In an early essay in *The Champion*, Fielding laid down the rule governing moderation and balance in literary affairs in terms very similar to those which he used years later in his discussion of humour:

> As there was never a better Rule for the Conduct of Human Life than what is convey'd in that excellent short Sentence—*Ne quid nimis*, so there is none so seldom observed . . . . Men often become ridiculous or odious by over-acting even a laudable part: For Virtue itself, by growing too exuberant, and (if I may be allowed a Metaphor) by running to Seed changes its very Nature, and becomes a most pernicious Weed of a most beautiful Flower (No. 26).

It was on this principle that he composed the scale of values represented by the thermometer of wit (No. 27). On this scale good sense (or judgement), is the middle point. One may rise above it to true wit, by means of 'a Degree of Fire', or sink below it to gravity because of a lack of intellectual liveliness. Immoderate rise and fall alike lead to faults which are objectionable, ultimately to the extremes of madness and stupidity. On the scale of literary quality which corresponds to this scale of wit in the writer, the place of good sense is taken by Nature, as the proper subject of art, that of madness by fantasy, that of stupidity by dullness. Good sense and nature throughout Fielding's work are presented as standards, deviation from which is permissible only on the strictly limited conditions which genius alone can fulfil.

Fielding frequently refers to a similar scale of values in his later work, in the introductory chapters to *Tom Jones* and the Preface to *The Journal of A Voyage to Lisbon*, where he defines true history as the middle point between the extremes of prosaic dullness and fantasy. In the Preface he expresses most strongly his dislike for any departure from the standards of Nature, criticizing Homer and Hesiod, and saying that he would have preferred them to have written in prose. At the same time, he attacks the opposite abuse of mere reportage, condemning those travel-writers 'who waste their time and paper with recording things and facts of so common a kind that they challenge no other right of being remembered than as they had the honour of having happened to the author' (No. 30). The same criteria are used throughout the introductory chapters to *Tom Jones*, where he criticizes Homer for his use of the marvellous and condemns the dullness of contemporary historians. In Book II, ch. i, when he is discussing his 'new province of writing', he distinguishes between the true history and the work of 'the painful and voluminous historian' whose accounts 'in reality very much resemble a newspaper, which consists of just the same number of words, whether there be any news in it or not' (No. 63). On the same principle, in the Preface to *Joseph Andrews* and *Tom Jones*, Book IV, ch. i, as well as in the Preface to *The Journal* . . ., he condemns 'those idle romances' which present an idealized view of human life, 'the productions not of nature but of distempered brains' . . .

Fielding attacked dullness and fantasy throughout his career, though after he had become a novelist he more frequently discussed those forms which affected the writing of fictitious history. Even then he was not prepared to persist in his theory beyond the reach of sense. Homer and Hesiod might be open to theoretic criticism, but their work was clearly to be distinguished from the heroic romances and praised because it possessed that sheer imaginative power which can make fiction into reality:

> They are not indeed so properly said to turn reality into fiction, as fiction into reality. Their paintings are so bold, their colours so

> strong, that every thing they touch seems to exist in the very manner they represent it . . . (No. 30).

On the whole, however, the novelist insisted that 'Man . . . is the highest subject . . . which presents itself to the pen of our historian, or of our poet . . .' (No. 66). Good sense, moderation and order were essential parts of his concept of literary art.

These qualities are shown nowhere more clearly than in Fielding's own reaction to the work of his rival for contemporary success. *Shamela* followed shortly after Richardson's *Pamela* (1740), and showed Fielding's strong distaste for what he saw as the imposition of a specious morality on a human situation which actually revealed something different, and for the ridiculously overdone 'puffing' of the introductory material. A few months later the appearance of *Joseph Andrews* showed that Fielding thought a burlesque of his fellow novelist's crude and over-simple presentation of human nature was an appropriate starting-point for a work which investigated the full complexity of the relationship between theory and fact in human behaviour. When *Clarissa* appeared, his reaction was equally swift and equally positive, and he praised it with sincere enthusiasm: 'Such Simplicity, such Manners, such deep Penetration into Nature; such Power to raise and alarm the Passions, few writers, either antient or modern, have been possessed of' (No. 42). His letter of praise might, one imagines, have satisfied even Richardson. Yet Fielding's enthusiasm was never blind. His last remarks, in the Preface to *The Journal of A Voyage to Lisbon*, suggest a detached judgement of Richardson's theory of fiction and his crude idea of the relationship between morality and art.

No two works of genius could be much farther apart in character tendency and tone than *Clarissa* and *Tom Jones*, and it is a strong indication of the quality of Fielding's mind that he was not only able, but also willing, to recognize the achievement of his rival. In literary matters Fielding's judgement was always unbiased and rarely at fault. He respected the ancients, but not at the expense of the moderns; he praised his friends, but chose no enemies except those whose work he was obliged to criticize. Though he never presented his readers with a system of philosophy or a system of criticism, he did provide them with the materials to make one for themselves. From authors who wrote in Latin, Greek, French, Spanish and English, on literature history, divinity, law and ethics, he drew together the materials of an attitude to life and presented them with a consistent unity of tone. The high praise which one of these writers gave to another belongs equally to him:

> [He] would teach us, to conquer our Vices, to rule our Passions, to follow Nature, to limit our Desires, to distinguish True from False, and Ideas from Things, to forsake Prejudice, to know throughly the Principles, and Motives of all our Actions, and to shun that Folly which is in all Men, who are bigotted to the Opinions they have imbibed under their Teachers, which they keep obstinately without examining whether they are well-grounded. In a Word, he endeavours to make us happy for our selves, agreeable, and faithful to our Friends, easie, discreet, and honest to all, with whom we are oblig'd to live.[21]

As a description of Fielding himself, this passage is deficient only in that it makes no reference to the quality which is perhaps, after all, most uniquely his—the firm combination of wit and and dignity which pervades his criticism and his fiction. *Tom Jones*, which demands such flexibility of response, which contains so elusive a balance between moral judgement and play of mind, is the highest achievement of Fielding's art. But the reader of *Tom Jones* will recognize these qualities in Fielding's essays and Prefaces, throughout the criticism which deals with the world he saw before him, as well as that which he so completely created. What Fielding wrote at one time and in one way is the best background to what he wrote at another. His criticism of literature and manners is the best introduction to his 'criticism of life'.

Chronological List of Contents

Appendices

PART ONE

The Theatre

Fielding thought of the theatre as an important social centre, a reflector of cultural and moral standards rather than a source of mere entertainment. For people like John Rich and Theophilus Cibber, who used it merely as a means of making money, with no concern for cultural standards, he had a sharp contempt. Though his career as a dramatist was virtually over by 1737, he maintained his interest in the stage until the end of his life and kept up his theatrical connections—especially through his friendship with David Garrick. The prefaces, essays and letters in this section all belong to the early part of his career, but the opinions which they contain are to be met with elsewhere in Fielding's work. Many other references to plays, actors, actresses and incidents at the theatre are scattered throughout this volume.

1 Preface to *Tom Thumb: a Tragedy . . .*

1730

Fielding's mock-reply to the critics of *Tom Thumb . . .* is the vehicle of his earliest attack on Colley Cibber. It is also directed at modern prefaces in general.

Tom Thumb . . . was first performed on April 24, 1730, and a text of this version was published on the same day. This was followed by a second edition on May 1, 1730, from which the Preface reprinted here is taken.

A Preface is become almost as necessary to a Play, as a Prologue: It is a Word of Advice to the Reader, as the other to the Spectator: And as the Business of a Prologue is to commend the Play, so that of the Preface is to Compliment the Actors.

A Preface requires a Style entirely different from all other Writings; A Style for which I can find no Name in either the Sublime of *Longinus*, or the Profund [*sic*] of *Scriblerus*:[1] which I shall therefore venture to call the Supernatural, after the celebrated Author of *Hurlothrumbo:* who, tho' no Writer of Prefaces, is a very great Master of their Style.[2]

As *Charon* in *Lucian* suffers none to enter his Boat till stripped of every thing they have about them,[3] so should no Word by any means enter into a Preface till stripped of all its Ideas. Mr. *Lock* complains of confused Ideas in Words, which is entirely amended by suffering them to give none at all:[4] This may be done by adding, diminishing, or changing a Letter, as instead of *Paraphernalia*, writing *Paraphonalia*: For a Man may turn *Greek* into Nonsense, who cannot turn Sense into either *Greek* or *Latin*.[5]

A Second Method of stripping Words of their Ideas is by putting half a dozen incoherent ones together: Such as *when the People of our Age shall be Ancestors*, &c.[6] By which means one discordant Word, like a surly Man in Company, spoils the whole Sentence, and makes it entirely Prefatical.

Some imagine this Way of Writing to have been originally

introduced by *Plato*, whom *Cicero* observes to have taken especial Pains in wrapping up his Sentiments from the Understandings of the Vulgar.[7] But I can in no wise agree with them in this Conjecture, any more than their deriving the Word Preface, *quasi Plaface, a Plato*: whereas the Original Word is *Playface, quasi Players Face*: and sufficiently denotes some Player, who was as remarkable for his *Face*, as his Prefaces, to have been the Inventor of it.

But that the Preface to my Preface be not longer than that to my Play: I shall have done with the Performances of others, and speak a Word or two of my own.

This Preface then was writ at the Desire of my Bookseller, who told me that some Elegant Criticks had made three great Objections to this Tragedy: which I shall handle without any Regard to Precedence: And therefore I begin to defend the last Scene of my Play against the third Objection of these* *Kriticks*, which is, to the destroying all the Characters in it, this I cannot think so unprecedented as these Gentlemen would insinuate, having my-self known it done in the first Act of several Plays: Nay, it is common in modern Tragedy for the Characters to drop, like the Citizens in the first Scene of *Œdipus*, as soon as they come upon the Stage.[8]

Secondly, they Object to the killing a Ghost. This (say they) far exceeds the Rules of Probability; perhaps it may; but I would desire these Gentlemen seriously to recollect, whether they have not seen in several celebrated Plays, such Expressions as these, *Kill my Soul, Stab my very Soul, Bleeding Soul, Dying Soul, cum multis aliis*, all which visibly confess that for a Soul or Ghost to be killed is no Impossibility.

As for the first Objection which they make, and the last which I answer, *viz.* to the Subject, to this I shall only say, that it is in the Choice of my Subject I have placed my chief Merit.

It is with great Concern that I have observed several of our (the *Grubstreet*) Tragical Writers, to Celebrate in their Immortal Lines the Actions of Heroes recorded in Historians and Poets, such as *Homer* or *Virgil, Livy* or *Plutarch*, the Propagation of whose Works is so apparently against the Interest of our Society; when the Romances, Novels, and Histories, *vulgo* call'd Story-Books, of our own People, furnish such abundant and proper Themes for their Pens, such are *Tom Tram, Hickathrift*, &c.[9]

And here I congratulate my Cotemporary[10] Writers, for their having enlarged the Sphere of Tragedy: The ancient Tragedy seems to have

**Prefatical Language.*

had only two Effects on an Audience, *viz*. It either awakened Terror and Compassion, or composed those and all other uneasy Sensations, by lulling the Audience in an agreeable Slumber. But to provoke the Mirth and Laughter of the Spectators, to join the Sock to the Buskin, is a Praise only due to Modern Tragedy.

Having spoken thus much of the Play, I shall proceed to the Performers, amongst whom if any shone brighter than the rest it was *Tom Thumb*. Indeed such was the Excellence thereof, that no one can believe unless they see its Representation, to which I shall refer the Curious: Nor can I refrain from observing how well one of the Mutes set off his Part: So excellent was his Performance, that it out-did even my own Wishes: I gratefully give him my share of Praise, and desire the Audience to refer the whole to his beautiful Action.

And now I must return my hearty Thanks to the Musick, who, I believe, played to the best of their Skill, because it was for their own Reputation, and because they are paid for it: So have I thrown little *Tom Thumb* on the Town, and hope they will be favourable to him, and for an Answer to all Censures, take these Words of *Martial*,

> *Seria cum possim, quod delectantia malim*
> *Scribere, Tu, Causa es*——[11]

2 Preface to *The Tragedy of Tragedies; or the Life and Death of Tom Thumb the Great*

1731

This Preface is a parody of the techniques of some contemporary critics, especially John Dennis and Richard Bentley, with burlesque references to heroic tragedy.

The expanded version of *Tom Thumb* was first performed on March 24, 1731, and published the same day, 'With Annotations of H. SCRIBLERUS SECUNDUS'. This was the third version and the fourth edition of the play.

H. Scriblerus Secundus,
HIS PREFACE

The Town hath seldom been more divided in its Opinion, than concerning the Merit of the following Scenes. Whilst some publickly affirmed, That no Author could produce so fine a Piece but Mr. *P*[*ope*], others have with as much Vehemence insisted, That no one could write any thing so bad, but Mr. *F*[*ielding*].

Nor can we wonder at this Dissention about its Merit, when the learned World have not unanimously decided even the very Nature of this Tragedy. For tho' most of the Universities in *Europe* have honoured it with the Name of *Egregium & maximi pretii opus, Tragœdiis tam antiquis quam novis longe anteponendum;*[1] Nay Dr. *B*[*entley*] hath pronounced, *Citiùs Mavii Aneadem quam Scribleri istius Tragœdiam hanc crediderim cujus Autorem Senecam ipsum tradidisse haud dubitârim;*[2] and the great Professor *Burman* hath stiled *Tom Thumb, Heroum omnium Tragicorum facilè Principem.*[3] Nay, tho' it hath, among other Languages, been translated into *Dutch*, and celebrated with great Applause at *Amsterdam* (where Burlesque never came) by the Title of *Mynheer Vander Thumb*, the Burgomasters receiving it with that reverent and silent Attention, which becometh an Audience at a deep Tragedy: Notwithstanding all this, there have not been wanting some who have represented these Scenes in a ludicrous Light; and Mr. *D[ennis]*[4] hath been heard to say with some Concern, That he wondered a Tragical and Christian Nation would permit a Representation on its Theatre, so visibly designed to ridicule and extirpate everything that is Great and Solemn among us.

This learned Critick and his Followers, were led into so great an Error, by that surreptitious and piratical Copy, which stole last Year into the World;[5] with what Injustice and Prejudice to our Author, I hope will be acknowledged by every one who shall happily peruse this genuine and original Copy. Nor can I help remarking, to the great Praise of our Author, that however imperfect the former was, still did even that faint Resemblance of the true *Tom Thumb*, contain sufficient Beauties to give it a Run of upwards of Forty Nights, to the politest Audiences. But, notwithstanding that Applause which it received from all the best Judges, it was as severely censured by some few bad ones: and I believe, rather maliciously than ignorantly, reported to have been intended a Burlesque on the loftiest Parts of Tragedy, and designed to banish what we generally call fine Things from the Stage.

Now, if I can set my Country right in an Affair of this Importance, I shall lightly esteem any Labour which it may cost. And this I the rather undertake, First, as it is indeed in some measure incumbent on me to vindicate myself from that surreptitious Copy before mentioned, published by some ill-meaning People, under my Name: Secondly, as knowing my self more capable of doing Justice to our Author, than any other Man, as I have given my self more Pains to arrive at a thorough Understanding of this little Piece, having for ten Years together read nothing else; in which Time, I think I may modestly presume, with the Help of my *English* Dictionary, to comprehend all the Meanings of every Word in it.

But should any Error of my Pen awaken *Clariss Bentleium*[6] to enlighten the World with his Annotations on our Author, I shall not think that the least Reward or Happiness arising to me from these my Endeavours.

I shall wave at present, what hath caused such Feuds in the learned World, Whether this Piece was originally written by *Shakespear*, tho' certainly that, were it true, must add a considerable Share to its Merit; especially, with such who are so generous as to buy and to commend what they never read, from an implicit Faith in the Author only: A Faith! which our Age abounds in as much, as it can be called deficient in any other.

Let it suffice, that the *Tragedy of Tragedies*, or, *The Life and Death of Tom Thumb*, was written in the Reign of Queen *Elizabeth*. Nor can the Objection made by Mr. *D*[*ennis*], That the Tragedy must then have been antecedent to the History, have any Weight, when we consider, That tho' the *History of Tom Thumb*, printed by and for *Edward M*[*idwinte*]*r*, at the Looking Glass on *London-Bridge*,[7] be of a later Date; still must we suppose this History to have been transcribed from some other, unless we suppose the Writer thereof to be inspired: A Gift very faintly contended for by the Writers of our Age. As to this History's not bearing the Stamp of Second, Third or Fourth Edition, I see but little in that Objection; Editions being very uncertain Lights to judge of Books by: And perhaps Mr. *M*[*idwinte*]*r* may have joined twenty Editions in one, as Mr. *C*[*url*]*l* hath ere now divided one into twenty.[8]

Nor doth the other Argument, drawn from the little Care our Author hath taken to keep up to the Letter of the History, carry any greater Force. Are there not Instances of Plays, wherein the History is so perverted, that we can know the Heroes whom they celebrate by no other Marks than their Names? Nay, do we not find the same Character placed by different Poets in such different Lights, that we can discover not the least Sameness, or even Likeness in the Features. The *Sophonisba* of *Mairet*, and of *Lee*, is a tender, passionate, amorous Mistress of *Massinissa*; *Corneille*, and Mr. *Thomson* give her no other Passion but the Love of her Country, and make her as cool in her affection to *Massinissa* as to *Syphax*. In the two latter, she resembles the Character of Queen *Elizabeth*; in the two former, she is the Picture of *Mary* Queen of *Scotland*. In short, the one *Sophonisba* is as different from the other, as the *Brutus* of *Voltaire*, is from the *Marius* Jun. of *Otway*; or as the *Minerva* is from the *Venus* of the Ancients.[9]

Let us now proceed to a regular Examination of the Tragedy before us. In which I shall treat separately of the Fable, the Moral, the Characters, the Sentiments, and the Diction. And first of the

Fable; which I take to be the most simple imaginable; and, to use the Words of an eminent Author, 'One, regular and uniform, not charged with a Multiplicity of incidents, and yet affording several Revolutions of Fortune; by which the Passions may be excited, varied, and driven to their full Tumult of Emotion.'[10]——Nor is the *Action* of this Tragedy less great than uniform. The Spring of all, is the Love of *Tom Thumb* for *Huncamunca*, which causeth the Quarrel between their Majesties in the first Act; the Passion of Lord *Grizzle* in the Second; the Rebellion, Fall of Lord *Grizzle* and *Glumdalca*, Devouring of *Tom Thumb* by the Cow, and that bloody Catastrophe in the Third.

Nor is the *Moral* of this excellent Tragedy less noble than the *Fable*; it teaches these two instructive Lessons, *viz.* That human Happiness is exceeding transient and, That Death is the certain End of all Men; the former whereof is inculcated by the fatal End of *Tom Thumb*; the latter by that of all the other Parsonages [*sic*].

The *Characters* are, I think, sufficiently described in the *Dramatis Personæ*; and I believe we shall find few Plays, where greater Care is taken to maintain them throughout, and to preserve in every Speech that characteristical Mark which distinguishes them from each other. 'But (says Mr. *D*[*ennis*]) how well doth the Character of *Tom Thumb*, whom we must call the Hero of this Tragedy, if it hath any Hero, agree with the Preceps of *Aristotle*, who defineth *Tragedy to be the Imitation of a short, but perfect Action, containing a just Greatness in it self*, &c. What Greatness can be in a Fellow, whom History relateth to have been no higher than a Span?' This Gentleman seemeth to think, with Serjeant *Kite*, that the Greatness of a Man's Soul is in Proportion to that of his Body,[11] the contrary of which is affirmed by our *English* Physognominical Writers. Besides, if I understand *Aristotle* right, he speaketh only of the Greatness of the Action, and not of the Person.

As for the *Sentiments* and the *Diction*, which now only remain to be spoken to; I thought I could afford them no stronger Justification than by producing parallel Passages out of the best of our *English* Writers. Whether this Sameness of Thought and Expression which I have quotted [*sic.*] from them, proceeded from an Agreement in their Way of Thinking; or whether they have borrowed from our Author, I leave the Reader to determine. I shall adventure to affirm this of the Sentiments of our Author; That they are generally the most familiar which I have ever met with, and at the same Time delivered with the highest Dignity of Phrase; which brings me to speak of his *Diction*.——Here I shall only beg one Postulatum, *viz.* That the greatest Perfection of the Language of a Tragedy is, that it is not to be understood; which granted (as I think it must be) it will necessary [*sic*] follow, that the only ways [*sic*] to avoid this, is by being too high or too low for the Understanding, which will comprehend every thing within its Reach. Those two Extremities of Stile Mr. *Dryden* illustrates by the familiar Image of two Inns, which I shall term the Aerial and the Subterrestrial.[12] *Horace* goeth farther, and sheweth when it is proper to call at one of these Inns, and when at the other.

Telephus & Peleus, cum pauper & exul uterque,
Projicit Ampullas & Sesquipedalia Verba.[13]

That he approveth of the *Sesquipedalia Verba*, is plain; for had not *Telephus & Peleus* used this sort of Diction in Prosperity, they could not have dropt it in Adversity. The Aerial Inn, therefore (says *Horace*) is proper only to be frequented by Princes and other great Men, in the highest Affluence of Fortune; the Subterrestrial is appointed for the Entertainment of the poorer Sort of People only, whom *Horace* advises,

—— *dolere Sermone pedestri.*[14]

The true Meaning of both which Citations is, That Bombast is the proper Language for Joy, and Doggrel for Grief, the latter of which is literally imply'd in the *sermo pedestris*, as the former is in the *Sesquipedalia Verba.*

Cicero recommendeth the former of these; *Quid est tam furiosum vel tragicum quàm verborum sonitus inanis, nullâ subjectâ Sententiâ neque Scientiâ.*[15] What can be so proper for Tragedy, as a Set of big sounding Words, so contrived together, as to convey no Meaning; which I shall one Day or other prove to be the Sublime of *Longinus*. *Ovid* declareth absolutely for the latter Inn:

Omne genus scripti gravitate Tragœdia vincit.[16]

Tragedy hath of all Writings the greatest Share in the *Bathos*, which is the Profound of *Scriblerus*.

I shall not presume to determine which of these two Stiles be properer for Tragedy.—— It sufficeth that our Author excelleth in both. He is very rarely within sight through the whole Play, either rising higher than the Eye of your Understanding can soar, or sinking lower than it careth to stoop. But here it may perhaps be observed, that I have given more frequent Instances of Authors who have imitated him in the Sublime, than in the contrary. To which I answer, First, Bombast being properly a Redundancy of Genius, Instances of this Nature occur in Poets, whose Names do more Honour to our Author, than the Writers in the Doggrel, which proceeds from a cool, calm, weighty way of thinking. Instances whereof are most frequently to be found in Authors of a lower Class. Secondly, That the Works of such Authors are difficultly found at all. Thirdly, That it is a very hard Task to read them, in order to extract these Flowers from them. And Lastly, It is very often difficult to transplant them at all; they being like some

Flowers of a very nice Nature, which will flourish in no Soil but their own: For it is easy to transcribe a Thought, but not the Want of one. The *Earl of Essex*,[17] for Instance, is a little Garden of choice Rarities, whence you can scarce transplant one Line so as to preserve its original Beauty. This must account to the Reader for his missing the Names of several of his Acquaintance, which he had certainly found here, had I ever read their Works; for which, if I have not a just Esteem, I can at least say with *Cicero*, *Quæ non contemno, quippè quæ nunquam legerim.*[18] However, that the Reader may meet with due Satisfaction in this Point, I have a young Commentator from the University, who is reading over all the modern Tragedies, at five Shillings a Dozen, and collecting all that they have stole from our Author, which shall shortly be added as an Appendix to this Work.

3 Prolegomena to *The Covent Garden Tragedy*

1732

The Covent Garden Tragedy was first performed on June 1, 1732, and published on June 24, 1732. The text is reprinted from the first edition.

The Prolegomena consists mainly of a parody of *The Grub-street Journal's* attack on the play; see note 3, p. 13.

It hath been customary with Authors of extraordinary Merit, to prefix to their Works certain Commendatory Epistles in Verse and Prose, written by a Friend, or left with the Printer by an unknown Hand; which are of notable Use to an injudicious Reader, and often lead him to the Discovery of Beauties, which might otherwise have escaped his Eye. They stand like Champions at the Head of a Volume, and bid Defiance to an Army of Criticks.[1]

As I have not been able to procure any such Panegyricks on the following Scenes from my Friends, nor Leisure to write them myself, I have, in an unprecedented manner, collected such Criticisms as I could meet with on this Tragedy, and have placed them before it; but I must at the same time assure the Reader, that he may shortly expect an Answer to them.

The first of these Pieces, by its Date, appears to be the Production of some fine Gentleman, who plays the Critick for his Diversion, tho' he has not spoil'd his Eyes with too much reading. The latter will be easily discover'd to come from the Hands of one of that Club, which hath determin'd to instruct the World in Arts and Sciences, without understanding any; who

> With less Learning than makes Felons 'scape
> Less human Genius than God gives an Ape.

Are resolv'd

> ——— ——— —— ——— in Spite
> Of Nature, and their Stars to write.[2]

DEAR JACK,—Since you have left the Town, and no rational Creature except myself in it, I have applied myself pretty much to my Books; I have, besides the *Craftsman* and *Grubstreet Journals*, read a good deal in Mr. *Pope's Rape of the Lock*, and several Pages in *the History of the King of Sweden*, which is translated into *English*; but fancy, I shou'd understand more of it, if I had a better Map: for I have not been able to find out *Livonia* in mine.[3]

I believe, you will be surpriz'd to hear, I have not been twice at the Play-House since your Departure: But alas! what Entertainment can a Man of Sense find there now? The *Modern Husband*, which we hiss'd the first Night, had such Success, that I began to think it a good Play, till the *Grubstreet Journal* assured me it was not.[4] *The Earl of Essex*, which you know is my Favourite of all *Shakespeare's* Plays, was acted the other Night; but I was kept from it by a damn'd Farce which I abominate, and detest so much, that I have never either seen it, or read it.

Last *Monday* came out a new Tragedy, called, *The Covent-Garden Tragedy*, which I believe, I may affirm to be the worst that ever was written. I will not shock your good Judgment by any Quotations out of it. To tell you the Truth, I know not what to make of it: One wou'd have guess'd from the Audience, it had been a Comedy: For I saw more People laugh than cry at it. It adds a very strong Confirmation to your Opinion, That it is impossible, any thing worth reading shou'd be written in this Age.

St. *James's* Coffee-House.[5]

I am, &c

A CRITICISM on the *Covent-Garden Tragedy*, originally intended for the *Grubstreet Journal*

I have been long sensible, that the Days of Poetry are no more, and that there is but one of the Moderns, (who shall be nameless)[6] that can write either Sense or *English*, or Grammar: For this Reason, I have pass'd by unremarked, generally unread, the little, quaint, short-lived Productions of my Cotemporaries: For it is a Maxim with my Bookseller, that no Criticism on any Work can sell, when the Work itself does not.

But when I observe an Author growing into any Reputation, when I see the same *Play*, which I had liberally hiss'd the first Night, advertised for a considerable Number of Nights together; I then begin to look about me, and to think it worth criticizing on: A Play that runs twelve Nights, will support a temperate Critick as many Days.

The Success of the *Tragedy of Tragedies*, and the *Modern Husband* did not only determine me to draw my Pen against those two Performances, but hath likewise engaged my Criticism on every thing which comes from the Hands of that Author, of whatever nature it be,

Seu Græcum sive Latinum,[7]

The *Covent-Garden Tragedy* bears so great an Analogy to the Tragedy of *Tom Thumb*, that it needs not the Author's Name to assure us from what Quarter it had its Original. I shall beg leave therefore to examine this Piece a little, even before I am assured what Success it will meet with. Perhaps, what I shall herein say, may prevent its meeting with any.

I shall not here trouble the Reader with a laborious Definition of Tragedy drawn from *Aristuttle* or *Horase*, for which I refer him to those Authors. I shall content myself with the following plain Proposition. 'That a Tragedy is a Thing of five Acts, written Dialogue-wise, consisting of several fine Similies, Metaphors, and Moral Phrases, with here and there a Speech upon Liberty. That it must contain an Action, Characters, Sentiments, Diction, and a Moral.' Whatever falls short of any of these, is by no means worthy the Name of a Tragedy.

Quæ Genus aut Flexum variant, quæcunque novato
Ritu deficiunt superantve, Heteroclita sunto.[8]

I shall proceed to examine the Piece before us on these Rules, nor do I doubt to prove it deficient in them all,

Quæ sequitur manca est Numero Casuque Propago.[9]

As for an Action, I have read it over twice, and do solemnly aver, I can find none, at least none worthy to be called an Action. The Author, indeed, in one Place seems to promise something like an Action, where *Stormandra*, who is enraged with *Lovegirlo*, sends *Bilkum* to destroy him, and at the same time threatens to destroy herself! But alas! what comes of all this Preparation!—Why, *parturiunt montes*[10]—the Audience is deceived according to Custom, and the two murdered People appear in good Health: for all which great Revolution of Fortune, we have no other Reason given, but that the one has been run through the Coat, and the other has hung up her Gown instead of herself.—*Ridiculum*!

The Characters, I think, are such as I have not yet met with in

Tragedy: I believe all Monsters of the Poet's own Brain. First, for the Character of Mother *Punchbowl*; and, by the way, I cannot conceive why she is called Mother. Is she the Mother of any Body in the Play? No. From one Line one might guess she was a Bawd, *Leathersides* desires her to procure two Whores, *&c.* but then is she not continually talking of Virtue? How can she be a Bawd? In the third Scene of the second Act she appears to be *Stormandra's* Mother.

Punchb. *Daughter, you use the Captain too unkind.*

But, if I mistake not in the Scene immediately preceding, *Bilkum* and she have mother'd and son'd it several times. Sure, she cannot be Mother to them both, when she wou'd put them to bed together. Perhaps, she is Mother-in-law to one of them, as being married to her own Child: But of this the Poet shou'd (I think) have given us some better Assurance than barely intimating, that they were going to bed together, which People in this our Island have been sometimes known to do, without going to Church together.

What is intended by the Character of *Gallono*, is difficult to imagine. Either he is taken from Life, or he is not. Methinks, I cou'd wish he had been left out of the Dance,* nothing being more unnatural than to conceive so great a Sot to be a Lover of Dancing; nay, so great a Lover of Dancing, as to take that Woman for a Partner whom he had just before been abusing. As for the Characters of *Lovegirlo* and *Kissinda*, they are poor Imitations of the Characters of *Pyrrhus* and *Andromache* in the *Distrest Mother*, as *Bilkum* and *Stormandra* are of *Orestes* and *Hermione*.[11]

——*Sed quid morer istis.*[12]

As for Mr. *Leathersides*, he is indeed an Original, and such a one, as I hope will never have a Copy. We are told (to set him off) that he has learnt to read, has read Play-Bills, and writ the *Grubstreet Journal*. But how reading Play-Bills, and writing *Grubstreet* Papers can qualify him to be a Judge of Plays, I confess, I cannot tell.[13]

The only Character I can find entirely faultless, is the Chair-Man: for first we are assur'd,

*The Critic is out in this Particular, it being notorious *Gallono* is not in the Dance; but to shew how careful the Author was to maintain his Character throughout, the said *Gallono* during the whole Dance is employ'd with his Bottle and his Pipe.

He asks but for his Fare,

When the Captain answers him,

Thy Fare be damn'd.

He replies in the gentlest manner imaginable,

This is not acting like a Gentleman.

The Captain upon this threatens to knock his Brains out. He then answers in a most intrepid and justifiable Manner:

Oh! that with me, &c.

I cannot help wishing, this may teach all Gentlemen to pay their Chair-Men.

Proceed we now to the Sentiments. And here, to shew how inclin'd I am to admire rather than dislike, I shall allow the beautiful Manner wherein this Play sets out. The first five Lines are a mighty pretty Satyr on our Age, our Country, Statesman, Lawyers, and Physicians: What did I not expect from such a Beginning? But alas! what follows? No fine Moral Sentences, not a Word of Liberty and Property, no Insinuations, that Courtiers are Fools, and Statesmen Rogues. You have indeed a few Similies, but they are very thin sown.

Apparent rari nantes in Gurgite vasto.[14]

The Sentiments fall very short of Politeness every where; but those in the Mouth of Captain *Bilkum* breathe the true Spirit of *Billingsgate*. The Courtship that passes between him and *Stormandra* in the second Act is so extremely delicate, sure the Author must have serv'd an Apprenticeship there, before he cou'd have produced it. How unlike this was the beautiful manner of making Love in Use among the Ancients, that charming Simplicity of Manners which shines so apprently in all the Tragedies of *Plautus*,* where,

——*petit & prece blandus amicam.*[15]

But alas! how shou'd an illiterate Modern imitate Authors he has never read.

To say nothing of the Meanness of the Diction, which is some degrees lower than I have seen in any Modern Tragedy, we very often meet with Contradictions in the same Line. The Substantive is so far from shewing the Signification of its Adjective as the latter requires.

*I suppose these are lost, there remaining now no more than his Comedies.

An Adjective requires some Word to be joined to it to shew its Signification. vid. Accidence.[16]

That it very often takes away its Meaning, as particularly *virtuous Whore*. Did it ever enter into any Head before, to bring these two Words together. Indeed, my Friend, I cou'd as soon unite the Idea of your sweet self, and a good Poet.

Forth from your empty Head I'll knock your Brains.

Had you had any Brains in your own Head you never had writ this Line.

Yet do not shock it with a Thought so base.

Ten low Words creep here in a Line indeed.

——Monosyllabla nomina quædam,
Sal, sol, ren et splen, car, ser, vir, vas.——[17]

Virgal Rod, Grief-stung Soul, &c.

I wou'd recommend to this Author (if he can read) that wholesome little Treatise, call'd, *Gulielmi Lilii Monita Pædagogica*, where he will find this Instruction.

——*Veluti Scopulos, barbara verba fuge.*[18]

Much may be said on both sides of this Question;
Let me consider what the Question is;

Mighty pretty, faith! resolving a Question first, and then asking it.

——————thou hast a Tongue
Might charm a Bailiff to forego his Hold.

Very likely indeed! I fancy, Sir, if ever you were in the Hands of a Bailiff, you have not escap'd so easily.

Hanover-Square shall come to Drury-Lane.

Wonderful!

Thou shalt wear Farms and Houses in each Ear.

Oh! *Bavius*! oh! Conundrum, is this true! Sure the Poet exaggerates; What! a Woman wear Farms and Houses in her Ear, nay, in each Ear, to make it still the more incredible. I suppose these are poetical Farms and Houses, which any Woman may carry about her without being the heavier. But I pass by this and many other Beauties of the like Nature, *quæ lectio juxta docebit*,[19] to come to a little Word which is worth the whole Work.

Nor Modesty, nor Pride, nor Fear, nor REP.[20]

Quid sibi vult istud REP?—I have looked over all my Dictionaries, but in vain,

Nusquam reperitur in usu.[21]

I find indeed such a Word in some of the *Latin* Authors, but as it is not in the Dictionary, I suppose it to be obsolete. Perhaps it is a proper Name, if so, it shou'd have been in *Italicks*. I am a little inclined to this Opinion, as we find several very odd Names in this Piece, such as *Hackabouta*, &c.

I am weary of raking in this Dirt, and shall therefore pass on to the Moral, which the Poet very ingenuously tells us, is, he knows not what, nor any one else I dare swear. I shall however allow him this Merit, that except in the five Lines abovementioned, I scarce know any Performance more of a Piece. Either the Author never sleeps, or never wakes throughout.

ASS in præsenti perfectum format in avi.*[22]

Gul. Lilius* reads this Word with a single ***s.*

4 A Letter to *The Daily Post*

Monday, July 31, 1732; signed 'Philateles'

In this letter Fielding continues his defence against the attacks of *The Grubstreet Journal.*

Men' moveat Crinex Pantilius? aut crucier, quod
Vellicet absentem Demetrius? aut quod ineptus
Fannius Hermogenis lædat Conviva Tigelli?
HOR.[1]

SIR, I have read, with the Detestation it deserves, *an infamous Paper* call'd *the Grubstreet Journal:*[2] A Paper written by a Set of obscure Scriblers in the true Style and Spirit of Billingsgate, without either Learning, Wit, Decency, or often common Sense, and design'd to vilify and defame the Writings of every Author, except a few, whose Reputation is already too well establish'd for their Attacks, the Characters of whom they have, in the Opinion of all wise Men, blacken'd more with their Applause, than they have the others with their Censures.

The Love of *Scandal* is so *general an Appetite*, that no one can wonder at the Success of any Nonsense or Ribaldry which hath that to recommend it: To this all the infamous Scriblers of the Age owe a very comfortable Maintenance; and to this, and this only, the *Grubstreet Journal* owes its Being.

I believe every Man of good Sense and good Nature hath view'd with Abhorrence the scandalous undeserv'd Attacks, which they have lately so often repeated on a Gentleman, to whom the Town hath owed so much Diversion, and to whose Productions it has been so very favourable: An Attack which the Favour of the Town, and the good Reception he hath met with from the Players, hath drawn on him.

This Torrent of Ribaldry hath come abroad under several Names, such as *Dramaticus, Prosaicus, Publicus, &c.*[3] Whether these be the same Person is insignificant to determine; however, as they have all said the same Things, or rather call'd the same Names, an Answer to one will serve them all.

Mr. *Publicus* (whom by the ingenious and cleanly Metaphors he takes from the Streets, such as *Nastiness, Dirt, Kennel, Billingsgate, Stews, &c.* one would have imagin'd to have sometime thrown Dirt with other Instruments than a Pen) sets out with a most *notorious Falshood*, where he says *the two Performances* (*the Tragedy and Debauchees*)[4] met with the *universal Detestation of the Town*; whereas the *Debauchees* was received with as *great Applause* as was ever given on the Theatre: The Audience, which, on most Nights of its Representation, was as numerous as hath been known at that Season of the Year, seem'd in continual Good-Humour, and often in the highest Raptures of Approbation; and, except on the first Night, and ev'n then in one particular Scene, there never was one Hiss in the House.

He goes on, *Many that were there* (at the Tragedy) *had neither so much Taste, nor so little Modesty, as to sit it out*; as a Proof of which, three Ladies of the Town made their Exit in the first Act, while several of the first Rank and Reputation saw the Curtain fall: And this, had he not wanted common Sense, or common Honesty, he never had wonder'd, or pretended to have wonder'd, at; for why should any Person of Modesty be offended at seeing a Set of *Rakes* and *Whores* exposed and set in the most *ridiculous Light*? Sure the Scene of a Bawdy-house may be shewn on a Stage without shocking the most modest Woman; such I have seen sit out that Scene in the *Humorous Lieutenant*,[5] which is quoted and commended by one of the finest Writers of the last Age.

The Author is said to recommend *Whoring and Drunkenness*; how! Why a Rake speaks against Matrimony, and a Sot against Sobriety: So Molière in *Don Juan* recommends all Manner of Vices, and every Poet (I am sure every good one) that hath exposed a vicious Character, hath by this Rule contributed to debauch Mankind.

After the following excellent Remark, *Methinks the Writer tho' might as well have left Seas of Sulphur and Eternal Fire out of the mad Joke, for Fear he should meet with them in sober Sadness*, he proceeds to *the Epilogue*, where he says the Author tells the Ladies, without any Ceremony, *that there's no Difference betwixt the best of them, and the Bawdy-house Trulls they had been seeing on the Stage*; *and that pretend what they would, they were all a Parcel of Errant Whores*: This is *a most infamous Lye*, as any one who reads the Epilogue to the *Covent Garden Tragedy* must see, where nothing more is asserted, than that it is natural for one Sex to be fond of the other,

In short you (Men) are the Business of our Lives,
To be a Mistress kept the Strumpet strives,
And all the modest Virgins to be Wives.

This is the Compliment for which he hopes the Ladies will reward him the next Benefit Night. I am sorry any Man so well born as this Author, should be obliged to receive a Benefit Night; but should be much more sorry that he should depend on such Ladies as this Critick's Wife and Daughter to support it: However, the Wish is human enough, and shews how void of Malice the Writer is.

But he is not contented with representing the Poet as having abus'd the Ladies, (which I believe the Poet is so much a Gentleman as to think the worst Thing could be said of him) the Critick, after having terribly mangled the Play by tearing out several Passages, without inserting the whole Speeches, or making the Reader acquainted with the Character of the Speaker, accuses the Author with being free with the Bible; how free with the Bible? Why he has given a ridiculous Description of Purgatory: Well, and hath Purgatory any Thing more to do with the Bible than a Description of the Infernal Shades or Elisian Fields of the Heathens, or of the Paradise of the Mahometans. If the Critick had shewn as much Sense as Malice, I should have imagin'd the *Popish Priest* had peep'd forth in this Place; for sure *any Protestant, but a Nonjuring Parson, would be asham'd* to represent a Ridicule on Purgatory as a Ridicule on the Bible, or the Abuse of *Bigotted Fools* and *Roguish Jesuits* as an Abuse on Religion and the English Clergy.[6]

Not having vented enough of his Malice on these two Pieces, he adds, *Had I either Leisure or Inclination I could go a little farther with this Writer, and make it appear from all his Performances, that his Pen is not only void of Wit, Manners and Modesty, and likewise of the most common Rules of Poetry, but even Grammar*: This is a most barbarous Assertion; how true it is I shall leave to the Opinion of the World: As for the strict Rules which some Criticks have laid down, I cannot think an Author obliged to confine himself to them; for the Rules of Grammar, the Education which the Author of the *Debauchees* is known to have had, makes it unlikely he should err in those, or be able to write such wretched Stuff as, *I used to offer in its Behalf, &c.* A Sense wherein that Verb is never found in any good Writer of the English Language; nor indeed will its Derivation from the Latin *Utor* at all admit of it. Again, *Trulls they had been seeing*, Expressions a Boy in the second Form at Eaton would have been whipt for: As for the other Part of the Charge,

I must tell our Critick, there is a Vein of Good Humour and Pleasantry which runs through all the Works of this Author, and will make him and them amiable to a good-natur'd and sensible Reader, when the low, spiteful, false Criticisms of a *Grub-street Journal* will be forgotten.

Yours,

PHILALETHES.

P.S. Whether his Scurrility on the *Mock Doctor* be just or no, I leave to the Determination of the Town, which hath already declared loudly on its Side. Some Particulars of the Original are omitted, which the Elegance of an English Audience would not have endur'd; and which, if the Critick had ever read the Original, would have shewn him that the chaste *Molière* had introduced greater Indecencies on the Stage than the Author he abuses: I may aver he will find more in *Dryden*, *Congreve*, *Wycherly*, *Vanbrugh*, *Cibber*, and all our best Writers of *Comedy*, nay in the Writings of almost every Genius from the Days of *Horace*, to those of a most *Witty*, *Learned*, *and Reverend Writer* of *our own Age*.[7]

5 A Letter to *Common Sense*[1]: *or, The Englishman's Journal*, No. 16

Saturday, May 21, 1737; signed 'Pasquin'

Here Fielding is replying to an article in *The Daily Gazeteer* (supposed to have been written by Lord Hervey) in which, as the author of *Pasquin*, he was threatened with the introduction of censorship.

SIR,—As I have yet no Vehicle of my own,[2] I shall be obliged to you if you will give the following a Place in the next Stage, and am,

Your humble Servant.

To the Author of the *Gazetteer* of May 7.[3]

SIR,—Though the Paper you have attacked me in be so little read, that should you print a Libel in it, you could scarce be said to have published it; yet, as you are pleased to style yourself an Adventurer in Politicks, and as I know a certain Person whom that Appellation will exactly fit,[3] I shall take a little Notice of what you have advanced. This I undertake, not with Regard of what is written, but out of Respect to the Person whom I suppose the Author. And here, if I should happen to mistake you, I hope I shall not offend: For my Lord *Shaftesbury* well observes, that a judicious Beggar, when he addresseth himself to a Coach, always supposeth that there is a Lord in it; seeing, that should there be no Lord there, a private Gentleman will never be offended by the Title.[4]

You set out, Sir, with a pretty Panegyrick on the Lenity of the Administration, whence you draw this Conclusion, That it is ungenerous to attack it, because it will not crush you for so doing. *To abuse the Lenity of Power, when Men know it will not hurt them* (say you) *is like talking Obscenity to a Woman who will not defend herself, and* MUST *hear it.* The Comparison between the Attack of a Ministry, and that of a Woman, might afford some pleasant Remarks; I shall only say, I suppose you do not mean an old Woman, seeing, that to talk a little smuttily to such, would be no great Insult, if the common Saying be true, which however I do not believe, that all old Women love B[awd]y.

You are pleased to say, Sir, that *no Argument whatever can be alledged to support the bringing of Politicks on the Stage*. If you mean by Politicks, those Secrets of Government which, like the *Mysteries* of the *Bona Dea*,[6] are improper to be beheld by vulgar Eyes, such as Secret Service, &c. I must answer, your Caution is unnecessary, at least to me, who cannot expose to others, what I have not found out myself. But if by your Politicks, you mean a general Corruption (one of the greatest Evils (you are pleased to own) our Constitution is subject to) I cannot think such Politicks too sacred to be exposed. But *Pasquin* was not (as you insinuate) the first Introducer of Things of this Kind; we have several Political Plays now extant: And had you ever read *Aristophanes*, you would know that the gravest Matters have been try'd this Way. A Method which a great Writer (I think, Mr. *Bayle*) seems to approve; where he represents Ridicule as a kind of Fiery Trial, by which Truth is most certainly discovered from Imposture.[7] Indeed, I believe, there are no Instances of bringing Politicks on the Stage 'in those Neighbouring Nations' where, you say, that 'we may see disguised Informers in almost every Publick Place, with blank *Lettres de Cachet*, ready to fill up with the Names of such as dare barely inquire, in a manner different from the Sense of the Court, into the State of Affairs, and a *Bastile* always open to receive them:' Nor where you tell us, that 'a Holy Inquisition, and the Gallies, offer their Service to the *State*, as well as to Religion.'

But pray, Sir, what do you intend by mentioning these? I hope not to threaten us, nor to insinuate that any Thing will make it *necessary* to introduce such damned Engines of Tyranny among us.

But you seem to think, Sir, that to ridicule Vice, is to serve its Cause. And you mention the late ingenious Mr. *Gay*, who, you say, in his *Beggars Opera*[8] hath made Heroes and Heroines of Highwaymen and Whores. Are then Impudence, Boldness, Robbery, and picking Pockets the Characteristicks of a Hero? Indeed, Sir, we do not always approve what we laugh at. So far from it, Mr. *Hobbes* will tell you that Laughter is a Sign of Contempt.[9] And by raising such a Laugh as this against Vice, *Horace* assures us we give a sorer Wound, than it receives from all the Abhorrence which can be produced by the gravest and bitterest Satire.[10] You will not hardly, I believe, persuade us, how much soever you may desire it, that it is the Mark of a great Character to be laughed at by a whole Kingdom.

I shall not be industrious to deny, what you are so good to declare, that I am buoy'd up by the greatest Wits, and finest Gentlemen of the Age; and Patroniz'd by the Great, the Sensible, and the Witty in the Opposition. Of such Patrons I shall be always proud, and to such shall be always glad of the Honour of owning an Obligation. Nor is it a small Pleasure to me, that my Heart is conscious of none to certain Persons who are in the Opposition to those Characters by which you have been pleased to distinguish my Patrons.[11]

The *Historical Register*, and *Eurydice Hiss'd*, being now publish'd, shall answer for themselves against what you are pleas'd to say concerning them; but as you are pleased to assert, that I have insinuated that all Government is a *Farce*, and perhaps a damn'd one too, I shall quote the Lines on which you ground your Assertion; and, I hope, then you will be so good as to retract it.

—*Wolsey's* Self, that mighty Minister,
In the full Height and Zenith of his Power,
Amid a Crowd of Sycophants and Slaves,
Was but (perhaps) the Author of a *Farce*,
Perhaps, a damn'd one too.

I am far from asserting that all Government is a *Farce*, but I affirm that, however the very Name of Power may frighten the Vulgar, it will never be honoured by the Philosopher, or the Man of Sense, unless accompany'd with Dignity. On the contrary, nothing can be more Burlesque than Greatness in mean Hands. Mr. *Penkethman* never was so ridiculous a Figure, as when he became **Penkethman the Great*.[12]

I shall only make a Remark or two, and conclude.

First, I have not ridiculed Patriotism, but have endeavoured to shew the several Obstructions to a proper exerting this Noble Principle; and that Corruption alone is equal to all the rest. I have endeavoured to represent the Consequence thereof, and to shew, that whoever gives up the Interest of his Country, in Fact gives up his own.

Secondly, I must observe, Sir, that if we are not (as you say) to expose evil or weak Measures, for fear of informing our Neighbours, this Argument will extend in its full Force to the Press; and I think I remember to have seen it formerly used on that Occasion. But it will not hold in either Case; for I do not believe Foreign Ministers to be so weak, as to remain in an entire stupid Ignorance of what we are

*In the Burlesque of Alexander.

doing; nor do I think if well considered, a more ridiculous Image can enter into the Mind of Man, than that of all the Ambassadors of *Europe* assembling at the *Hay Market* Playhouse to learn the Character of our Ministry.[13]

Lastly, you insinuate, that *the same Poet*, who (you say) *now prostitutes the Muses* (that is, by laughing at Vice and Folly) may hereafter attack future Administrations (tho', by the by, I am far from owning that he hath attacked the present). To this, Sir, I must beg Leave to say, without any Reflection on our present Ministry, that, I believe, there are now amongst those Gentlemen who are styled the *Opposition*, Men in Genius, Learning, and Knowledge so infinitely superior to the rest of their Countrymen, and of Integrity so eminent, that should they, *in process of Time*, be in the Possession of Power, they will be able to triumph over, and trample upon all the Ridicule which any Wit or Humour could level at them: For Ridicule, like *Ward's* Pill,[14] passes innocently through a sound Constitution; but when it meets with a Complication of foul Distempers in a gross corrupt Carcase, it is apt to give a terrible Shock, to work the poor Patient most immoderately; in the Course of which Working, it is ten to one but he bes——ts his Breeches. I am,

Sir,

Your humble (tho' not obliged) Servant,

PASQUIN.

6 *The Champion; or, the Evening Advertiser,* No. 129

Tuesday, September 9, 1740

Fielding began *The Champion* on November 15, 1739, under the title of *The Champion; or, British Mercury*, and conducted it with the help of James Ralph. The title was changed when it became an evening paper on April 10, 1740. Fielding's contributions ceased after June 1741.

For *The Champion* Fielding created the persona of the choleric Captain Hercules Vinegar, whose self-acting club was supposed to cast fear into the hearts of all offenders against social conventions and the laws of good behaviour. Various members of the Captain's family helped him to conduct his Court of Censorial Enquiry (see e.g. below, No. 13).

Pugnat ad Exemplum primi minor ordine Pili.

TIBULLUS.[1]

Notwithstanding the frequent Hints and Petitions I have receiv'd to take the Theatre under my Protection, I have hitherto declined it from an Opinion, that its Condition was absolutely desperate, that it was degenerated to Farce and Shew, and sunk beneath the Dignity of my censorial Notice.

However, I was prevail'd on last *Saturday* Night to take my Club with me into the Pit, where I found myself agreeably deceiv'd: The House, which was that Night open'd for the Season, is beautified in a very elegant Manner: The Audience was very numerous, and more polite than the Scarcity of Company, at present in Town, could have promised: The Play, which was *Shakespear's*, very decently and regularly perform'd, and Mr. *Milward*,[2] who perform'd the Character of *Hamlet*, acquitted himself with so much Art, that, I believe, since Mr. *Betterton* he hath not been excell'd, and the whole Audience exprest private Satisfaction, as well as public Applause at his Action, seeming to hope that the Loss of Mr. *Wilks* will be at lest repair'd, by one whom Nature hath every Way qualified for an excellent Actor.[3]

Mr. *Quin* is so greatly eminent in Parts of a superior Cast, that it is an invaluable Compliment to say, that he excell'd in that of the Ghost: But what greatly pleas'd me, and occasion'd this Essay, was a Piece of News communicated to me at the House, and which, I hope, wants no Confirmation, *viz.* that the future Conduct of that Theatre is committed to his Care.[4]

The Stage is, in Miniature, a Resemblance of the grand Theatre of the World, to which it hath been often compar'd, and nothing can conduce more to the Welfare of the former as the latter, than to have its Management committed to one of proper Abilities, Knowledge, and Character. As Mr. *Quin*, therefore, is at the Head of his Profession, as he is a Man of Sense and Spirit, the Actors will consequently depend on, and readily submit to his Direction; and we may expect to see the Theatre flourish, and, arising from its late despised and declining State, again recover its ancient Honour and Reputation.

Mr. *Fletewood* is a Gentleman of Birth and Fortune, and hath had an Education foreign to theatrical Affairs; the late disorderly Conduct of the Theatre therefore, the Occasion of the many Insults which the Actors have sufferr'd from the Town, as well as the Advantages gain'd over it by its neighbouring Stage, are not properly to be imputed to him, whose Interest it undoubtedly is that the Trade of his own People (for such his Actors are) should flourish: He will forgive me, therefore, if I imagine he trusted the Conduct of his Stage to some mean, low Rascal, who was probably bribed by those in an opposite Interest, to excite the Indignation of the Town by raising the Prices, and giving them nothing for their Money.[5]

Since then, Mr. *Fletewood*, hath fallen into this wise Conduct, as every Thing, is best shewn by its Foil or its opposite, let us consider what would have been the Consequence of a contrary Behaviour, if, instead of making his best Actor his Prime Minister, he had conferr'd that Office on some illiterate, shabby Fellow, without any other Merit, than that of flattering his Master, and suffering himself to be kicked as often as he pleased.

First, all good Authors would have abandoned his Cause, and instead of writing for the Stage would have writ against it, and exposed it by Wit and Ridicule, to the Contempt and Derision of every one, whilst their Places would have been supplied with Persons of the Meridian of the Deputy Manager's Understanding, Scriblers who would have only exposed him who set them to work, for Instance, such as the Authors of the *Gazetteer*, &c.

Secondly, such a dirty Manager would have had some Relations, and Adherents, on whom all the principal Parts would have been conferred without any Regard to their Capacity: These Figures would have strutted about to the utmost Scorn of the Spectators, who must have looked on every Exhibition in the Light of *Alexander* burlesqu'd, where *Penkethman* formerly played the Part of *Alexander the Great*;[6] whilst such Performers as Mr. *Quin*, Mr. *Milward*, and Mrs. *Clive*,[7] would have been neglected, or perhaps offered the Parts of Footmen and Chambermaids, which they would have refused with Contempt. The natural and necessary Consequence of which is, that the others would have been hissed off the Stage, and tho' perhaps some of the fine People, at the other End of the Town, from a Friendship to the principal Manager, would have born with it, yet the City, who are the chief Supporters of the Theatre, would not have sent one Shilling of their Money into it.

Thirdly, raising the Prices perpetually for miserable Farces, below the Dignity of the Theatre, such as fresh Recruits of Mr. *Bayes's* Forces, Hobby-Horse-Fights; the *Devil to pay*, *the Lottery*, *Tom Thumb the Great*, *An Hospital for Fools*, &c.[8] which additional Prices, tho' they have a Way at the Playhouse of cramming down the People's Throats; yet they are always received with grumbling, hissing, catcalling, groaning and other Methods of exploding, that are generally found to produce Mischief in the End. And, for what Purpose are these advanc'd Prices intended, but to enrich the Deputy Manager, who by means of having his own Creatures in all the Offices, is enabled the better to cheat both his Master and the Town?

Now, what must have been the Consequence of these Measures, but a total Decay of the Business in that Theatre, which should be so conducted; a Reduction of Profits to the Manager, and an absolute impoverishing the Actors: So that if any had ventured abroad, they would have been constantly taken, nay, the Enemy* would have ventured to nab them even within their own Walls. A Rival Theatre would have run away with all their Trade, nay, a Company of contemptible *French* Comedians, whom we formerly starv'd as often as they ventured amongst us, might in Time have become formidable to the Theatre Royal.[9]

But, besides the Incapacity and paultry corrupt Dealings of these low Tools, the Contempt of their Superiors encreases the Mischief: For, can we imagine that great Actors will accept of Parts under the

*Bailiffs so call'd in theatrical Language.

Direction of a Candle-Snuffer, or one who is qualified for no higher an Office. Thus the poor Wretch would, whether willing or no, be necessitated to employ sad Strol[l]ers in the chief Characters. The Consequence of which would be, the quickly laying aside the old *English* Drama, and introducing Scenes of *Italian* and *French* Buffoonery on the Stage, whose Performers the Pit would soon hiss or perhaps kick off, notwithstanding the weak Defence of a few Soldiers, who would hardly be brought to fire on their Countrymen, while they were exerting the Priviledges of *Englishmen*.

But I am glad Mr. *Fletewood* hath acted a wiser Part, and I am convinc'd, he will very shortly triumph over the weak Attempts of his Rivals: He will find that the late Mismanagement of the Theatre, not any Animosity against him in the Town, was the Occasion of all the Confusion the latter End of last Season.

Indeed, to look into the World at large, and *parvis componere magna*,[10] we shall eternally find every Order of Men to thrive according to the Abilities and the Character of him who is at the Head of it. Thus conquered our Armies under the Duke of *Marlborough*, thus are Fleets victorious under *Vernon*: Thus our Law thrives under a *Hardwick*,[11] and thus, if we were to turn over our Annals, we shall find the Commonwealth itself flourishing or declining, as the Helm hath been guided by an able and an upright, or a weak and corrupt Ministry.

But to return from my Digression, and conclude as I begun with the Theatre, I once more congratulate the Town with the Prospect of restoring so innocent, so agreeable, and so useful a Diversion, and, instead of Rope-dancing and Tumbling, Farce and Puppet-shew, of being once more entertain'd in *Drury-Lane* in a Manner equal to what our Ancestors have been.

L.

N.B. We shall shortly present our Readers with some Papers addressed to the Electors of *Great Britain*, written by a very eminent Hand, who hath thought fit to honour us by the introducing them into the World thro' our Hands. As these are calculated to do public Service, we hope those who wish well to their Country, will take all possible Care to spread them universally.

7 *The True Patriot: and The History of Our Own Times*, No. 18

From Tuesday, February 25, to Tuesday, March 4, 1746

Fielding began *The True Patriot* on November 5, 1745, and continued it until January 17, 1746. The journal was mainly political, designed to serve as a rallying point for patriot feeling during the 1745 Rebellion.

Majores nusquam Rhonchi juvenesque senesque
Et Pueri nasum Rhinocerotis habent.

MARTIAL[1]

I was pleased the other Night with the ingenious Confession of a Gentleman, who sat by me at the Oratorio;[2] who, after having expressed a Dislike to the Composition, and declared that the Opera was in his Opinion greatly its Superior, very shortly assured us all, that he had not the least Taste or Judgment in Music.

It might be wished, that several pretended Connoisseurs in other Sciences had the Grace to follow so good an Example: But, on the contrary, the more ignorant and incapable these are, the more self-sufficient we generally find them; the worst Judges, in Cases of this Nature, being the most rigid Asserters of their own Jurisdiction.

This is a dreadful Discouragement to all Men of true Genius, who are often contented to bury their Talents under a Bushel, rather than by producing them in Public, to trust the Decision of their Merit to a Tribunal, where Numbers, Noise and Power, too often carry the Question against Sense and Reason.

Painters as well as Musicians have complained, and not without Reason, of the Census past on their Works by Men who have not the least Skill in their Art. Here, I am informed, the general Rule of judging, among ignorant Critics, is from the apparent Antiquity of the Piece. One celebrated Connoisseur in particular is said never to have given his Suffrage for a Picture, unless where the Colours were so sunk and faded, that no one could possibly discover what it was the Picture of.

The Professors of Literature, Prose-writers as well as Poets, labour under this Calamity of being try'd by Judges who never read the Laws over which they preside. This is more particularly the Fate of Dramatic Authors. Every one hath heard of THE TOWN; a Name which the Play-House Critics gave their Body, and under which they sat many Years in Judgment on all Dramatic Pieces exhibited to the Public. This Office of Criticism belonged formerly to another Body of Critics called THE PIT, so named from the Part of the Theatre which they occupied, whereas THE TOWN, their Successors, disposed themselves alike in all Parts of the Theatre, except the Boxes.

These Critics, like the Mohocs of old,[3] were long known only to the Members of their Society, and various were the Opinions concerning them. Some of the Ladies conceived, that this *Town* was a single Person who sat in the uppeı Gallery; for in that Part they always posted one of their Number, who was most remarkable for the Deepness of his Voice and the Shrillness of his Cat-call. And according to this Opinion, I remember a young Fellow gave an Account of a Hiss at a Play about two Years ago. 'The Town, says he, was resolved the Play should not go on, and hissed. Then Mr. *Mills* came forward, and offered to speak, and the Town cry'd, *Hear him, hear him*; but upon his offering to excuse *Fleetwood*, the *Town* presently took up an Apple and flung at his Head.'[4] From this Relation I at first concluded, that *the Town* was some impudent Rascal, who deserved to have been turned out of the House; but I afterwards found that the *Town* was *Nomen Collectivum*, and that the young Gentleman who told us the Story, was himself one of the Number meant by it.

Others imagined that *the Town* meant the Men of Learning and Taste; and others again concluded, that by *the Town* was understood every Man in the Town, at least all those who frequented such Entertainments, and that the Votes and Sentiments of all such were included in the Determinations made at the Play-House.

The Town ruled many Years with absolute Sway, till at last growing wanton with their Power, and insisting on a prescriptive Right to break the Heads of the Actors, and to pull down the House, or set it on fire, as often as they pleased; by which Means the Ladies and all others, except only the *Town*, were terrified from going to Plays, the Manager was obliged to take a List of *the Town*, in order to apply to a Court of Justice for Redress. Which being done, *the Town* appeared to consist chiefly of young Gentlemen who were Apprentices to several Trades, mixed with some few who were *designed for* the Law, and half a dozen young Members of the Army. Most of them being of that Age to which the Law assigns the Appellation of Infant.

Upon this Discovery a Prosecution was commenced, on which it appearing that this prescriptive Right was not good in Law, the Town hath been since restrained within more moderate Bounds, and claim no Right of disturbing an Audience, except at a new Play, where they still maintain their ancient Privilege of Hissing, Cat-calling, &c.[5]

It might be perhaps questioned, whether these young Gentlemen are all complete Judges of Dramatic Merit, and whether they do not sometimes pass the Censure of vile Stuff and *lowe*, (a Word in great Use in the Upper Gallery)[6] a little improperly; but what is still worse, Corruption as well as Ignorance prevails too often in this Court of Criticism, and the Cat-call is discharged not at the Play, but at its Author.

An Instance of this occurs to my Memory, at one of these Exhibitions, when I happened to sit next a Youth who was a most perfect Master of the Cat-call, and played upon it almost without Intermission. As the Performance did not, in my Opinion, deserve quite so severe a Treatment, I took an Occasion of remonstrating to my Neighbour, who without Hesitation swore he was resolved to damn the Play; for that the Author was in Possession of a very pretty Girl, for whom he had himself a violent Affection. Ay, damn him, says another who overheard us, and who had hitherto accompanied the instrumental with very loud vocal Music, *I hate the Fellow, because he's a Whig*.

Without staying to comment on these mean Artifices of Revenge, the Baseness of which is sufficiently apparent, I cannot help observing, that some Persons have taken a Hint from the Town, and espouse and decry the Productions of Men of Learning, as the Author is or is not of their Party. This Method begins to prevail so much, that it will shortly be no more possible for a Man to gain Reputation in the Republic of Letters, without the Assistance of great Men, than it hath formerly been to procure a Place or Pension. Indeed, I think it will soon become no improper Application, to some of these, *Sir, I desire you will let me be a great Poet, or be pleased to let me have a great deal of Wit and Humour, in my Writings.*

As this is truly the Case, it certainly imports *The True Patriot* to warn his honest Readers against such Proceedings. A Man, who is determined to adhere to no Party longer than their Views are consistent with the Interest of his Country, and to oppose any who by their Principles or Practice are manifestly its Enemies, must necessarily expect that all Parties, who are guided by such base Politics, will unite in denying, or to borrow a Phrase from *the Town* above-mentioned, on this Occasion, *in damning his* Writings.

We have indeed already received Advice of some Persons, who have ventured to nibble at our Paper, and in private Corners to whisper several disrespectful Matters against some of our most approved Performances, and against the Voice of the People.[7]

The Public, for whose Sake this Paper was instituted, and the more sensible Part of it, for whose Entertainment it is calculated, will not withdraw their Favour from our Endeavours, while we continue to deserve it. The Reason therefore of this Admonition is less intended for our own Sake, than to caution such Persons from persisting any longer in their base Purposes: For, however secretly they may imagine they have conducted their Malice, we assure them their Names are well known, and unless they immediately alter their Conduct towards us, they must shortly expect to find themselves gibbeted in our Papeı, and exposed to the same universal Derision with the *Par nobile fratrum*, whom we have lately hung forth as Objects of public Scorn and Contempt.[8]

PART TWO

Colley Cibber: Prince of Dunces

Colley Cibber (1671–1757), joint manager of the Theatre Royal, Drury Lane, from 1710 to 1732, dramatist and Poet Laureate, was one of the best-known characters of his generation, and is now remembered for his part in the *Dunciad* (1742). Fielding's relations with him began when he offered his first play, *Love in Several Masques*, to Drury Lane in 1728. By 1730, for reasons which are not clear, Fielding had fallen out with Cibber and Wilks, his co-manager, and retired to the Haymarket, from whence he ridiculed Cibber in *The Author's Farce* (1730) and the Preface to *Tom Thumb* (1730). By December 1731, however, he was back at Drury Lane, reconciled with Cibber and Wilks. During 1732 Cibber acted in several of Fielding's plays and, with his son Theophilus, was praised in the Preface to *The Mock Doctor* (1732). After Cibber's retirement and Theophilus Cibber's withdrawal from Drury Lane, the relationship changed again, and Fielding attacked both the Cibbers throughout the rest of his career, particularly in the revised version of *The Author's Farce* (1734), in *Shamela* (1741) and probably in *The Apology for the Life of Theophilus Cibber* (1740).

References to Cibber in *The Champion* are very frequent. Fielding remarked caustically on *The Apology for the Life of Mr. Colley Cibber, Comedian* (1740) even before it was published. When the book appeared he made a consistent attack on its style and content. Though Cibber had attacked him in *The Apology*, Fielding's motive was not personal. Apart from the fact that *The Apology* was, in many ways, an obvious target for ridicule, its author had attempted to defend the Government of Sir Robert Walpole, against which *The Champion* was directed.

8 *The Champion; or, the Evening Advertiser,* No. 69

Tuesday, April 22, 1740

—— *melius non tangere clamo.*
HOR.[1]

It may, I believe, be affirmed that the Generality of Mankind, (I mean such as are at all acquainted with History) know much more of former Times than their own. Most of us may be considered like the Spectators of one of Mr. *Rich's* Entertainments; we see Things only in the Light in which that truly ingenious and learned *Entertainmatic* Author is pleased to exhibit them, without perceiving the several Strings, Wires, Clock-work, &c. which conduct the Machine; and thus we are diverted with the Sights of Serpents, Dragons and Armies, whereas indeed those Objects are no other than Pieces of stuff'd Cloth, painted Wood, and Hobby-Horses, as such of his particular Friends as are admitted behind the Scenes, without any Danger of *interrupting his Movements*, very well know.[2]

In the same Manner we are deceived in the Grand Pantomimes played on the Stage of Life, where there is often no less Difference between the Appearances and Reality of Men and Things, and where those who are utter Strangers to the Springs of the political Motion, judging by Habits, Posts or Titles, have actually mistaken Men for Heroes, Patriots and Politicians, who have been in fact as mere Machines as any used by the aforesaid Mr. *Rich*: for when a Man is absolutely void of Capacity, it matters not whether his Skin be stuff'd with *Guts* or Straw, or whether his Face be made of Wood or Brass.[3]

As History cannot furnish any Instance of Political Pantomime equal with the following, I shall set it down at length for the Entertainment of my unlearned Readers, as I have concisely translated it from *Suetonius* in his Life of *Caligula*.[4]

This Heroe (says my Author) having sent a few of his Guards over the *Rhine*, where they were to conceal themselves, ordered an Alarm to be brought to him after Dinner, of the Enemy's Approach in vast Numbers. Upon which he presently hastned with his chief Officers, and a Party of the *Pretorian* Horse into the next Wood, whence he returned with the sham Trophies of a Victory, upbraiding the Cowardice of those who stayed behind, and crowning the Companions and Partakers of his Victory with Chaplets of a new Name and Species. Another Time, having privately sent forth some of his Hostages, he arose hastily from his Supper and brought them back in Chains, boasting of his Pantomime Adventure in the most extravagant Manner, desiring those who told him that all the Troops were returned from the Expedition, to sit down in their Armour, and ridiculously repeating to them a celebrated Verse of *Virgil*; in which *Æneas* encourages his Followers to *persevere in encountering all Dangers and Toils in Hopes of their future Happiness*; inveighing bitterly at the same time against the Senate, and those *Romans* who were absent, and enjoyed the Pleasures of *Rome*, whilst *Cæsar* exposed himself to such eminent Dangers. *Lastly*, He drew out his Army on the Sea-shore, and disposed every thing as for a Battel, no one knowing or even guessing what he intended, when suddenly he ordered all the Soldiers to fill their Helmets with Cockles, which he called the Spoils of the Ocean, worthy of a Place in the *Roman* Temples. Here, after he had built a Tower as a Monument of his Victory, the Remains of which are still extant, according to *Pitiscus*,[5] called by the *English* the *Old Man*, he rewarded his Soldiers with 100 *Denarii per Man*; and, not contented yet with all this Pageantry, he writ to *Rome* to demand a Triumph.

Ridiculous as this Parade now appears, it is probable not a few of the more ignorant *Romans* were imposed on by it, and looked on *Caligula* as a real Conqueror; a Circumstance, which, if we consider the several Tricks played since by Ministers and Statesmen, will not appear so strange or incredible. It is History which strips off the Mask, and shews things in their true Light; but this is not written, or at least publish'd 'till the ensuing Age, and for the Good of Posterity. I often lament that, being an old Man, I have but little Hopes of seeing those Histories of their own Times, which two of our Cotemporaries, of very great Genius, are said to be compiling.[6]

But, at the same time, I cannot help the felicitating my self and my Countrymen that one learned Man hath thought fit to indulge his own Age with the History of his Times: for tho' from a peculiar Modesty which *shines* in all the Actions of this great Man, he calls it only an *Apology for his own Life*, and tho' some imagin'd it would have been confined only to the Theatre, yet certain it is that this valuable Work hath much greater Matters in View, and may as properly be stiled an Apology for the Life of ONE who hath played a very comical Part, which, tho' Theatrical, hath been Acted on a much larger Stage than *Drury Lane*.

And here I cannot help mentioning some whimsical Opinions, which perhaps the Novelty of the Attempt may have occasioned; for tho' the Offspring be of such a Bulk as is generally thought a Security from being soon buried in a Band box, and the good Parent seems to imagine that he hath produced, as well as my Lord *Clarendon* a *Κτῆμα ἐς αιεὶ*;[7] for he refuses to quote any thing out of *Pasquin*, lest he should *give it a Chance of being remembered*;[8] yet some imagined there is great Reason to apprehend with him in *Horace*, *Ne sit superstes*;[9] for Goody —— the Midwife hath been seen to shake her Head, and Nurse *Lewis* complains that it lies in a heavy Lump in the Nursery,[10] and cannot be carried abroad even this fine Weather: Nay, several Grammatical Physicians have not scrupled to say that the Child is produced from *Mala Stamina*, and instead of being born with all its Senses, hath indeed no Sense in it. As for the Vulgar, they are as incredulous with Regard to this, as to some other Births, and will not believe there was any Off-spring at all; to justify which Suspicion, they alledge that a Guinea hath been insisted on for the Sight of it, a Price which it is improbable any one would give barely *to satisfy his Curiosity*; they pretend that the vast Difference between the pale Countenances of those Children, which at all resemble the Father, such as Master *Cæsar* in *Egypt*, the *Heroic Daughter*, the *Refusal*, and *Love in a Riddle*, all dead long ago, and the stronger Complexion of some others, have brought the Chastity of his Muse into Question;[11] Nay, they aver that his Muse herself hath been long incapable of bringing any thing to the least Form; for that, of late Years, she hath only *miscarried* of strange Lumps called *Odes* and *Gazetteers*.[12] Lastly, They affirm that the old Gentleman hath been dead some time, and that the Laurel (the Heir Loom of the Family) hath fallen down on the Head of his Son.

But notwithstanding such malicious Suggestions, I have the Pleasure to assure the Reader, (to drop the Allegory) that there is such a Book to be had at Mr. *Lewis's* in *Covent-Garden*, treating of all manner of Matters promiscuously; that is to say, of Ministers and Actors, Parliaments and Play-houses, of Liberty, Operas, Farces, *C. C. R. W.*[13] and many other good things; amongst which there are several Particulars which no one can know without reading it, and which very probably may not reach Posterity in any other History. If therefore the Opinion, that this Book will have but a short Duration, should be true, it may be attended with two remarkable Circumstances; for the present Age will not only equal, but exceed Posterity in the Knowledge of their own Times, and the Author may have a very singular Fate; and, if he creeps into *no other Record*, out-live the History of his own Life.

I shall very shortly (for we must enjoy good things whilst we have them) give the Reader some Taste of this invaluable Performance; I shall here only obviate a flying Report, taken from a confident Assertion of some Persons, that whatever Language it was writ in, it certainly could not be *English*; an Opinion which may possibly, together with the Price, have obstructed the Sale and prevented any Extracts from it in the *Farthing-Post*, whose Author may not be good at Translation.[14] Now I shall prove it to be *English* in the following Manner. Whatever Book is writ in no other Language, is writ in *English*. This Book is writ in no other Language, *Ergo*, It is writ in *English*: Of which Language the Author hath shewn himself a most absolute Master; for surely he must be absolute Master of that whose Laws he can trample under Feet, and which he can use as he pleases. This Power he hath exerted, of which I shall give a *barbarous* Instance in the Case of the poor Word *Adept**; a Word which I apprehend no School-Boy hath ever wantonly employed, unless to signify the utmost Perfection; for Ignorance they cannot plead who have gone beyond the Accidence, since they must then find that *adipiscor vult adeptus*:[15] Nay an *Englishman* may learn from *Hudibras*,

> In *Rosicrucian* lore, as learned
> As he that *verè Adeptus* earned.[16]

This Word our great *Master* hath tortured and wrested to signify a *Tyro* or *Novice*, being directly contrary to the Sense in which it hath been hitherto used.

This Spirit of absolute Power is generally whipt out of Boys at School, and I could heartily wish our *Adept* had been in the *Way* of such Castigation. And perhaps it is on this Account that one of our Poets

**The Author's Words are these: 'Mrs.* Tofts, *who first took her first Grounds of Musick in her own Country, was then* BUT *an ADEPT in it: Yet whatever Defect the* fashionable Skilful *might find in her Manner, she had, in the* general Sense *of her Spectators, Charms that few of the most learned Singers ever arrive at. The Beauty of her fine proportioned Figure, and the exquisitely sweet* silver Tone *of her Voice, with that peculiar* rapid Swiftness of her Throat, *were Perfections not to be imitated by Art or Labour.' Thus I have transcribed the whole Paragraph, which, I think, abounds with many Flowers of that* exquisitely sweet silver *Stile called the Profound, and with* Perfections *purely the Gifts of Genius, not to be imitated by Art or Labour.*
(Vid. Col. Cibb. *Apol.* fol. 226)

says, *That he who never felt* BIRCH, *should never wear* BAYS,[17] *i.e.* That no Man should be trusted with a Pen who will take this Method to shew us HIS GREAT COMMAND OF WORDS.

C.

9 *The Champion; or, the Evening Advertiser*, No. 72

Tuesday, April 29, 1740

Mandare quenquam Literis Cogitationes suas, qui eas nec disponere nec illustrare possit, —— *hominis est intemperanter abutentis & Otio & Literis*

Cic., *Tusc. Quaest.*[1]

Notwithstanding the Opinion of *Cicero* in my Motto, That he who commits his Thoughts to Paper without being able methodically to range them, or properly to illustrate them, gives us an Instance of the most intemperate Abuse of his own Time and of Letters themselves; and tho' *Quintilian* hath asserted, that Grammar is the Foundation of all Science;[2] Nay *Horace* himself denies anything to be in the Power of Genius without Improvement, notwithstanding these Authorities, I say, I have very often suspected whether Learning be of such Consequence to a Writer as it is imagined. This, however, I have hitherto kept to my self, and, perhaps, tho' *Horace* hath, in another Place, taken up the contrary side to what he declares above, and hath enumerated many Advantages arising to a State from the Custom of Writing as well without, as with Learning.[3] I might perhaps have never ventured publicly to have declared my Opinion, had I not found it supported by one of the *Greatest Writers* of our own Age: I mean Mr. *Colley Cibber*, who, in the Apology for his Life, tells us, That *we have frequently Great Writers that cannot read.*[4]

But as by not reading, our Author explains himself not to mean such as do not know their great A, but those who cannot read Theatrically; so by not reading I mean such as we generally say *can hardly write and read*, or in other Words, a Man *barely* qualified to be a Member of the R[oyal] S[ociet]y.[5]

Our Author, who is a Great Writer every Inch of him, hath, as well as *Longinus*, given us an Example of what he asserts, for I am apprehensive that some Persons who know him only by his Book, may really doubt whether he can read or no. As this may possibly be a controverted Point, I wish when he told us he had gone through a School, he had also told us what Books they read in the upper Form; since there are, I believe, some Schools where the Forms are numbered by the Numbers of Syllables which make one Word more difficult to spell than another. However, tho' his History no where expressly declares his *ne plus ultra* in Learning; there is a passage in it which though it may be overlook'd by an ordinary Reader, brings this Point within a very narrow Compass of Certainty: *Wherever the* VERB OUTDO *comes in,* (says our Author) *the* PLEASANT ACCUSATIVE CASE OUTDOING is *sure to follow*. Now, as I have shewn in a former Paper that his Learning could have gone very little beyond the Accidence, I think it is plain from this Instance that he must have learnt as far as the *pleasant Accusative Case*, and not quite so far as the *Participles*. A Part of Speech which if he had known would certainly have made its Appearance here.[6]

Having settled this Point, I proceed to shew the little Advantage of Learning, or Grammar, to an Author, which I shall demonstrate two Ways: *First*, I shall shew that he is generally to be understood without, and *secondly*, That he is sometimes not to be understood with it. And of both these I shall (as it lies in my Way) give Instances from the GREAT WRITER above-mentioned. Thus, when he says (*Fol.* 23) Satire is *angrily* particular, every Dunce of a Reader knows he means angry with a particular Person, or when he says (*page* 25.) a *Moral* Humanity, can't you strike Moral out and let Humanity stand by it self, or put Virtue in its Place? When in *page* 42. we read, *Beauty* SHINES INTO *equal Warmth the Peasant and the Courtier*, do we not know what he means though he hath made a Verb active of SHINE, as in *Page* 117, he hath of REGRET, *nothing could more painfully regret a judicious Spectator*. So in Page 43. *The People met us* in *Acclamation*. Page 55. *What Pleasure is not languid to Satiety?* Page 70. Betterton *excels himself*. Page 71. Was not *equal to his former self*. Page 78. *The Trial of Lord* Mohun *printed among* THOSE OF THE STATE. 72. *An Acute and piercing Tone which struck every Syllable of his Words distinctly upon the Ear*. 109. *One side of the Cause grew weary*. 114. *A fair Promise to my being in Favour*. 132. *The Tragedians seemed to think their Rank as much above the Comedians as in the Characters they severally acted*. ibid. Dogget *could not with Patience look upon the costly Trains and Plumes of Tragedy, in which knowing himself to be useless, he thought were all a vain Extravagance*. 134. *Never to pay their People when the Mony did not come in, nor then neither, but in such Proportions,* &c.—*This would induce the Footmen to come all Hands aloft in the Crack of our Applauses*. 139. *Studying Perfect*. 154. *The* Utile Dulci *was of old equally the Point*. 157. *The Flatness of many miserable*

Prologues—seemed wholly UNEQUAL *to the few good ones*, &c. 175. *Public Approbation is the warm Weather of a Theatrical Plant*. 176. *Mrs.* Oldfield *threw out such new Proffers of a Genius*. 202. *Melts into Pangs of Humanity*. 220. *So exotic a Partner*. 243. Farinelli *singing to an Audience of five and thirty Pounds*. 261. *The Decadence of* Betterton's *Company*. 288. *A Man may be Debtor to Sense or Morality*. 297. *Our Enemies made a Push of a good round Lie upon us*. Now in all these Instances, tho' a Boldness of Expression is made use of, which none but great Masters dare attempt, and which a School Boy would run a great Hazard by imitating, yet we may with some little Difficulty, without the least Help of Grammar, give a Guess at his Meaning. But there are other Parts of this Work so very sublime, that Grammar offers you its Aid in vain; the following Stile carries a *Βίανἄμαχον*, according to *Longinus*, along with it, *and absolutely overpowers* the Reader, as the Poets in *Horace*,

Animum quocunq; volunt Auditoris agunto.

So can our Author; this Stile comes upon you, says the former Critic like a *Thunderbolt*, or, to use a Word which may give a more familiar Idea to my Reader, like a *Blunderbuss*, and carries all before it.[7] I shall produce some Instances of this sublime kind. *Page* 42. 'So *clear an Emanation* of Beauty. *&c. struck* me into a Regard that had something softer than the most profound Respect in it. *Page* 62. *Some Actors* heavily drag the Sentiment along with a long-toned Voice and absent Eye. *Page* 65. Many a barren brained Author has streamed into a frothy flowing Style, pompously rolling into founding Periods, signifying roundly nothing. 66. The strong Intelligence of his Attitude and Aspect, drew you into an impatient Gaze. 67. There is even a kind of Language in agreeable Sounds, which, like the Aspect of Beauty, without Words, speaks and plays with the Imagination. 69. Let our Conception of whatever we are to speak, be ever so just, or Ear ever so true, yet, when we are to deliver it to an Audience, (I will leave Fear out of the Question) there must go along with the whole, a natural Freedom and becoming Grace, which is easier to conceive than to describe: for without this inexpressible Somewhat, the *Performance will come out oddly disguised, or somewhere defectively, unsurprizing to the Hearer*. 76. The Wit of the Poet seemed to come from him *extempore*, and *sharpened into more Wit* by his Delivery. 101. In all the chief Parts she acted, the desirable was so predominant, that no Judge could be cold enough to consider from what other particular Excellence she became delightful. 158. His Accents were frequently too sharp and violent, which sometimes occasioned his eagerly cutting off half the Sound of Syllables, that ought to have been gently melted into the Melody of Metre. 176. A forward and sudden Step into Nature. 185. Not long before this Time, the *Italian* Opera began first to steal into *England*; but in as rude a Disguise and unlike it self as possible; in a lame hobbling Translation into our own Language, with false Quantities or METRE OUT OF MEASURE to its original Notes sung by our own unskilful Voices. 209. The Mind of Man is naturally free, and when he is compelled or menaced into any Opinion that he does not readily conceive, he is more apt to doubt the Truth of it, than when his Capacity is led by Delight into Evidence and Reason. 210. A Spectacle for Vacancy of Thought to gaze at. 216. Attention enough for any four Persons. *Lastly, Out of his Depth with his simple Head above Water.*' Which Idea of our Author that we may leave in our Reader, we will quote no more from him, since I apprehend what was at first asserted is fully made out, *viz.* That it is needless for a GREAT WRITER to understand his Grammar: for as we can generally guess his Meaning without it, so when his Genius (to speak in our Author's Stile) ascends into the elevated and nervously pompous Elements of the Sublime, the Ladder of Grammar offers it self in vain to the Feet of the Reader's Understanding: for tho' the Words, which may be called the Brick and Mortar of Speech, are regularly conglutinated together, so as to erect the extraneous Frontispiece of a delicate, excessively-sweet Sugar-Loaf of a Pile; yet if there be no Sentiment, no aspiring, animating, softly, sweetly tempered Spirit, this Pile is only a naked Building, void of Furniture, where the wearied Understanding of the long-travelled Reader will find no Featherbed to repose himself on.

As we have not Room in this Paper to enumerate all the particular Beauties of this Author, we shall be obliged to divert the Reader once more with him, when we shall attempt, in his own Stile, which with vast Industry we have made our selves Masters of, to draw his own Character; seeing there are some Parts of it which either through Haste or Inadvertency, he hath himself omitted.

L.

10 *The Champion; or, the Evening Advertiser,* No, 75

Tuesday, May 6, 1740

——ὄφῤ εὖ εἰδῆς,
Ὅσσον φέρτερός εἰμὶ σέθεν, στυγέη δὲ καὶ ἄλλος

HOMER.[1]

It is the Remark of a judicious Critic, That there is a certain Particularity in the Stile of every great Writer which distinguishes him from all others.[2] Nay, it is a common Phrase to signify our Esteem of an Author, *That he has a Stile*. This is a kind of Touchstone used by Commentators, to try what Parts of a Great Man's Works are truly his own; by which Guide the learned *Bentley* hath made such wholesome and delightful Defalcations from *Milton*.[3]

The *Great Writer*, whose Character I am to attempt, hath given us the strongest Instance of this Kind. His Stile is so very singular that one might almost say, *He hath even a Language to himself*, (an Honour never before attributed to any Author.) This Particularity of Stile is so evident, that it will be impossible for the Writers of his own or a subsequent Age, to introduce any of their Works under his Name; nay, I question whether some of his own Works, written before he arrived at this Perfection, may not be *suspected* by some future *Theobald*; and do a little doubt, whether *even* the *Careless Husband*, or *Love's last Shift*, will be thought equal to the *Apology*.[4]

I have premised this little, as an Excuse for those Defects which I am too sensible of in the following Imitation; in which, as I have endeavoured to use my Author's own Words in the same Sense which he hath attributed to them, as often however as I am capable of finding it out, so I have distinguished all these Words so used in *Italics*, that since I am not equal to his Merit, I may not be guilty of stealing any Portion of his Fame.

The Author of the *Apology* made *his first forward Step into Nature* in *Nov.* 1671. In 1682, he went to a Free-School, *where he staid till he got through it, and such Learning as that School could give, is the most he pretends to; which tho' he hath not utterly forgot, he hath not much improved by*

Study. We find little remarkable of him till he came to the Stage, unless that *The Fate of King* James, *The Prince of* Orange, *and himself, were all at once upon the Anvil: That he narrowly escaped being a General or a Bishop*; and once on a Time fell in Love *with the Emanation of Beauty*. Soon after his Ascendant on the Stage, he was *possest by so full a Vanity and Content*, that he stands compared in the *Apology, to Alexander the Great, and Charles the* XIIth. In the Roll of Time, he sprung into Excellence in several Parts, those in which he *shone* the Audience *into* the greatest Admiration, were of a duplex Kind, *viz*. In Tragedy, *those Parts which had not the least Proffer of the Amiable in them*; and in Comedy, in such as were made up of *well-bred Vices*. Indeed, the latter seem to have sat with a more full and easy Fashion upon him, as his Voice, where there was a too large Infusion of the *Monotone*, interwoven with a regrating Acidity, wanted that *harmonious, pleasing, sound Melody, which the Throws and Swellings of Honour and Ambition require*; whereas he became the *Foppington* so well, that *the Roars* of the Audience frequently sounded forth what the *cooler* Judge afterwards acknowledged, that he was the truest and most compleat Coxcomb ever seen. As his actorial Excellence is so well known, we shall proceed *with Rapidity* to survey him as an Author. His Learning, as far as it regards Languages, hath been already spoken to; we will therefore examine him in the Sciences. In Arithmetic he seems to have made no Immensity of Progress: For he says, *Apol. fol*. 42. That he attended but to TWO Words which were SOME WINE AND WATER: and in 225, he talks of an EIGHTH PART MORE THAN HALF. In Architecture he seems to be something more an *Adept*. He says, *page* 241, 'That the Area of the old Stage projected about four Feet forwarder in a semi-oval Figure, parallel to the Benches of the Pit;' and in 242, 'Not only from the Stage's being shortned in Front, but likewise from the additional Interposition of those Stage Boxes, the Actors, (*in Respect to the Spectators that fill them*) are kept so much more backward from the main Audience.' In Philosophy he declares himself a *Stoic*; but indeed, though he differs from all others of this Kind, by asserting that *Fire*, AIR, *and Water, are opposite to each other*, yet if it is necessary to rank him among the Philosophers, I should rather think him a Natural than any other. In Politics he is truly *facilè Princeps:* for, to omit the dignified Reasons which he gives for restraining the Liberty of the Stage; namely, that bad Ministers may be more effectually hurt there, than by the Press; and his Method of proving the superior Worth of a Minister, by his being the *longest railed at*; there is one Stroke beyond all the *Osbornes, Walsinghams, Sidneys, Freemans*,[5] all the Bob-tail Writers of the Age, *viz.* That *we had but a contested Right to any Liberty before the Revolution.* This is a Discovery, which, if it had entered into the Head of the Jacobitical Writers in King *William's* Reign, would have done their Business at once; for, if we had no Right to Liberty before the Revolution, none but our great Biographer can tell us what Right we had to the Revolution. But his political Principles seem every where to be the *Babylonish*, which like the *Babylonish* Dialect in *Hudibras*, are a party-colour'd Mixture of patched and pie-balled Principles,[6] from whose jarring and repugnant Atoms is struck out a *Silver*, or rather Golden-*toned* Utility: *Which, like dung thrown on a Meadow, leaves an involuntary Crop behind it.* But no more of *these serious Matters*, which our Biographer (*page* 168.) says he only enters upon *to give the Public a true Portrait of his Mind, and fairly to let them see how far he is, or is not a* Blockhead; a Point in which the Reader is, I doubt not, by this time well settled. Indeed I apprehend his Character as a Writer, is now so established, that he may write on to Eternity without any Danger of hurting it. This I think is pretty certain that no one will ever attempt to attack him any more. Nay, to say the Truth, as rich Things are the soonest apt to surfeit, we are almost as desirous to have done with him, as he himself, out of an Aversion to so much Praise, can be that we should: we shall therefore only give a few Instances of one particular Beauty in this Work, which, as it may be ranged under one Head, we did not confound with the Miscellaneous Olio[7] in our last, namely, his Similies. Not to mention our Author's Comparisons of himself to King *James*, the Prince of *Orange*, *Alexander the Great*, *Charles* the XIIth, and *Harry* IV. of *France*, his favourite, Simile is a Lion, thus *page* 39. we have a Satisfied Presumption, that *to drive* England *into Slavery is like teaching* an old Lion to Dance. 104. *Our new Critics are like Lions Whelps that dash down the Bowls of Milk*, &c. besides a third Allusion to the same Animal: and this brings into my Mind a Story which I once heard from *Booth*, that our Biographer had, in one of his Plays in a Local Simile, introduced this generous Beast in some Island or Country where Lions did not grow; of which being informed by the learned *Booth*, the Biographer replied, *prithee tell me then where there is a Lion, for God's Curse, if there be a Lion in* Europe, Asia, Africa, *or* America, *I will not lose my Simile.* Another Observation which I have made on our Author's Similies is, that they generally have an Eye towards the Kitchen. Thus *page* 56. *Two Play-Houses are like two* Puddings *or two* Legs of Mutton. 224. *To plant young Actors is not so easy as to plant* Cabbages. To which let me add a

Metaphor in *page* 57. where *unprofitable Praise can hardly give Truth a* SOUP MAIGRE. As we cannot draw the sarcastical Conclusion which would attend a less rich Author, we must necessarily conclude that our Biographer is too much inclined to write on a full Stomach.

After so many Commendations of this Work, the Author will permit me to find a few Faults. The *pages* 217 and 218 are almost entirely taken up to inform the Reader that the *Biographer* lent Colonel *Brett* his clean Shirt. This brings to my Mind a Story in Dr. *South*'s Letter to *Sherlock*, which is in Substance as follows. 'Once on a Time a Gentleman and his Servant were travelling together, and the Gentleman called out to his Man, and said unto him, *John*, get thee down from thy Horse, and I will get me down from my Horse, then take off the Saddle that is on thy Horse, and afterwards take off the Saddle that is on my Horse. Then take thou the Saddle that was on my Horse, and put on thy Horse, and the Saddle that was on thy Horse put thou on my Horse. Lord, Sir, says *John*, could you not have said, change Saddles.'[8] So might our *Biographer* have said change shirts. The other two little Exceptions I shall make are such, as, if this Work had been *a little lower and worse than it is*, would not have been observed, but a Scar is immediately seen in Beauty, or a Coal in a white Pudding. *Page* 326. *It is an ill Bird that —— ——*,[9] and 332. *The Pills began to Gripe him.* Both these Passages seem to allude to a Part of the human Body, which no wise Author will ever put his Reader in mind of.

Thus I have done with this excellent Work, which is really a Suet Pudding full of Plumbs; and as the Stile or Diction is perfectly new, I shall conclude with a concise Description thereof. It is a Fluid of the galacteous or milky Kind; on which, as on Milk, there is a Cream, or rather Froth swimming on the Top: This being once skimmed off, the whole becomes quite clear, without any Sediment at the Bottom. A Circumstance in some Measure owing to the Rapidity of its Current; by which, as in a rapid Stream, the Waves of Words pass by so quick, that it is very difficult to separate or fix distinct Ideas on any particular Body of Water; You cannot distinguish one Wave from another, and you have from the whole, only an Idea of a River. So here the Periods smoothly, softly, sweetly roll and flow along; nor is the Reader able to collect any other Idea, than that it is a Book abounding with Excellencies, from *the best of which* (to use our Author's own Words, *page* 75) *he plainly sees the* whole *but a Lesson given him to get by Heart some great Author whose Sense is deeper than the* Reader's *Understanding*.

11 *The Champion: or, the Evening Advertiser,* No. 80

Saturday, May 17, 1740

——*Audacem fugat hoc terretque Poetam.*
Hor.[1]

Proceedings *at a Court of Censorial Enquiry held before Capt.* Hercules Vinegar, *Great Champion and Censor of* Great-Britain. *On* Monday *the 12th Instant, being the first Court held in the first Year of his Censorship.*

A.P. Esq;[2] was indicted for that He, being a Person to whom Nature had bequeath'd many Talents, in Order and with Design that he might well and duly give People their own; nevertheless, he the said *A.P.* the said good Talents and Design neglecting and no Ways regarding, but having too much Fear before his Eyes, one *Forage*, alias *Brass*, alias *his Honour*,[3] and many other sad Fellows to the Jurors unknown, all Sorts of Roguery to commit and perpetrate did allow and suffer, without giving to the said *Brass*, &c. any Thing of their own, and by these Means he the said *A.P.* did encourage, comfort, aid, abet, and receive the said *Brass*, &c.

The Prisoner being called on to plead, his Council stood up and spoke in the following Manner:

Council. May it please you, Mr. *Captain*, and you, Gentlemen of the Jury, I am of Council for the Prisoner, and I do apprehend it will be needless to trouble you, Mr. *Captain*, with any of the manifold Exceptions which might be taken to this Indictment, since the Crime alledg'd against the Prisoner is such, that, was it never so fully charged, or was he ever so clearly convicted of it, no Judgment would, I conceive, be given against him: For what is it we are accused of, but of holding our Tongue, or, in a legal Phrase, of not giving People their own? Now we hope, Mr. *Captain*, you will not punish any one for not doing that which he would be punish'd in other Courts for doing. We therefore desire to read the Statute of *Noli me tangere*,[4] by which it will appear that the Prisoner could act in no other Manner, without bringing himself into visible Danger, which the Law will not oblige any Man to incur.

Court. Read the Statute.

Council. Begin at Page 10. *And if any Person,* &c.

Clerk Reads. 'And if any Person shall presume to speak or write any Thing against the said *Brass,* such Person, his Wife, his Children, and all other his Relations whatever, together with all those of the said Name, shall be ruined and starved.'

Court. (Shaking his Head.) 'The Prisoner must be discharged.'

2. T. Pistol *was called to the Bar, but the Goaler answered, that he had been that Morning taken out of his Custody by the Officer of another Court, the said* Pistol *being at this Time in almost every Court of the Kingdom.*[5]

3. *Col.* Apol. *was then sent to the Bar.*

Clerk. Col. *Apol.* hold up your Hand.

Some Time was spent before the Prisoner could be brought to know which Hand he was to hold up.[6]

You stand indicted here by the Name of Col. *Apol.* late of *Covent Garden,* Esq; for that you, not having the Fear of Grammar before your Eyes, on the of at a certain Place, called the**Bath,* in the County of *Somerset,* in *Knights-Bridge,* in the County of *Middlesex,* in and upon the *English* Language an Assault did make, and then and there, with a certain Weapon called a Goose-quill, value one Farthing, which you in your left Hand then held, several very broad Wounds but of no Depth at all, on the said *English* Language did make, and so you the said Col. *Apol.* the said *English* Language did murder. To which the Prisoner pleaded, *Not guilty.*

Several Exceptions were taken to the Indictment, as that the Wounds were not described and the English *Language was not said to have died,* &c. *but they were all over-ruled.*

Anne Applepie sworn. The Prisoner is my Master. I have often seen him with a Goose-quill in his Hand, and a Bottle full of Liquor before him, into which he dipped the Weapon, and then made several scratches on white Paper, but with what Design I can't tell, he would often ask me how I spelt several Words, upon which I told him I had never been at School, and he answered, he had been at School, but had almost forgot what he learned there.

**What if an Obligation bear Date at* Bourdeaux, *in* France, *where shall it be sued? Answer is made, it may be alledged in a certain Place called* Bourdeaux in France in Islington in the County of Middlesex. *Co. Lyt.*, 261. b.[7]

Prisoner. Have you not often seen me look in a Book?

Anne Applepie, Yes, Sir.

Court. What Book?

Anne Applepie. I can't read myself, but my Master used to call it *Bailey's Dicksnary*.[8]

At which there was a great Laugh.

Thomas Trott, sworn. An't please your Honour, my Lord, I lived with the Prisoner several Years. About four Years ago, my Master the Prisoner, and I, were riding together towards the *Bath*, *Tam*, says my Master, for so he used to call me, what dost think? Sir, says I, I can't tell. Why, says he, I am going to write my Life; dost think 'twill sell? Ay, be sure, Sir, says I: For I had heard my Fellow-Servants say, my Master was a great Writer, and *Poet-Horreat*, which they said was the Top Poet in the Kingdom. And so an't please your Honour, my Lord, as we jogged on, my Master passing by a River, called to me, *Tam*, says he, dost thou see the *exquisite sweet Flowings* of that Water, so sweetly will my Life flow. These were his very Words, but I little thought he meant any Harm, 'though I did not understand him. And so, my Lord, we came to an Inn, and I observed the Prisoner reading something that was written upon the Window, and crying out, That will do, an excellent Thing for my Book, Stap my Vitals!

Prisoner. Did I not write something down in my Pocket-Book, at the same Time?

Thomas Trott. You did so.

Prisoner. You see, Sir, what Book was meant. It was my usual Custom to collect those scattered Pieces of Wit, which, by repeating in Company, I often gave a sparkling Turn to the delicate Adroitness of Conversation; and sometimes by writing the same on other Windows, I have transconvey'd the fiery Rays of a lucid Understanding from one Town to another.

Thomas Trott. I know no more of the Matter, but that I heard among the Neighbours t'other Day, that my Master had made a terrible Business on't, and that he would be devilishly worked for it in the *Champion*.

Then J. Watts, *Mr.* Leuis [*sic*] *and some others were sworn and brought the Fact home on the Prisoner, after which three Numbers of the* Champion *were read, and the several Quotations compared with the Original.*[9]

Court. Well, Mr. Col. *Apol.* what have you to say for yourself.

Prisoner. Sir, I am as innocent as the Child which hath not yet enter'd into Human Nature of the Fact laid to my Charge. This Accusation is the forward Spring of Envy of my Lawrel. It is impossible I should have any Enmity to the *English* Language, with which I am so little acquainted; if therefore I have struck any Wounds into it, they have rolled from Accident only. I confess in my Book, that *when I am warmed with a Thought, my Imagination is apt to run away with me, and make me talk Nonsense.*[10] Besides, if the *English* Language be destroyed, it ought not to be laid to my Charge, since I can evidently demonstrate that other *Literati* have used the said Language more barbarously than I have. I desire a Critical Operator may be sworn.

A Critic sworn. Sir, I can affirm on my Oath, that the *English* Language has had more Violence done it by a very great and Eminent Physician who is MD. CR. Ed S. and FRS.[11] than by the Prisoner at the Bar, for though the Prisoner certainly left several *sore* places in it, yet in the Condition he left it, it might be understood, and sometimes expressed itself with much Vigour; but the M.D. *&c.* hath so mangled and mauled it, that when I came to examine the Body, as it lay in Sheets in a Bookseller's Shop, I found it an expiring heavy Lump, without the least Appearance of Sense. I shall give you one Instance, Sir, of this barbarous Treatment. 'Perhaps the primitive animal Body might consist of the first pure, specific and hallowed Elements, harmoniously combined, and elegantly ranged in their original Natures, of which our present patched gross Bodies, are only the confused dense Kind; as our present Globe of Earth, its Water, Salt, Air, Light and Earth, are but probably the putrified Carcase of the primitive Planet; but both may continue to have some remote Analogy to one another, as a Carcase hath to a living Beauty, or an *Egyptian* Mummy to a *Cleopatra.*'* After this Instance no one will I believe lay the Murder of the *English* Language to the Prisoner's Charge, since it may be more properly called the Murder of the Language to bring Sentences together without any Meaning, than to make their Meaning obscure by any Slip in Grammar or Orthography.

The Prisoner then called several Persons to his own and his Book's Character, as to his own they all gave him a very good one, and particularly a certain fat Gentleman, who often told the Court that he was a *pleasant Companion.*[12]

As to the Book, they all agreed it was a very entertaining one; that

*See Cheyne's *Philosophical Conjectures, Discourse the First,* Page 8.

several Parts of it were really excellent, and that if he had not, from the Warmth of his Imagination, run into Nonsense, nor, from the Coldness of either his Circumstances or his Principles had *crawled* out of his Way into Politics, his Book would have been perfect in its Kind. That, even as it was, the Author had discover'd a Genius, though he appears neither in his Head or his Heart to be much of a true *Englishman*.

The Captain then summed up the Evidence, and, just before he concluded, Mrs. *Joan* whisper'd in his Ear, that the *Apology* was ordered by the Author to be twice advertis'd in the *Champion*, upon which the Captain, not from the Motive of a Bribe, but of the Prisoner's Submission to his Correction, and likewise considering that he had stood already three Times in the censorial Pillory, and been well pelted, directed the Jury in his Favour, and they found it *Chance-Medley*.[13]

Brass was then brought to the Bar, but it being late, and his Indictment so very long, that it would have reached from *Westminster* to the *Tower*, his Trial was deferred, and the Court adjourned to the next Day. But before they rose Dr. *Cheyne's* late Book was ordered to be immediately taken into custody.

L.

PART THREE

The Art of Criticism

False criticism was a common subject of Fielding's satire. At the beginning of his career he parodied the pedantry of Richard Bentley, John Dennis, and Lewis Theobald; later he parodied textual criticism generally in his treatment of *Hamlet* (No. 15). Most frequently he attacked the spirit of meanness, unfairness, partiality of modern critics, associating their activities with the growth of party spirit in politics and the general decline of cultural standards.

12 *The Champion; or, the Evening Advertiser,* No. 3

Tuesday, November 20, 1739

Fielding was very conscious of the perversion of nature which resulted from a slavish obedience to contemporary fashion and taste. In this paper he discusses the misapplication of talent which resulted in the 'ugly Beaus, and illiterate Critics' of his generation.

Nihil decet invitâ Minervâ, id est repugnante Natura, sic ut decorum conservare non possis, si aliorum Naturam imiteris, omittas tuam.

CIC., *de Off.*[1]

The Study of our own Minds, hath been recommended by the Wise of all Ages, as the most beneficial to which a Man could apply himself. The ancient Precept of *Nosce Teipsum*, is not only necessary to the Pursuit of Virtue; but we shall find a very strict search into the Powers and Faculties of our Mind, to be the only sure Method by which we can propose to arrive at any Perfection whatsoever.

Cicero, in several Parts of his Works, and particularly those *de Officiis*, takes frequent Occasion to advise every Man, before he engaged in any Art or Science, to examine thoroughly into his particular Talents, *Quo ferat Natura videre*,[2] to observe which Way his Genuis leads him; nor can any one ever reap considerable Fruit of his Labours, unless when they are employed with due Subservience to this great Guide.

The excellent Lord *Shaftsbury*, in his *Advice to an Author*, councils him to frequent Communications with himself in order to this Discovery, That before he embark in any Work, he may thoroughly understand.

——*Quid valeant Humeri, quid ferre recusent.*[3]

Fewer Men have failed in the World through Want of sufficient Application, than through applying their Labour in direct Opposition to their Genius: For Want of this strict Examination, which those great

Authors, abovecited, recommend, Men often mistake their Genius, and become ridiculous Triflers in one Art, who might have been glorious Professors of another. *Many a Man (says Dr.* South*) would have made a very good Pulpit, who hath made a very bad Figure in it.*[4]

Parents are often faulty in this Point. They are apter to consider their own Inclinations, than those of their Children. The Humour of a Father in an *English* Comedy, who is determined at all Events to breed his Son a Lawyer, is not so extravagant as it at first appears. Men of all Professions are generally desirous to educate their Children to their own Business, without examining into their Genius, or enquiring whether Nature hath given them proper Talents, and as it were predestinated them for that Profession. Men who have arrived at any great Excellence, are commonly said to have been born for such and such Ends: And I know not, if what is said of Poetry, *That he, who is not so by Nature, will never become so by Art,*[5] may not also be affirmed of every other Art and Science. It is said by *Quintilian,* —— *That Nature must begin whatever Art consummates; whatever is undertaken otherwise, is a Building without a firm Foundation, Labour entirely thrown away.*[6]

But it is still more surprising, that we often mistake our own Talents; the greater Part of Mankind are fond of exerting themselves in Characters for which Nature hath rendered them utterly unfit, while they neglect such as they have Abilities to shine in. I believe there are few Instances where Nature hath been so very sparing, but that she hath bestowed some one Quality or other, which might have enabled its Possessor, had he strictly applied himself to it, to have arrived at some Degree of Eminence, and been in some Kind serviceable to himself and others; at the same time, that she hath never been so bounteous, but to leave some Part of her Work unfinished, some particular Talent so imperfect, that the Man might have contended his whole Life in vain, to have exerted it with any Success. Yet it would be endless to give Examples of such as seem to have been her greatest Darlings, to have possessed the most and greatest Faculties, who have not been contented therewith, but have (a while at least) forsaken the noble Roads wherein they were so well enabled to travel on to the highest Degrees of Happiness and Honour, that they might pursue superficial Praise in Ways much beneath them, and which, with all their superior Powers, they have never been able to attain.

Cicero, who is so justly commended by *Rapin,* for not having imitated *Demosthenes* in those Excellencies, which would not have become his own.[7] This very Person, who here appears so thoroughly to have understood the Strength and Bent of his Genius, and who hath so well advised others to that Study, could not refrain from sometimes applying himself to those Muses with whom he was so entirely unacquainted, and suffering the Name of an excellent Orator, to be joined to that of a very indifferent Poet.

But, not to fetch Instances from ancient History, which is every where full of them, I shall mention some Writers of our own, who have erred in the same Manner.

Wycherly, whom I have always esteemed one of the best of our comic Writers, left the *Drama*, where he had acquired so great and so just an Applause, to write some of the worst Poems that any Age hath produced; and *Congreve*, who will always be esteemed by those who have a polite Taste in Comedy, could not forbear attempting Reputation, in a Manner for which he was so disqualified, that he produced a Tragedy (notwithstanding its Success) little superior to those of our worst Writers.[8]

The Remark, that Bullies are always the greatest Cowards, may be extended to every other Virtue as well as Courage. Men are so far from following that excellent Advice of my Lord *Bacon*, to shelter their Vices under those Virtues which seem nearest a-kin to them, that they always fly to those that are entirely opposite.[9] Thus the Coward, instead of aiming at Humility, the Reputation of which he might perhaps easily acquire, is ever aiming at that of Valour, which his Nature hath rendered impossible for him to be ever eminent in; and the covetous Man, slighting the Estimation of Frugality, commonly contends for that of Liberality.

As nothing is so ridiculous, so nothing is more common, than to see Men acting Parts for which they are every Way unfit. I remember a certain Dancing-Master, sufficiently excellent in his Art, and who seemed happily to have blundered on the only little Talent, by which Nature had enabled him to procure a Livelihood. There was hardly a Man or Woman, in the Town wherein he lived, whose Heels had not at one Time or other been under his Command. This Gentleman, who was in a very fair Way of dancing into a Fortune, took it into his Head in his latter Days to commence Politician, and spent so much Time in reading Histories and News-Papers, that he lost most of his Scholars to a young Rival, who troubled his Head with no other Motions of the *French* Court, than those which were made to the Sound of a Fiddle.

How many ugly Beaus, and illiterate Critics, swarm every where in this City? How many awkward People are the Jest of the Court, who might have harangued with good Success in *Westminster-Hall*?[10] And how many contemptible Members are there in our learned Societies, who might have shined out very illustriously in an Assembly of the Ladies? Many a Physician, have starved with Infamy, by doing that Execution with his Pen, which, he would have arrived at with great Profit and Honour, by having done with his Sword. And the same Spirit, which hath made a Divine a Curse to his Country, would have made a Soldier a Blessing to it.

The Players, whom I used to converse with much in my younger Days, have often told me, that those who succeeded best among them in comic Parts, were continually desirous of appearing in tragical; and their best Tragedians were usually as certain in their own Opinions, of gaining the greatest Applause in Comedy.

This, I believe, all those who were acquainted with the Theatre, while under the Regulation of that Triumvirate,[11] so famous in Dramatic History, can recall to their Memory several Instances of: But what had still a worse Effect on the Stage at that Time, was, that those Triumvirs, while they cautiously concealed the Abilities of such Actors, whose Capacities they imagined might rival or eclipse their own, very zealously introduced into Characters of Dignity and Consequence, several of their own Favourites and Relations, who were generally, with great Contempt, hissed off the Stage.

As a Misapplication of Talents in private Life, always renders the Person guilty of it ridiculous, so in a public Capacity it makes a whole Nation so. Let us fancy to ourselves a Country, where the several Parts in the Government should be bestowed as the Characters in *Alexander the Great* once were; in which *Penkethman* personated that illustrious Hero, and *Dicky Norris*, *Statira*; would not such a People make as burlesque a Figure in the World, as that celebrated Piece did on the Stage?[12]

13 *The Champion; or, the Evening Advertiser,* No. 5

Tuesday, November 27, 1739

Thoughtless and malicious criticism was, Fielding thought, unchristian. His attacks on the critics of his day are connected with his condemnation of party spirit, cruelty and malice. In this paper he quotes from an early version of his poem *On Good Nature*.

—— *Nescis Dominæ Fastidia Romæ*
Crede mihi, nimium *Martia Turba sapit.*
Majores nusquam Ronchi juvenesque senesque
Et Pueri Nasum Rhinocerotis habent.
MART.[1]

There are two Sorts of Persons, who, may, in some Sense, be said to feed on the Breath which goeth out of the Mouth of Man; namely, the Soldier and the Author. But here I would not be understood to mean, by Soldier, such wise Military Men, who justly despising this thin Diet, are content to receive from five hundred to two thousand Pounds a Year, for appearing now and then in a red Coat with a Sash, in the Parks and Market-Places of this Kingdom, and who never saw an Enemy, unless the old Officers and Soldiers of their own Regiments, who disdain to have such Commanders at their Head; nor, by Authors, would I be supposed to cast any Reflection on such as have found a Method by Panegyric, to cram themselves with more substantial Food. The Kind of Persons here hinted at, may be seen in St. *James's* Park in a foggy Morning in shabby red and black Coats, with open Mouths eagerly devouring the Fog for Breakfast. Such Soldiers as an Acquaintance of mine, who, after he had served many Campaigns in *Flanders*, and been wounded in *Spain*, with a generous Heart and an empty Pocket died in the *King's-Bench*; and such Authors as *Butler*, who, after he had published his inimitable *Hudibrass*, was starved to Death in a Garret.[2]

Now what did these obtain, or what can their Followers promise themselves besides Fame, which is but the Breath of Man? A Dainty, however unsubstantial, on which *Horace* assures us, a Poet will grow extremely fat.

Palma negata macrum donata reducit opimum.[3]

Here I am aware, it will be objected, that I confer this Reward too soon, and the same Epistle of *Horace*, with Dr. *Bentley's Ingentia FATA*,[4] will be produced against me, and many other Authorities, to prove that they taste not this Delicacy till after their Death: For which Reason it may be told me I should have imitated the Style of the Author of *Tom Thumb*,* and asserted that that there were the Ghosts of two Sorts of Persons, *&c.* who fed on the Breath of Man. To which I only answer, that tho' Envy, which, according to *Ovid*, only preys on the Living,[5] may have robbed some of their just Fame during their Lives; yet several Instances may be produced to the contrary. That Verse of the Poet:

Præsenti tibi maturos largimur Honores.[6]

May have been applyed to many more than him for whom it was first intended. But those who do not care to allow any Praise to a living Author, may if they please consider him as feeding on the Hopes of it; the one being almost as substantial as the other.

Indeed the Soldier is in this Point happier than the Poet, as he generally receives his Portion of Fame sooner. *Alexander* had the immediate Honours of his Victories, and perhaps much more than they deserved; but poor *Homer* was, during his Life, reputed little better than a Ballad-singer; and *Plutarch*, in the Life of *Lycurgus*, tells us, that his Poems were scarce heard of in *Greece* till many Years after his Death. Yet the Poet hath some Advantage in his Turn; for his Works, if not his Name, will outlive the others; to which we may add Sir *William Temple's* Observation, that the World hath produced a thousand equal to *Alexander*, but scarce one capable of writing an *Iliad*.[7]

But to drop the Soldier, with whom we have no more to do at present, and stick to the Author. If Fame be, as I have said, his Food, (and perhaps in a litteral Sense it may be often so called) how cruel must they be, who rashly, inconsiderately, and often wantonly take

*An Author who dealt so much in Ghosts, that he is said to have spoiled the *Hay-Market* Stage, by cutting it all into Trap Doors.

the Bread out of his Mouth, since it seldom happens that they are such as can ever put it into their own?

This is a Cruelty of which all the good Writers, from the Days of *Horace* to the present Time, have complained, and for which bad Authors have in all Ages been stigmatized; some of whom, like the Wretch who burnt the Temple at *Ephesus*,[8] have been immortalized for their Infamy, and owed such their Immortality, to those very Poets whom they have traduced. Thus *Virgil* hath recorded the Names of *Mævius* and *Bavius*;[9] and thus *Pope* (whose Works will be coeval with the Language in which they are writ) hath condescended to transmit to Posterity many Heroical Persons, who, without his kind Assistance, would have never been known to have dared lift their Pens against the greatest Poet of his Time. Bad Writers therefore seem to have a Sort of prescriptive Privilege to abuse good ones; in which I the rather indulge them for the great Inoffensiveness thereof; such Calumny being seldom read, and never believed.

Leaving, therefore, all such as utterly incorrigible, I shall here address myself only to those who never have nor ever intend to write, and consequently can propose no Interest in ruining the Reputation of those who do. I would recommend to all Persons (except bad Writers) to be extremely cautious in the Use of the Words *Low*, *Dull*, *Stupid*, *Sad Stuff*, *Grub-street*, &c. which, with some few more, I wish heartily were banished out of our Language, and that it was reckoned as certain a Mark of Folly to use them, as it would be of Indency to use some others. Tho' I must own at the same Time, this might be as fatal to Criticism, as the Banishment of indecent Words hath been to Gallantry; and that some Persons of admired Judgment would be as hard put to it to talk critically without the one, as some noted Beaus are to talk wantonly without the other.

I should be sorry to think there was in Mankind the Principle pointed at in the following Lines, which I have taken from a Poem not yet communicated to the Public.

> Nor in the Tyger's Cave, nor Lion's Den,
> Dwells our Malignity. For selfish Men,
> The Gift of Fame like that of Money deem;
> And think they lose, whene'er they give Esteem.[10]

I rather impute unjust Censure to Ignorance than Malice, and very sincerely believe Men when they say *I don't understand a Word of all this*; which they may probably say with great Truth of the whole *Iliad*.

And one may apply to these Persons what *Dacier* said of a *French* Critic, who abused the last mentioned Poem. *That he found it more easy to censure him than to read him.*[11]

However, as it is certain they are not always understood in this Light, and that the emptiest Fellows have sometimes done Harm (as my Bookseller terms it) *to the Sale of a Work* I shall, as a Terror to all such Persons, as well as an Information to those who have been abused by them, communicate to the Public the Opinion of Mr. Counsellor *Vinegar*, on the following Case.

Q. If a Man says of an Author that he is dull, or hath no Wit, (seeing that Wit is his Property, according to a noble Lord who hath more of that Property than any Man) will not an Action lie for the said Author?[12]

Moy semble quod si ascun dit de J. S. eteant un Poete quod est Dull. Action bien volt gyser et le Resolution de le Case, 1 R. A. 55 S. 16. Bien agree ove ceo ubi Action fuit port per ten Apprentice del Ley et Plt declare quod Deft avoit dit de luy quod est Dunce, and will get nothing by the Law. Et le Opinion del Court, fuit quod Action bien gist, car Home Poet estte Heavie, et nemy tam pregnant come ascuns auters sont et encore un bon Lawyer. Mes quia il avoit dit que il ne volt get ascun chose per la Ley. Action gist. Sic icy car si Poete soit Heavite ou dull non volt gett ascun chose en le World.[13]

WIL. VINEGAR.

But, in the mean Time, as such Action may not be soon brought or soon decided, it may be proper to put some immediate stop to the present Currency of Criticism. In order thereto, having consulted with the Elders of my Family, I have determined, by Virtue of that Authority with which I have invested myself, to lay down some Qualifications, without which no Person shall henceforth presume to censure any Performance whatever.

And here he, who shall consider the Derivation of this Word Criticism, which is from a *Greek* Word, implying no less than Judgment, or shall reflect on the vast Abilities which have been possest by the Professors of this Art, and what hath been required by those who have given Rules for it, particularly Mr. *Pope* in his most excellent Essay thereon;

Let those teach others who themselves excell,
And censure freely who have written well.[14]

And in many other Places of that charming Poem, he I say, who will weigh all these Particulars, will doubtless think me extremely reasonable in the following Particulars.

First, I expect henceforward, that no Person whatever, be his Qualifications what they will, presume to give his Opinion against any literary Production, without having first read one Word of it.

Secondly, That no *Man* under the Age of fourteen, shall be entitled to give a Definitive Opinion (unless in the Play-house).

Thirdly, That no Person shall be allowed to be a perfect Judge in any Work of Learning, who hath not advanced as far as the End of the Accidence; unless at the Coffee-Houses West of *Charing-Cross*, where such Deficiencies shall be supplied by a proper Quantity of Lace and Embroidery.

As to Prejudice, I mention it not, seeing that the only Persons in whom we can suspect so base a Motive, are either those Authors beforementioned, who have my Leave to abuse me or any one else as much as they please, or such as are sworn Enemies to all Literature in General, and have entered into Bonds among themselves, to give no Encouragement to any Genius whatever. Of some of whom I have lately heard, and may possibly describe to the Public, that whatever they hereafter say may go for nothing.

Lastly, It being well known that some Men have a Way of communicating their critical Sentiments by Winks, Nods, Smiles, Frowns, and other Signs and Tokens, without the Assistance of Speech; and having heard of a certain Person in this Kingdom, whose Nod could convey more meaning than the most significant Words of any other,[15] I prohibit all People of no Consequence from using any of these Signs, and do expressly forbid any Man hereafter to shake his Head, who is universally known among his Acquaintance to have nothing in it.

C.

14 *The Covent Garden Journal*, No. 3

Saturday, January 11, 1752

The Covent Garden Journal was Fielding's last newspaper. He began it on January 4, 1752, and ended it on November 25 of the same year.

This paper on criticism was probably directed at the critics of *Amelia*; see below, No. 72, headnote.

Majores nusquam Rhonchi; Juvenesque, Senesque,
Et Pueri Nasum Rhinocerotis habent.

MARTIAL.

In English,

No Town can such a Gang of Critics shew,
Ev'n Boys turn up that Nose they cannot blow.[1]

By a Record in the Censors Office, and now in my Custody, it appears, that at a censorial Inquisition, taken *Tricesimo qto. Eliz.* by one of my illustrious Predecessors, no more than 19 Critics were enrolled in the Cities of London and Westminster; whereas at the last Inquisition taken by myself, 25°. *Geo. 2di.* the Number of Persons claiming a Right to that Order, appears to amount to 276302.[2]

This immense Encrease is, I believe, to be no otherwise accounted for, than from the very blameable Negligence of the late Censors, who have, indeed, converted their Office into a mere Sinecure, no Inquisition, as I can find, having been taken since the Censorship of Isaac Bickerstaffe, Esq; in the latter End of the Reign of Queen Anne.[3]

To the same Neglect are owing many Encroachments on all the other Orders of the Society. That of *Gentlemen* in particular, I observe to have greatly increased, and that of *Sharpers* to have decreased in the same Proportion within these few Years.

All these Irregularities it is my firm Purpose to endeavour at reforming, and to restore the high Office with which I am invested to its ancient Use and Dignity. This, however, must be attempted with

Prudence and by slow Degrees: For habitual and inveterate Evils are to be cured by slow Alteratives, and not by violent Remedies. Of this the good Emperor Pertinax will be a lasting Example. 'This worthy Man' (says Dion Cassius) 'perished by endeavouring too hastily to reform all the Evils which infested his Country. He knew not, it seems, tho' otherwise a Man of very great Knowledge, that it is not safe, nor indeed possible, to effect a Reformation in too many Matters at once. A Rule which, if it holds true in private Life, is much more so when it is applied to those Evils that affect the Public.'[4]

I thought it, therefore, not prudent, in the Hurry of my above Inquisition to make any Exceptions, but admitted all who offered to be enrolled. This is a Method which I shall not pursue hereafter, being fully resolved to enquire into the Qualifications of every Pretender.

And that all Persons may come prepared to prove their Right to the Order of Critics, I shall here set down those several Qualifications which will be insisted on before any will be admitted to that high Honour. In doing this, however, I shall strictly pursue the excellent Rule I have cited, and shall act with most perfect Moderation; for I am willing to throw open the Door as wide as I can, so that as few as possible may be rejected.

It is, I think, the Sentiment of Quinctilian, that no Man is capable of becoming a good Critic on a great Poet, but he who is himself a great Poet.[5] This would, indeed, confine the Critics on Poetry, at least, to a very small Number; and would, indeed, strike all the Antients, except only Horace and Longinus off the Roll; of the latter of whom, tho' he was no Poet, Mr. Pope finely says,

> Thee, great Longinus, all the Nine inspire,
> And bless their Critic with a Poet's Fire.[6]

But with Respect to so great a Name as that of Quinctilian, this Rule appears to me much too rigid. It seems, indeed, to be little less severe than an Injunction that no Man should criticize on Cookery but he who was himself a Cook.

To require what is generally called Learning in a Critic, is altogether as absurd as to require Genius. Why should a Man in this Case, any more than in all others, be bound by any Opinions but his own? Or why should he read by Rule any more than eat by it? If I delight in a Slice of Bullock's Liver or of Oldmixon,[7] why shall I be confined to Turtle or to Swift?

The only Learning, therefore, that I insist upon, is, That my Critic

BE ABLE TO READ; and this is surely very reasonable: For I do not see how he can otherwise be called a Reader; and if I include every Reader in the Name of Critic, it is surely very just to confine every Critic within the Number of Readers.

Nor do I only require the Capacity of Reading, but the actual Exercise of that Capacity; I do here strictly forbid any Persons whatever to pass a definitive Sentence on a Book BEFORE THEY HAVE READ AT LEAST TEN PAGES IN IT, under the Penalty of being for ever rendered incapable of Admission to the Order of Critics.

Thirdly, all Critics who from and after the First Day of February next, shall condemn any Book, shall be ready to give some Reason for their Judgment: Nor shall it be sufficient for such Critic to drivel out, *I don't know not I, but all that I know is, I don't like it.* Provided, nevertheless, that any Reason how foolish or frivolous soever, shall be allowed a good and full Justification; except only the Words POOR STUFF, WRETCHED STUFF, BAD STUFF, SAD STUFF, LOW STUFF, PAULTRY STUFF. All which STUFFS I do forever banish from the Mouths of all Critics.

Provided also, that the last-mentioned Clause do extend only to such Critics as openly proclaim their Censures; for it is our Intention, that all Persons shall be at Liberty to dislike privately, whatever Book they please, *without understanding, or reading one Word of it*, any Thing therein or herein contained to the contrary notwithstanding.

But as it is reasonable to extend this Power of judging for themselves, no farther in this Case of Criticism, than it is allowed to Men in some others, I do here declare, that I shall not, for the future, admit any Males to the Office of Criticism till they be of the full Age of 18, that being the Age when the Laws allow them to have a Capacity of disposing personal Chattles: for, before that Time, they have only the Power of disposing of themselves in the trifling Article of Marriage. Females, perhaps, I shall admit somewhat earlier, provided they be either witty or handsome, or have a Fortune of 5000 *l.* and upwards.

Together with Childhood, I exclude all other civil Incapacities; and here I mean not only legal but real Lunatics, and Ideots. In this Number I include all Persons who, from the whole Tenour of their Conduct, appear to be incapable of discerning Good from Bad, Right from Wrong, or Wisdom from Folly, in any Instance whatever.

There are again some Persons whom I shall admit only to a partial Exercise of this Office; as, for Instance, Rakes, Beaux, Sharpers, and fine Ladies, are strictly forbidden, under Penalty of perpetual Exclusion, to presume to criticise on any Works of Religion, or Morality. All

Lawyers, Physicians, Surgeons, and Apothecaries, are strictly forbidden to pass any Judgment on those Authors who attempt any Reformation in Law, or Physic. Officers of State, and wou'd-be Officers of State, (honest Men only excepted,) with all their Attendants, and Dependents, their Placemen, and wou'd-be Placemen, Pimps, Spies, Parasites, Informers, and Agents, are forbidden, under the Penalty aforesaid, to give their Opinions of any Work in which the Good of the Kingdom, in general, is designed to be advanced; but as for all Pamphlets which anywise concern the great Cause of WOODALL OUT, and TAKEALL IN, Esqs;[8] full Liberty is left to both Parties, and the one may universally cry up, and commend, and the other may universally censure and condemn, as usual. All Critics offending against this Clause, are to be deemed infamous, and their several Criticisms are hereby declared to be entirely void, and of none Effect.

No Author is to [be] admitted into the Order of Critics, until he hath read over, and understood, Aristotle, Horace, and Longinus, in their original Language; nor then without a Testimonial that he hath spoken well of some living Author besides himself.

Lastly, all Persons are forbid, under the Penalty *of our highest Displeasure*, to presume to criticise upon any of those Works with which WE OURSELVES shall think proper to oblige the Public; and any Person who shall presume to offend in this Particular, will not only be expunged from the Roll of Critics, but will be degraded from any other Order to which he shall belong; and his Name will be forthwith entered in the Records of Grub-Street.

A.

ALEXANDER DRAWCANSIR.

15 *The Covent Garden Journal*, No. 31

Saturday, April 18, 1752

This paper might be read in conjunction with the scenes in *A Journey from this World to the Next* (1743), ch. viii, where the narrator describes Shakespeare's reaction to a dispute about his meaning.

Qui Bavium non odit, amet tua Carmina, Mævi.

VIRGIL.[1]

He who doth not hate one bad Commentator, let him love a worse.

SIR,—You are sensible, I believe, that there is nothing in this Age more fashionable, than to criticise on Shakespeare: I am indeed told, that there are not less than 200 Editions of that Author, with Commentaries, Notes, Observations, &c. now preparing for the Press; as nothing therefore is more natural than to direct one's Studies by the Humour of the Times, I have myself employed some leisure Hours on that great Poet. I here send you a short Specimen of my Labours, being some Emendations of that most celebrated Soliloquy in *Hamlet*, which, as I have no Intention to publish Shakespeare myself, are very much at the Service of any of the 200 Critics abovementioned.

I am, &c.

Hamlet, Act III. Scene 2

To be, or not to be, that is the question.

This is certainly very intelligble; but if a slight Alteration were made in the former Part of the Line, and an easy Change was admitted in the last Word, the Sense would be greatly improved. I would propose then to read thus;

To be, or not. To be! That is the BASTION.

That is the strong Hold. The Fortress. So Addison in *Cato*.

Here will I hold——[2]

The military Terms which follow, abundantly point out this Reading.

> Whether 'tis nobler in the *Mind* to *suffer*
> The *Slings* and Arrows of outragious Fortune,
> Or *to take Arms against a Sea* of Troubles,
> And by opposing end them.

Suffering is, I allow, a Christian Virtue; but I question whether it hath ever been ranked among the heroic Qualities. Shakespeare certainly wrote BUFFET; and this leads us to supply Man for Mind; Mind being alike applicable to both Sexes, whereas Hamlet is here displaying the most masculine Fortitude. *Slings* and *Arrows* in the succeeding Line, is an Impropriety which could not have come from our Author; the former being the Engine which discharges, and the latter the Weapon discharged. To the Sling, he would have opposed the Bow; or to Arrows, Stones. Read therefore WINGED ARROWS; that is, feathered Arrows; a Figure very usual among Poets: So in the classical Ballad of Chevy Chase;

> The Grey-Goose Wing that was thereon
> In his Heart's Blood was wet.

The next Line is undoubtedly corrupt—to take Arms against a Sea, can give no Man, I think, an Idea; whereas by a slight Alteration and Transposition all will be set right, and the undoubted Meaning of Shakespeare restored.

> Or *tack* against an *Arm 'oth' Sea* of Troubles,
> And by composing end them.

By composing himself to Sleep, as he presently explains himself. What shall I do? says Hamlet. Shall I *buffet* the Storm, or shall I tack about and go to Rest?

> —— *To die*, to sleep;
> No more; and by a Sleep to say we end
> The Heart-ach, and the thousand natural Shocks
> The Flesh is Heir to; 'tis a *Consummation*
> Devoutly to be wished. *To die*, to sleep;
> To sleep, perchance to dream;——

What to die first, and to go to sleep afterwards; and not only so but to dream too?—— But tho' his Commentators were dreaming of

Nonsense when they read this Passage, Shakespeare was awake when he writ it. Correct it thus;

——To lie to sleep.

i.e. To go to sleep, a common Expression; Hamlet himself expressly says he means *no more*; which he would hardly have said, if he had talked of Death, a Matter of the greatest and highest Nature: And is not the Context a Description of the Power of Sleep, which every one knows puts an End to the Heart-ach, the Tooth-ach, Head-ach, and indeed every Ach? So our Author in his *Macbeth*, speaking of this very Sleep, calls it

Balm of hurt Minds, great Nature's *second Course*.[3]

Where, by the bye, instead of second Course, I read SICKEN'D DOSE; this being, indeed, the Dose which Nature chuses to apply to all her Shocks, and may be therefore well said *devoutly to be wished for*; which surely cannot be so generally said of Death.—— But how can Sleep be called a *Consummation*?—— The true Reading is certainly *Consultation*; the Cause for the Effect, a common Metonymy, *i.e.* When we are in any violent Pain, and a Set of Physicians are met in a *Consultation*, it is to be hoped the Consequence will be a sleeping Dose. Death, I own, is very devoutly to be apprehended, but seldom wished, I believe, at least by the Patient himself, at all such Seasons.

For natural *Shocks*, I would read *Shakes*; indeed I know only one Argument which can be brought in Justification of the old Reading; and this is, that *Shock* hath the same Signification, and is rather the better Word. In such Cases, the Reader must be left to his Choice.

For in that Sleep of Death what Dreams may come
When we have *shuffled* off this mortal *Coil*,
Must give us Pause——

Read and print thus:

For in that Sleep, of Death what Dreams may come?
When we have *scuffled* off this mortal *Call*,
Must give us Pause——

i.e. Must make us stop. *Shuffle* is a paultry Metaphor, taken from playing at Cards; whereas *scuffle* is a noble and military Word.

The Whips and Scorns of Time.

Undoubtedly *Whips* and *Spurs.*

> When he himself might his *Quietus* make
> With a bare *Bodkin.*

With a bare *Pipkin.* The Reader will be pleased to observe, that Hamlet, as we have above proved, is here debating whether it were better to go to sleep, or to keep awake; as an Argument for the affirmative, he urges that no Man in his Senses would bear *The Whips and Scorns of Time, the Oppressor's Wrong,* &c. when he himself, without being at the Expence of an Apothecary, might make his *Quietus, or sleeping Dose,* with a bare PIPKIN, the cheapest of all Vessels, and consequently within every Man's Reach.

> ——Who would Fardles bear,
> To groan and sweat under a weary Life?

Who indeed would bear anything for such a Reward? The true Reading is

> ——Who would for th' Ales bear
> To groan, &c.

Who would bear the Miseries of Life, for the Sake of the Ales. In the Days of Shakespeare, when Diversions were not arrived at that Degree of Elegance to which they have been since brought, the Assemblies of the People for Mirth were called by the Name of an ALE. This was the Drum or Rout of that Age, and was the Entertainment of the better Sort, as it is at this Day of the Vulgar. Such are the *Easter-Ales* and the *Whitsun-Ales,* at present celebrated all over the West of England. The Sentiment therefore of the Poet, is this; *Who would bear the Miseries of Life, to enjoy the Pleasures of it*; which latter Word is by no forced Metaphor called THE ALES OF LIFE.

> And makes us rather bear the Ills we have,
> Than fly to others that we know not of.

This, I own, is Sense as it stands; but the Spirit of the Passage will be improved, if we read

> Than try *some others,* &c.
> ——Thus the native Hue of Resolution,
> Is sicklied o'er with the pale Cast of Thought.

Read,

—Thus the native Blue of Resolution,
Is pickled o'er in a stale Cask of Salt.

This restores a most elegant Sentiment; I shall leave the Relish of it therefore with the Reader, and conclude by wishing that its Taste may never be obliterated by any future Alteration of this glorious Poet.

A.

PART FOUR

Pertaining to Grub Street

Fielding's great battle with the inhabitants of Grub Street, the literary hacks of his time, is described in the opening numbers of *The Covent Garden Journal*, but he maintained a running fight against them throughout his career. Fielding was by no means as willing to dismiss modern productions as either Swift or Pope, or to pillory individual authors. He was unstinting in his praise for modern authors of whom he approved, but had nothing but scorn for those who helped to depreciate cultural and moral standards for financial and party reasons. He attacked the practice of puffing literary works, the tricks of unscrupulous booksellers, the hack translator who was ignorant of languages, the empty newspaper, and the prevailing taste for slander and indecency. Throughout his attacks on Grub Street he maintains the dignity of the world of letters against the sordid literary underworld of eighteenth-century London.

16 *The Champion; or, the Evening Advertiser,* No. 47

Saturday, March 1, 1740

In this paper Fielding attacks the art of 'puffing'—that is, the contemporary techniques of advertisement as practised by booksellers like the notorious Edmund Curll.

——*Heu Plebes Scelerata & prava Favoris?*
SIL ITAL.[1]

I have, in a former Paper, remarked the Partiality by which we are governed in our Dealings with Trades and Professions, and shewed that we are led entirely by Fashion to prefer this or that individual Member to all the rest of his Calling.[2] This hath given Rise to a common Expression of *Getting a Name*, and to the common Custom of hanging out Names on a Sign, by which we are sometimes not only informed where Mr. *A. B.* now lives, but likewise of the Place from whence he came. There is one of these Names in *Fleet-street*, which seems to be hung out as the Rival of St. *Dunstan's* Clock.[3]

This Partiality arises from one or both of these amiable Originals, *viz.* Pride and Ignorance; for as there are several wise People who are vain of being the Bubbles[4] of eminent Men, so there are others, who, tho' they are very pretty Gentlemen and very fine Ladies, are unluckily so ignorant, that they do not know when they are imposed on.

As Pride and Ignorance reign the most absolute in the learned World, so this Prejudice is felt more severely by us Authors than by any other Set of Men. I believe of the present Encouragers and Advancers of Wit and Learning not one in twenty hath ever been at School, and of those who have, very few have brought away any other Marks but those of the Rod with them. So that what *Horace* says of Writers, *That the Learned and Unlearned become such indifferently*,[5] may be more properly applied to Readers of whom, according to Mr. *Pope*,

Ten censure wrong to one who writes amiss.[6]

But Pride hath at least an equal Share with Ignorance in the Matter.

Writing seems to be understood an arrogating to yourself a Superiority (which of all others will be granted with the greatest Reluctance) of the Understanding. In which, as the Pre-eminence is not so apparent as in Beauty or Riches, Pride is often able in our own Minds a long while to maintain the weaker Side of the Argument. *The Understanding, like the Eye,* (says Mr. *Lock*) *whilst it makes us see and perceive all other Things, takes no Notice of itself; and it requires Art and Pains to set it at a Distance and make it its own Object.*[7] This Comparison, fine as it is, is inadequate: For the Eye can contemplate itself in a Glass, but no *Narcissus* hath hitherto discovered any Mirrour for the Understanding, no Knowledge of which is to be obtained but by the Means Mr. *Lock* prescribes, which as it requires Art and Pains, or in other Words, a very good Understanding to execute, it generally happens that the Superiority in it, is a Cause tried on very dark and presumptive Evidence, and a Verdict commonly found by self Love for ourselves.

But, to pursue this philosophical Enquiry no farther, it is certain that a Man no where meets with such Opposition as in an Attempt to acquire Reputation by Writing, which the World always with-holds from him as long as it is able, and seldom allows him till he is past the Enjoyment of it. The Lawrel, like the Cypress, being generally thrown into the Grave.

This Malignancy hath given Rise to several Inventions among Authors, to get themselves and their Works a Name. And has introduc'd that famous Art call'd Puffing, which, as it is brought to great Perfection in this Age, affords us a constant Article in one Column of our Paper.[8]

It would be endless to run through the several Branches of this Art, by which we are inform'd that certain Works have been very much admired by Persons of great Distinction and Judgment, or at other Times of their great Usefulness, and often that they are prohibited at certain Places, the Author run away, or banish'd, or hang'd, all which are thought to give an additional Value to his Works.

But the chief Art of Book-puffing is that which may be very properly call'd *Getting a Name* to a Book, I mean that Method which had flourish'd much of late of borrowing a Name for its Author.

Numberless are the Arts which the Street-walking-Muses make use of to lay their Bastards at the Doors of their Betters, or in other Words by which Booksellers and their bad Authors endeavour to steal the Names of good ones. This Stratagem hath been long practised on the Dead, and since the Restoration of Learning and the Invention of

Printing, most of the celebrated Authors of Antiquity have been forced to adopt as their own, the Offspring not only of several Ages beyond them, but even of such as have not had the least Affinity to them. I remember about twelve Years ago, upon the Success of a *new* Play of *Shakspeare's*, *said* to have be found somewhere by Some-body, the Craft set themselves to searching, and soon after I heard that several more Plays of *Shakspeare*, *Beaumont* and *Fletcher*, and *Ben Johnson* were *found*, and the Town to be *entertain'd* with them; but the Players, for I know not what Reason, discouraging this Practice, it hath since ceased.[9]

But the great Improvement of this Art is said to be the Growth of the present Age; namely, the borrowing the Name of an Author while he is alive, which is done several Ways.

One Bookseller is reported to have maintained certain Writers in his Garret, because they had the same Names with some of their eminent Cotemporaries. Others have contented themselves with concealing the Name of the Author in the Title-Page, and only spreading Whispers through the Coffee-Houses, that he is a very considerable Person, my Lord, or Mr. Such-a-one, which the Whisperer hath discovered by his Stile, or been credibly informed of by some who have seen the Manuscript. But the most usual Way is to throw out certain Hints in the Advertisements, such as by a Lady of Quality. By a celebrated Physician. By *D*[*octo*]*r S*[*wif*]*t*. By a certain Dean, *&c.* By all which Means a very spurious Issue are propagated in the learned World. Thus *Gay* becomes Dull, *Addison* publishes *B*[*awd*]*y* Poems, and *D*[*ea*]*n S*[*wif*]*t* hath writ more Nonsense than *C*[*olle*]*y C*[*ibbe*]*r*.

But the most remarkable Piece of Ingenuity, if it had been done by Design, was exhibited this Winter, in which a Poem was publish'd with the following Title Page, printed in the same Manner as it is here inserted

Seventeen
Hundred Thirty Nine,
Being the Sequel of

Seventeen
Hundred Thirty Eight.
Written

by Mr. Pope

If this had been publish'd by any other Bookseller but Mr. *C*[*url*]*l*, we should have believed that it was intended to impose the Year Nine on the World as a Work of Mr. *Pope's*, who is I think avowedly the Author of the Year Eight; but the said Mr. *C*[*url*]*l* is too well known to have any such Attempt suspected, both from the Nicety of his Conscience and his Judgment, which could not suffer him to hope that he should be able to exhibit the Pop of a *Pistol* for the Fire of a Canon.[10]

I have been often desired by my Bookseller to give a *Name* (as he calls it) to this Paper: For which Purpose, he hath drawn up several Advertisements. One signifying, that the late Mr. *Addison* left a large Quantity of Papers behind him, some of which were entitled *Essays on several Subjects*. Another importing that the Author of this Paper was in *Wales* at the Time that Sir *Richard Steel* died. Or suppose (says he) it should be insinuated that you was lately come from *Ireland*. Ah! you might have thrown in a Hint about *Lais's* Wash. Or else if you should say you had a Lodging near *Twickenham* last Summer.[11] Any of these Things would do. Nay, he hath carried it so far as to desire me to go to several Coffee-Houses where I am little known, and assert roundly that my Lord *B*[*olingbro*]*ke* was the Author of the *Champion*, assuring me that he would whisper it to every one who came into his Shop; and he was sure it would do: For that the same Scheme had been successfully tried by another.

In short, it would be tedious to run through the several Persons which by Hints, Tokens, and initial Letters, he would have intimated to be the Authors of the *Champion*, indeed almost every one that the present Age hath ever read with Admiration. Nor did he confine himself to single Persons, he was desirous to insinuate that some Papers were composed by the C[olle]dge of Ph[ysicia]ns, others by the R[oy]al Soc[ie]ty, and others by that admired Body the Soc[ie]ty for Advancement of L[earning].[12]

I answered him, that I scorned to impose false Colours on the World, that if my Paper could not succeed by the Merit, he should not owe its Success to the Roguery of the Author. In short, that, like some tender Parents, I had such a Fondness for my Offspring, that I would not part with them to another even for their own Advantage.

However, to pacify him, I was forced to condescend to agree, that in order to make my Paper appear like a *Spectator*, it should for the Future be adorned with a Capital Letter at the End, as well as a Motto at the Beginning.[13]

C.

17 *The Champion; or, the Evening Advertiser,* No. 147

Tuesday, October 21, 1740

This paper, together with the passage selected from *Amelia* (No. 18, below), represents Fielding's views on translation and quotation by modern authors.

Quem recitas meus est, O Fidentine, Libellus,
Sed malè cum recitas, incipit esse tuus.
MART.[1]

I am very well pleas'd (said the ingenious Mr. *Addison*) *when I find any beautiful Passage in an ancient Author, which hath not been* blown upon *by any succeeding Writer.*[2] Indeed, there are very few which have not undergone this Fate. *Homer* and *Virgil, Plato* and *Aristotle, Cicero* and *Demosthenes,* have been torn (if I may be allow'd the Expression) Limb from Limb, and divided as lawful Spoil among the Poets and Philosophers of later Ages: And, I believe, there is not a Sentiment, not a Line in *Horace,* which is not at present extant in the Works of our modern Essay-Writers.

The *Greek* Authors would have been infinitely securer than the *Latin* from these Depredations, and *Plato* and *Aristotle* might have remain'd, perhaps, pretty entire to this Day, had not their Armour been taken from them, and their Works left exposed by the Attacks of Translators, by which means they have become liable to the Insults of several who could not have come at them, while they were entrench'd in their own Language. *Montagne* (who of all others abounds the most in Quotations) calls quoting an Author *transplanting his Sentiments into his own Works*; a Term, in my Opinion, very elegantly adapted to this Practice:[3] For, as we see Trees, *&c.* transplanted to an improper Soil, fade and decay, so must it fare with the Product of a rich and fertile Imagination, transplanted into the sterile Pages of a Blockhead. The fruit of *Athens* cannot flourish with any Strength, or Beauty, in the Soil of *Grubstreet.*

This some of our Moderns are so sensible of, that, in order to adapt them to their Works, they change as much as in them lies, the very Nature of these elegant Flowers before they transplant them, by lopping, maiming, and altering. Insomuch, that by that time a Sentiment of *Homer* hath been scourged by Translators, thro' two or three Languages, and receiv'd afterwards the *Coup-de-Grace* of a Transcriber, it may possibly fit very well the Place to which it is transplanted, and may seem more properly the Product of the Soil it is transplanted to, than that it was taken from. Dr. *South* says of these Writers, *That their Quotations are to be* trusted no farther than they are seen *in the Original.*[4]

But there is another Sort of Writers, quite different from these, who are so far from being beholding to the Ancients, or borrowing any Thing from them, that they rather chuse out of the Abundance of their Stock to lend to, and lay Obligations on the said Ancients. I mean those Authors, who very generously attribute certain elegant Sentiments to them, which are no where to be found in their Works, and are indeed no other than the lawful Issue of their own Brains: A Charity very frequent among the Moderns, who seem to find all the Pleasure in bestowing, which the best Christian ever could boast of. It is common with these Gentlemen, after having introduced some very plain and obvious Reflection into their Works, to add, *as* Plato *very well observes*, or, *as* Plutarch *somewhere has it*; nay, I have known the Obligation conferr'd on the whole Body of the Ancients together, and have seen an honest, downright *English* Sentiment set out with *I have somewhere read in an ancient Writer*. I remember a Writer, some Years ago, who was so exceeding liberal to the ancient Philosophers, that I question whether he did not prove *Cicero's* Words to be true, *That there was no Absurdity so great, but that some Philosopher had maintain'd it.*[5]

Nothing can appear more comprehensive than the Liberality of these Gentlemen, who at once lay an Obligation on Antiquity, by accumulating on it these additional Honours; and on Posterity, by transmitting to it such Fragments, as the whole Works of these Authors could by no means supply it with.

But Charities, however good their Intentions, do not always answer the End proposed; on the contrary, they sometimes prove, like the Legacies which some generous Physicians leave to their Country, of greater Hurt than Benefit. Besides my Bookseller informs me, that notwithstanding the Liberality, which at first Sight appears in these Authors, it is not to enhance the Fame of the Ancients, that they lend them their Sentiments, but to enhance their own Profit, they borrow their Names. Nor am I well assured, that the said Ancients are not more hurt than advantaged by these Practices. I have, therefore, on mature Deliberation, drawn up the following Advertisement, in the Stile of the justly celebrated Mr. *Pinchbeck*,[6] which I shall follow the Example of the abovemention'd Writers, and publish in the Name of the Ancients.

This is to acquaint all Gentlemen, that they may not be imposed upon for the future, as they hitherto have been, by Authors, Booksellers, Hawkers and Pedlars in and about this Town.

NOTICE IS HEREBY GIVEN,

That the Ancients do not dispose of one Grain of their curious Metal to any modern Authors whatever, nor are the Works composed of the said Metal, to be had of any but themselves: Therefore, Gentlemen are desired to be aware of Impostors, who do, or may pretend to sell the said Metal, for all their Pretensions are Fictions and a notorious Imposition on the Public, the said Ancients being the only Makers of the true genuine Metal, the Secret whereof they discovered, and have communicated to none. They, therefore, desire all Gentlemen, who intend to favour them with their Custom, to take particular Notice of the following Words, written in the Front of their Works, *viz*. *ΤΗΣ ΟΜΗΡΟΥ*,[7] &c. P. VIRGILII, &c.

There being Counterfeits abroad which have occasioned several Persons to make very great Mistakes.

Gentlemen are instructed how to apply to the said Ancients, by several Persons at *Eton*, *Westminster* and *Winchester*, and at the two Universities.

Their best Works may be had of Mr. *John Nourse*, at his Shop without *Temple Bar*, he being a Person very intimate with the said Ancients.[8]

N.B. They are not the Ancients who keep the Shop in *R—— Street*, nor —— nor —— for the Works of the said Ancients are not made up in that slight, ordinary, cheap Manner, as such Goods must be that are hawked about.[9]

C

18 From *Amelia* (1751), Book VIII, ch. v, 'Comments upon Authors'

Amelia was published on December 18, 1751; the text reprinted here is from the first edition. In this extract Fielding uses Booth's encounter with a contemporary hack author as an opportunity for an attack on several abuses in the literary world.

CHAP. V
Comments upon Authors

Having left *Amelia* in as comfortable a Situation as could possibly be expected, her immediate Distresses relieved, and her Heart filled with great Hopes from the Friendship of the Colonel; we will now return to *Booth*, who when the Attorney and Serjeant had left him, received a Visit from that great Author of whom honourable Mention is made in our second Chapter.

Booth, as the Reader may be pleased to remember, was a pretty good Master of the Classics: For his Father, tho' he designed his Son for the Army, did not think it necessary to breed him up a Blockhead. He did not perhaps imagine that a competent Share of *Latin* and *Greek* would make his Son either a Pedant or a Coward. He considered likewise, probably, that the Life of a Soldier is in general a Life of Idleness, and might think that the spare Hours of an Officer in Country Quarters would be as well employed with a Book, as in sauntring about the Streets, loitering in a Coffee House, sotting in a Tavern, or in laying Schemes to debauch and ruin a Set of harmless ignorant Country Girls.

As *Booth* was therefore what might well be called, in this Age at least, a Man of Learning, he began to discourse our Author on Subjects of Literature. 'I think, Sir,' says he, 'that Doctor *Swift* hath been generally allowed by the Critics in this Kingdom, to be the greatest Master of Humour that ever wrote. Indeed, I allow him to have possessed most admirable Talents of this Kind; and if *Rabelais* was his Master, I think he proves the Truth of the common *Greek* Proverb—That the Scholar is often superior to the Master. As to *Cervantes,* I do not think we can make any just Comparison; for tho' Mr. *Pope* compliments him with sometimes taking *Cervantes*' serious Air.' 'I remember the Passage,' cries the Author.

> Oh thou, whatever Title please thy Ear,
> *Dean, Drapier, Bickerstaff* or *Gulliver*;
> Whether you take Cervantes' serious Air,
> Or laugh and shake in Rabelais' easy Chair.[1]

'You are right, Sir,' said *Booth*; 'but tho' I should agree that the Doctor hath sometimes condescended to imitate *Rabelais,* I do not remember to have seen in his Works the least Attempt in the Manner of *Cervantes.* But there is one in his own Way, and whom I am convinced he studied above all others—— You guess, I believe, I am going to name *Lucian.* This Author, I say, I am convinced he followed; but I think he followed him at a Distance; as, to say the Truth, every other Writer of this Kind hath done in my Opinion: For none, I think, hath yet equalled him. I agree, indeed, entirely with Mr. *Moyle* in his Discourse on the Age of the Philopatris, when he gives him the Epithet of the incomparable *Lucian*;[2] and incomparable I believe he will remain as long as the Language in which he wrote shall endure. What inimitable Piece of Humour is his *Cock.*'[3]—— 'I remember it very well,' cries the Author, 'his Story of a Cock and a Bull is excellent.' *Booth* stared at this, and asked the Author what he meant by the Bull? 'Nay,' answered he, 'I don't know very well upon my Soul. It is a long time since I read him. I learnt him all over at School, I have not read him much since. And pray, Sir,' said he, 'how do you like his *Pharsalia*? Don't you think Mr. *Rowe's* Translation a very fine one?'[4] *Booth* replied, 'I believe we are talking of different Authors. The *Pharsalia* which Mr. *Rowe* translated was written by *Lucan*; but I have been speaking of *Lucian,* a *Greek* Writer, and in my Opinion the greatest in the Humorous Way, that ever the World produced.' 'Ay!' cries the Author, 'he was indeed so, a very excellent Writer indeed. I fancy a Translation of him would sell very well.' 'I do not know, indeed,' cries *Booth.* 'A good Translation of him would be a valuable Book. I have seen a wretched one published by Mr. *Dryden,* but translated by others, who in many Places have misunderstood *Lucian's* Meaning, and have no where preserved the Spirit of the Original.'[5] 'That is great Pity,' says the Author. 'Pray, Sir, is he well translated into *French*?' *Booth* answered, he could not tell; but that he doubted it very much, having never seen a good Version into that Language, out of the *Greek*. 'To confess the Truth, I believe,' said he, 'the *French* Translators have generally consulted the *Latin* only; which, in some of the few *Greek* Writers I have read, is intolerably bad. And as the *English* Translators, for the most Part, pursue the *French*, we may easily guess, what Spirit those Copies of bad Copies of bad Copies must preserve of the Original.'

'Egad, you are a shrewd Guesser,' cries the Author, 'I am glad the Booksellers have not your Sagacity. But how should it be otherwise, considering the Price they pay by the Sheet? The *Greek*, you will allow, is a hard Language; and there are few Gentlemen that write, who can read it without a good Lexicon. Now, Sir, if we were to afford Time to find out the true Meaning of Words, a Gentleman would not get Bread and Cheese by his Work. If one was to be paid, indeed, as Mr. *Pope* was for his *Homer*.[6] Pray, Sir, don't you think That the best Translation in the World?'

'Indeed, Sir,' cries *Booth*, 'I think, tho' it is certainly a noble Paraphrase, and of itself a fine Poem, yet, in some Places, it is no Translation at all. In the very Beginning, for Instance, he hath not rendered the true Force of the Author. *Homer* invokes his Muse in the five first Lines of the *Iliad*; and, at the End of the fifth, he gives his Reason.

Διος δ' ἐτελείετο βγλή,

'For all these Things,' says he, 'were brought about by the Decree of *Jupiter*; and, therefore, he supposes their true Sources are known only to the Deities. Now, the Translation takes no more Notice of the *ΔE*,[7] than if no such Word had been there.'

'Very possibly,' answered the Author; 'it is a long Time since I read the Original. Perhaps, then, he followed the *French* Translations. I observe, indeed, he talks much in the Notes of Madam *Dacier* and Monsieur *Eustathius*.'[8]

Booth had now received Conviction enough of his Friend's Knowledge of the *Greek* Language; without attempting, therefore, to set him right, he made a sudden Transition to the *Latin*. 'Pray, Sir,' said he, 'as you have mentioned *Rowe's* Translation of the *Pharsalia*; do you remember, how he hath rendered that Passage in the Character of *Cato*?

——Venerisque huic maximus Usus
Progenies; urbi Pater est, urbique Maritus.

For I apprehend that Passage is generally misunderstood.'

'I really do not remember,' answered the Author.—'Pray, Sir, what do you take to be the Meaning?'

'I apprehend, Sir,' replied *Booth*, 'that, by these Words, *Urbi Pater est, Urbique Maritus, Cato* is represented as the Father and Husband to the City of *Rome*.'

'Very true, Sir,' cries the Author, 'very fine, indeed.—Not only the Father of his Country, but the Husband too; very noble, truly.'

'Pardon me, Sir,' cries *Booth*, 'I do not conceive that to have been *Lucan's* Meaning. If you please to observe the Context: *Lucan* having commended the Temperance of *Cato*, in the Instances of Diet and Clothes, proceeds to venereal Pleasures; of which, says the Poet, his principal Use was Procreation: Then he adds, *Urbi Pater est, Urbique Maritus*, That he became a Father and a Husband, for the Sake only of the City.'

'Upon my Word, that's true,' cries the Author, 'I did not think of it. It is much finer than the other—*Urbis Pater est*—what is the other?—ay—*Urbis Maritus*.—It is certainly as you say, Sir.'

Booth was, by this, pretty well satisfied of the Author's profound Learning; however, he was willing to try him a little further. He asked him, therefore, what was his Opinion of *Lucan* in general, and in what Class of Writers he ranked him.

The Author stared a little at this Question; and after some Hesitation, answered, 'Certainly, Sir, I think he is a fine Writer, and a very great Poet.'

'I am very much of the same Opinion,' cries *Booth*; 'but where do you class him, next to what Poet do you place him?'

'Let me see,' cries the Author, 'where do I class him! next to whom do I place him!—Ay!—why!—why, pray, where do you yourself place him?'

'Why, surely,' cries *Booth*, 'if he is not to be placed in the first Rank, with *Homer*, and *Virgil*, and *Milton*—I think clearly, he is at the Head of the second; before either *Statius*, or *Silius Italicus*.—Tho' I allow to each of these their Merits; but, perhaps, an Epic Poem was beyond the Genius of either. I own I have often thought, if *Statius* had ventured no farther than *Ovid* or *Claudian*, he would have succeeded better: For his *Sylvæ* are, in my Opinion, much better than his *Thebais*.'[9]

'I believe I was of the same Opinion formerly,' said the Author.

'And for what Reason have you altered it?' cries *Booth*.

'I have not altered it,' answered the Author; 'but, to tell you the

Truth, I have not any Opinion at all about these Matters at present. I do not trouble my Head much with Poetry: For there is no Encouragement to such Studies in this Age. It is true, indeed, I have now and then wrote a Poem or two for the Magazines; but I never intend to write any more: For a Gentleman is not paid for his Time. A Sheet is a Sheet with the Booksellers; and, whether it be in Prose or Verse, they make no Difference; tho' certainly there is as much Difference to a Gentleman in the Work, as there is to a Taylor, between making a plain and a laced Suit. Rhimes are difficult Things; they are stubborn Things, Sir. I have been sometimes longer in tagging a Couplet, than I have been in writing a Speech on the Side of the Opposition, which hath been read with great Applause all over the Kingdom.'

'I am glad you are pleased to comfirm that,' cries *Booth*: 'For I protest, it was an entire Secret to me till this Day. I was so perfectly ignorant, that I thought the Speeches, published in the Magazines, were really made by the Members themselves.'

'Some of them, and I believe I may, without Vanity, say, the best,' cries the Author, 'are all the Production of my own Pen; but, I believe, I shall leave it off soon, unless a Sheet of Speech will fetch more than it does at present. In Truth, the Romance Writing is the only Branch of our Business now, that is worth following. Goods of that Sort have had so much Success lately in the Market, that a Bookseller scarce cares what he bids for them. And it is certainly the easiest Work in the World; you may write it almost as fast as you can set Pen to Paper; and if you interlard it with a little Scandal, a little Abuse on some living Characters of Note, you cannot fail of Success.'

'Upon my Word, Sir,' cries *Booth*, 'you have greatly instructed me. I could not have imagined, there had been so much Regularity in the Trade of Writing, as you are pleased to mention; by what I can perceive, the Pen and Ink is likely to become the Staple Commodity of the Kingdom.'

'Alas! Sir,' answered the Author, 'it is over-stocked.—The Market is over-stocked. There is no Encouragement to Merit, no Patrons. I have been these five Years soliciting a Subscription for my new Translation of *Ovid's Metamorphoses*, with Notes explanatory, historical, and critical; and I have scarce collected five hundred Names yet.'

The Mention of this Translation a little surprised *Booth*; not only as the Author had just declared his Intentions to forsake the tuneful Muses; but for some other Reasons, which he had collected from his Conversation with our Author, he little expected to hear of a Proposal to translate any of the *Latin* Poets. He proceeded, therefore, to catechise him a little farther; and by his Answers was fully satisfied, that he had the very same Acquaintance with *Ovid*, that he had appeared to have with *Lucan*.

19 *The Covent Garden Journal*, No. 4

Tuesday, January 14, 1752

In this paper Fielding attacks, by means of the abuse of words, the degeneration of contemporary society. The connection between the two ideas was the reason for his attacks on the authors of Grub Street, whom he considered primarily responsible for the debasement of values.

——Nanum cujusdam Atlanta vocamus:
Æthiopem Cygnum: parvam extortamque puellam
Europen. Canibus pigris Scabieque vetusta
Laevibus, et siccae lambentibus Ora lucernae
Nomen erit Pardus, Tigris, Leo; si quid adhuc est
Quod fremat in Terris violentius.——

JUV., *Sat.* 8.[1]

'One may observe,' says Mr. Locke, 'in all Languages, certain Words, that, if they be examined, will be found, in their first Original, and their appropriated Use, not to stand for any clear and distinct Ideas.' Mr Locke gives us the Instances 'of Wisdom, Glory, Grace. Words which are frequent enough (says he) in every Man's Mouth; but if a great many of those who use them, should be asked what they mean by them, they would be at a Stand, and not know what to answer: A plain Proof, that tho' they have learned those Sounds, and have them ready at their Tongue's End; yet there are no determin'd Ideas laid up in their Minds, which are to be expressed to others by them.'[2]

Besides the several Causes by him assigned of the Abuse of Words, there is one, which, tho' the great Philospher hath omitted it, seems to have contributed not a little to the Introduction of this enormous Evil. This is That Privilege which Divines and moral Writers have assumed to themselves of doing Violence to certain Words, in Favour of their own Hypotheses, and of using them in a Sense often directly contrary to that which Custom (the absolute Lord and Master, according to Horace, of all the Modes of Speech) hath allotted them.[3]

Perhaps, indeed, this Fault may be seen in somewhat a milder Light, (and I would always see the Blemishes of such Writers in the mildest.) It may not, perhaps, be so justly owing to any designed Opposition to Custom as a total Ignorance of it. An Ignorance which is almost inseparably annexed to a collegiate Life, and which any Man, indeed, may venture to own without blushing.

But whatever may be the Cause of this Abuse of Words, the Consequence is certainly very bad: For whilst the Author and the World receive different Ideas from the same Words, it will be pretty difficult for them to comprehend each other's Meaning; and hence, perhaps, it is that so many Gentlemen and Ladies have contracted a general Odium to all Works of Religion or Morality; and that many others have been Readers in this Way all their Lives without understanding what they read, consequently without drawing from it any practical Use.

It would, perhaps, be an Office very worthy the Labour of a good Commentator to explain certain hard Words which frequently occur in the Works of Barrow, Tillotson, Clark,[4] and others of this Kind. Such are Heaven, Hell, Judgment, Righteousness, Sin, *Etc.* All which, it is reasonable to believe, are at present very little understood.

Instead, however, of undertaking this Task myself, at least, at present, I shall apply the Residue of this Paper to the Use of such Writers only. I shall here give a short Glossary of such Terms as are at present greatly in Use, and shall endeavour to fix to each those exact Ideas which are annexed to every of them in the World; for while the Learned in Colleges do, as I apprehend, consider them all in a very different Light, their Labours are not likely to do much Service to the polite Part of Mankind.

A MODERN GLOSSARY

ANGEL. The Name of a Woman, commonly of a very bad one.

AUTHOR. A laughing Stock. It means likewise a poor Fellow, and in general an Object of Contempt.

BEAR. A Country Gentleman; or, indeed, any Animal upon two Legs that doth not make a handsome Bow.

BEAUTY. The Qualification with which Women generally go into Keeping.

BEAU. With the Article A before it, means a great Favourite of all Women.

BRUTE. A Word implying Plain-dealing and Sincerity, but more especially applied to a Philosopher.

CAPTAIN. } Any Stick of Wood with a Head to it, and a Piece of
COLONEL. } black Ribband upon that Head.

CREATURE. A Quality Expression of low Contempt, properly confined only to the Mouths of Ladies who are Right Honourable.

CRITIC. Like *Homo*, a Name common to all human Race.

COXCOMB. A Word of Reproach, and yet, at the same Time, signifying all that is most commendable.

DAMNATION. A Term appropriated to the Theatre; though sometimes more largely applied to all Works of Invention.

DEATH. The final End of Man; as well of the *thinking Part of the Body*, as of all the other Parts.

DRESS. The principal Accomplishment of Men and Women.

DULNESS. A Word applied by all Writers to the Wit and Humour of others.

EATING. A Science.

FINE. An Adjective of a very peculiar Kind, destroying, or, at least, lessening the Force of the Substantive to which it is joined: As *fine* Gentlemen, *fine* Lady, *fine* House, *fine* Cloaths, *fine* Taste;—in all which *fine* is to be understood in a Sense somewhat synonymous with useless.

FOOL. A complex Idea, compounded of Poverty, Honesty, Piety, and Simplicity.

GALLANTRY. Fornication and Adultery.

GREAT. Applied to a Thing, signifies Bigness; when to a Man, often Littleness, or Meanness.

GOOD. A Word of as many different Senses as the Greek Word *῎Εχω*, or as the Latin *Ago*: for which Reason it is but little used by the Polite.[5]

HAPPINESS. Grandeur.

HONOUR. Duelling.

HUMOUR. Scandalous Lies, Tumbling and Dancing on the Rope.

JUDGE. } An old Woman.
JUSTICE. }

KNAVE. The Name of four Cards in every Pack.

KNOWLEDGE. In general, means Knowledge of the Town; as this is, indeed, the only Kind of Knowledge ever spoken of in the polite World.

LEARNING. Pedantry.

LOVE. A Word properly applied to our Delight in particular Kinds of Food; sometimes metaphorically spoken of the favourite Objects of all our *Appetites*.

MARRIAGE. A Kind of Traffic carried on between the two Sexes, in which both are constantly endeavouring to cheat each other, and both are commonly Losers in the End.

MISCHIEF. Funn[*sic*], Sport, or Pastime.

MODESTY. Aukwardness, Rusticity.

NO BODY. All the People in Great Britain, except about 1200.

NONSENSE. Philosophy, especially the Philosophical Writings of the Antients, and more especially of Aristotle.

OPPORTUNITY. The Season of Cuckoldom.

PATRIOT. A Candidate for a Place at Court.

POLITICS. The Art of getting such a Place.

PROMISE. Nothing.

RELIGION. A Word of no Meaning; but which serves as a Bugbear to frighten Children with.

RICHES. The only Thing upon Earth that is really valuable, or desirable.

ROGUE. }
RASCAL. } A Man of a different Party from yourself.

SERMON. A Sleeping-Dose.

SUNDAY. The best Time for playing at Cards.

SHOCKING. An Epithet which fine Ladies apply to almost every Thing. It is, indeed, an Interjection (if I may so call it) of Delicacy.

TEMPERANCE. Want of Spirit.

TASTE. The present Whim of the Town, whatever it be.

TEASING. Advice; chiefly that of a Husband.

VIRTUE. }
VICE. } Subjects of Discourse.

WIT. Prophaneness, Indecency, Immorality, Scurrility, Mimickry, Buffoonery. Abuse of all good Men, and especially of the Clergy.

WORTH. Power. Rank. Wealth.

WISDOM. The Art of acquiring all Three.

WORLD. Your own Acquaintance.

A.

20 *The Covent Garden Journal*, No. 5

Saturday, January 18, 1752

This is the first meeting of the Court of Censorial Enquiry in the *Covent Garden Journal.* Compare the procedure in Captain Hercules Vinegar's Court in *The Champion* (e.g. above, No. 11) and that of John Trottplaid's in *The Jacobite's Journal* (see below, Nos. 43 et seq.).

At a Court *of* Censorial Enquiry *now held this* 18th *of* January, 1752, *before the truly respectable* Sir ALEXANDER DRAWCANSIR, *Knt. Censor of* Great Britain.

The Court was opened by the Censor, with a very learned and elegant Speech; setting forth the great Antiquity, and Usefulness of this Court, and the many Inconveniences which had attended the Society by the long Discontinuance; but as he hath been pleased to give the Public much of the Substance of this Speech in his Essay of To-day, we will not here transcribe it at large.

The Court then came to several Resolutions.

First, It was resolved, That it of Right belongs to this Court to hear, and determine, all manner of Causes, which in anywise relate to the Republic of Letters. To examine, try, recommend, or condemn, all Books, and Pamphlets, of whatever Size, or on whatever Subject.

Secondly, That it is at the Discretion of this Court to pass any of the following Sentences on such Book, or Pamphlet, as shall, after a full and fair Hearing, be judged worthy of Condemnation; that is to say, 1. To be imprisoned on the Shelf, or in the Warehouse of the Bookseller. 2. To be immediately converted into waste Paper. 3. To be burnt by the Hands of the common Hangman, or by those of some common Publisher of Scandal, which are, perhaps, much the more infamous.

Thirdly, That after any such Judgment passed by this Court, it shall not be lawful for any Person whatever, to purchase, or read, the said

Book, or Pamphlet, under the Penalty of being considered as in Contempt.

Fourthly, For the more easy carrying on our Design of examining all Books which shall, from Time to Time, be made public, it is ordered, that all Booksellers do, previous to their publishing, or vending, any Book, or Pamphlet, present unto our Clerk in Court, for our Use, one fair Copy of all such Books, and Pamphlets; and that (in Case it be a Book) the same be well bound and gilt, and do contain, in gilt Letters on the Back, the Name, or Title, of the said Book.

Fifthly, Resolved, That both the Theatres, and all other Places of Diversion and Resort, are under our Protection; and every thing which passes at any of these, is subject to our Cognizance and Jurisdiction. For which Reason, we do most earnestly and seriously recommend to all our trusty and well beloved People to send us immediate Notice of any Misconduct or Misbehaviour that shall happen in any of the Managers of these Places of Diversion, or in any of the Performers or Spectators.

Sixthly, Resolved, That all Places of general Rendezvous, tho' at a private House, shall be deemed public Places, and the Masters and Mistresses of all such Houses shall be considered in the same Light as the Managers of our public Theatres; and shall be equally subject to the Jurisdiction of this Court.

Seventhly, Whereas, by the Statute of Good-Breeding, the wearing a Hat in the Boxes, at the Play-House, before or behind the Ladies, is a very great Offence, that swearing or talking loud, is, likewise, under very severe Penalty forbidden by the said Statute; all our Officers in the Pit are strictly charged to see the said Law carried into vigorous Execution.

Eighthly, In the Statute of Gallantry, are these Words, 'Provided that for the future, a fierce Cock of the Hat be not considered as any Mark of Valour in any Person whatever, save only in Attorney's Clerks, Apprentices, Gamblers, and Bullies.' Resolved, therefore, that it shall be lawful for any honest and sober Man, at all Times to remove all such Hats from the Blocks on which they are displayed, with absolute Impunity, saving to the said Clerks their antient Right.

Ninthly, Resolved, That laughing, grinning, whispering, and staring Modesty out of Countenance, are to be reputed Wit in any Ale-House, and at Sadler's Wells;[1] but at no other Place whatsoever.

Tenthly, Resolved, That to give an Affront or Offence at any public Place, to sober and grave Persons, to the Ladies, or to the Clergy, is a very high Crime and Misdemeanor, strictly forbidden by the Laws of Decency; and whoever is convicted thereof, will be struck out of the Order of Gentlemen, at the next Inquisition to be taken of that Order.

Adjourned.

21 *The Covent Garden Journal*, No. 6

Tuesday, January 21, 1752

This is one of Fielding's most ironic essays, in which he takes the role of a lover of modern learning.

Quam multi tineas pascunt, blattasque diserti!
Et redimunt soli carmina docta coci!
Nescio quid plus est quod donat secula chartis,
Victurus genium debet habere liber.

MART. LIB. 6.[1]

How many fear the Moth's and Bookworm's Rage,
And Pastry-Cooks, sole Buyers in this Age?
What can these Murtherers of Wit controul?
To be immortal, Books must have a soul.

There are no human Productions to which Time seems so bitter and malicious an Enemy, as to the Works of the learned: for though all the Pride and Boast of Art must sooner, or later, yield to this great Destroyer; though all the Labours of the Architect, the Statuary, and the Painter, must share the same Mortality with their Authors; yet, with these, Time acts in a gentler and milder Manner, allows them generally a reasonable Period of Existence, and brings them to an End by a gradual and imperceptible Decay: so that they may seem rather cut off by the fatal Laws of Necessity, than to be destroyed by any such Act of Violence, as this cruel Tyrant daily executes on us Writers.

It is true, indeed, there are some Exceptions to this Rule; some few Works of Learning have not only equalled, but far exceeded, all other human Labours in their Duration; but alas! how very few are these, compared to that vast Number which have been swallowed up by this great Destroyer. Many of them cut off in their very Prime; others in their early Youth; and others, again, at their very Birth; so that they can scarce be said ever to have been.

And, as to the few that remain to us, is not their long Existence to be attributed to their own unconquerable Spirit, and rather to the Weakness, than to the Mercy of Time? Have not many of their Authors foreseen, and foretold, the Endeavours which would be exerted to destroy them, and have bodly asserted their just Claim to Immortality, in Defiance of all the Malice, all the Cunning, and all the Power of Time?

Indeed, when we consider the many various Engines which have been employed for this destructive Purpose, it will be Matter of Wonder, that any of the Writings of Antiquity have been able to make their Escape. This might almost lead us into a Belief, that the Writers were really possessed of that Divinity, to which some of them pretended, especially as those which seem to have had the best Pretensions to this Divinity, have been almost the only ones which have escaped into our Hands.

And here, not to mention those great Engines of Destruction which Ovid so boldly defies,[2] such as Swords, and Fire, and the devouring Moths of Antiquity, how many cunning Methods hath the Malice of Time invented, of later Days, to extirpate the Works of the Learned, and to convert the Invention of Paper, and even of Printing, to the total Abolition of those very Works which they were so ingeniously calculated to perpetuate.

The first of these, Decency will permit me barely to hint to the Reader. It is the Application of it to a Use for which Parchment and Vellum, the antient Repositories of Learning, would have been utterly unfit. To this cunning Invention of Time, therefore, Printing and Paper have chiefly betrayed the Learned; nor can I see, without Indignation, the Booksellers, those great Enemies of Authors, endeavouring by all their sinister Arts to propagate so destructive a Method: for what is commoner than to see Books advertised to be printed *on a superfine, delicate, soft Paper*, and again, *very proper to be had in all Families*, a plain Insinuation to what Use they are adapted, according to these Lines.

Lintott's for gen'ral Use are fit,
For some Folks read, but all Folks——.[3]

By this abominable Method, the whole Works of several modern Authors have been so obliterated, that the most curious Searcher into Antiquity, hereafter, will never be able to wipe off the Injuries of Time.

And, yet, so truly do the Booksellers verify that old Observation, *dulcis odor lucri ex re qualibet*,[4] that they are daily publishing several Works, manifestly calculated for this Use only; nay, I am told, that one of them is, by Means of a proper Translator, preparing the whole Works of Plato for the B——.

Next to the Booksellers are the Trunk-makers, a Set of Men who have of late Years made the most intolerable Depredations on modern Learning. The ingenious Hogarth hath very finely satyriz'd this, by representing several of the most valuable Productions of these Times on the Way to the Trunk-maker. If these Persons would line a Trunk with a whole Pamphlet, they might possibly do more Good than Harm; for then, perhaps, the Works of last Year might be found in our Trunks, when they were possibly to be found no where else; but so far from this, they seem to take a Delight in dismembring Authors; and in placing their several Limbs together in the most absurd Manner. Thus while the Bottom of a Trunk contains a Piece of Poetry, the Top presents us with a Sheet of Romance, and the Sides and Ends are adorned with mangled Libels of various Kinds.

The third Species of these Depredators, are the Pastry Cooks. What Indignation must it raise in a Lover of the Moderns, to see some of their best Performances stain'd with the Juice of Gooseberries, Currants, and Damascenes![5] But what Concern must the Author himself feel on such an Occasion; when he beholds those Writings, which were calculated to support the glorious Cause of Disaffection or Infidelity, humbled to the ignoble Purpose of supporting a Tart or a Custard! So, according to the Poet,

> Great Alexander dead, and turn'd to Clay,
> May stop a Hole to keep the Wind away.[6]

But, besides the Injuries done to Learning by this Method, there is another Mischief which these Pastry Cooks may thus propagate in the Society: For many of these wondrous Performances are calculated only for the Use and Inspection of the few, and are by no means proper Food for the Mouths of Babes and Sucklings. For Instance, that the Christian Religion is a mere Cheat and Imposition on the Public, nay, that the very Being of a God is a Matter of great Doubt and Incertainty, are Discoveries of too deep a Nature to perplex the Minds [of] Children with; and it is better, perhaps, till they come to a certain Age, that they should believe quite the opposite Doctrines. Again, as Children are taught to obey and honour their Superiors, and to keep their Tongues from Evil-speaking, Lying, and Slandering, to what good Purposes can it tend to shew them that the very contrary is daily practised and suffered and supported in the World? Is not this to confound their Understandings, and almost sufficient to make them neglect their Learning? Lastly, there are certain Arcana Naturæ, in disclosing which the Moderns have made great Progress; now whatever Merit there may be in such Denudations of Nature, if I may so express myself, and however exquisite a Relish they may afford to *very* adult Persons of both Sexes in their Closets, they are surely too speculative and mysterious for the Contemplation of the Young and Tender, into whose Hands Tarts and Pies are most likely to fall.

Now as these three Subjects, namely, Infidelity, Scurrility, and Indecency, have principally exercised the Pens of the Moderns, I hope for the future, Pastry Cooks will be more cautious than they have lately been. In short, if they have no Regard to Learning, they will have some, I hope, to Morality.

The same Caution may be given to Grocers and Chandlers; both of whom are too apt to sell their Figs, Raisins, and Sugar to Children, without enough considering the poisonous Vehicle in which they are conveyed. At the waste Paper Market, the Cheapness of the Commodity is only considered; and it is easy to see with what Goods that Market is likely to abound; since tho' the Press hath lately swarmed with Libels against our Religion and Government, there is not a single Writer of any Reputation in this Kingdom, who hath attempted to draw his Pen against either.

But to return to that Subject from which I seem to have a little digressed. How melancholy a Consideration must it be to a modern Author, that the Labours, I might call them the Offspring of his Brain, are liable to so many various Kinds of Destruction, that what Tibullus says of the numerous Avenues to Death may be here applied.

——Leti mille repente viæ.
To Death there are a thousand sudden Ways.[7]

For my own Part, I never walk into Mrs. Dodd's Shop,[8] and survey all that vast and formidable Host of Papers and Pamphlets arranged on her Shelves, but the noble Lamentation of Xerxes occurs to my Mind; who, when he reviewed his Army, on the Banks of the Hellespont, is said to have grieved, for that not one of all those Hundreds of Thousands would be living an Hundred Years from that Time.[9] In the same Manner, have I said to myself, 'How dreadful a Thought is it, that of all these numerous and learned Works, none will survive to the next Year?' But, within that Time,

——All will become,
Martyrs to Pyes, and Relicts of the B——.[10]

I was led into these Reflections by an Accident which happened to me the other Day, and which all Lovers of Antiquity will esteem a very fortunate one. Having had the Curiosity to examine a written Paper, in which my Baker inclosed me two hot Rolls, I have rescued from Oblivion one of the most valuable Fragments, that I believe is now to be found in the World. I have ordered it to be fairly transcribed, and shall very soon present it to my Readers, with my best Endeavours, by a short Comment, to illustrate a Piece which appears to have remained to us from the most distant and obscure Ages.[11]

A.

22 *The Covent Garden Journal*, No. 15

Saturday, February 21, 1752

This paper and the one which follows are connected in subject-matter and style; they are examples of the legalistic play in which Fielding frequently indulges.

Proceedings at the Court of Censorial Enquiry, *Etc.*

The Censor gave his Opinion in the Cause of B—— T——,[1] against whom there was an Information on the Statute of Dulness,

That this Court hath no Jurisdiction over any of the Subjects of Grubstreet, unless in Cases of Blasphemy, Sedition, Scurrility and Indecency.

That the Corporation of Grubstreet had existed from Time, whereof the Memory of Man was not to the contrary, and for all that Time had enjoyed and used the Privilege of being dull.

That tho' by the Carelessness of the Clerks, all the Records of Grubstreet were lost, so that it was scarce possible to find any of a single Year's standing, yet it well appeared by incontestable Authorities, that there had been a Grubstreet even in Greece itself, where as appears from Longinus, there were Dealers in the Turgid, the Puerile, the Vapid and other the known Wares of Grubstreet.

That Grubstreet was in a flourishing State in Rome, hath been proved by many Citations from Juvenal and Horace; and even from a Line of Virgil himself, who advises the Admirers of one Grubstreet Writer, to be likewise the Admirers of another.[2]

Mr. Censor added, that all these Proofs were taken from the Writings of Men who were avowed Enemies to the Grubstreet Cause, and were consequently the most unquestionable Evidence.

Mr. Censor said, he was sorry to confess that Grubstreet had very fully made out its Title to a much greater Antiquity, than the Kingdoms of Wit and Learning. That the two last had arisen from the first, and not that from these.

That before the first Beginners of the Reformation, all was Grubstreet; and Darkness had overspread the Face of the whole Kingdom.

That tho' the Dominions of Grubstreet had been lessened since the Rise of the Kingdom of Wit and Learning, still had the low Republic continued a great and mighty Power.

That the Subjects of this Republic had never paid any, not even the least Acknowledgments to the Kingdom of Wit; but that on the contrary, the Subjects of the latter had always paid certain Tributes to Grubstreet. That Shakespear himself was obliged to this Composition; for that all his Admirers had ever accounted for certain Passages in his Works, from his having been forced to comply with the absurd Taste of his Audience, in other Words, to pay a Tribute to Grubstreet.

That Ben Johnson was compelled to pay the same Acknowledgments, and very plainly writ some of his Plays, with no other View than that of offering a Tribute to the Republic; and Beaumont and Fletcher often contented themselves with two Scenes of Wit, and filled the rest with Dulness from the same Motive.

That Dryden is another Instance of the same Tribute exacted and complied with; witness several of his Plays; in writing which he could apparently have no other Design, than what is here alledged.

I need not, said the Censor, run through all the Proofs. Even Swift himself as the late noble Writer of his Life seems to allow, suffered some Pieces to be inserted in his Works, as a Tribute to the same Republic. This is an Instance equal to all the rest, if we consider either the Temper of the Man, or his known Antipathy to the Cause of Grubstreet.

The last Example I shall produce, is that of Pope, who begins the last Book of his *Dunciad* with an Address to Dulness.

> Yet, yet a Moment, one dim Ray of Light,
> Indulge, dread Chaos and eternal Night,
> Of Darkness visible so much be lent,
> As Half to shew, half veil the deep Intent!
> Ye Pow'rs, whose Mysteries restor'd I sing,
> To whom Time bears me on his rapid Wing;
> Suspend awhile your Force inertly strong,
> Then take at once the Poet and the Song.[3]

Here the Poet confesses the great Power of Grubstreet, and seems to allow explicitly that the greatest Wits write only through the Indulgence of that Republic.

Upon the whole as Mr. Cibber, that great and profound Lawyer, long since discovered that we had no Right to any Liberty before the Revolution,[4] so it appears to me that no Wits were at Liberty to write without paying a Tax to Grubstreet, 'till this was stipulated for them by the late Treaty of Covent-Garden.[5]

On the contrary, no single Instance hath been shewn where any Author of Grubstreet hath paid any Tribute to the Kingdom of Wit, but have in all Ages claimed, had, and used the full Privilege of being as dull as they please, and this Privilege is secured to them by the above Treaty.

For all which Reasons Judgment was ordered to be entered for the Defendant.

(*Adjourned.*)

23 *The Covent Garden Journal,* No. 23

Saturday, March 21, 1752

Οὐκ ἀγαθὸν πολυκοιρανὶη εςἶ ϐοίη κοίρανος ἔστω
Εἶς Βασιλεύς, ὦ δωκε Κρόνου παῖς ἀγκυλομήτεω
Σκῆπτρόν τ᾽ ἠδὲ θὲμιστας, ἳνα σφὶσο ἐμβασιλέυη.

HOMER.

——————Here is not allow'd,
That worst of Tyrants, an usurping Crowd.
To one sole Monarch, Jove commits the Sway;
His are the Laws, and him let all obey.[1]

POPE.

Tho' of the three Forms of Government acknowledged in the Schools,[2] all have been very warmly opposed, and as warmly defended; yet, in this Point, the different Advocates will, I believe, very readily agree, that there is not one of the three which is not greatly to be preferred to a total Anarchy; a State in which there is no Subordination, no lawful Power, and no settled Government; but where every Man is at Liberty to act in whatever Manner it pleaseth him best.

As this is in Reality a most deplorable State, I have long lamented, with great Anguish of Heart, that it is at present the Case of a very large Body of People in this Kingdom. An assertion which, as it may surprize most of my Readers, I will make Haste to explain, by declaring that I mean the Fraternity of the Quill, that Body of Men to whom the Public assign the Name of AUTHORS.

However absurd Politicians may have been pleased to represent the *Imperium in Imperio*, it will here, I doubt not, be found on a strict Examination to be extremely necessary.[3] The Commonwealth of Literature being indeed totally distinct from the greater Commonwealth, and no more dependant upon it than the Kingdom of England is on that of France. Of this our Legislature seems to have been at all Times sensible, as they have never attempted any Provision for the Regulation or Correction of this Body. In one Instance, it is true, there are (I should rather, I believe, say there were) some Laws to restrain them: For Writers, if I am not mistaken, have been formerly punished for Blasphemy against God, and Libels against the Government; nay I have been told, that to slander the Reputation of private Persons, was once thought unlawful here as well as among the Romans, who as Horace tells us, had a severe Law for this Purpose.[4]

In enacting these Laws (whatever may be the Reason of suffering them to grow obsolete) the State seem to have acted very wisely; as such Kind of Writings are really of most mischievous Consequence to the Public; but alas! there are many Abuses, many horrid Evils, daily springing up in the Commonwealth of Literature, which appear to affect only that Commonwealth, at least immediately, of which none of the political Legislators have ever taken any Notice; nor hath any Civil Court of Judicature ever pretended to any Cognizance of them. Nonsense and Dulness are no Crimes in *Foro Civili*:[5] No Man can be questioned for bad Verses in Westminster-Hall; and amongst the many Indictments for Battery, not one can be produced for breaking poor Priscian's Head, tho' it is done almost every Day.[6]

But tho' immediately, as I have said, these Evils do not affect the greater Commonwealth; yet as they tend to the utter Ruin of the lesser, so they have a remote evil Consequence, even on the State itself; which seems by having left them unprovided for, to have remitted them, for the Sake of Convenience, to the Government of Laws, and to the Superintendence of Magistrates of this lesser Commonwealth; and never to have foreseen or suspected that dreadful State of Anarchy, which at present prevails in this lesser Empire; an Empire which hath formerly made so great a Figure in this Kingdom, and that indeed almost within our own Memories.

It may appear strange, that none of our English Historians have spoken clearly and distinctly of this lesser Empire; but this may be well accounted for, when we consider that all these Histories have been written by two Sorts of Persons; that is to say, either Politicians or Lawyers. Now the former of these have had their Imaginations so entirely filled with the Affairs of the greater Empire, that it is no Wonder the Business of the lesser should have totally escaped their Observation. And as to the Lawyers, they are well known to have been very little acquainted with the Commonwealth of Literature, and to have always acted and written in Defiance to its Laws.

From these Reasons it is very difficult to fix, with Certainty, the exact Period when this Commonwealth first began among us. Indeed if the Originals of all the greater Empires upon Earth, and even of our own, be wrapped in such Obscurity that they elude the Enquiries of the most diligent Sifters of Antiquity, we cannot be surprized that this Fate should attend out little Empire, opposed as it hath been by the Pen of the Lawyer, overlooked by the Eye of the Historian, and never once *smelt after* by the Nose of the Antiquarian.

In the earliest Ages, the literary State seems to have been an Ecclesiastical Democracy: For the Clergy are then said to have had all the Learning among them; and the great Reverence paid at that Time to it by the Laity, appears from hence, That whoever could prove in a Court of Justice that he belonged to this State, by only reading a single Verse in the Testament, was vested with the highest Privileges, and might do almost what he pleased; even commit Murder with Impunity. And this Privilege was called the Benefit of the Clergy.[7]

This Commonwealth, however, can scarce be said to have been in any flourishing State of old Time, even among the Clergy themselves; inasmuch as we are told, that a Rector of a Parish going to Law with his Parishioners about paving the Church, quoted this Authority from St. Peter, *Paveant illi, non paveam ego*. Which he construed thus: *They are to pave the Church, and not I.* And this by a Judge, who was likewise an Ecclesiastic, was allowed to be very good Law.

The Nobility had clearly no antient Connection with this Commonwealth, nor would submit to be bound by any of its Laws, witness that Provision in an old Act of Parliament; 'that a Nobleman shall be entitled to the Benefit of his Clergy (the Privilege abovementioned) *even tho' he cannot read.*' Nay the whole Body of the Laity, tho' they gave such Honours to this Commonwealth, appear to have been very few of them under its Jurisdiction; as appears by a Law cited by Judge Rolls in his Abridgement, with the Reason which he gives for it. 'The Command of the Sheriff,' says this Writer, 'to his Officer by Word of Mouth, and without writing is good; for it may be, that neither the Sheriff or his Officer can write or read.'[8]

But not to dwell on these obscure Times, when so very little authentic can be found concerning this Commonwealth, let us come at once to the Days of Henry the Eighth, when no less a Revolution happened in the lesser than in the greater Empire: For the literary Government became absolute together with the Political, in the Hands of one and the same Monarch; who was himself a Writer, and dictated not only Law but Common-Sense too, to all his People; suffering no one to write or speak but according to his own Will and Pleasure.

After this King's Demise, the literary Commonwealth was again separated from the Political; for I do not find that his Successor on the greater Throne, succeeded him likewise in the lesser. Nor did either of the two Queens, as I can learn, pretend to any Authority in this Empire, in which the Salique Law hath universally prevailed;[9] for tho' there have been some considerable Subjects of the Female Sex in the Literary Commonwealth, I never remember to have read of a Queen.

It is not easy to say with any great Exactness what Form of Government was preserved in this Commonwealth during the Reigns of Edward VI, Queen Mary and Queen Elizabeth; for tho' there were some great Men in those Times, none of them seemed to have affected the Throne of Wit: Nay Shakespear, who flourished in the latter end of the last Reign, and who seemed so justly qualified to enjoy this Crown, never thought of challenging it.

In the Reign of James I, the literary Government was an Aristocracy, for I do not chuse to give it the evil Name of Oligarchy, tho' it consisted only of four, namely, Master William Shakespear, Master Benjamin Johnson, Master John Fletcher and Master Francis Beaumont. This Quadrumvirate, as they introduced a new form of Government, thought proper according to Machiavel's Advice, to introduce new Names,[10] they therefore called themselves THE WITS, a Name which hath been affected since by the reigning Monarchs in this Empire.

The last of this Quadrumvirate enjoyed the Government alone during his Life;[11] after which the Troubles that shortly after ensued, involved this lesser Commonwealth in all the Confusion and Ruin of the greater, nor can any Thing be found of it with sufficient Certainty, till the WITS in the Reign of Charles the Second, after many Struggles among themselves for Superiority, at last agreed to elect JOHN DRYDEN to be their King.

This King John had a very long Reign, tho' a very unquiet one; for there were several Pretenders to the Throne of Wit in his Time, who formed very considerable Parties against him, and gave him great Uneasiness, of which his Successor hath made mention in the following Lines:

> Pride, Folly, Malice, against Dryden rose,
> In various Shapes, of Parsons, Critics, Beaus.[12]

Besides which, his Finances were in such Disorder, that it is affirmed his Treasury was more than once entirely empty.

He died nevertheless in a good old Age, possessed of the Kingdom of Wit, and was succeeded by King ALEXANDER, sirnamed POPE.

This Prince enjoyed the Crown many Years, and is thought to have stretched the Prerogative much farther than his Predecessor: He is said to have been extremely jealous of the Affections of his Subjects, and to have employed various Spies, by whom if he was informed of the least Suggestion against his Title, he never failed of branding the accused Person with the Word DUNCE on his Forehead in broad Letters; after which the unhappy Culprit was obliged to lay by his Pen forever; for no Bookseller would venture to print a Word that he wrote.

He did indeed put a total Restraint on the Liberty of the Press: For no Person durst read any Thing which was writ without his Licence and Approbation; and this Licence he granted only to four during his Reign, namely, to the celebrated Dr. Swift, to the ingenious Dr. Young to Dr. Arbuthnot, and to one Mr. Gay, four of his principal Courtiers and Favourites.

But without diving any deeper into his Character, we must allow that King Alexander had great Merit as a Writer, and his Title to the Kingdom of Wit was better founded at least than his Enemies have pretended.

After the Demise of King Alexander, the Literary State relapsed again into a Democracy, or rather indeed into downright Anarchy; of which, as well as of the Consequences, I shall treat in a future Paper.

A.

The Covent Garden Journal, No. 46

Tuesday, June 9, 1752

Fielding's attack on pertness in modern literature owes its form to Pope's *Art of Sinking* (1728). Behind both works lies Longinus's treatise *On the Sublime.*

Nec pudor obstabit.
Juv.[1]

Let not your Modesty hurt you.

TO THE
CENSOR of Great Britain.

Mr. Censor,—As you was pleased to publish my last Letter,[2] I have sent you the further Productions of my Friend on the same Subject. Without further Preface then, my Friend after having vindicated the Honour of the Moderns, as being, tho' not the Inventors of the Pert, yet the undoubted Improvers and Enlargers thereof, and its Introductors into almost every Species of Writing, proceeds, like a true systematick Writer, to enquire what Geniuses are the fittest to receive, imbibe, and digest, the Doctrine of the Pert; and to shine most in the practical Application and Exercise thereof. In this Disquisition, which is pretty prolix, he displays an extensive Knowledge of the human Heart, as well as of the human Understanding; and at last concludes, that those are the most susceptible of the Efficacy of his Precepts, who have the best Opinion of themselves; and, on the other Hand, that those will profit least by his Instructions, who are most deeply tinctured with that aukward shame-faced Thing called Modesty. What he adds is somewhat extraordinary. 'If a young Writer,' saith he, 'entertains a mean Opinion of his own Abilities, and is at the same Time, what is commonly called a Man of Sense, I despair of him, and I pronounce him incorrigible, and utterly incapable of relishing and profiting by my Instructions and Advices. He will jog on like a Mule at his own Pace, regardless of extrinsic Direction. But if he hath a tolerable Share of Folly, I have some Hopes of him, let him be ever so modest. Tho' he has a poor Opinion of his own Parts at present, yet, ten to one, he will change his Mind in Time, and come to think himself a pretty mettled Fellow.' And a little farther on, 'that Man,' continues he, 'who after having hastily run through *King Arthur*,[3] fancies himself qualified to compose a better Epic Poem than the *Æneid*; or who because he was in the Battle of ——, (no Matter whether he stood or fled) undertakes to write a System of the military Art; or who, by dipping in a Tindal and Bollingbroke,[*sic*][4] feels himself animated by a strong Impulse to subvert the Religion of his Country; that Man I admire, so promising a Genius I revere, and hail with a

Macte, nova virtute, puer.[5]

That Writer, if he attends to, and diligently follows my Instructions, will in Time make a wonderful Figure; he will climb up to the Pinnacle of the true Pert.'

Having shewn that a good Opinion of ones own Parts is an indispensible Requisite in such as aspire to the Height of the Tharsus,[6] and to be all-accomplished in the Art of Swaggering in Print, he earnestly recommends and inculcates an unwearied Zeal and restless Efforts, to entertain, cherish and increase that hopeful and profitable Disposition; towards which, he says, nothing conduces more than the diving into, dwelling on, and exaggerating the Faults and Defects of Writers, especially those that are reputed the most excellent of their Kind, whether Ancient or Modern. And that the Pupil may see and perceive these the more fully and distinctly, he advises him to keep their Beauties and Excellencies out of his View as much as possible. His reasoning on this Head is curious, and, for ought I know, original. 'As the natural Eye,' saith he, 'when accommodated to view minute Objects, is rendered unfit to take in large Prospects; so the Understanding when strained to find out and canvass Faults, becomes disqualified for comprehending Excellencies. And as those Artists, who daily pore upon Miniatures, become near-sighted, their Eyes being by Force of Habit rendered unable to descry Hills, Woods or Palaces, at a Distance; so the true Critic, whose Business it is to spy out every little Flaw or Blemish in a great Work, of course becomes incapable of perceiving the Beauties of its Disposition, and its principal Parts, they lying far beyond the Reach of his Discernment. But this Contractedness of Comprehension is so far from being a Loss to our Disciple of the Pert, that it is of double Advantage to him. For while it enables him to see the Faults of Writers distinctly and fully, as through a magnifying Glass, it removes their Excellencies from his View, and gives him the solid Pleasure of exulting and triumphing in his own Talent, while he reflects upon the Faults of others, from which he imagines himself free; without being mortified by the Images of unatainable[*sic*] Perfections, of which he can have no Idea.'

My Friend next passes to the Consideration of such Helps, as our young Adventurer may use with Success for his improvement in this fundamental Article; to wit, the spying out and magnifying the Faults of Writers. 'For altho,' says he, 'nothing will do here without a suitable Genius, yet the Horation Precept *Doctrina vim promovet insitam*, is of eternal and unlimited Truth.'[7] And therefore he recommends the reading of such Authors, as have been most diligent, and most perspicacious in detecting and exposing the Imperfections of celebrated Authors. Upon this Occasion he pathetically laments the Loss all true Critics have sustained by the Shipwreck of the Works of the immortal Zoilus. 'Of what amazing Penetration, as well as Freedom of Thought,' says he, 'must that Man have been, who in a learned and enlightened Age, and in the Neighbourhood of the wittiest People that ever flourished, could spy out what no Body else so much as suspected; to wit, Spots and Blemishes in that Son[*sic*] of Poetry the idolized Homer? How invincible was his Fortitude, who durst publish his Discoveries at a Time, when, by so doing, he ran the Risk of being pelted, or knocked down by every Body he met with in the Streets, from the Prince to the Porter or Apple-woman? And do we hesitate to proclaim him the Father of Criticism, the Parent of the Pert? But, adds he a little farther on, this Loss, great as it is, is not a little alleviated by the celebrated Abbé Terraçon's Dissertations on the *Iliad*,[8] which I can never sufficiently praise and recommend to my hopeful Pupil; this invaluable Work I would have him

Nocturna versare manu, versare diurna.'[9]

He afterwards mentions many other Authors of the same Stamp, amongst which Dennis, of acutely austere Memory, shines with a distinguished Lustre; but he laments the Scarcity of their Works, and ardently wishes they were re-published. But that, he says, is *optandum potius quam sperandum*.[10]

'But,' continues he, 'tho' the Pupil may draw unspeakable Advantage from the Dead, he may no less profit by the Living. The rising

Generation of both Sexes furnishes a numerous Army of Critics, who swarm in all Places of Rendezvous; amongst whom he will always find a dead Majority on his Side, the Dissentients being so very few that they scarce dare open their Mouths in promiscuous Companies; but are reduced either to ruminate alone in their Garrets upon their own antiquated Notions, or, when they can afford to make Holiday, to give them vent over a Mug of Beer with their Fellows. But let my hopeful Disciple herd with the modish Majority; let him, with erected Ears, greedily drink in; let him retain, meditate upon, and digest their free, easy, and airy Effusions; Effusions not smelling of the Lamp but perfumed with a natural, unlaboured Essence; quickened with a light volatile Spirit, and gratefully acidulated with the poignant Juice of Cavil.'

Yours, &c.

MISOTHARSUS.

25 *The Covent Garden Journal*, No. 59

Saturday, August 15, 1752

Here Fielding ironically promises to write a prose *Dunciad* in order to preserve the names of modern writers from oblivion.

——Illachrymabiles
Urgentur, ignotique longa
Nocte, carent quia Vate Sacro.

HOR.[1]

Without a Tear they fall, without a Name,
Unless some sacred Bard records their Fame.

There is a certain Affection of the Mind, for which tho' it be common enough in the People of this Country, we have not, I think, any adequate Term in our Language. The Greeks, tho' they likewise want a Name for the Abstract, called a Man so affected *ΥΠΕΡΦΡΩΝ*, a Word which I shall not attempt to translate otherwise than by a Paraphrase; I understand by it a Man so intoxicated with his own great Qualities, that he despises and overlooks all other Men. In this Sense the Participle passive of the Verb *ὑπερφρονέω* is used in Thucydides, *ὑπὸ τῶν εὐπραγούντων ὑπερφρονούμενος*.[2] The Sentiment is in the Mouth of Alcibiades, and it is a very fine one. *As no Man*, says he, *will even speak to us when we are unfortunate, so must they bear in their Turn* to be despised by us when we are intoxicated with our Successes.

This disdainful Temper, notwithstanding its haughty Aspect, proceeds, if I am not much mistaken, from no higher Principle than rank Timidity. We endeavour to elevate ourselves and to depress others, lest they should be brought into some Competition with ourselves. We are not sufficiently assured of our own Footing in the Ascent to Greatness, and are afraid of suffering any to come too near us, lest they should pull us down, and advance into our Place.

Of this pitiful Temper of Mind, there are no Persons so susceptible as the Brethren of the Quill. Not only such Authors as have been a little singular in their Opinions concerning their own Merit, and in whom it seems more excusable to bear a jealous Eye towards others; but even those who have far out stripped their fellow Coursers in the Race of Glory, stretch their scornful Eyes behind them, to express their Disdain of the poor Wretches who are limping and crawling on at however great a Distance.

Many are the Methods by which this Passion is exerted. I shall mention only one, as it is much the most common and perhaps the most invidious. This is a contemptuous Silence. A Treatment not much unlike to that with which the Buccaneers formerly used to treat their conquered Enemies, when they sunk, or as they phrased it, hid them in the Sea.

How many Names of great Writers may we suppose to have been Sunk by this base Disposition! Homer, as I remember, hath not perpetuated the Memory of a simple Writer, unless that of Thersites, who was, I make no Doubt, from the Character given of him in the *Iliad*, an Author of no small Estimation. And yet there were probably as many of the Function in those Days, as there are in this; nay Homer himself in his *Odyssey*, mentions the great Honours which Poets then received in the Courts of all Princes,[3] whence we may very reasonably conclude that they swarmed in those Courts, and yet the Names of three only of his Cotemporaries have triumphed over the Injuries of Time, and the Malice of their Brethren so as to reach our Age.[4]

The learned Vossius, who seems to have employed no little Pains in the Matter, hath not been able to preserve to us many more than two hundred down to the Death of Cleopatra,[5] and yet we are assured, that the famous Alexandrian Library contained no less than six hundred Thousand Volumes, of which, as the Humour of those Ages ran, we may conceive a sixth Part at least to have consisted of Poetry.

Among the Latins how many great Names may we suppose to have been hid by the affected Taciturnity of Virgil, who appears to have mentioned only those Writers of Quality to whom he made his Court! Of his Friend Horace he had not the Gratitude to take any Notice; much less to repay those Praises which this latter Poet had so liberally bestowed on him.

Horace again tho' so full of Compliments to Virgil, of poor Ovid is altogether as cruelly and invidiously silent.

Ovid, who was, I am confident, one of the best natured of Human kind, was of all Men most profuse in the Praises of his Cotemporaries; and yet even he hath been guilty of Sinking. Numberless were the

Poets in his Time, whose Names are no where to be found in his Works; nay he hath played the Buccaneer with two, one of whom is celebrated by Horace, and both of them by Virgil. The learned Reader well knows I mean the Illustrious Names of Bavius and Maevius; whose Merits were so prevalent with Virgil, that tho' they were both his bitter Revilers, he could not refrain from transmitting them to Posterity.[6] I wish he had dealt as generously by all his Censurers, and I make no Doubt but we should have been furnished with some hundreds of Names, *quæ nunc premit Nox.*[7]

Among our own Writers, too many have been guilty of this Vice. Had Dryden communicated all those who drew their Pens against him, he would have preserved as many Names from Oblivion as a Land Tax Act;[8] but he was, I am afraid, so intoxicated with his own Merit, that he overlooked and despised all the great Satyrists who constantly abused, I had almost said libelled, his Works, unless they were some other way eminent, besides by their Writings, such as Shadwell, who was Poet Laureat, and Buckingham, who was a Duke.[9]

Of all the chief Favorites and Prime Ministers of the Muses, the late ingenious Mr. Pope was most free from this scornful Silence. He employed a whole Work for the Purpose of recording such Writers as no one without his Pains, except he had lived at the same Time and in the same Street, would ever have heard of. He may indeed be said to have raked many out of the Kennels[10] to Immortality, which, tho' in somewhat a stinking Condition, is to an ambitious Mind preferable to utter Obscurity and Oblivion; many, I presume, having, with the Wretch who burnt the Temple of Ephesus,[11] such a Love for Fame, that they are willing even to creep into her common Shore.

In humble Imitation of this Great Man, in the only Instance of which I am capable of imitating him, I intend shortly to attempt a Work of the same kind, in Prose I mean, and to endeavour to do Justice to a great Number of my Cotemporaries, whose Names, for far the greater Part, are much less known than they deserve to be. And that I may be the better enabled to execute this generous Purpose, I have employed several proper Persons to find out these Authors. To this End I have ordered my Bookseller to send me in the Names of all those Apprentices and Journeymen of Booksellers and Printers who at present entertain and instruct the Town with their Productions. I have besides a very able and industrious Person who hath promised me a complete List of all the Hands now confined in the several Bridewells[12] in and about this City, which carry on the Trade of Writing, in any of the Branches of Religion, Morality, and Government; in all which every Day produces us some curious Essay, Treatise, Remarks, &c. from those Quarters.

I shall conclude this Paper with some very fine Lines from the third Book of the *Dunciad*, which gave indeed the first Hint to my charitable Design: For what a melancholy Consideration is it, that all *these Armies* there spoken of should perish in the Jaws of utter Darkness, and that the Names of such Worthies should be as short lived as their Works!—The Verses are Part of the Speech of Settle to his Son Cibber.

And see, my Son! the Hour is on its Way
That lifts our Goddess to Imperial Sway.
This fav'rite Isle long sever'd from her Reign,
Dove-like she gathers to her Wings again.
Now look thro' Fate! behold the Scene she draws!
What Aids, what Armies to assert her Cause!
See all her Progeny, illustrious Sight!
Behold, and count them as they rise to Light.
As Berecynthia, while her Offspring vye
In Homage to the Mother of the Sky,
Surveys around her, in the blest Abode,
An hundred Sons, and ev'ry Son a God:
Not with less Glory mighty Dulness crown'd,
Shall take thro' Grubstreet her triumphant Round;
And her Parnassus glancing o'er at once,
Behold an hundred Sons, and each a Dunce.[13]

A

PART FIVE

The Laws of Good Writing

Fielding made many incidental statements and reflections concerning the standards of good writing, though he never approached the subject formally. The keystone of his theory is the idea that balance, moderation, proportion, relevance of subject and style should be maintained at all costs, at the risk of turning wit into absurdity (see Introduction).

26 *The Champion; or, the Evening Advertiser,* No. 53

Saturday, March 15, 1740

The revulsion from excess of any kind was deeply rooted in Fielding's mind. This paper contains one of his most important statements of the idea of moderation and balance in literature.

Excessit Medecina Modum.——
LUCAN.[1]

It will be found, I believe, a pretty just Observation, that many more Vices and Follies arrive in the World through Excess than Neglect. Passion hurries ten beyond the Mark, for one whom Indolence holds short of it. As there never was a better Rule for the Conduct of human Life than what is convey'd in that excellent short Sentence —— *Ne quid nimis*,[2] so there is none so seldom observed. No Character is oftner represented on the Stage of the World than that of Justice *Overdo* in the *Nest of Fools*;[3] Men often become ridiculous or odious by over-acting even a laudable Part: For Virtue itself, by growing too exuberant, and (if I may be allowed a Metaphor) by running to Seed changes its very Nature, and becomes a most pernicious Weed of a most beautiful Flower.

Nothing can be more becoming than Modesty in Women. Indeed, she who wants it is a Kind of Monster in Nature, a Sort of frightful Prodigy; yet even this amiable Quality may be carried too far, may be distorted into Affectation and Prudery, and make a Woman, what Sir *Richard Steel* calls, *outragiously virtuous*.[4]

Civility or Complacence is a Quality entirely necessary to the humanizing Mankind, without which they would degenerate into Brutes and Savages; yet this when too extravagant, renders the Possessor ridiculous in himself and troublesome to others. I have known two Men catch cold, by contending which should go last out of the Rain; and have seen an elegant Dish spoiled at an Entertainment, while the well bred Guests have been shifting it from one to t'other. This troublesome

Overdoing in Civility proceeds generally from a well-inclined Temper, encouraged by a narrow Education, and is entirely abandoned by all the well-bred People of our Age.

Friendship and Love, in Persons who want Delicacy, become often nauseous and distastful. We have a vulgar Phrase, by which we express our Contempt for Excess in the latter, by saying, such a Man pins himself to his Wife's Girdle. I have known some Couples so extravagantly fond of each other, that their whole Acquaintance have been Witnesses of their tenderest Endearments: But I must remark here, that as this Excess is not very common, so it seldom lasts long.

Most Professions lose their Merit, and become useless or hurtful to Mankind by this Talent in their Professors.

Physicians have dosed more People out of the World, than have ever died for want of Medicines. The Apothecary in *Garth*, tells the Doctor.

> Your Ink descends in such excessive Show'rs,
> 'Tis plain you can regard no Health but ours.[5]

Molière, who was the severest Enemy to this Faculty, hath levelled his sharpest Satire against this Part of their Character.

Religion and Laws have been adulterated with so many needless and impertinent Ceremonies, that they have been too often drawn into Doubt and Obscurity. Some Divines and Lawyers have by one Faculty of Overdoing, contributed as much as in them lay, to deprive Mankind of the Benefit arising from those invaluable B[l]essings. The liberal Arts have suffered from the same Cause.

Cicero tells us, that *Apelles* imputed the Faults of most of the Painters of his Time to their over-doing.——*Pictores eos errare dicebat Qui non sentirent quid esset satis.*[6]

Few have deserved that Praise which *Pliny* gives to a certain Painter named *Timai*. In all whose Works (says he) there is more to be understood than is expressed.[7]

Homer, who hath been stiled the Prince of Poets, is too often inclined to overdoing. He is too prolix in his Narrations, and much too frequent in his Repetions; insomuch, that a very excellent Critic accuses him of an *Intemperance of Words.*[8] This was a Fault from which *Virgil* was entirely clear, and yet *Augustus* in his Orders to *Tucca* and *Varius*, concerning the Edition of his Works, gives them full Leave to retrench any Superfluities therein, but by no means to insert any Addition. Such an Esteem had that polite Prince of Conciseness, and such a Detestation of all Redundancy in Writing.

Ovid hath been justly censured for his Exuberance, of Fancy, he hath been guilty of the same Multiplication of Ideas which *Homer* hath of Words. In his *Metamorphosis*, he is always unwilling to quit his Subject. His Description of the Flood of *Deucalion* is a perfect Chaos of Images. It is the glaring Blemish in that admirable Work, wherein there is scarce a Page but what abounds with Instances of this Nature.

Young Authors, and all those who have more Imagination than Judgment, are continually guilty of this Vice. They think they have never said enough on a Subject, and are apt to heap Idea on Idea till they have tired and confused their Readers.

That laborious Tribe the Commentators, are to a Man full of this over-doing Quality. They ever

> Explain a Thing till all Men doubt it,
> And write about it, Goddess, and about it,[9]

Which is so just an Observation, that the Mind of a Reader, who should examine the Commentaries on *Virgil* or *Horace*, would be in as perplexed a Condition as that of Judge *Gripus*, who very humourosly complains that every new Evidence only tends to darken and embarass a Case which was plain enough before.[10]

It hath been the Tenet of some Philosophers, that the original Matter of the whole Universe might be reduced within the Compass of a Nutshell. I shall not assert into what narrow Bounds all that is truly excellent in Authors might be reduced, but I am confident the very best might be retrenched within much fewer Pages than they at present consist of. We may, I believe, notwithstanding what I have observed before of the *Æneid*, conclude, that had *Virgil* lived to the compleating it, it would have been not a little shorter than it now is. It was well answered by Archbishop *Tillotson* to King *William*, when he complained of the Shortness of his Sermon.— 'Sir,' said the Bishop, 'could I have bestowed more Time on it, it would not have been so long.'[11]

Horace, in his Art of Poetry, particularly recommends an exact and severe Defalcation of all superfluous Members in Poetry.[12] He himself practices this Rule every where with the greatest exactness; so much dreading the contrary, that in one of his Epistles, when he apprehends himself in Danger of running into too great a Length, he stops short, and ends in almost an abrupt Manner,

> ——*Ne me verbosi serinia Lippi*
> *Compilasse putes—Verbum non amplius addam.*[13]

Juvenal reprehends this Vice as the very first in his *Codrus*——

Impune diem comsumpserit Ingens
Scriptus & in Tergo nec dum finitus Orestes.[14]

This will be eternally found in all bad Authors.

That I may not be guilty of the Vice I am declaiming against, I shall end this Torrent of Quotations, into which I have been unavoidably drawn, by recommending this Golden Rule of Conciseness, or as it is somewhere called the Golden Mean, to all my Readers. Since it is certain, that by the contrary Method, whatever is truly excellent loses half its Praise, and whatever is ridiculous or odious receives double the Aggravation.

L.

27 *The True Patriot and The History of Our Own Times*, No. 22

From Tuesday, March 25, to Tuesday, April 1, 1746

The standards implied in this humorous paper relate to those more fully explained in the Preface to *The Journal of A Voyage to Lisbon* (No. 30), where Fielding stresses the need for a balance between the extremes of fantasy and dullness. Here sense is represented as the middle point between madness and stupidity.

To the TRUE PATRIOT.

Crane-Court, March 25, 1746.[1]

SIR,—I am one of those People to whom the World usually give the Title of *Virtuosi*. And tho' I am very sensible that the Generality of Mankind are apt to entertain a low and contemptible Opinion of us, as an useless Sett [*sic*] of People, yet that they have little Reason for doing so, I hope will appear from what I am going to relate.

I have formerly been a very great Traveller, and when I was in *Germany*, some Years ago, I happened to make an Acquaintance with a celebrated Alchymist, who had spent a great Part of his Life in search of the *Philosopher's Stone*. It has often happened, that altho' the Virtuosi of this Sort have failed in their principal Attempt; yet the accidental Discovery of some Secret, which they never aimed at, has fully recompensed them for the Labour of the Undertaking. This was the Case of my worthy Friend abovementioned. He was obliged, by an *untimely Death*, to leave the GREAT WORK unfinished; but it is owing to his Industry, that I am become Master of a SECRET, of equal, if not of superior Importance.[2]

My Acquaintance with this Gentleman commenced but a little before his Death; but he had taken such a Liking to me, in this short time, that by his last Will he bequeathed to me all his Books and Curiosities. It would be tedious to give an Account of all the *Rarities* which I thus became Master of; but amongst the rest was a curious Machine, which at first sight I took to be a *Thermometer*. It was constructed in the usual form, but very small, the Glass Tube being not above three Inches long. This Tube was filled with a red transparent Liquor, and behind it was an Ivory Scale, upon which the Degrees of *Heat and Cold* (as I then thought) were delineated with the greatest Nicety; but there was no Inscription upon it to point out the Changes of the Air, as is usually done on the Common Thermometers, by the Words *Hot*, *Temperate*, &c. I took this Instrument home with me, and placed it on the Table in my Study. That Night the Weather changed, as it does frequently in that Climate, from temperate to very cold. I was eager to see my Thermometer the next Morning, in Expectation that it would have very exactly shewn this Change; but I had no sooner cast my Eye upon it, but I saw that the Spirits stood exactly where they had done the Day before. I could not tell what to make of this; however, I had a Mind to make a farther Trial of it, and therefore placed it on my Table, near the Fire, to see if the Heat would make the Spirits rise. It is my constant Custom, in a Morning, while my Breakfast is getting ready, to entertain myself with a Book; and I generally take up one or other of the Classic Authors for this Purpose. That Morning I happened to take up a *Virgil*. I had no sooner began to read, but I saw the *Spirits* mount up suddenly in the Thermometer, from whence I concluded, but there must have been a very sudden Alteration of the Air; but upon laying the Book aside, to observe the Instrument more exactly, the *Spirits* immediately subsided to their former Pitch. This Accident surprized me pretty much; but I had greater Reason for Admiration when I observ'd, that the Moment I began to read on, the *Spirits* began to ascend again, and that they sunk as soon as ever I left off. I imagined, at first, that my Breath was the Cause of this sudden Change; but I soon laid aside that Thought, as I observ'd, that there was the same Appearance, whether I read aloud or to myself; and whether I was near to, or at a Distance from the *Glass*. Whilst I was in this Perplexity, I took up the first Book which came to hand, which happen'd to be a Volume of Sermons, which had been given me by an Eminent Divine, when I first went abroad. I had scarcely dipp'd into it, when I saw, to my great Astonishment, that the Liquor, instead of rising, sunk down of a sudden to the very Bottom of the Tube, and ascended again as suddenly, upon my laying the Book aside. Most People, had they been in my Place, would have attributed this *Phænomenon to Magic*. And for my own Part, I must freely own, that I do not comprehend what secret Properties this Liquor has, nor how it is prepared, but must leave that Matter to be discuss'd by the Philosophers and Naturalists of the Age; all I can say to it is, that by making a great many Experiments of the like kind, I always found, that the *Spirits* in the Tube rose or fell, in proportion to *Altitude* or *Depression* of the Author's Genius.

As most great Inventions have been owing originally to Chance, so I may be said, by mere Accident, to have found out the Use of an *Instrument*, which may properly be stiled, *The Test of Understanding*; or, *The Weather-Glass of Wit*: As it shews the Degree of *Heat* or *Coldness* in the *Understanding*, with as much Certainty, as the Common Thermometers do that of the Atmosphere. And, by the exactest Observations I have been able to make, it appears, that the different Degrees of *Sense* are ranged according to the ensuing Scale, which, for that Reason, I have affix'd to the *Thermometer*.

MADNESS.

WILDNESS.

TRUE WIT, OR FIRE.

VIVACITY.

GOOD-SENSE.

GRAVITY.

PERTNESS.

DULLNESS.

STUPIDITY, OR FOLLY.[3]

If any Objection should be made to my placing the different Degrees of Understanding at equal distances from each other, I must acquaint the Objector, that it did not proceed from my own Invention, but that it was the Result of several long and careful Experiments, which I made of the rising and falling of the *Spirits* in my Thermometer. Whenever I read a plain sensible Production of any Author, I always observed that the *Spirits* kept exactly to the *middle Point*. If Good Sense was mix'd with here and there a lively Stroke, they rose to *Vivacity*. A Degree more of *Heat* raises the Thermometer to *Fire*; which is always the more laudable Quality in an Author, the more steadily and equably it burns. Too great a Degree of Fire degenerates into *Wildness*, or Extravagance, which last is but one Degree below *Madness*, or the *raving* Point. The lower part of the Scale points out the different Degrees of *Coldness* in the Understanding. *Good Sense*, by a farther Degree of Cold, is *condensed* into *Gravity*: Gravity, as appears from my Glass, falling just as much short of Good-Sense, as Vivacity does of true Wit, or Fire; and, as they are but one Degree distant from each other, this may probably be the Reason why the Man of *Vivacity* is often mistaken for a *Wit*, and the *grave Man* for a *Man of Sense*. The next Degree below *Gravity* is *Pertness*: This Quality of the Mind is oftentimes called *Wit*; and indeed they appear, by my Scale, to be equally distant from Good-Sense; but with this Difference, that as true Wit is two Degrees above, so Pertness is just as many below that Point; for the witty Writer borders upon Extravagance, but the *pert* one is but one Degree above being *dull*.

I may, perhaps, hereafter communicate to you the Observations which I have made, from Time to Time, upon different Kinds of Writers, by the help of my Thermometer; for I have brought it to so great a Degree of Exactness, that I can tell, to the *Twelfth Part of an Inch*, how much Wit there is in any Author. But I shall wave this Point at present, to acquaint you, That I seldom go into Company without taking my Glass along with me; and whilst others are employ'd in gazing upon it, and observing the Inscription, which is in a Character of my own Invention, somewhat resembling the *Chinese*, I have an Opportunity of examining the *Height* or *Depth* of their Capacities.

Give me Leave now to mention some of the many Advantages which the Public may reap from the Use of this *Machine*, and which may intitle the Inventor to your Encouragement, as a *True Patriot*. It will readily be allowed me, I presume, that my Thermometer may be rendered of the utmost Use to the Managers of the two Theatres, by furnishing them with a certain Rule, by which they may judge of the Merit of new *Dramatic* Performances. I humbly hope, therefore, that those Gentlemen will constitute me *Surveyor-General* of Plays: And I submit to their Discretion, Whether it would not be proper, upon the first Night of a new Play, to give out *Bills*, in which the Quantity of Wit contain'd in each Scene should be marked down. For by this Means the Audience would be enabled to *clap* or *hiss* in the proper Place. And I believe most Authors, who have written for the Stage, will agree with me, that this is a Thing which is very much wanted at this

Time, and which would greatly tend to promote a good Harmony between the *Poet* and the *Pitt* [*sic*].

My *Thermometer* may still be of further Use, by enabling Readers of all Kinds, *gentle* as well as *simple*, to judge of the Merit of new Books, as well as of new Plays.—I have oftentimes secretly lamented, that the Generality of Readers have no certain Rule of doing this; and at the same Time pitied the Fate of young Authors, whose Works, for Want of some such Rule, have many Times been stifled, as one may say, at their very Birth.—The common Way of judging of new Performances, I know, is to cast an Eye upon the Title-page, to see what *capital* Letters are added at the End of the Author's Name: For the more or fewer there are of these, the greater or less is the Merit of the Work.—I have sometimes known the whole Impression of a Book sold off, in a few Days Time, by the Help of a *D.D.* an *F.R.S.* or *C.M.L.S.*[4] in the Title-page, when it would, perhaps, have lain upon the Bookseller's Hands for Years together, nay, and perhaps have been sent to the *Pastry Cooks* at last, if it had wanted this Addition. There is another Way of judging of the Excellency of a Book, *viz.* by observing whom it is dedicated to: And it can hardly be imagined what an Effect a Dedication to his Grace of——, my Lord *C*——, or Dr. *M*——, *&c.*[5] has sometimes had, in filling the Bookseller's *Pocket*, and inhancing the *Reputation* of the Author. There is a third Way of determining the Worth of a Book, which I prefer to either of the former, namely, by observing whom it is printed for. A very ingenious Friend of mine, whom I was lately talking with about the Character of a new Pamphlet, assured me, that it must be a very good one, because it was printed for *J.* and *P. K*——, in *L——te Street.*[6]—And this is the general Way of judging of all anonymous Pieces whatever. Now, although I allow each of these Methods to have its Use, yet, in my humble Opinion, the Value of Books may be more certainly ascertained by Means of my Thermometer, than by any of the three.

From what I have said of the Properties of my Weather-glass, you will perceive, that no Body is better qualified than myself, to carry into Execution a Project which wou'd be of universal Benefit, and which, for a long Time past, I have had in my Thoughts; *viz.* To erect *an Office for assaying Wit*, or trying whether it be *Standard*. I intend to take the Office of *Assay Master* on myself, and do hereby advertise all Booksellers, Publishers, *&c.* who deal in *Literary Wares*, that, by applying to my Office, they may have the *Metal*, which they traffic in, *assayed*, for a small Gratuity, in order to discover whether it be *true* or *counterfeit*. As you have profess'd yourself a *True Patriot*, I hope you will give Encouragement to my Scheme, by recommending it to the Public; and, in Return for the Favour, I shall be ready, at any Time, to *assay* your *Paper*, *gratis*; and to give you any farther Assistance which is in my Power. And I flatter myself that my Assistance will not be thought inconsiderable; since, by taking my Glass along with me into all Companies, from the Ministers *Levee* down to the City Club, I have found out the Means of penetrating into the true Characters and Abilities of most of the considerable Persons in this Kingdom; and can, at any Time, furnish you with an exact Calculation of the Quantity of Wisdom and Folly which is to be found in this Metropoli.

I am, &c.

TORRICELLI, Junr.

28 Preface to *Familiar Letters on David Simple . . .*

1747

The *Familiar Letters . . .*, by Fielding's sister, Sarah Fielding, followed her *David Simple* (1744, see below, No. 62). This volume, to which Fielding contributed five letters, was published on April 10, 1747; the text is taken from the first edition.

PREFACE

Written by a Friend of the Author

The Taste of the Public, with regard to Epistolary Writing, having been much vitiated by some modern Authors, it may not be amiss to premise some short matter concerning it in this Place, that the Reader may not expect another Kind of Entertainment than he will meet with in the following Papers, nor impute the Author's designed Deviation from the common Road, to any Mistake or Error.

Those Writings which are called Letters, may be divided into four Classes. Under the first Class may be ranged those Letters, as well antient as modern, which have been written by Men, who have filled up the principal Characters on the Stage of Life, upon great and memorable Occasions. These have been always esteemed as the most valuable Parts of History, as they are not only the most authentic Memorials of Facts, but as they serve greatly to illustrate the true Character of the Writer, and do in a manner introduce the Person himself to our Acquaintance.

A Second Kind owe their Merit not to Truth, but to Invention; such are the Letters which contain ingenious Novels, or shorter Tales, either pathetic or humorous; these bear the same Relation to the former, as Romance doth to true History; and, as the former may be called short Histories, so may these be styled short Romances.

In the next Branch may be ranked those Letters, which have past between Men of Eminence in the Republic of Literature. Many of these are in high Estimation in the learned World, in which they are considered as having equal Authority to that, which the political World allows to those of the first Class.

Besides these three Kinds of Letters, which have all their several Merits, there are two more, with which the Moderns have very plentifully supplied the World, tho' I shall not be very profuse in my Encomiums on either: These are Love-Letters, and Letters of Conversation, in which last are contained the private Affairs of Persons of no Consequence to the Public, either in a political or learned Consideration, or indeed in any Consideration whatever.

With these two Kinds of Letters the *French* Language in particular so vastly abounds, that it would employ most of the leisure Hours of Life to read them all; nay, I believe indeed, they are the principal Study of many of our fine Gentlemen and Ladies, who learn that Language.

And hence such Readers have learnt the critical Phrases of a *familiar easy Style*, a *concise epistolary Style*, *&c.* and these they apply to all Letters whatever.

Now, from some polite modern Performances, written I suppose by this Rule, I much doubt, whether these *French* Readers have any just and adequate Notion of *this epistolary Style*, with which they are so enamoured. To say the truth, I question whether they do not place it entirely in short, abrupt, unconnected Periods; a Style so easy, that any Man may write it, and which, one would imagine, it must be very difficult to procure any Person to read.

To such Critics therefore I would recommend *Ovid*, who was perhaps the ablest Writer of *les Lettres Galantes*, that ever lived. In his *Arte amandi* they will find the following Rule,

——*præsens ut videare loqui.*[1]

viz. that these Letters should preserve the Style of Conversation; and in his Epistles they will see this excellently illustrated by Example. But if we are to form our Idea of the Conversation of some modern Writers from their Letters, we shall have, I am afraid, a very indifferent Opinion of both.

But in reality, this Style of Conversation is only proper, at least only necessary to these, which I have called Letters of Conversation; and is not at all requisite, either to Letters of Business, which in After-ages make a Part of History, or to those on the Subject of Literature and Criticism.

Much less is it adapted to the Novel or Story-Writer; for what difference is there, whether a Tale is related this or any other way? And sure no one will contend, that the epistolary Style is in general the most proper to a Novelist, or that it hath been used by the best Writers of this Kind.[2]

It is not my Purpose here to write a large Dissertation on Style in general, nor to assign what is proper to the Historian, what to the Romance, and what to the Novel-Writer, nor to observe in what manner all these differ from each other; it is sufficient to have obviated an Objection, which, I foresaw, might be made to these little Volumes by some, who are in truth as incapable of knowing any of the Faults, as of reaping any of the Beauties of an Author; and I assure them, there is no Branch of Criticism, in which Learning, as well as Good-sense is more required, than to the forming an accurate Judgment of Style, tho' there is none, I believe, in which every trifling Reader is more ready to give his Decision.

Instead of laying down any Rules for the use of such Tyros in the critical Art, I shall recommend them to one, who is a Master of Style, as of every other Excellence.[3] This Gentleman in his *Persian* Letters, many of which are written on the most important Subjects in Ethics, Politics, and Philosophy, hath condescended to introduce two or three Novels: in these they will find that inimitable Writer very judiciously changing the Style which he uses on other Occasions, where the Subjects of his Letters require the Air and Style of Conversation; to preserve which, in relating Stories that run to any length, would be faulty in the Writer, and tiresome to the Reader.

To conclude this Point, I know not of any essential Difference between this, and any other way of writing Novels, save only, that by making use of Letters, the Writer is freed from the regular Beginnings and Conclusions of Stories, with some other Formalities, in which the Reader of Taste finds no less Ease and Advantage, than the Author himself.

As to the Matter contained in the following Volumes, I am not perhaps at liberty to declare my Opinion: Relation and Friendship to the Writer may draw upon me the Censure of Partiality, if I should be as warm, as I am inclined to be in their Commendation.

The Reader will however excuse me, if I advise him not to run them over with too much Haste and Indifference; such Readers will, I promise them, find little to admire in this Book, whose Beauties (if it have any) require the same Attention to discover them, with which the Author herself hath considered that Book of Nature, whence they are taken. In Books, as well as Pictures, where the Excellence lies in the Expression or Colouring only, the first Glance of the Eyes acquaints us with all the Perfection of the Piece; but the nicest and most delicate Touches of Nature are not so soon perceived. In the Works of *Cervantes* or *Hogarth*, he is, I believe, a wretched Judge, who discovers no new Beauties on a second, or even a third Perusal.

And here I cannot controll myself from averring, that many Touches of this kind appear to me in these Letters; some of which I cannot help thinking as fine, as I have ever met with in any of the Authors, who have made Human Nature their Subject.

As such Observations are generally supposed to be the Effects of long Experience in, and much Acquaintance with Mankind, it may perhaps surprize many, to find them in the Works of a Woman; especially of one, who, to use the common Phrase, hath *seen so little of the World*: and I should not wonder on this account, that these Letters were ascribed to another Author, if I knew any one capable of writing them.

But in reality the Knowledge of Human Nature is not learnt by living in the Hurry of the World. True Genius, with the help of a little Conversation, will be capable of making a vast Progress in this Learning; and indeed I have observed, there are none who know so little of Men, as those who are placed in the Crouds, either of Business or Pleasure. The Truth of the Assertion, that Pedants in Colleges have seldom any Share of this Knowledge, doth not arise from any Defect in the College, but from a Defect in the Pedant, who would have spent many Years at *St. James's* to as little Purpose:[4] for daily Experience may convince us, that it is possible for a Blockhead to see much of the World, and know little of it.

The Objection to the Sex of the Author hardly requires an Answer: It will be chiefly advanced by those, who derive their Opinion of Women very unfairly from the fine Ladies of the Age; whereas, if the Behaviour of their Counterparts the Beaus, was to denote the Understanding of Men, I apprehend the Conclusion would be in favour of the Women, without making a Compliment to that Sex. I can of my own Knowledge, and from my own Acquaintance bear Testimony to the Possibility of those Examples, which History gives of Women eminent for the highest Endowments and Faculties of the Mind. I shall only add an Answer to the same Objection, relating to *David Simple*, given by a Lady of very high Rank, whose Quality is however less an Honour to her than her Understanding. *So far*, said she, *from doubting David Simple to be the Performance of a Woman, I am well convinced, it could not have been written by a Man.*[5]

In the Conduct of Women, in that great and important Business of their Lives, the Affair of Love, there are Mysteries, with which Men are perfectly unacquainted: their Education being on this head in Constraint of, nay, in direct Opposition to, Truth and Nature, creates such a constant Struggle between Nature and Habit, Truth and Hypocrisy, as introduce often much Humour into their Characters; especially when drawn by sensible Writers of their own Sex, who are on this Subject much more capable, than the ablest of ours.

I remember it was the Observation of a Lady, for whose Opinion I have a great Veneration, that there is nothing more generally unnatural, than the Characters of Women on the Stage, and that even in our best Plays: If this be fact, as I sincerely believe it is, whence can it proceed, but from the Ignorance in which the artificial Behaviour of Women leaves us, of what really passes in their Minds, and which, like all other Mysteries, is known only to the Initiated?

Many of the foregoing Assertions will, I question not, meet with very little Assent from those great and wise Men, who are not only absolute Masters of some poor Woman's Person, but likewise of her Thoughts. With such Opposition I must rest contented; but what I more dread, is, that I may have unadvisedly drawn the Resentment of her own lovely Sex against the Author of these Volumes, for having betrayed the Secrets of the Society.

To this I shall attempt giving two Answers: First, that these nice Touches will, like the Signs of Masonry, escape the Observation and Detection of all those, who are not already in the Secret.

Secondly, if she should have exposed some of those nicer Female Foibles, which have escaped most other Writers, she hath at the same time nobly displayed the Beauties and Virtues of the more amiable Part, which abundantly overbalances in the account. By comparing these together, young Ladies may, if they please, receive great Advantages: I will venture to say, no Book extant is so well calculated for their Instruction and Improvement. It is indeed a Glass, by which they may dress out their Minds, and adorn themselves with more becoming, as well as more lasting Graces, than the Dancing-Master, the Manteau-Maker, or the Millener [*sic*] can give them. Here even their Vanity may be rendered useful, as it may make them detest and scorn all base, mean, shuffling Tricks, and admire and cultivate whatever is truly amiable, generous and good: Here they must learn, if they will please to attend, that the Consummation of a Woman's Character, is to maintain the Qualities of Goodness, Tenderness, Affection and Sincerity, in the several social Offices and Duties of Life; and not to unite Ambition, Avarice, Luxury, and Wantonness in the Person of a Woman of the World, or to affect Folly, Childishness and Levity, under the Appelation of a fine Lady.

To conclude, I hope, for the Sake of my fair Country-Women, that these excellent Pictures of Virtue and Vice, which, to my Knowledge, the Author hath bestowed such Pains in drawing, will not be thrown away on the World, but that much more Advantage may accrue to the Reader, than the Good-nature and Sensibility of the Age have, to their immortal Honour, bestowed on the Author.

29 *The Covent Garden Journal*, No. 62

Saturday, September 16, 1752

Here Fielding, from beneath the mask of a Bedlam lunatic, defends modern drama against an attempt to apply neo-classic rules.

Insanire parat certe ratione modoq;[1]

To Sir ALEXANDER DRAWCANSIR, Knt.
Censor of Great Britain.

Bedlam, Apr. 9, 1752.

SIR,—I have been confined in this Place four Years; my Friends, that is, my Relations, but, as I call them, my *Enemies*, think me Mad, but to show you I am not, I'll send you a Specimen of my Present State of Mind.—About a Week ago, a grave Gentleman came to the Grate of my Cell and threw me in a Pamphlet, written it seems by a Gent. of Cambridge. I read it over, and approve the Drama much, but I must send you some Thoughts that occur'd to me from Reading the Prefix'd Five Letters[2]—the Author it seems lives at Pembroke-Hall, in Cambridge, where Sophocles, Euripides, and Æschilus, have, I don't doubt, been his darling Studies, not forgetting the abominable Rules of Aristotle, who indisputably wrote very properly concerning Dramatic Poetry at his Time of Day, but what a Figure wou'd a Modern Tragedy make with his three Unities!—if Shakespeare had observed them—he wou'd have flown like a *Paper-Kite*, not *soar'd like an Eagle*.—Again, Sir, as to his *Chorus* he is so fond of, why that did very well amongst the Greek Writers; but methinks this *Mr. Chorus* would be a very impertinent Fellow if he was to put in his Observations on any of Shakespeare's interesting Scenes; as for Example, what do you think of this same *Chorus*, if he was to be upon the Stage when, in the Play of *Othello*, Iago is imprinting those exquisite Tints of Jealousy upon Othello's Mind in the third Act; or suppose when Desdemona drops the fatal Handkerchief, the *Chorus* was to call after her to bid her take it up again, or tell the Audience what was to happen in Case she did not.—— Or suppose, Sir, this same *Chorus* was to stand by, and tell us Brutus and Cassius were going to differ, but that they would make it up again—would not this prevent the noble Anxiety this famous Scene in *Julius Cæsar* raises in the Minds of a sensible Audience? Another Use this ingenious Gentleman finds out for the *Chorus*, and that is, to explain the Characters and Sentiments of the several Personages in the Drama, to the Audience. Now, Sir, there is a Nation in the World which has found out a way of doing this very effectually without *interrupting the Action*——and that is, *the Chinese*; these People always make the Characters of the Drama come upon the Stage before the Play begins, and tell who they are, as thus Sir.

Enter Dramatis Personæ.

1. I am Taw-Maw-shaw, King of Tonchin, Brother to Hunfish, am to be dethroned by my Brother, and killed with the Sabre of the renowned Schimshaw.

2. I am Hunfish, Brother to Taw-Maw-shaw, I am to dethrone him, and usurp his Crown.

3. I am Schimshaw Master of the great Sabre which is to kill the King Taw-Maw-shaw.

Thus, Sir, do these wise People let you into the Characters of the Drama; which is to be sure a much wiser way, than by a *Chorus*, who interrupt the Actors to cram in their stupid Remarks—— Indeed, when Dramatic Poetry first appeared, the whole was represented *by one Person*, and there it was necessary the *Chorus* should come in, to give the poor Solo Speaker a little Breath, but as I have half a dozen Plays by me which I intend to bring upon the Stage, I beg you will insist upon it that this learned Cantab says no more about his *Chorus*, for it would be very hard upon me if I had not the same Indulgence which has been shewn *to all my Cotemporaries*; which is to let the Audience find out the Meaning of my Characters if they can, of themselves; if not, let them depart as wise as they came.——

I am,

Sir, Yours in clean Straw,

TRAGICOMICUS.

N.B. I have no Objection to the Choruses of the immortal Handel.[3]

If you observe, Sir, this learned Gentleman finds fault with Shakespeare's *Chorus* in Harry the Vth, and says it would do better in other Metre.—— If I had him here, I believe I should do him a Mischief.

30 Preface to *The Journal of A Voyage to Lisbon*

1755

Fielding's journal was published after his death by his brother John on February 25, 1755; the text is taken from the first edition.

The Preface to *The Journal* . . . is one of the last pieces which Fielding wrote. It contains material which relates very closely to some of the arguments in the introductory chapters of *Tom Jones*—particularly the idea of history. The argument in general, however, reflects on Fielding's basic convictions about all literary art.

There would not, perhaps, be a more pleasant, or profitable study, among those which have their principal end in amusement, than that of travels or voyages, if they were writ, as they might be, and ought to be, with a joint view to the entertainment and information of mankind. If the conversation of travellers be so eagerly sought after as it is, we may believe their books will be still more agreeable company, as they will, in general, be more instructive and more entertaining.

But when I say the conversation of travellers is usually so welcome, I must be understood to mean that only of such as have had good sense enough to apply their peregrinations to a proper use, so as to acquire from them a real and valuable knowledge of men and things; both which are best known by comparison. If the customs and manners of men were every where the same, there would be no office so dull as that of a traveller: for the difference of hills, valleys, rivers; in short, the various views in which we may see the face of the earth, would scarce afford him a pleasure worthy of his labour; and surely it would give him very little opportunity of communicating any kind of entertainment or improvement to others.

To make a traveller an agreeable companion to a man of sense, it is necessary, not only that he should have seen much, but that he should have overlooked much of what he hath seen. Nature is not, any more than a great genius, always admirable in her productions, and therefore the traveller, who may be called her commentator, should not expect to find every where subjects worthy of his notice.

It is certain, indeed, that one may be guilty of omission as well as of the opposite extreme: but a fault on that side will be more easily pardoned, as it is better to be hungry than surfeited, and to miss your dessert at the table of a man whose gardens abound with the choicest fruits, than to have your taste affronted with every sort of trash that can be pick'd up at the green-stall, or the wheel-barrow.

If we should carry on the analogy between the traveller and the commentator, it is impossible to keep one's eye a moment off from the laborious much read doctor Zachary Grey, of whose redundant notes on *Hudibras* I shall only say, that it is, I am confident, the single book extant in which above five hundred authors are quoted, not one of which could be found in the collection of the late doctor Mead.[1]

As there are few things which a traveller is to record, there are fewer on which he is to offer his observations: this is the office of the reader, and it is so pleasant a one, that he seldom chuses to have it taken from him, under the pretence of lending him assistance. Some occasions, indeed, there are, when proper observations are pertinent, and others when they are necessary; but good sense alone must point them out. I shall lay down only one general rule, which I believe to be of universal truth between relator and hearer, as it is between author and reader; this is, that the latter never forgive any observation of the former which doth not convey some knowledge that they are sensible they could not possibly have attained of themselves.

But all his pains in collecting knowledge, all his judgment in selecting, and all his art in communicating it, will not suffice, unless he can make himself, in some degree, an agreeable, as well as an instructive companion. The highest instruction we can derive from the tedious tale of a dull fellow scarce ever pays us for our attention. There is nothing, I think, half so valuable as knowledge, and yet there is nothing which men will give themselves so little trouble to attain; unless it be, perhaps, that lowest degree of it which is the object of curiosity, and which hath therefore that active passion constantly employed in its service. This, indeed, it is in the power of every traveller to gratify; but it is the leading principle in weak minds only.

To render his relation agreeable to the man of sense, it is therefore necessary that the voyager should possess several eminent and rare talents; so rare, indeed, that it is almost wonderful to see them ever united in the same person.

And if all these talents must concur in the relator, they are certainly in a more eminent degree necessary to the writer: for here the narration admits of higher ornaments of stile, and every fact and sentiment offers itself to the fullest and most deliberate examination.

It would appear therefore, I think, somewhat strange, if such writers as these should be found extremely common; since nature hath been a most parsimonious distributer of her richest talents, and hath seldom bestowed many on the same person. But on the other hand, why there should scarce exist a single writer of this kind worthy our regard; and whilst there is no other branch of history (for this is history) which hath not exercised the greatest pens, why this alone should be overlooked by all men of great genius and erudition, and delivered up to the Goths and Vandals as their lawful property, is altogether as difficult to determine.

And yet that this is the case, with some very few exceptions, is most manifest. Of these I shall willingly admit Burnet and Addison;[2] if the former was not perhaps to be considered as a political essayist, and the latter as a commentator on the classics, rather than as a writer of travels; which last title perhaps they would both of them have been least ambitious to affect.

Indeed if these two, and two or three more, should be removed from the mass, there would remain such a heap of dulness behind, that the appelation of voyage-writer would not appear very desirable.

I am not here unapprized that old Homer himself is by some considered as a voyage-writer; and indeed the beginning of his *Odyssy* may be urged to countenance that opinion, which I shall not controvert. But whatever species of writing the *Odyssy* is of, it is surely at the head of that species, as much as the *Iliad* is of another; and so far the excellent Longinus would allow, I believe, at this day.[3]

But, in reality, the *Odyssy*, the *Telemachus*,[4] and all of that kind, are to the voyage-writing I here intend, what romance is to true history, the former being the confounder and corrupter of the latter. I am far from supposing, that Homer, Hesiod, and the other antient poets and mythologists, had any settled design to pervert and confuse the records of antiquity; but it is certain they have effected it; and, for my part, I must confess I should have honoured and loved Homer more had he written a true history of his own times in humble prose, than those noble poems that have so justly collected the praise of all ages; for though I read these with more admiration and astonishment, I still read Herodotus, Thucydides and Xenophon, with more amusement and more satisfaction.

The original poets were not, however, without excuse. They found the limits of nature too strait for the immensity of their genius, which they had not room to exert, without extending fact by fiction; and that especially at a time when the manners of men were too simple to afford that variety, which they have since offered in vain to the choice of the meanest writers. In doing this, they are again excusable for the manner in which they have done it,

Ut speciosa dehinc miracula promant.[5]

They are not indeed so properly said to turn reality into fiction, as fiction into reality. Their paintings are so bold, their colours so strong, that every thing they touch seems to exist in the very manner they represent it: their portraits are so just, and their landscapes so beautiful, that we acknowledge the strokes of nature in both, without enquiring whether nature herself, or her journeyman the poet, formed the first pattern of the piece.

But other writers (I will put Pliny[6] at their head) have no such pretensions to indulgence: they lye for lying sake, or in order insolently to impose the most monstrous improbabilities and absurdities upon their readers on their own authority; treating them as some fathers treat children, and as other fathers do lay-men, exacting their belief of whatever they relate, on no other foundation than their own authority, without ever taking the pains of adapting their lies to human credulity, and of calculating them for the meridian of a common understanding; but with as much weakness as wickedness, and with more impudence often than either, they assert facts contrary to the honour of God, to the visible order of the creation, to the known laws of nature, to the histories of former ages, and to the experience of our own, and which no man can at once understand and believe.

If it should be objected (and it can no where be objected better than where, I now write,* as there is no where more pomp of bigotry) that whole nations have been firm believers in such most absurd suppositions; I reply, the fact is not true. They have known nothing of the matter, and have believed they knew not what. It is, indeed with me no matter of doubt, but that the pope and his clergy might teach any of those Christian Heterodoxies, the tenets of which are the most diametrically opposite to their own; nay, all the doctrines of Zoroaster,

* At Lisbon.

Confucius, and Mahomet, not only with certain and immediate success, but without one catholick in a thousand knowing he had changed his religion.

What motive a man can have to sit down, and to draw forth a list of stupid, senseless, incredible lies upon paper, would be difficult to determine, did not Vanity present herself so immediately as the adequate cause. The vanity of knowing more than other men is, perhaps, besides hunger, the only inducement to writing, at least to publishing, at all: why then should not the voyage-writer be inflamed with the glory of having seen what no man ever did or will see but himself? This is the true source of the wonderful, in the discourse and writings, and sometimes, I believe, in the actions of men. There is another fault of a kind directly opposite to this, to which these writers are sometimes liable, when, instead of filling their pages with monsters which no body hath ever seen, and with adventures which never have nor could possibly have happened to them, they waste their time and paper with recording things and facts of so common a kind, that they challenge no other right of being remembered, than as they had the honour of having happened to the author, to whom nothing seems trivial that in any manner happens to himself. Of such consequence do his own actions appear to one of this kind, that he would probably think himself guilty of infidelity, should he omit the minutest thing in the detail of his journal. That the fact is true, is sufficient to give it a place there, without any consideration whether it is capable of pleasing or surprising, of diverting or informing the reader.

I have seen a play (if I mistake not, it is one of Mrs. Behn's, or of Mrs. Centlivre's) where this vice in a voyage-writer is finely ridiculed. An ignorant pedant, to whose government, for I know not what reason, the conduct of a young nobleman in his travels is committed, and who is sent abroad to shew My Lord the world, of which he knows nothing himself, before his departure from a town, calls for his journal, to record the goodness of the wine and tobacco, with other articles of the same importance, which are to furnish the materials of a voyage at his return home.[7] The humour, it is true, is here carried very far; and yet, perhaps, very little beyond what is to be found in writers who profess no intention of dealing in humour at all.

Of one or other or both of these kinds are, I conceive, all that vast pile of books which pass under the names of voyages, travels, adventures, lives, memoirs, histories, &c. some of which a single traveller sends into the world in many volumes, and others are, by judicious booksellers, collected into vast bodies in folio, and inscribed with their own names, as if they were indeed their own travels; thus unjustly attributing to themselves the merit of others.

Now from both these faults we have endeavoured to steer clear in the following narrative: which, however the contrary may be insinuated by ignorant, unlearned, and fresh-water critics, who have never travelled either in books or ships, I do solemnly declare doth, in my own impartial opinion, deviate less from truth than any other voyage extant; my lord Anson's alone being, perhaps, excepted.[8]

Some few embellishments must be allowed to every historian: for we are not to conceive that the speeches in Livy, Sallust,[9] or Thucydides, were literally spoken in the very words in which we now read them. It is sufficient that every fact hath its foundation in truth, as I do seriously aver is the case in the ensuing pages; and when it is so, a good critic will be so far from denying all kind of ornament of stile or diction, or even of circumstance to his author, that he would be rather sorry if he omitted it: for he could hence derive no other advantage than the loss of an additional pleasure in the perusal.

Again, if any merely common incident should appear in this journal, which will seldom, I apprehend, be the case, the candid reader will easily perceive it is not introduced for its own sake, but for some observations and reflections naturally resulting from it; and which, if but little to his amusement, tend directly to the instruction of the reader or to the information of the public; to whom if I chuse to convey such instruction or information with an air of joke and laughter, none but the dullest of fellows will, I believe, censure it; but if they should, I have the authority of more than one passage in Horace to alledge in my defence.[10]

Having thus endeavoured to obviate some censures to which a man, without the gift of fore-sight, or any fear of the imputation of being a conjurer, might conceive this work would be liable, I might now undertake a more pleasing task, and fall at once to the direct and positive praises of the work itself; of which indeed I could say a thousand good things: but the task is so very pleasant that I shall leave it wholly to the reader; and it is all the task that I impose on him. A moderation for which he may think himself obliged to me, when he compares it with the conduct of authors, who often fill a whole sheet with their own praises, to which they sometimes set their own real names, and sometimes a fictitious one. One hint, however, I must give the kind reader; which is, that if he should be able to find no sort of amusement in the book, he will be pleased to remember the public utility which will arise from it. If entertainment, as Mr. Richardson observes, be but a secondary consideration in a romance;[11] with which Mr. Addison I think agrees, affirming the use of the pastry-cook to be the first;[12] if this, I say, be true of a mere work of invention, sure it may well be so considered in a work founded, like this, on truth; and where the political reflections form so distinguishing a part.

But perhaps I may hear, from some critic of the most saturnine complexion, that my vanity must have made a horrid dupe of my judgment, if it hath flattered me with an expectation of having any thing here seen in a grave light, or of conveying any useful instruction to the public, or to their guardians. I answer with the great man, whom I just now quoted, that my purpose is to convey instruction in the vehicle of entertainment; and so to bring about at once, like the revolution in *The Rehearsal*,[13] a perfect reformation of the laws relating to our maritime affairs: an undertaking, I will not say more modest, but surely more feasible, than that of reforming a whole people, by making use of a vehicular story, to wheel in among them worse manners than their own.

PART SIX

On Wit and Humour

Fielding greatly appreciated the value of ridicule as a tool of the critic and moralist, but he was apprehensive about its being wrongly directed. He tried, in the Preface to *Joseph Andrews* (No. 59) and the papers reprinted in this section, to analyse wit and humour in order to show their proper relationship to morality. (See also Introduction.)

31 *The Champion; or, the Evening Advertiser,* No. 52

Thursday, March 13, 1740

The subject of this paper—'roasting'—had already been considered by Swift in his *Hints towards an Essay on Conversation* (not published until 1763), where he wrote: 'It now passeth for Raillery to run a Man down in Discourse, to put him out of Countenance, and make him ridiculous, sometimes to expose the Defects of his Person, or Understanding; on all which Occasions he is obliged not to be angry, to avoid the Imputation of not being able to take a Jest. It is admirable to observe one who is dexterous at this Art, singling out a weak Adversary . . .' (*Polite Conversation, etc.*, ed. H. Davis and L. Landa, 1964, 91). See also *Spectator*, No. 422, Friday, July 4, 1712.

———*Torrere parant*———

VIRG.[1]

There is a certain Diversion called Roasting, which, notwithstanding it is in some Vogue with the polite Part of the World, I have no Notion of. This Term is well known to be taken from Cookery, from whence those who are great Adepts in the Art, borrow also several others; such as putting the Person to be roasted on the Spit, turning him round till he is done enough, *&c.*

But though this, as I have said before, is thought a very delicate Entertainment by some People of good Taste, yet, as it is attended with great Pain and Torment, to the poor Wretch who is thus roasted alive, I have always thought it too barbarous a Sacrifice to Luxury. Nor have I ever more willingly given into it, than into those Cruelties which are executed on particular Animals, in order to heighten their Flavour; I am an utter Enemy to all roasting alive, from this which is performed on one of our own Species, to that which is practised on a Lobster.

It hath been thought, that this Custom of Man-Roasting was originally introduc'd among us from some Nation of Cannibals: It is indeed more than probable that our savage Ancestors us'd to eat the

Flesh of their Enemies roasted in this Manner; tho' this latter Custom hath been so long left off, that we find no Traces thereof in our Annals.

A learned Antiquarian of my Acquaintance, does not carry the Original of this Custom so high: He derives it only from the roasting of Heretics, in use among the *Roman* Church, and fancies it an unextirpated Remain of that barbarous Execution. He brings, as a Strengthener of this his Opinion, the Choice which we make of an odd Creature, or, in his own Words, a Heretic to the common Forms of Behaviour to perform it on. He is a great Enemy to this Practice, being, as he thinks, more consistent with the Principles of Jesuitism, than true Christianity.

But, for my Part, I imagine this Term of roasting to have been given to this Diversion, from the Torments which the Person spitted is supposed to endure in his Mind, even equal to those Bodily Pains which he would undergo, was he to be roasted alive.

Now the Pleasure which we take in such Amusements as this, must arise either from a great Depravity of Nature, which delights in the Miseries and Misfortunes of Mankind, or from a Pride which we take in comparing the Blemishes of others with our own Perfections.

As for the first, my Lord *Shaftsbury* says, 'There is an Affection nearly related to Inhumanity, which is a gay and frolicsome Delight in what is injurious to others, a Sort of wanton Mischievousness and Pleasure in what is destructive, a Passion, which, instead of being retrain'd, is encourag'd in Children, so that it is indeed no Wonder if the Effects of it are very unfortunately felt in the World: For it will be hard, perhaps, for any one to give a Reason, why that Temper, which was us'd to delight in Disorder, and Ravage when in a Nursery, should not afterwards find Delight in other Disturbances, and be the Occasion of equal Mischiefs in Families among Friends and in the Public.'[2] I advise all Parents to whip this Spirit out of their Children, the doing which may be truly call'd, *a wholesome Severity*.

And, surely, if we thoroughly search'd the Bottom of our own Minds, few of us would have frequent Cause of Triumph in these Comparisons. Perhaps, indeed, we are without that particular Blemish which we ridicule in another; but at the same Time, let us carefully consider whether we have not as great Imperfections of another Kind. I have often observ'd in Life, the Person roasted to be infinitely superior to those who (to use a Word of their own) have enjoy'd him. To say the Truth, the least Oddity in Behaviour, the most inoffensive Peculiarity often exposes a Man of Sense and Virtue, to the Ridicule of those who are in every Degree his Inferiors. These seem to lay in wait for, and catch at every Opportunity to pull down a Man, whom Nature hath placed so far above them.

But, though the Generality of Roasters be of this Kind, and the Buffoons they use such as may be very aptly call'd Turnspits, the lowest and most despicable of their Kind, yet I have known some of Sense and Goodnature too forwardly give in to this Diversion. Men, who would by no Means have consented to do any other Injury, reputing this innocent and harmless. These, did they consider the Nature and Consequence of their pursuing this Amusement, would, I believe, soon condemn it.

If a Man be wholly insensible of his being the Jest and Scorn of the Company, if he be so unaffected with it, as to be quite easy and contented, and satisfied with himself this while, such a Person can be little more than a direct Ideot, and is a melancholly, not a pleasant Spectacle: For my Part, I have always shunn'd the Sight of a Monster, an Abortion or Imperfection in Nature. I consider myself as a Son of this great and general Mother, I feel a Kind of filial Pity, and can by no Means be delighted with any of her monstrous Births. And surely a human Creature without Understanding, is a more horrible Object than one born without Arms, Legs, or any other of its Members. Such a one is the Object of Pity, not of Scoff and Merriment; nor should I entertain a good Opinion of him, who could go to *Bedlam*, and divert himself with the dreadful Frenzies, and monstrous Absurdities, of the Wretches there.

But, if we conceive the Subject of our Ridicule to be of a more sensible Composition, that he sees in himself the Deformity, or perhaps, incurable Oddity which renders him the Object of Contempt; it will be difficult to illustrate his Misery by any lively Comparison. Contempt is, I believe, of all Things the most uneasily to be endur'd by the Generality of Men. It gnaws and preys on our very Vitals, and by how much less the Person so affected discovers it, by so much he often feels it the more acutely. I have seen a Man in the highest Agony, and even in a cold Sweat, from being display'd by some ridiculous Buffoon, who hath at the same Time, as they call it, play'd him off with such Nicety, that it was impossible for the other to take hold of any Thing for which he might call him to an Account. I am always apt, at such Times, to pity the Person who is thus turn'd into Ridicule, and seldom or never join the Laugh against him. Nay, it is not unusual with me, to attack the Turnspit himself, in which I have been often so successful, that I have turn'd the whole Current of Laughter that Way. I cannot but observe, with great Pleasure, the double Delight of the Company on these Occasions: For nothing ever roasts so kindly as a Turnspit.

Some Persons have fallen into this Way, in order to establish a Reputation of Wit, though with great Absurdity: For nothing is so sure a Sign of wanting it, as flying to these mean Resources to appear to have it. A Roaster gives me as low an Idea of his Wit, as a Bully does of his Courage. These beautiful Qualities, where they are, will always appear. They are the Fool and the Coward, who are continually searching out weak Objects on whom to display their mock Talents with Safety. And it is generally in the dullest Company that this most abounds.

If we consider this Diversion in the worst Light, it will appear to be no other than a Delight in seeing the Miseries, Misfortunes, and Frailties of Mankind display'd; and a Pleasure and Joy conceiv'd in their Sufferings therein. A Pleasure, perhaps, as inhuman, and which must arise from a Nature as thoroughly corrupt and diabolical, as can possibly pollute the Mind of Man.

L.

32 Preface to *Plutus, The God of Riches. A Comedy. Trans. from the Original Greek of Aristophanes: With Large Notes Explanatory and Critical*

1742

This translation, published on May 31, 1742, was by Fielding and the Reverend William Young. The Preface owes a great deal to Mme. Dacier's introduction to her translation of the play (1684).

As we intend, if we proceed in this Work, to prefix to it a very large Dissertation on the Nature and End of Comedy, with an Account of its Original, Rise, and Progress to this Day; which will include a full View of the *Grecian* Stage: We shall at present confine ourselves to a very few Words, in Recommendation of our Author himself, and in Apology for this Translation.

ARISTOPHANES was born about 460 Years before CHRIST, most probably in an Island called *Ægina* near *Athens*, where it is certain he had an Estate. He is one of the oldest Professors of the Comic Art, and indeed lived so very near the Original of the Drama, that, besides the Admiration due to his deep Discernment in Human Nature, to the incomparable Humour of his Characters, to his Wit, Style, Numbers, *&c.* which have received great Elogiums both from antient and modern Critics; we must be astonished at the Regularity and Order of his Comedies, to which in more than two thousand Years successive Poets have been able to add so little.

We have not Room here to relate half, which hath been written in Praise of our Author, the Honours which he received not only from his own Countrymen, who ordered his Name to be enrolled above those of all his Cotemporaries; but from the Emperor of *Persia*, who considered him merely from the Force of his Wit, and the Uses he applied it to, as a Person of the greatest Consequence in *Athens*.[1]

But as the Esteem of one great, and wise, and good Man, is infinitely preferable to the giddy Shouts of the Rabble, or to the capricious Favour of Kings, we hasten to the Account given by *Olympiodorus* in his Life of *Plato*; who tells us, that a very intimate Acquaintance subsisted between the Philosopher and the Poet; and that the former learnt from the Writings of the latter, the Art of adapting in his Dialogues the Diction to the Character of the Speaker.[2] Indeed it is impossible to read the Works of both with any Attention, without observing the most striking Similitude in their Expression; both being remarkable for that *Attic* Purity of Language, and the elegant Use of those Particles, which, though they give such an inexpressible nervous Force to the Diction of these Authors, have been represented as Expletives, and useless by the Ignorance of Posterity.

The Affection of *Plato* for *Aristophanes* is reported to have been so extremely strong, that after the Death of the Philosopher a Volume of the other's Comedies were found in his Bed. The following Epigram likewise is said to have been his:

᾿Αι Χάριτες τέμενός τι λαβεῖν ὅπερ ἐχὶ πεσεῖται
Ζητε͂σαι, Ψυχὴν εὗρον Αριστοφάνες.

The Graces *endeavouring to obtain a never-falling Temple, found one in the Genius of* Aristophanes.

We know that *Plato*, in his *Phædon*, speaks against a Comic Poet with the utmost Vehemence; and, in his Apology for *Socrates*, mentions *Aristophanes* among his false Accusers by Name; and that *Ælian* ascribes the Death of *Socrates* to the Ridicule brought on him by the Comedy of *the Clouds*; with which *Diogenes Laertius* seems to assent:[3] But we question not refuting this Story, if ever it be our Fortune to translate that Play.

But farther, the Elegance of his Style, and the Justness of his Sentiments, recommended him, notwithstanding his Impurities, to the Primitive Fathers of the Church. Thus we find him several times quoted by *Clemens Alexandrinus*;[4] and there is a Tradition, that St. *Chrysostom* held him in so great Favour, as never to sleep without one of his Comedies under his Pillow, in order to begin the next Day's Reading with the Works of the most correct Writer. And to this perhaps we may justly ascribe that Father's having surpassed all the rest in the Purity of his Diction; and hence likewise he probably drew that remarkable Acrimony of Style, in which he hath so severely exposed the Faults of the Fair Sex; which latter we the rather mention, as it takes off an ill-natured Observation, which might otherwise have insinuated, that the

Purity of our Author's Diction did not alone recommend him to the Father for a Bedfellow.[5]

To conclude this Part of our Preface, *Longinus* gives the Character of *Sublime* to our Author's Diction; *Horace* commends the Freedom and Justice with which he lashed the Vices of his Times: Indeed so great hath been always his Reputation, that, as M. *Dacier* observes, to deny his Merit, would be *to give the Lye to all Antiquity*.[6]

It may seem therefore impossible, that the Works of such an Author should fail of Success in any Language, unless through the Fault of the Translation; to which our Reader will, I suppose, if he finds this Play disagree with his Taste, impute it.

There are some, I am told, *profest* Admirers of *Aristophanes* in the *Greek*, who assert the Impossibility of translating him; which, in my Opinion, is asserting, in other Words, the Impossibility of understanding him: for sure a Man must have a very superficial Knowledge of his own Language, who cannot communicate his Ideas in it. If the Original conveys clear and adequate Ideas to me, I must be capable of delivering them to others in that Language which I am myself a perfect Master of. I am deceived therefore, if the Complaints of Translators do not generally arise from the same Cause with those I have often heard made in Conversation by Men, who have mistaken some floating imperfect Images in their Minds for clear and distinct Conceptions, and bitterly lament that they are *unable to express themselves*: Whereas a Man who conceives clearly, will, I apprehend, always express himself so.

I remember a Translation of a celebrated Line in *Lucan* into *French*, which is thus:

> *Victrix causa Deis placuit, sed victa Catoni.*
> *Les Dieux servent Cesar, mais Caton suit Pompée.*[7]

The Sense of the *Latin* is,

The Gods embraced the Cause of the Conqueror, but *Cato* that of the Conquered.

The Sense of the *French* is,

> The Gods preserved *Cæsar*, but *Cato* followed Pompey.

Will any Man say, that this *Frenchman* understood his Author, or that *Lucan* had conveyed the same Idea to him, which he himself had conceived when he wrote that excellent and beautiful Compliment to *Cato*.

To mention no more Instances, (for Thousands occur in most Translations) I am convinced that the Complaint of the Difficulty of rendering an Author in the Translator's own Language, arises commonly from the Difficulty of comprehending him.

I do not, however, affect to say, that a Translation labours under no Disadvantage, or that it can be entirely *alter & idem*.

On the contrary, I am sensible, that in this particular Undertaking we have three principal ones to encounter.

First, We are to render a purer and more copious Language in that which is impurer and more confined. This drives us often from literally pursuing the Original, and makes a Periphrasis necessary to explain a single Word, or the concisest Expression.

Secondly, There is in *Aristophanes* a great deal of that Wit which consists merely in the Words themselves, and is so inseparable from them, that it is impossible to transfer it into any others: But this is a Species of Wit, which our Readers of the better Taste will not much repine at being deprived of. It is indeed sometimes found in good Authors, where it appears like a Tinsel-Ornament on a beautiful Woman, to catch the Admiration of vulgar Eyes, and to offend Persons of real Taste. However, that we might oblige all, and be as faithful to our Author as possible, where we have not been able to preserve such Facetiousness in our Text, we have generally remarked it in our Notes.

The last Disadvantage I shall mention, is the Harmony which in many Places of the Original is excellently sweet. This, perhaps, I should have thought impossible to preserve, had not the inimitable Author of the *Essay on Man* taught me a System of Philosophy in *English* Numbers, whose Sweetness is scarce inferior to that of *Theocritus* himself: But

Non omnia possumus omnes.[8]

These are indeed Objections which can only be made by our most learned Readers, whom perhaps our close Adherence to our Author, and particularly *in the Simplicity of his Language*, may in some measure conciliate to us. The most dangerous and fatal Enemies we are to dread, are those whom this very Simplicity may offend; the Admirers of that pretty, dapper, brisk, smart, pert Dialogue, which hath lately flourished on our Stage. This was first introduced with infinite Wit by *Wycherley*, and continued with still less and less by his Successors, till it is at last degenerated into such sort of Pleasantry as this, in the *Provoked Husband*:

Manly. If that were my Case, I believe I should certainly sleep in another House.

L. Grace. How do you mean?

Manly. Only a Compliment, Madam.

L. Grace. A Compliment!

Manly. Yes, Madam, in rather turning myself out of Doors than her.

L. Grace. Don't you think that would be going too far?

Manly. I don't know but it might, Madam: for in strict Justice I think she ought rather to go than I.

Again.

L. Grace. Can a Husband love a Wife too well?

Manly. As easily, Madam, as a Wife may love her Husband too little.

L. Grace. 'Tis Pity *but* your Mistress should hear your Doctrine.

Manly. Pity me, Madam, when I marry the Woman *that* won't hear it, *&c. &c. &c.*[9]

This sort of Stuff, which is, I think, called genteel Comedy, and in which our Laureate succeeded so excellently well both as Author and Actor, had some Years ago taken almost sole Possession of our Stage, and banished *Shakespear*, *Fletcher*, *Johnson*, &c. from it; the last of whom, of all our *English* Poets, seems chiefly to have studied and imitated *Aristophanes*, which we have remarked more than once in our Notes. To such therefore of our Readers, whose Palates are vitiated with the theatrical Diet I have above-mentioned, I would recommend a Play or two of *Johnson's*, to be taken as a kind of Preparative before they enter on this Play; for otherwise the Simplicity of its Style, for want of being sweetned with modern Quaintness, may, like old Wine after Sugar-Plumbs, appear insipid, and without any Flavour. But our Readers of a purer Taste and sounder Judgment, will be able, we apprehend, to digest good Sense, manly Wit, just Satire, and true Humour, without those Garnishments which we could with infinitely greater Ease have supplied (as others have done) in the room of our Author's Meaning, than have preserved it in his own plain Simplicity of Stile.

It may be expected that we should here take some Notice of the other Translations of this Play, especially those two of M. *Dacier* and Mr. *Theobald*,[10] which we have sometimes taken the Liberty of dissenting from in our Translation, and on which we have commented with some Freedom in our Notes; but if we are right on these Occasions, little Apology will be required; if wrong, we shall gladly embrace Correction, nor persist obstinately in Error. I own, we have more to answer to the Memory of the Lady than to Mr. *Theobald*, who being a Critic of great Nicety himself, and great Diligence in correcting Mistakes in others, cannot be offended at the same Treatment. Indeed there are some Parts of his Work which I should be more surprised at, had he not informed us in his Dedication, that he was assisted in it by M. *Dacier*. We are not therefore much to wonder, if Mr. *Theobald* errs a little, when we find his Guide going before out of the Way.

We shall conclude our Preface with the Argument of this Play, as left us by Mr. *Addison* in his 464th *Spectator*.

33 *The Covent Garden Journal*, No. 10

Tuesday, February 4, 1752

In this discussion of wit, Fielding firmly subordinates entertainment to instruction: 'Diversion is a secondary consideration.'

At nostri Proavi Plautinos et numeros, et
Laudavêre Sales, nimium patienter utrumque,
Ne dicam Stulte, mirati.

HOR.[1]

Modernized:

In former Times this tasteless, silly Town
Too fondly prais'd Tom D'Urfey and Tom Brown.[2]

The present Age seems pretty well agreed in an Opinion, that the utmost Scope and End of Reading is Amusement only; and such, indeed, are now the fashionable Books, that a Reader can propose no more than mere Entertainment, and it is sometimes very well for him if he finds even this in his Studies.

Letters, however, were surely intended for a much more noble and profitable Purpose than this. Writers are not, I presume, to be considered as mere Jack-Puddings, whose Business it is only to excite Laughter: This, indeed, may sometimes be intermixed, and served up, with graver Matters, in order to titilate the Palate, and to recommend wholesome Food to the Mind; and, for this Purpose, it hath been used by many excellent Authors: *for why* (as Horace says) *should not any one promulgate Truth with a Smile on his Countenance? Ridicule, indeed,* as he again intimates, *is commonly a stronger and better Method of attacking Vice, than the severer kind of Satire.*[3]

When Wit and Humour are introduced for such good Purposes, when the agreeable *is blended with the useful, then* is the Writer said *to have succeeded in every Point. Pleasantry* (as the ingenious Author of Clarissa says of a Story) *should be made only the Vehicle of Instruction:*[4] and thus Romances themselves, as well as Epic Poems, may become worthy the Perusal of the greatest of Men: But when no Moral, no Lesson, no Instruction is conveyed to the Reader, where the whole Design of the Composition is no more than to make us laugh, the Writer comes very near to the Character of a Buffoon; and his Admirers, if an old Latin proverb be true,[5] deserve no great Compliments to be paid to their Wisdom.

After what I have here advanced, I cannot fairly, I think, be represented as an Enemy to Laughter, or to all those Kinds of Writing that are apt to promote it. On the contrary, few Men, I believe, do more admire the Works of those great Masters who have sent their Satire (if I may use the Expression) laughing into the World. Such are that great Triumvirate, Lucian, Cervantes, and Swift. These Authors I shall ever hold in the highest Degree of Esteem; not indeed for that Wit and Humour alone which they all so eminently possest, but because they all endeavoured, with the utmost Force of their Wit and Humour, to expose and extirpate those Follies and Vices which chiefly prevailed in their several Countries.

I would not be thought to confine Wit and Humour to these Writers. Shakespeare, Molière, and some other Authors, have been blessed with the same Talents, and have employed them to the same Purposes. There are some, however, who tho' not void of these Talents have made so wretched a Use of them, that had the Consecration of their Labours been committed to the Hands of the Hangman, no good Man would have regretted their Loss: Nor am I afraid to mention Rabelais, and Aristophanes himself in this Number. For if I may speak my Opinion freely of these two last Writers, and of their Works, their Design appears to me very plainly to have been to ridicule all Sobriety, Modesty, Decency, Virtue and Religion, out of the World.[6] Now whoever reads over the five great Writers first mentioned in this Paragraph, must either have a very bad Head, or a very bad Heart, if he doth not become both a wiser and a better Man.

In the Exercise of the Mind, as well as in the Exercise of the Body, Diversion is a secondary Consideration, and designed only to make that agreeable, which is at the same Time useful, to such noble Purposes as Health and Wisdom. But what should we say to a Man who mounted his Chamber Hobby,[7] or fought with his own Shadow for his Amusement only? How much more absurd and weak would he appear, who swallowed Poison because it was sweet.

How differently did Horace think of Study from our modern Readers.

Quid verum atque decens curo et rogo, et omnis in hoc sum: Condo et compono, quae mox depromere possim.

Truth and Decency are my whole Care and Enquiry. In this Study I am entirely occupied; these I am always laying up, and so disposing, that I can at any Time draw forth my Stores for my immediate Use.[8] The whole Epistle indeed, from which I have paraphrased this Passage, is a Comment upon it, and affords many useful Lessons of Philosophy.

When we are employed in reading a great and good Author, we ought to consider ourselves as searching after Treasures, which, if well and regularly laid up in the Mind, will be of use to us on sundry Occasions in our Lives. If a Man, for Instance, should be overloaded with Prosperity, or Adversity, (both of which Cases are liable to happen to us) who is there so very wise, or so very foolish, that, if he was a Master of Seneca and Plutarch, could not find great Matter of Comfort and Utility from their Doctrines? I mention these rather than Plato and Aristotle, as the Works of the latter, are not, I think, yet compleatly made English; and, consequently, are less within the Reach of most of my Countrymen.

But, perhaps, it may be asked, Will Seneca or Plutarch make us laugh? Perhaps not; but if you are not a Fool, my worthy Friend, which I can hardly with Civility suspect, they will both, (the latter especially) please you more than if they did. For my own Part, I declare, I have not read even Lucian himself with more Delight than I have Plutarch; but surely it is astonishing, that such Scriblers as Tom Brown, Tom D'Urfy, and the Wits of our Age should find Readers, whilst the Writing of so excellent, so entertaining, and so voluminous an Author as Plutarch remain in the World, and, as I apprehend, are very little known.

The Truth I am afraid is, that real Taste is a Quality with which Human Nature is very slenderly gifted. It is indeed so very rare, and so little known, that scarce two Authors have agreed in their Notions of it; and those who have endeavoured to explain it to others, seem to have succeeded only in shewing us that they knew it not themselves. If I might be allowed to give my own Sentiments, I should derive it from a nice Harmony between the Imagination and the Judgment; and hence perhaps it is, that so few have ever possessed this Talent in any eminent Degree. Neither of these will alone bestow it; nothing is indeed more common than to see Men of very bright Imaginations, and of very accurate Learning (which can hardly be acquired without

Judgment) who are entirely devoid of Taste; and Longinus, who of all Men seems most exquisitely to have possessed it, will puzzle his Reader very much if he should attempt to decide, whether Imagination or Judgment shine the brighter in that inimitable Critic.

But as for the Bulk of Mankind, they are clearly void of any Degree of Taste. It is a Quality in which they advance very little beyond a State of Infancy. The first Thing a Child is fond of in a Book, is a Picture; the second is a Story; and the third a Jest. Here then is the true *Pons Asinorum*,[9] which very few Readers ever get over.

From what I have said, it may perhaps be thought to appear, that true Taste is the real Gift of Nature only; and if so, some may ask, To what Purpose have I endeavoured to show Men that they are without a Blessing, which it is impossible for them to attain?

Now, tho' it is certain that to the highest Consummation of Taste, as well as of every other Excellence, Nature must lend much Assistance; yet great is the Power of Art almost of itself, or at best with only slender Aids from Nature; and to say the Truth, there are very few who have not in their Minds some small Seeds of Taste. *All Men* (says Cicero) *have a sort of tacit Sense of what is right or wrong in Arts and Sciences, even without the help of Arts.*[10] This surely it is in the Power of Art very greatly to improve. That most Men therefore proceed no farther than as I have above declared, is owing either to the want of any, or (which is perhaps yet worse) to an improper Education.

I shall, probably, therefore, in a future Paper, endeavour to lay down some Rules by which all Men may acquire at least some Degree of Taste.[11] In the mean while, I shall, (according to the Method observed in Innoculation) recommend to my Readers, as a Preparative for their receiving my Instructions, a total Abstinence from all bad Books; I do therefore most earnestly intreat all my young Readers, that they would cautiously avoid the Persual of any modern Book till it hath first had the Sanction of some wise and learned Man; and the same Caution I propose to all Fathers, Mothers, and Guardians.

Evil Communications corrupt good Manners, is a Quotation of St. Paul from Menander.[12] EVIL BOOKS CORRUPT AT ONCE BOTH OUR MANNERS AND OUR TASTE.

C.

34 *The Covent Garden Journal*, No. 18

Tuesday, March 3, 1752

In attacking false wit, Fielding elaborates on a metaphor suggested by Samuel Butler or Swift and compares it with imitation champagne.

Omnibus in terris, quæ sunt a gadibus usq;
Aurorem & Gangem, pauci dignoscere possunt
**VINA bona, atq; illis multum diversa*——

JUVENAL.[1]

From where Cornubia's hundred Boroughs end,
To where the Caledonian Shores extend,
How few are found with Taste to ascertain
The vilest Perry, and the best Champagne.

It is from a very common but a very false Opinion, that we constantly mix the Idea of Levity with those of Wit and Humour. The gravest of Men have often possessed these Qualities in a very eminent Degree, and have exerted them on the most solemn Subjects with very eminent Success. These are to be found in many Places in the most serious Works of Plato and Aristotle, of Cicero and Seneca. Not only Swift, but South hath used them on the highest and most important of all Subjects. In the Sermons of the Latter, there is perhaps more Wit, than in the Comedies of Congreve; and in his Controversy with Sherlock on the Trinity,[2] he hath not only exerted great Wit, but many Strokes of the most exquisite Drollery. Not to mention the Instance of St. Paul, whose Writings do in my Opinion contain more true Wit, than is to be found in the Works of the unjustly celebrated Petronius.[3]

In like Manner, and with like Error we unite the Ideas of Gravity with Dulness, as if the former was inseparably annexed to the latter. True indeed it is that Dulness appears in her own Form, and in her proper Dress, when she walks abroad in some tritical Essay on a grave Subject;

*So I chuse to read this Passage, at least on the present Occasion.

and many millions of Reams have in all Ages been sacrified to her by her Votaries in this Manner; but she doth not always preserve this solemn Air. She often appears in public in Essays of Entertainment, as the Booksellers chuse to call them; and sometimes in Print, as well as on the Stage, disguises herself in a Jack-pudding Coat, and condescends to divert her good Friends with sundry Feats of Dexterity and Grimace.

The late ingenious Dr. Swift, who was one of the greatest Enemies that Dulness ever had; and who hath traced her out and exposed her in all her various Disguises, likens these two different Appearances of Dulness to the different Qualities of small Beer in the Barrel, and small Beer in the Bottle.[4] The former of which is well known to be of all Things the most vapid, insipid and heavy; but the latter is altogether as airy, frothy, brisk and bouncing.

But tho' there is excellent Drollery in this Comparison, I have still another Liquor in my Eye, which will better match this airy and brisk Kind of Dulness; at least will give the Reader a more just Idea of that very Quality which we principally intend to remark in this Paper. The Liquor I mean, is that of Perry: for as this hath been often imposed on the injudicious Palate for Champagne, so hath this Kind of Dulness with no less Assurance been often vented to the Public under the Name of Wit.

As this is grown to be a very common Practice, and as the Consequence of it is very pernicious to the Society; the Understandings of Men being as capable of an Injury as their Health, and as every Taste is no more capable of distinguishing in the Case of Wit than in the Case of Champagne, I shall do, I think, no inconsiderable Service to the Public by giving them some Rules to direct their Judgment, and to arm them against this Imposition. And here I shall chiefly make use of the Words Champagne and Perry, instead of Wit and Dulness, as the two former seem the pleasanter and better sounding Words, and will equally explain my Meaning.

The first Caution I shall give my Reader on this Head, is to take Care of all Shops over the Door of which is writ in great Letters the following Word, BIBLIOPOLIUM. The true Reading of which is BIBITOPERRYUM. A Corruption which hath led many Men into an Error, and hath carried them into a Perry-shop by Mistake.

In the next Place, I caution all Persons to pay no Regard to the Labels with which the Perry Merchants constantly endeavour to put off the worst of their Stuff. Nothing indeed is more common than to see a Quantity of rank Perry, with a Label signifying, that it is the very best of Champagne, and approved of by all Persons of Taste. The Words *curious, eminent, learned, the 6th or seventh Edition. Done into English from the original French Vessels* &c. written upon the Label, are all of them certain Marks of Perry.

Nor is much more Regard to be had to the positive Assertion of the Merchant himself; for nothing is more usual in this Trade as well as with the Wine-Merchant, than to sell one Thing for another. Both of these make use indeed of the same Imposition, and as every Dealer in French Vinegar, hath the Names of the most excellent Wines always at his Tongue's End, and ready to be applied to the worst Goods in his Warehouse, so hath our Perry-Merchant constantly in his Mouth the Names of the most celebrated Authors; under one of which without any Scruple, he vends the genuine anonymous Productions of Grub-street; the Names of Swift, Addison, Pope, Dryden, Prior, &c. have been used by the one Kind of Merchant, as of Laseat, Latour, Bennet, &c.[5] have been by the other.

Having premised these Cautions, I come now to those Marks which may distinguish the true Champagne from Perry, even to those who are not vested with sufficient Taste to know the one from the other by their several Flavours.

The first Quality which is remarkable in Perry, is its extreme Frothiness, in which indeed it will sometimes almost wholly evaporate.

2dly, It is very apt to bounce and fly with much Noise, as it is truly little more than a Composition of Wind, and proceeded originally, according to the Observations of Butler, from the Author's Incapacity of sending his Wind downwards.[6]

An extraordinary Degree of Thinness is another manifest Sign of Perry. Let the Quantity be never so large, you can immediately see through it; nor is there ever any thing to be found at the Bottom.

There are perhaps some other Differences which do not at present occur to me; but indeed the surest Way of judging is by the opposite Consequences, which never fail to attend these two Liquors.

First, as Champagne is sure to raise the Spirits, and to fill almost every Man with Mirth and Gayety; so this is as certain to depress, and render those who swallow any Quantity more heavy and dull.

If, after a large Draught, you find yourself inclined to Irreligion and Blasphemy, never touch a Drop more, for this is a sure Sign of the very worst of all Perry.

Again, if after sitting to it (as is the Language of Drinking) an Hour or two, you find in yourself a Propensity to talking indecently, indeed to any Discourse which modest Ears should not hear; this is another manifest Indication. Nothing indeed being so very apt to corrupt the Minds of Youth, to make them unfit for civil Company, and to send them to the Brothels, than this Kind of Perry. In this Instance, indeed, the metaphorical Perry, which I have been here treating of, and that genuine Liquor which comes to us from Worcestershire, seem to bear a strict Analogy to each other. And for this Reason, I suppose, it is so sacred to the Brothel, that when a Bottle of Champagne is then called for, a Bottle of Perry is sure to be brought to the Customer; that being the only Champagne which is ever admitted into these Houses, from the Tendency no doubt which it hath to propagate that Kind of Filth in which they deal.

The last odious Quality of this Kind of Perry, and which most clearly distinguishes it from that which we here call true Champagne, is that it never fails to propagate gross Abuse and Scandal; so far indeed as to inspire Men to call Names, and to deal in all the Language of Billingsgate. So very rancorous is the Nature of Perry, that many eminent Dabblers in it have escaped the Cudgel or the Whipping Post from this Circumstance only, that they have been so absolutely intoxicated as to be unable to pronounce certain Syllables in an articulate Manner. Instead of Minister, Lord, Bishop, &c. they have only uttered such Sounds as may be imitated by pronouncing M—nst–r, L—d, B—sh—p, and so forth. Thus by stripping a Name or a Title of its Vowels, they securely strip the Owner of all his Virtues and good Qualities.[7]

Now Champagne, on the contrary, is known to inspire Men not only with the most sparkling Wit, but with the highest good Humour; and so far is it from filling the Head or Heart with Mischief and Rancour, that in France the Character which is given to the best Champagne, and that of a certain Age, is that it is *Ami d'homme*; A FRIEND TO MANKIND. An appellation which, as it is perhaps the most glorious of all, so hath it most justly belonged to those great Men in all Ages, whom Heaven hath been pleased to distinguish with those superior Talents which are properly said to constitute a true Genius.

A.

35 *The Covent Garden Journal*, No. 19

Saturday, March 7, 1752

This paper, together with the two which follow it, contains Fielding's definition of humour. Fielding drew largely on previous discussions by Jonson (*Every Man out of his Humour*, 1599), Sir William Temple ('On Poetry', 1690; see n. 2, p. 172), and William Congreve ('Concerning Humour in Comedy'. 1696; see n. 3, p. 173).

Non hæc jocosæ conveniunt Lyræ.
HOR.[1]

Such Matters are beyond a Jest.

If any Person should have the Assurance to exhibit a Set of Bristol Stones to the Public as real Diamonds;[2] or if another should call himself a China-Man, and deliver to his Customers some of the vilest Earthen-Ware, as the real Production of China or Dresden, the Consequence in both Cases is certain. The Imposition would be too gross to deceive a single Individual, and the Undertakers would immediately become the Objects of universal Ridicule and Contempt.

Again, should any Man, pretending to be a Conoisseur, go about the Town and abuse the finest Jewels in Mr. Lacan's Possession as mere Counterfeits, would not such a Person presently gain the Reputation of a Madman, and be soon ashamed of shewing his ridiculous Face in public?[3]

This, as I endeavoured to shew in my last Paper, is not the Case with the Dealers in Letters. The truest Brilliants often lie overlooked and neglected on the Booksellers Shelves, while the most impudent Counterfeits are received, admired, and encouraged. Milton himself (I am ashamed of my Country when I say it) very narrowly escaped from the Jaws of Oblivion; and, instead of shining for ever with those great Lights of Antiquity in whose Constellation he is now admitted, was like to have been bundled up with those *Ephemeran* insect Authors, of whom every Day almost sees both the Birth and the Funeral.

Now may we not hence conclude, that in the Distinction of Diamonds, China, and such like, from their Counterfeits, there are some certain well-known Criterions to form and direct our Judgment; and that in Matters of Invention and Learning, either there are no Rules to guide our Opinion, or that such Rules are but weakly established, and that we are in general very ignorant of them.

Hence must arise those different Notions which we so often find among Men, of the same Author and the same Work; and which Horace allegorically points at, when he says,

Tres mihi Convivæ prope dissentire videntur, &c.

Thus in one Company it is very common to hear the same Book extolled to the Skies, with the Epithets of fine, excellent, inimitable, and so forth; which in another is vilified and run down, as the lowest, dullest, and saddest Stuff that ever was writ.

Of all Kinds of Writing there is none on which this Variety of Opinions is so common as in those of Humour, as perhaps there is no Word in our Language of which Men have in general so vague and indeterminate an Idea. To speak very plainly, I am apt to question whether the greater Part of Mankind have any Idea at all in their Heads, when this Word drops (perhaps accidentally) from their Tongue.

I remember a Gentleman who used to have this Word very frequently in his Mouth, and bestowed it with great Liberality on most of his Acquaintance. I was sometimes inclined to wonder at his Taste, 'till I happened to be on board a Ship with him, when he rapt out a great Oath, and swore that the Ship had a great deal of Humour in it. I was now satisfied that with my Friend this Word had no Meaning at all.

What can we sometimes conceive of an Audience at a Play-House, where I have heard the dullest Chitchat between Gentlemen and Ladies called Humour, and applauded as such! On the other Side, *Albumazar* was but coldly received, and *the little French Lawyer* of Fletcher was hissed off the Stage.[5]

And here I cannot omit a pleasant Fact to which I was myself a Witness. A certain comic Author produced a Piece on Drury-Lane Stage, called *The Highland Fair*, in which he intended to display the comical Humours of the Highlanders; the Audience, who had for three Nights together sat staring at each other, scarce knowing what to make of their Entertainment, on the fourth joined in a unanimous exploding Laugh. This they had continued through an Act, when the Author, who unhappily mistook the Peels of Laughter which he heard for Applause, went up to Mr. Wilks, and, with an Air of Triumph, said——*Deel o' my Sal, Sare, they begin to tauk the Humour at last.*[6]

Whether the Audience or the Poet erred most on this Occasion, I shall not determine. Certain it is that it is no unusual Thing in the former, to make very gross Mistakes in this Matter, as great indeed as the late learned Bernard Lintott the Bookseller, who, having purchased the Copy of a Tragedy called *Phædra and Hypolitus*, lamented that the Author had not put a little more Humour in it; for that, he said, was the only Thing it wanted.[7]

In Truth, there is nothing so unsettled and incertain, as our Notion of Humour in general. The most common Opinion is, that whatever diverts or makes you laugh, is Humour; and in Proportion as Men are more or less risible in their Nature, they are more or less liberal in this Appellation. A merry Fellow, or a pleasant Companion as he is called (and, by the by, I have known many a dull Dog called so) never fails to obtain the Character of a Man of Humour, among his Acquaintance and Admirers. The Qualifications of these Gentlemen, are a facetious Countenance, a sagacious Leer, and somewhat of Drollery in the Voice; and their Performances are usually a merry (i.e. b[awd]y) Catch, or a long Story, with a Sting of the same Kind in the Tail.

I forbear to mention here the vast Variety of handy or practical Jests, as I have seen them touched elsewhere, all which are reputed to be Humour by the Vulgar. Such are Tweaks by the Nose, Kicks on the Backside, pulling away your Chair, snatching off your Wig, with many others.

But there is another Kind of Humour, on which I do not remember to have seen any Remarks. This is that tragical Humour which was perhaps intended by the learned Bookseller abovementioned; and which, tho' it may tend to raise Laughter in some, may however be said to have its Foundation in Tears.

As the Species of practical Humour, just before spoken of, are produced by doing little jocose Mischiefs to others, this tragical Humour consists in afflicting Men with the greatest and most serious Evils; in a Word, in ruining, destroying, and tormenting Mankind.

Histories abound with Examples of Men who have very eminently possessed this Kind of Humour. There hath scarce existed indeed a single Tyrant or Conqueror upon Earth, who, tho' otherwise perhaps extremely dull, was not a great Master this Way. Alexander the Great was much gifted with this Quality, of which we have many Instances in the Accounts of his Asiatic Expedition. His burning the City of Persepolis in particular, was a Performance of most exquisite Humour.

What were the Reigns of Caligula and Claudius, of Nero and Domitian, of Commodus, Caracalla, Heliogabalus, and all those Imperial Bucks or Bloods of Rome, but great tragical Farces in which one Half of Mankind was with much Humour put to Death and Tortures, for the Diversion of the other Half.

But of all the Performances of this Kind I have ever met with, I am most pleased with the common Story of Phalaris and Perillus.[8] The latter of these being desirous of recommending himself to the Favour of the Former, who was a great Tyrant, and consequently a great Lover of the tragical Humour, acquainted his Master Phalaris that he had, with much Invention and hard Labour, contrived an Entertainment for him which would produce the highest Sport and Pastime. It was thus to be performed; the Artist had made the brazen Image of a Bull, into the Belly of which a human Creature was to be conveyed. The Bull was then to be heated 'till it was red hot, by means of which the Person inclosed within, suffering the most intolerable Torments, would bellow in such a Manner that the Sound would very near imitate, or to speak in the present fashionable Taste, would admirably MIMIC, the Roaring of a Bull.

Phalaris highly approved the Project; but being himself a Man of great Humour, he was willing to add somewhat of his own to the Joke. He therefore chose Perillus, the Inventor, for the Person on whom the Experiment was first to be tried, and accordingly shut him up and roasted him in his own Bull.

From this, I suppose, that pleasant Humour called ROASTING was derived; for so not only the Term, but the Thing seems to intimate; this diverting Entertainment consisting in giving all the Torments possible to the Object, and may indeed be called Roasting him alive.

Hence likewise the pleasant Pastime of roasting Men's Characters may possibly take it's Original. Hence all that Torrent of Humour which flow[*sic*] so plentifully in Libels of all Kinds, in which, Names that we ought to tremble to think of, and others which highly deserve our Reverence and Honour, are pointed out as the Marks of Ridicule and Contempt; and, to use the common Expression, ROASTED for the Entertainment of the Public.

To conclude, as Tully long ago said, that there was no Absurdity which some of the Sophists had not maintained to be *true Philosophy*[9] so is there no Nonsense whatever, provided it be dashed with Abuse and Scurrility; which will not pass with many for TRUE HUMOUR.

C.

36 *The Covent Garden Journal,* No. 55

Saturday, July 18, 1752

——*Juvat integros accedere Fontes*
Atque haurire——

LUCRETIUS.[1]

————It is pleasant to handle
An untouched Subject.

It hath been observed, that Characters of Humour do abound more in this our Island, than in any other Country; and this hath been commonly supposed to arise from that pure and perfect State of Liberty which we enjoy in a degree greatly superior to every foreign Nation.[2]

This Opinion, I know, hath great Sanction, and yet I am inclined to suspect the Truth of it, unless we will extend the Meaning of the Word Liberty, farther than I think it hath been yet carried, and will include in it not only an Exemption from all Restraint of municipal Laws, but likewise from all Restraint of those Rules of Behaviour which are expressed in the general Term of good Breeding. Laws which, tho' not written, are perhaps better understood, and tho' established by no coercive Power, much better obeyed within the Circle where they are received, than any of those Laws which are recorded in Books, or enforced by public Authority.

A perfect Freedom from these Laws, if I am not greatly mistaken, is absolutely necessary to form the true Character of Humour; a Character which is therefore not to be met with among those People who conduct themselves by the Rules of good Breeding.

For indeed good Breeding is little more than the Art of rooting out all those Seeds of Humour which Nature had originally implanted in our Minds.

To make this evident it seems necessary only to explain the Terms, a Matter in which I do not see the great Difficulty which hath appeared to other Writers. Some of these have spoken of the Word Humour, as if it contained in it some Mystery impossible to be revealed, and no one, as I know of, hath undertaken to shew us expresly [*sic*] what it is, tho' I scarce doubt but it was amply done by Aristotle in his Treatise on Comedy, which is unhappily lost.

But what is more surprizing, is, that we find it pretty well explained in Authors who at the same Time tell us, they know not what it is. Mr. Congreve, in a Letter to Mr. Dennis, hath these Words. *We cannot certainly tell what Wit is, or what Humour is,* and within a few Lines afterwards he says, *There is great Difference between a Comedy wherein there are many things humorously, as they call it, which is pleasantly spoken, and one where there are several Characters of Humour, distinguished by the particular and different Humours appropriated to the several Persons represented, and which naturally arise from the different Constitutions, Complexions, and Dispositions of Men.* And again *I take Humour to be a singular and unavoidable Manner of saying or doing any thing peculiar and natural to one Man only; by which his Speech and Actions are distinguished from those of other Men. Our Humour hath Relation to us, and to what proceeds from us, as the Accidents have to a Substance; it is a Colour, Taste, and Smell diffused through all; tho' our Actions are ever so many, and different in Form, they are all Splinters of the same Wood, and have naturally one Complexion,* &c.[3]

If my Reader hath any doubt whether this is a just Description of Humour, let him compare it with those Examples of humorous Characters which the greatest Masters have given us, and which have been universally acknowledged as such, and he will be perhaps convinced.

Ben Johnson, after complaining of the Abuse of the Word, proceeds thus,

> Why Humour (as 'tis Ens) we thus define it,
> To be a Quality of Air, or Water,
> And in itself holds these two Properties,
> Moisture and Fluxure; as for Demonstration,
> Pour Water on this Floor, 'twill wet and run;
> Likewise the Air forc'd thro' a Horn or Trumpet
> Flows instantly away, and leaves behind
> A kind of Dew; and hence we do conclude,
> That whatsoe'er hath Fluxure and Humidity,
> As wanting Power to contain itself,
> Is Humour. So in every human Body,
> The Choler, Melancholy, Phlegm and Blood,

By Reason that they flow continually
In some one Part, and are not continent,
Receive the Name of *Humours*. 'now thus far
It may, by Metaphor, apply itself
Unto the general Disposition:
As when some one peculiar Quality
Doth so possess a Man, that it doth draw
All his Effects, his Spirits, and his Powers,
In their Confluxions all to run one Way,'
This may be truly said to be a Humour.
But that a Rook by wearing a py'd Feather,
The Cable Hatband, or the three piled Ruff, .
A Yard of Shoe-tie, or the Switzer's Knot
On his French Garters should affect a Humour!
O! it is more than most ridiculous.[4]

This Passage is in the first Act of *Every Man out of his Humour*; and I question not but to some Readers, the Author will appear to have been *out of his Wits* when he wrote it; but others I am positive will discern much excellent Ore shining among the Rubbish. In Truth his Sentiment when let loose from that stiff Boddice in which it is laced, will amount to this that as the Term Humour contains in it the Ideas of Moisture and Fluxure, it was applied to certain moist and flux Habits of the Body, and afterwards metaphorically to peculiar Qualities of the Mind, which when they are extremely prevalent, do, like the predominant Humours of the Body, flow all to one Part, and as the latter are known to absorb and drain off all the corporeal Juices and Strength to themselves, so the former are no less certain of engaging the Affections, Spirits, and Powers of the Mind, and of enlisting them as it were, into their own Service, and under their own absolute Command.

Here then we have another pretty adequate Notion of Humour, which is indeed nothing more than a violent Bent or Disposition of the Mind to some particular Point. To enumerate indeed these several Dispositions would be, as Mr. Congreve observes, as endless as to sum up the several Opinions of Men; nay, as he well says, the *Quot homines tot sententiæ*[5] may be more properly interpreted of their Humours, than their Opinions.

Hitherto there is no Mention of the Ridiculous, the Idea of which, tho' not essential to Humour, is always included in our Notions of it.

The Ridiculous is annexed to it these two ways, either by the Manner or the Degree in which it is exerted.

By either of these the very best and worthiest Disposition of the Human Mind may become ridiculous. Excess, says Horace, even in the Pursuit of Virtue, will lead a wise and good Man into Folly and Vice[6]——So will it subject him to Ridicule; for into this, says the judicious Abbe Bellegarde, a Man may tumble headlong with an excellent Understanding, and with the most laudable Qualities.[7] Piety, Patriotism, Loyalty, Parental Affection, &c. have all afforded Characters of Humour for the Stage.

By the Manner of exerting itself likewise a Humour becomes ridiculous. By this Means chiefly the Tragic Humour differs from the Comic; it is the same Ambition which raises our Horror in *Macbeth*, and our Laughter at the drunken Sailors in the *Tempest*; the same Avarice which causes the dreadful Incidents in the *Fatal Curiosity* of Lillo, and in the *Miser* of Molière;[8] the same Jealousy which forms an Othello, or a Suspicious Husband.[9] No Passion or Humour of the Mind is absolutely either Tragic or Comic in itself. Nero had the Art of making Vanity the Object of Horror, and Domitian, in one Instance, at least, made Cruelty ridiculous.[10]

As these Tragic Modes however never enter into our Notion of Humour, I will venture to make a small Addition to the Sentiments of the two great Masters I have mentioned, by which I apprehend my Description of Humour will pretty well coincide with the general Opinion. By Humour, then I suppose, is generally intended a violent Impulse of the Mind, determining it to some one peculiar Point, by which a Man becomes ridiculously distinguished from all other Men.

If there be any Truth in what I have now said, nothing can more clearly follow than the manifest Repugnancy between Humour and good Breeding. The latter being the Art of conducting yourself by certain common and general Rules, by which Means, if they were universally observed, the whole World would appear (as all Courtiers actually do) to be, in their external Behaviour at least, but one and the same Person.

I have not room at present, if I were able, to enumerate the Rules of good Breeding: I shall only mention one, which is a Summary of them all. This is the most golden of all Rules, no less than that *of doing to all Men as you would they should do unto you.*[11]

In the Deviation from this Law, as I hope to evince in my next, all that we call Humour principally consists. I shall at the same Time, I think, be able to shew, that it is to this Deviation we owe the general Character mentioned in the Beginning of this Paper, as well as to assign the Reasons why we of this Nation have been capable of attracting to ourselves such Merit in Preference to others.

A.

37 *The Covent Garden Journal*, No. 56

Saturday, July 25, 1752

Hoc Fonte derivata.

HOR.[1]

These are the Sources.

At the Conclusion of my last Paper, I asserted that the Summary of Good Breeding was no other than that comprehensive and exalted Rule, which the greatest Authority hath told us is the Sum Total of all Religion and all Morality.

Here, however, my Readers will be pleased to observe that the subject Matter of good Breeding being only what is called Behaviour, it is this only to which we are to apply it on the present Occasion. Perhaps therefore we shall be better understood if we vary the Word, and read it thus: *Behave unto all Men, as you would they should behave unto you.*

This will most certainly oblige us to treat all Mankind with the utmost Civility and Respect, there being nothing which we desire more than to be treated so by them. This will most effectually restrain the Indulgence of all those violent and inordinate Desires, which, as we have endeavoured to shew, are the true Seeds of Humour in the Human Mind: the Growth of which Good Breeding will be sure to obstruct; or will at least so overtop and shadow, that they shall not appear. The Ambitious, the Covetous, the Proud, the Vain, the Angry, the Debauchee, the Glutton, are all lost in the Character of the Well-Bred Man; or if Nature should now and then venture to peep forth, she withdraws in an Instant, and doth not shew enough of herself to become ridiculous.

Now Humour arises from the very opposite Behaviour, from throwing the Reins on the Neck of our favorite Passion, and giving it a full Scope and Indulgence. The ingenious Abbè, whom I quoted in my former Paper, paints this admirably in the Characters of Ill-Breeding, which he mentions as the very first Scene of the Ridiculous. 'Ill-Breeding' (*L'Impolitesse*) says he, 'is not a single Defect, it is the Result of many. It is sometimes a gross Ignorance of Decorum, or a stupid

Indolence, which prevents us from *giving to others what is due to them.* It is a peevish Malignity which inclines us to oppose the Inclinations of those with whom we converse. It is the Consequence of a foolish Vanity, which hath no Complaisance for any other Person: *The Effect of a proud and whimsical Humour, which soars above all the Rules of Civility*; or, lastly, it is produced by a melancholly Turn of Mind, which pampers itself (*qui trouve du Ragoût*) with a rude and disobliging Behaviour.'[2]

Having thus shewn, I think very clearly, that Good Breeding is, and must be, the very Bane of the Ridiculous, that is to say, of all humorous Characters; it will perhaps be no difficult Task to discover why this Character hath been in a singular Manner attributed to this Nation.

For this I shall assign two Reasons only, as these seem to me abundantly satisfactory, and adequate to the Purpose.

The first is that Method so general in this Kingdom of giving no Education to the Youth of both Sexes; I say general only, for it is not without some few Exceptions.

Much the greater Part of our Lads of Fashion return from School at fifteen or sixteen, very little wiser, and not at all the better for having been sent thither. Part of these return to the Place from whence they came, their Fathers Country Seats; where Racing, Cock fighting, Hunting, and other rural Sports, with Smoaking, Drinking, and Party become their Pursuit, and form the whole Business and Amusement of their future Lives. The other Part escape to Town in the Diversions, Fashion, Follies and Vices of which they are immediately initiated. In this Academy some finish their Studies, while others by their wiser Parents are sent abroad to add the Knowledge of the Diversions, Fashions, Follies, and Vices of all Europe, to that of those of their own Country.

Hence then we are to derive two great general Characters of Humour, which are the Clown and the Coxcomb, and both of these will be almost infinitely diversified according to the different Passions and natural Dispositions of each Individual; and according to their different Walks in Life. Great will be the Difference; for Instance, whether the Country Gentleman be a Whig or a Tory, whether he prefers Women, Drink, or Dogs; so will it be whether the Town Spark be allotted to serve his Country as a Politician, a Courtier, a Soldier, a Sailor, or possibly a Churchman, (for by Draughts from this Academy, all these Offices are supplied); or lastly whether his Ambition shall be contented with no other Appellation than merely that of a Beau.

Some of our Lads however, are destined to a further Progress in Learning; these are not only confined longer to the Labours of a School, but are sent thence to the University. Here if they please, they may read on, and if they please they may (as most of them do) let it alone, and betake themselves as their Fancy leads, to the Imitation of their elder Brothers either in Town or Country.

This is a Matter which I shall handle very tenderly, as I am clearly of an Opinion that an University Education is much the best we have; for here at least there is some Restraint laid on the Inclinations of our Youth. The Sportsman, the Gamester, and the Sot, cannot give such a Loose to their Extravagance, as if they were at home and under no manner of Government; nor can our Spark who is disposed to the Town Pleasures, find either Gaming-houses or Play-houses, nor half the Taverns or Bawdy-houses which are ready to receive him in Covent-Garden.

So far however I hope I may say without Offence, that among all the Schools at the Universities, there is none where the Science of Good-Breeding is taught; no Lectures like the excellent Lessons on the Ridiculous, which I have quoted above, and which I do most earnestly recommend to all my young Readers. Hence the learned Professions produce such excellent Characters of Humour; and the Rudeness of Physicians, Lawyers, and Parsons, however dignified or distinguished, affords such pleasant Stories to divert private Companies, and sometimes the Public.

I come now to the beautiful Part of the Creation, who, in the Sense I here use the Word, I am assured can hardly (for the most Part) be said to have any Education.

As to the Counterpart of my Country Squire, the Country Gentlewoman, I apprehend, that except in the Article of the Dancing-Master, and perhaps in that of being barely able to read and write, there is very little Difference between the Education of many a Squire's Daughter, and that of his Dairy Maid, who is most likely her principal Companion; nay the little Difference which there is, is, I am afraid, not in the Favour of the Former; who, by being constantly flattered with her Beauty and her Wealth, is made the vainest and most selfconceited Thing alive, at the same Time that such Care is taken to instil into her the Principles of Bashfulness and Timidity, that she becomes ashamed and afraid of she knows not what.

If by any Chance this poor Creature drops afterwards, as it were, into the World, how absurd must be her Behaviour! If a Man looks at her, she is confounded, and if he speaks to her, she is frightened out of her Wits. She acts, in short, as if she thought the whole Sex was engaged in a Conspiracy to possess themselves of her Person and Fortune.

This poor Girl, it is true, however she may appear to her own Sex, especially if she is handsome, is rather an Object of Compassion, than of just Ridicule; but what shall we say when Time or Marriage have carried off all this Bashfulness and Fear, and when Ignorance, Aukwardness, and Rusticity, are embellished with the same Degree, tho' perhaps not the same kind of Affectation, which are to be found in a Court. Here sure is a plentiful Source of all that various Humour which we find in the Character of a Country Gentlewoman.

All this, I apprehend, will be readily allowed; but to deny Good-Breeding to the Town-Lady, may be the more Dangerous Attempt. Here, besides the Professors of Reading, Writing, and Dancing, the French and Italian Masters, the Music Master, and of Modern Times, the Whist Master, all concur in forming this Character. The Manners Master alone I am afraid is omitted. And what is the Consequence? not only Bashfulness and Fear are entirely subdued, but Modesty and Discretion are taken off at the same Time. So far from running away from, she runs after the Men; and instead of blushing when a modest Man looks at her, or speaks to her, she can bear, without any such Emotion to state an impudent Fellow in the Face, and sometimes to utter what, if he be not very impudent indeed, may put him to the Blush.—— Hence all those agreable [*sic*] Ingredients which form the Humour of a Rampant Woman of —— the Town.

I cannot quit this Part of my Subject, in which I have been obliged to deal a little more freely than I am inclined with the loveliest Part of the Creation, without preserving my own Character of Good-Breeding, by saying that this last Excess, is by much the most rare; and that every Individual among my Female Readers, either is already, or may be, when she pleases, an Example of a contrary Behaviour.

The second general Reason why Humour so much abounds in this Nation, seems to me to arise from the great Number of People, who are daily raised by Trade to the Rank of Gentry, without having had any Education at all; or, to use no improper Phrase, Without having served an Apprenticeship to this Calling. But I have dwelt so long on the other Branch, that I have no Room at present to animadvert on this; nor is it indeed necessary I should, since most Readers with the Hints I have already given them, will easily suggest to themselves, a great Number of humorous Characters with which the Public have been furnished this Way. I shall conclude by wishing, that this excellent Source of Humour may still continue to flow among us, since tho' it may make us a little laughed at, it will be sure to make us the Envy of all the Nations of Europe.

A.

PART SEVEN

Approbations

Fielding was generous in his approval of other writers, both ancient and modern, including Shakespeare, Jonson, Pope, Dryden, James Thomson, George Lillo, and Edward Moore. This section contains assessments of two of the authors who most influenced him, Homer and Lucian, and praise of two of his contemporaries, Samuel Richardson and Charlotte Lennox.

38 From *Joseph Andrews*, Book V, ch. ii

Joseph, Fanny and Parson Adams arrive by night at the home of Mr. Wilson. The latter, suspicious as to the identity of Adams, begins a literary conversation in order to establish whether he is a clergyman. This gives the Parson an opportunity for his apostrophe to Homer.

Joseph Andrews was published on February 22, 1742. The text printed here is taken from 'The SECOND EDITION: Revised and Corrected with *Alterations* and *Additions* by the AUTHOR', published August, 1742.

The Master of the House, notwithstanding the Simplicity which discover'd itself in *Adams*, knew too much of the World to give a hasty Belief to Professions. He was not yet quite certain that *Adams* had any more of the Clergyman in him than his Cassock. To try him therefore further, he asked him, 'if Mr. *Pope* had lately published any thing new?' *Adams* answer'd, 'he had heard great Commendations of that Poet, but that he had never read, nor knew any of his Works.' 'Ho! ho!' says the Gentleman to himself, 'have I caught you?' 'What,' said he, 'have you never seen his *Homer*?' *Adams* answer'd, 'he had never read any Translation of the Classicks.' 'Why truly,' reply'd the Gentleman, 'there is a Dignity in the *Greek* Language which I think no modern Tongue can reach.' 'Do you understand *Greek*, Sir,' said *Adams* hastily. 'A little, Sir,' answered the Gentleman. 'Do you know, Sir, cry'd *Adams*, where I can buy an *Æschylus*, an unlucky Misfortune lately happened to mine.' *Æschylus* was beyond the Gentleman, tho' he knew him very well by Name; he therefore returning back to *Homer*, asked *Adams* 'what Part of the *Iliad* he thought most excellent.' *Adams* return'd, 'His Question would be properer, what kind of Beauty was the chief in Poetry, for that *Homer* was equally excellent in them all.

'AND indeed,' continued he, 'what *Cicero* says of a complete Orator, may well be applied to a great Poet; *He ought to comprehend all Perfections.*[1] *Homer* did this in the most excellent degree; it is not without Reason therefore that the Philosopher, in the 22d Chap. of his *Poeticks*, mentions him by no other Appellation than that of *The Poet:* He was the Father of the Drama, as well as the Epic: Not of Tragedy only, but of Comedy also; for his *Margites*, which is deplorably lost, bore, says *Aristotle*, the same Analogy to Comedy, as his *Odyssey* and *Iliad* to Tragedy.[2] To him therefore we owe *Aristophanes*, as well as *Euripides*, *Sophocles*, and my poor *Æschylus*. But if you please we will confine ourselves (at least for the present) to the *Iliad*, his noblest Work; tho' neither *Aristotle*, nor *Horace* give it the Preference, as I remember, to the *Odyssey*. First then as to his Subject, can any thing be more simple, and at the same time more noble? He is rightly praised by the first of those judicious Critics, for not chusing the whole War, which, tho' he says, it hath a compleat Beginning and End, would have been too great for the Understanding to comprehend at one View. I have therefore often wondered why so correct a Writer as *Horace* should in his Epistle to *Lollius* call him the *Trojani Belli Scriptorem.*[3] Secondly, his Action, termed by *Aristotle Pragmaton Systasis*;[4] is it possible for the Mind of Man to conceive an Idea of such perfect Unity, and at the same time so replete with Greatness? And here I must observe what I do not remember to have seen noted by any, the *Harmotton*, that agreement of his Action to his Subject: For as the Subject is Anger, how agreeable is his Action, which is War? from which every Incident arises, and to which every Episode immediately relates. Thirdly, His Manners, which *Aristotle* places second in his Description of the several Parts of Tragedy, and which he says are included in the Action; I am at a loss whether I should rather admire the Exactness of his Judgment in the nice Distinction, or the Immensity of his Imagination in their Variety. For, as to the former of these, how accurately is the sedate, injured Resentment of *Achilles* distinguished from the hot insulting Passion of *Agamemnon*? How widely doth the brutal Courage of *Ajax* differ from the amiable Bravery of *Diomedes*; and the Wisdom of *Nestor*, which is the Result of long Reflection and Experience, from the Cunning of *Ulysses*, the Effect of Art and Subtilty only. If we consider their Variety, we may cry out with *Aristotle* in his 24th Chapter, that no Part of this divine Poem is destitute of Manners. Indeed I might affirm, that there is scarce a Character in human Nature untouched in some part or other. And as there is no Passion which he is not able to describe, so is there none in his Reader which he cannot raise. If he hath any superior Excellence to the rest, I have been inclined to fancy it is in the Pathetick. I am sure I never read with dry Eyes, the two Episodes, where *Andromache* is introduced, in the former lamenting the Danger, and in the latter the Death of *Hector*.[5] The Images are so extremely tender in these, that I am convinced, the Poet had the worthiest and best Heart imaginable. Nor can I help observing how short *Sophocles* falls of the Beauties of the Original, in that Imitation of the dissuasive Speech of *Andromache*, with [*sic*] he hath put into the Mouth of *Tecmessa*.[6] And yet *Sophocles* was the greatest Genius who ever wrote Tragedy, nor have any of his Successors in that Art, that is to say, neither *Euripides* nor *Seneca* the Tragedian been able to come near him. As to his Sentiments and Diction, I need say nothing; the former are particularly remarkable for the utmost Perfection on that Head, namely Propriety; and as to the latter, *Aristotle*, whom doubtless you have read over and over, is very diffuse. I shall mention but one thing more, which that great Critic in his Division of Tragedy calls *Opsis*, or the Scenery,[7] and which is as proper to the Epic as to the Drama, with this difference, that in the former it falls to the share of the Poet, and in the latter to that of the Painter. But did ever Painter imagine a Scene like that in the 13th and 14th Iliads? where the Reader sees at one View the Prospect of *Troy*, with the Army drawn up before it; the *Grecian* Army, Camp, and Fleet, *Jupiter* sitting on Mount *Ida*, with his Head wrapt in a Cloud, and a Thunderbolt in his Hand looking towards *Thrace*; *Neptune* driving through the Sea, which divides on each side to permit his Passage, and then seating himself on Mount *Samos*: The Heavens open'd, and the Deities all seated on their Thrones. This is Sublime! This is Poetry!'

39 A Letter from Fielding to Samuel Richardson

October 15, 1748

This letter from Fielding to Richardson praising the fifth volume of *Clarissa* is evidence for Fielding's generosity and willingness to respond to the work of his contemporaries. It may be compared with his parody of *Pamela* in *Shamela* and his other published allusions to Richardson's work (see Nos. 30 and 42).

Dear S^{r}/Oct. 15. (1748) I have read over your 5th Vol.[1] In all the Accounts which Loveless Gives of the Transactions at Hampstead, you preserve the same vein of Humour which hath run through the preceding Volumes. The new Characters you Introduce are natural and entertaining, and there is much of the true Comic Force in the Widow Bevis. I have seen her often, and I Promise you, you have drawn her with great exactness. The Character of Loveless is heightened with great Judgment. His former Admirers must lose all Regard for him on his Perseverance, and as this Regard Ceases, Compassion for Clarissa rises in the same Proportion. Hence we are admirably prepared for what is to follow.—Shall I tell you? Can I tell you what I think of the latter part of your Volume? Let the Overflowings of a Heart which you have filled brimfull speak for me.

When Clarissa returns to her Lodgings at St. Clairs the Alarm begins, and here my Heart begins its Narrative. I am Shocked; my Terrors ar[e ra]ised, and I have the utmost Apprehensions for the poor betrayed Creature.—But when I see her enter with the Letter in her Hand, and after some natural Effects of Despair, clasping her Arms about the Knees of the Villain, call him her Dear Lovelace, desirous and yet unable to implore his Protection or rather his mercy; I then melt into Compassion, and find what is called an Effeminate Relief for my Terror to continue to the End of the Scene. When I read the next Letter I am Thunderstruck; nor can many Lines explain what I feel from Two.

What I shall [*sic*] say of holding up the Licence? I will say a finer Picture was never imagined. He must be a Glorious Painter who can do it Justice on Canvas, and a most wretched one indeed who could not do much on such a Subject. The Circumstance of the Fragments is Great and Terrible; but her [Clarissa's] Letter to Lovelace is beyond any thing I have ever read. God forbid that the Man who reads this with dry Eyes should be alone with my Daughter when she hath no Assistance within Call. Here my Terror ends and my Grief begins which the Cause of all my Tumultuous Passions soon changes into Raptures of Admiration and Astonishment by a Behaviour the most Elevated I can possibly conceive, and what is at the same time most Gentle and most natural. This Scene I have heard hath been often objected to. It is well for the Critick that My Heart is now writing and not my Head. During the Continuance of this Vol. my Compassion is often moved; but I think my Admiration more. If I had rec'd no Hint or Information of what is to succeed I should perceive you paving the way to load our admiration of your Heroine to the Highest Pitch, as you have before with wonderfull Art prepared us for both Terror and Compassion on her Account. This last seems to come from the Head. Here then I will end: for I assure you nothing but my Heart can force me to say Half of what I think of *the* Book. And yet what hinders me? I cannot be suspected of Flattery. I know the Value of that too much to throw it away, where I have no Obligation, and where I expect no Reward. And sure the World will not suppose me inclined to flatter one whom they will suppose me to hate if the[y] will be pleased to recollect that we are Rivals for that coy Mrs. Fame. Believe me however if your Clarissa had not engaged my Affections more than this Mrs. all your Art and all your Nature had not been able to extract a single Tear: for as to this Mrs. I have ravished her long ago, and live in a settled cohabitation with her in defiance of that Public Voice which is supposed to be her Guardian, and to have alone the Power of giving her away. To explain this Riddle. It is not that I am less but more addicted to Vanity than others; so much that I can wrap my self up as warmly in my own vanity, as the Ancient could involve himself in his Virtue. If I have any Merit I certainly know it and if the World will not allow it me, I will allow it my self. I would not have you think (I might say know) me *to be* so dishonest as to assert that I despise Fame; but this I solemnly aver that I love her as coldly, as most of us do Heaven, so that I will sacrifice nothing to the Pursuit of her. much less would I bind my self, as all her Passionate Admirers do, to harbour in my Bosom that monster Envy which of all Beings either real or imaginary I most heartily and sincerely abhor. You will begin to think I believe, that I want not much external Commendation. I will conclude then with assuring you. That I heartily wish you Success. That I sincerely think you in the highest manner deserve it. And that if you have it not, it it [*sic*] would be in me unpardonable Presumption to hope for Success, and at the same time almost contemptible Humility to desire it.

I am Dear S^r^ yrs. most Affectionately Hen. Ffielding.

I beg you to send me immediately the two remaining Vols.

40 *The Covent Garden Journal*, No. 24

Tuesday, March 24, 1752

Charlotte Lennox (1720–1806), the friend of Johnson and Goldsmith, produced several novels after *The Female Quixote* (1752), none of which were very successful. *The Female Quixote* is the story of a young girl who has formed her idea of life by reading the heroic romances and who is brought to reason after a series of painful experiences by the arguments of a worthy divine.

Proceedings at the Court of Censorial Enquiry, *&c.*

The Censor was pleased to deliver himself as follows:

I have perused a Book called, THE FEMALE QUIXOTE, OF THE ADVENTURES OF ARABELLA; and I shall give my Opinion of it with no less Sincerity than Candour.

This is an Imitation of the famous Romance of Cervantes called *The Life and Actions of that ingenious Gentleman Don Quixote of the Mancha*, &c. A Work originally written in Spanish, and which hath been translated into most of the Languages, and admired in most of the Countries in Europe.

I will here very frankly declare my Opinion in what Particulars the Imitation falls short; in what it equals, and in what it excels its illustrious Original.

In the first Place, Cervantes hath the Advantage of being the Original; and consequently is intitled to that Honour of Invention, which can never be attributed to any Copy however excellent. An Advantage which Homer will always claim, and which is perhaps the only one that he can claim, over Virgil and Milton.

In the next Place Cervantes is to be considered as an Author who intended not only the Diversion, but the Instruction and Reformation of his Countrymen: With this Intention he levelled his Ridicule at a vicious Folly, which in his Time universally prevailed in Spain, and had almost converted a civilized People in a Nation of Cut-throats.

In this Design he imitated the three glorious Poets I have mentioned. The first of whom placed the particular Good of Greece, the second the Honour of Rome, and the third the great Cause of Christianity before their Eyes, when they planned their several Poems. And the Success of none of them was perhaps equal to that of Cervantes.

Here again the Spanish Romance hath the Advantage of the English.

Thirdly, the Character of Don Quixote himself, as well as that of Sancho Pancha, are superior to those of Arabella and her Maid.

Fourthly, some of the Incidents in the Original are more exquisitely ridiculous than any which we find in the Copy. And those I think, are all the Particulars in which an impartial Critic can give the Preference to the Spaniard. And as to the two last, I cannot help observing, they may possibly be rather owing to that Advantage, which the Actions of Men give to the Writer beyond those of Women, than to any Superiority of Genius. Don Quixote is ridiculous in performing Feats of Absurdity himself; Arabella can only become so, in provoking and admiring the Absurdities of others. In the former Case, the Ridicule hath all the Force of a Representation; it is in a Manner subjected to the Eyes; in the latter it is conveyed, as it were, through our Ears, and partakes of the Coldness of History or Narration.

I come now to speak of those Parts in which the two Authors appear to me upon an Equality. So they seem to be in that Care which both have taken to preserve the Affection of their Readers for their principal Characters, in the midst of all the Follies of which they are guilty. Both Characters are accordingly represented as Persons of good Sense, and of great natural Parts, and in all Cases, except one, of a very sound Judgement, and what is much more endearing, as Persons of great Innocence, Integrity and Honour, and of the highest Benevolence. Again the Fidelity and Simplicity of Sancho Pancha, are well matched by these Qualities in Arabella's Handmaid. Tho' as I have before observed, I do not think the Character of Sancho is here equalled. It is perhaps a Masterpiece in Humour of which we never have, nor ever shall see the like.

There are probably more Instances under this Head, which I shall leave to the discerning Reader. I will proceed in the last Place to those Particulars, in which, I think, our Countrywoman hath excelled the Spanish Writer.

And this I am not afraid to declare, she hath done in my Opinion, in all the following Particulars.

First, as we are to grant in both Performances, that the Head of a very sensible Person is entirely subverted by reading Romances, this Concession seems to me more easy to be granted in the Case of a young Lady than of an old Gentleman. Nor can I help observing with what perfect Judgment and Art this Subversion of Brain in Arabella is accounted for by her peculiar Circumstances, and Education. To say Truth, I make no Doubt but that most young Women of the same Vivacity, and of the same innocent good Disposition, in the same Situation, and with the same Studies, would be able to make a large Progress in the same Follies.

Secondly, the Character of Arabella is more endearing than that of Quixote. This will undoubtedly be the Case between a beautiful young Lady and an old Fellow, where equal Virtues in both become Candidates for our Favour.

Thirdly, the Situation of Arabella is more interesting. Our Hearts are engaged very early in good Wishes for the Success of Mr. Glanville; a Character entirely well drawn, as are indeed many others; for in this Particular, the English Author hath doubtless the Preference.

Fourthly, here is a regular Story, which, tho' possibly it is not pursued with that Epic Regularity which would give it the Name of an Action, comes much nearer to that Perfection than the loose unconnected Adventures in *Don Quixote*; of which you may transverse the Order as you please, without any Injury to the whole.

Fifthly, the Incidents, or, if you please, the Adventures, are much less extravagant and incredible in the English than in the Spanish Performance. The latter, in many Instances, approaches very near to the Romances which he ridicules. Such are the Stories of Cardenio and Dorothea, Ferdinand and Lucinda, &c. In the former, there is nothing except the Absurdities of the Heroine herself, which is carried beyond Common-Life; nor is there any Thing even in her Character, which the Brain a little distempered may not account for. She conceives indeed somewhat preposterously of the Ranks and Conditions of Men; that is to say, mistakes one Man for another; but never advances towards the Absurdity of imagining Windmills and Wine-Bags to be human Creatures, or Flocks of Sheep to be Armies.

I might add more on this Subject, but I will pursue it no further; having already, I apprehend, given a larger Dose to Malice, Envy, and Ignorance, than they will care to swallow; but I cannot omit observing, that tho' the Humour of Romance, which is principally ridiculed in this Work, be not at present greatly in fashion in this Kingdom, our Author hath taken such Care throughout her Work, to expose all those Vices and Follies in her Sex which are chiefly predominant in Our Days, that it will afford very useful Lessons to all those young Ladies who will peruse it with proper Attention.

Upon the whole, I do very earnestly recommend it, as a most extraordinary and most excellent Performance. It is indeed a Work of true Humour, and cannot fail of giving a rational, as well as very pleasing, Amusement to a sensible Reader, who will at once be instructed and very highly diverted. Some Faults perhaps there may be, but I shall leave the unpleasing Task of pointing them out to those who will have more Pleasure in the Office. This Caution, however, I think proper to premise, that no Persons presume to find many: For if they do, I promise them, the Critic and not the Author *will be to blame*.

41 *The Covent Garden Journal*, No. 52

Tuesday, June 30, 1752

The translation of Lucian, to be done by Fielding and William Young, was advertised in *The Covent Garden Journal*, but does not seem actually to have been begun. Had it been finished it would have been of great interest to students of Fielding, who consistently praised Lucian as the originator of the ironic techniques which he applied in the service of reason and truth.

Fielding's paper is not, however, the result of great learning. All his examples and most of his arguments occur in writers whom he mentions during the course of the essay.

Graiis Ingenium, Graiis dedit Ore rotundo
Musa loqui——

HOR.[1]

Her Wit, and flowing Eloquence, the Muse
Gave to the Greeks——

As a Proposal is now publish'd for a Translation of the Works of Lucian into our Mother-Tongue,[2] it may not be improper to acquaint our English Readers with the real Value of the Work which is offered to their Acceptance.

This Author may be almost called the Father of true Humour: Mr. Dryden says, he knows not whom he imitated, unless it might be Aristophanes.[3] This Supposition can certainly be meant only of that Attic Elegance of Diction, in which there is perhaps some Resemblance between these two Authors; and this is a Point, in which I am afraid we are at this time but little able to decide who deserves the Preference; the learned Photius gives the Palm of excelling all others in Diction, to our Author. *τὴν μέντοι φράσιν ἐστὶν ἄριστος*[4]. But surely our ingenious Countryman could not conceive, that Lucian in the exquisite Pleasantry of his Humour, in the Neatness of his Wit, and in the Poignancy of his Satire, did condescend to be the Imitator of a Writer, whose Humour is often extravagant, his Wit coarse, and his Satire unjust and immoral.[5] Indeed, Mr. Dryden himsel, in the short Character which he presently after gives of Lucian's Writings, shews he could not have imitated the Greek Comedian. 'Any one,' says he, 'may see, that our Author's chief Design was to disnest Heaven of so many immoral and debauched Deities: His next, to expose the mock Philosophers; and his last, to give us Examples of a good Life in the Persons of the true.'[6] Of the first of these we may find, I allow many Strokes in Aristophanes, how inferior to the Spirit of Lucian, I submit to the learned Reader; but as to the second, I remember no Instance: For I hope the base and barbarous Abuse of Socrates will not be allowed an Attempt to expose the mock Philosophers. The Truth is, that Species of Wretches, who were the Objects of Ridicule at Rome, and who gained a Livelihood by being so, being, as Suetonius tells us, the favourite Buffoons of the Emperors themselves, were unknown in the Days of Aristophanes. And as to *giving an Example of a good Life in the Persons of the true Philosophers*, this likewise could no more be learnt from Aristophanes, than a System of Ethics can be drawn from our modern Comedies.

And as I am thus unwilling to think that Lucian was the Imitator of any other, I shall not be much more ready to grant, that others have been the Imitators of him. The Person whom I esteem to be most worthy of this Honour is the immortal Swift. To say Truth, I can find no better Way of giving the English Reader an Idea of the Greek Author, than by telling him, that to translate Lucian well into English, is to give us another Swift in our own Language. I will add, however invidious it may appear, that when I allow to this excellent English Writer the Praise of imitating the Greek, I allow him that Praise only which the best Imitator can possibly claim, of being Second to his Original. Our Author will perhaps for ever continue to deserve the Title of inimitable, (*i.e.* unequaled) which the learned Mr. Moyle hath given him.[7]

In Fact, besides the Superiority of Genius which seems to me to appear in Lucian, when he is compared with any other humorous Writer, no other seems to have had such excellent Materials to work upon. What Fund of Pleasantry hath any Age produced equal to that Theology and to that Philosophy which he hath exposed!

Notwithstanding all his Merit, (I should perhaps rather say, as a Proof of his Merit,) this inimitable Author hath had his Critics, that is, as the Moderns use the Word, his Censurers. 'Of this Number,' says

Dryden, 'is the wretched Author of the *Lucien en belle Humeur*, who being himself as insipid as a Dutch Poet, yet arraigns Lucian for his own Fault, *&c.* but the best on't is, the Jaundice is only in his own Eyes, which makes Lucian look yellow to him. All Mankind will exclaim against his preaching this Doctrine against him.'[8] The learned indeed are unanimous in their Elogiums on him; such amongst others are Photius, Grævius, Erasmus, D'Ablancourt, Dryden, Mayn, and the learned Mr. Moyle whom I have mentioned above.[9]

To the Honour of Lucian it should be likewise remembred, that his Virtues and abilities recommended him to the Favour of that Glory of human Nature, Marcus Aurelius, by whom our Author was employed in a very considerable Post in the Government.[10] That great Emperor did not, it seems, think, that a Man of Humour was below his Notice, or unfit for Business of the gravest Kind.

Nor can I omit the Honour done him by some of the first Planters of Christianity, who embraced his Arguments and applied them with good Success against the Advocates for the Heathen Deities, who could not resist his Raillery. 'For my Part,' says Dryden, 'I know not to whose Writings we owe more our Christianity, where the true God has succeeded a Multitude of false; whether to the grave Confutation of *Clemens Alexandrinus*, *Arnobius*, *Justin Martyr*, *St. Augustin*, *Lactantius*, &c. or to the facetious Wit of *Lucian*: A Wit which is thus described by Monsr. *D'Ablancourt*. "Qui a par tout de la Mignardise & de l'Agreement avec un humeur gaye & enjouée, & cette *urbanité Attique* que nous appellerions en nôtre langue une raillerié fine & delicate,"[11] &c.—In a Word, I conclude, that all who have a true Taste of Humour must read Lucian with the most exquisite Pleasure, and those who have not, will find no other Means so proper to acquire that Taste.'

Such is the Author now proposed to be translated, I may truly say, to be first translated into our Language: For as to the two Attempts hitherto made, tho' one of them hath Mr. Dryden's Name to the Preface (for indeed he translated but little himself) they can give the Reader no more Idea of the Spirit of Lucian, than the vilest Imitation by a Signpost Painter can convey the Spirit of the excellent Hogarth.[12]

As to the Abilities of one of the Gentlemen who propose this Translation I shall be silent; I will only venture to say, that no Man seems so likely to translate an Author well, as he who hath formed his Stile upon that very Author. Nor shall I trespass upon the Modesty of a Gentleman greatly endow'd with that Virtue, by saying much of the other. In this I believe, I shall have the universal Concurrence of those learned Men of this Age to whom he is known, that no Man now alive is better versed in that Language in which the Wit of Lucian lies as yet concealed. I shall add, that I doubt not but the Public will find a Pleasure in shewing some Regard to two Gentlemen, who have hitherto in their several Capacities endeavoured to be serviceable to them, without deriving any great Emolument to themselves from their Labours.

C.

PART EIGHT

From *The Jacobite's Journal*

Fielding conducted *The Jacobite's Journal* from December 5, 1747, to November 5, 1748, under the pseudonym of John Trott-Plaid. The journal was political, designed to defend the Government against the attacks of Jacobites and other malcontents, though it contains a good deal of literary material in the correspondence column and the Court of Criticism. The separate passages reprinted in this section could well be divided among the other sections. They have been kept together partly because *The Jacobite's Journal* has never been reprinted before, and partly because they share a tone which differs from that of Fielding's other journals. *The Jacobite's Journal*, on the whole, is more particular in its treatment of the authors, critics, actors, and the Opposition Press than was usual with Fielding. The range of comment within the one journal also indicates his refusal to separate literature and politics and his tendency to treat them alike as aspects of human activity, subject to the same laws of decency and moderation.

42 A Letter from *The Jacobite's Journal*, No. 5

Saturday, December 26, 1747

Compare No. 39.

Sir,—I am glad to find a Man of Learning and Genius once more in the Character of a public Writer. As to Politics, whatever may be your Principles, I shall not dispute them; for I have applied none of my Time to that Study. Thirty Years ago, indeed, a general Cry that the Nation was undone, created some Terrors in me, and had almost made me a Politician; but as I have heard that Outcry ever since, it hath long ceased to have any Effect, and I now enjoy my Fortune without any Apprehensions.

My chief Delight hath always been in reading; and as Works of Imagination afford me the greatest Pleasure, you may easily imagine that I have many Years ago run through all the Books (for they are not numberless) which ancient or modern Authors have produced of that kind. Indeed I have read them all so often, that their Beauties, from too much Familiarity, begin to pall upon my Mind.

How charmed am I therefore when I meet with a new Production in the Region of Fancy, capable of giving me the same Delight which I have received from my most favourite Authors at my first Acquaintance with them. The most learned Botanist, who discovers a new Plant; or the surfeited Epicure, who invents a new Dish, may perhaps have some faint Idea of my Pleasure, at perusing such Works from any of my Cotemporaries.

When I tell you I have lately received this Pleasure, you will not want me to inform you that I owe it to the Author of *Clarissa*. Such Simplicity, such Manners, such deep Penetration into Nature; such Power to raise and alarm the Passions, few Writers, either ancient or modern, have been possessed of. My Affections are so strongly engaged, and my Fears are so raised, by what I have already read, that I cannot express my Eagerness to see the rest. Sure this Mr. *Richardson* is Master of all that Art which *Horace* compares to Witchcraft,

——Pectus inaniter angit,
Irritat, mulcet, falsis terroribus implet,
Ut Magus.——[1]

With what Indignation do I therefore hear the Criticisms made on this Performance. *Clarissa* is undutiful; she is too dutiful. She is too cold; she is too fond. She uses her Father, Mother, Uncles, Brother, Sister, Lover, Friend, too ill, too well. In short, there is scarce a Contradiction in Character, which I have not heard assigned from different Reasons to this poor Girl; who is as much the Object of Compassion as she can be, and as good as she should be described.

Do, pray, Sir, now and then lay aside your Politics, and take upon you to correct our Critics. Advise these Snarlers, of both Sexes, to improve their Heads a little, before they venture to sit in Judgment on the Merit of an Author. I wish likewise before they read any more of this Author, they would amend their Hearts; for this, I take it, is an Axiom: *That a* bad *Heart cannot taste the Productions of a* good *one.*

I am, Sir,
Yours, &c.

43 From *The Jacobite's Journal*, No. 6

Saturday, January 9, 1748

Compare Nos. 11 and 14, where Fielding instituted other Courts of Censorial Enquiry.

Whereas it hath been represented unto us, as well by the Letters of several of our Correspondents, as by the humble Petition of many of the most reputable Booksellers, and doth otherwise sufficiently appear, that a great Number of loose, idle, and disorderly Persons, calling themselves Authors, have lately assembled at a certain Ale-house of ill Fame in *Grub-street*, commonly known by the Name of the *Pen and Pitcher*, and have there conspired together to mix up great Quantities of Ribaldry and Nonsense; and have afterwards endeavour'd to their utmost to spread the said Mixtures abroad among the People, often under false Names and Colours; and by means of a certain wicked, base, deceitful and diabolical Art, vulgarly call'd Puffing, to the great Annoyance of his Majesty's good Subjects, often to the great Prejudice of the Reputation of Men of the best and most solemn Characters, and always to the Loss of both the Money and Time of the Reader; to the Prejudice of all honest Booksellers, to the utmost Abuse, Disgrace, and Discouragement of Literature, and, lastly, to the great Scandal of this Nation.

And whereas the said wicked Persons, tho' often within the Intent, are not literally within the Description either of the Black Act,[1] or of the Act against sending threatning Letters; nor can the said Mixtures be sufficiently suppress'd, nor the Mischiefs intended by them be obviated by any Laws now in Being, We have been therefore humbly requested, as well by our Correspondents as by the Booksellers aforesaid to erect a Court of Criticism for the well-ordering and inspecting all Matters any wise concerning the Republic of Literature, and for the due Correction and Punishment of all Abuses committed therein. All which doth belong, and from Time, whereof the Memory of Man is not to the contrary, hath belonged to that high Censorial Office, with which, for very wise Causes and Considerations, we have thought proper to invest ourselves.

Having therefore duly weigh'd the Premises, and being well convinced of the great Necessity of immediately reviving the said Court, to the long Suspension of which (even from the Time of our most dear Predecessor *Isaac Bickerstaff*, Esq; of facetious Memory)[2] may justly be imputed all the Abuses above complain'd of, we have graciously determined forthwith to revive the said Court; and do hereby give Notice, that the said Court will be held on *Thursday* next at our Bookseller's Shop, between the Hours of Twelve and Two; and with the Proceedings thereat the Public will be acquainted in this our Paper, between the Foreign and Domestic Articles of News.

In this Court we intend, moreover, to recommend all Books and Writings, which have the least Merit in them, to the Public: And do hereby strictly charge the said Public not to purchase any modern literary Productions whatever, till they have first read our Approbation.

Given at our Bookseller's Shop,
this 10th of Jan. 1748.[3] JOHN TROTT-PLAID.

44 From *The Jacobite's Journal*, No. 7

Saturday, January 16, 1748

Proceedings at the Court of Criticism, *held on* Thursday, Jan. 14, 1747, before JOHN TROTT-PLAID, *Esq*; *Censor of* Great Britain.

Several Persons applied to his Honour in order to obtain Offices in the said Court; most of whom being rejected, departed grumbling, and threatened to go into the Opposition.

A Petition from Orator *Handlie* was read, praying to be Crier of the Court, offering to write, preach, or swear any thing, and to profess any Party or Religion, at a cheap rate; rejected.[1]

A Petition of a small Body of Critics, signed THE TOWN, humbly praying that his Honour would take the Playhouse under his Inspection, was presented and read. Upon which the Court said, They would consider thereof; and the Managers of the said Playhouses were ordered to attend on *Thursday* next.

M. Cooper presented to the Court a Pamphlet entitled *An Historical Essay upon the Ballance* [*sic*] *of Civil Power in England, &c.* which was read. And it was ordered that an Extract from the Dedication be immediately printed in this Paper, and that the said Pamphlet be recommended to the Perusal of the Public.[2]

The Court was moved on the Behalf of the Paper Manufacture; which it was said would be considerably injured by that general Prohibition published in our Journal of the 9th Instant. It was suggested by a learned Council that, If so be, that how, a Book was perfectly inoffensive, it might be permitted to be suffered to be read. And besides that how a Book might have some Degree of Merit, without having sufficient to entitle it to the high Honour of the Recommendation of the Court. Why therefore then, it would be better to qualifie the generality of the Words of the Clause of the Prohibition; and to confine it then to this, that how, if so be, a Book be condemned by the Court, why therefore then, in that Case, nobody should be permitted to read it.

This Motion was opposed by a Council who said he was employ'd by the Pastry-Cooks and the Makers of Trunks and Band-boxes, who were more concerned in Interest to support the beforementioned Order in its full Extent, than the Paper Manufacturers could be to abridge it. He said it was true, that the Morals of the People, or the Reputations of Individuals, could not be injured by Books merely inoffensive; but that such might nevertheless rob the Public of both their Time and Money. He likewise urged, that it was not the printing, but the reading only of such Books, which was prohibited; and that he conceived there would not be one the less printed on account of the Prohibition; for as all Authors, good or bad, have the same good Opinion of their own Works, not one would despair of the Court's Recommendation to the Public. The principal Consequence, he said, would be, that his Clients the Pastry-Cooks, &c. would be served at a cheaper rate.[3]

The Court, conceiving this to be a Matter of great Moment, were unwilling to determine hastily, and therefore gave Day to the several Parties concerned in Interest, to wit, Thursday fortnight, when they will hear the Merits of the Cause on both sides.

After which the Court adjourned to Thursday next at 12 of the Clock.

45 From *The Jacobite's Journal*, No. 8

Saturday, January 23, 1748

In this leading article, writing under a pseudonym, Fielding puts self-seeking politicians and partial critics in the same category. They are treated similarly elsewhere in his work, but nowhere so frequently as in *The Jacobite's Journal*, written when he was being subjected to savage personal abuse by his political opponents and insulted as a literary hack.

Est iniqua in omni re accusanda, prœtermissis bonis, malorum enumeratio, vitiorumq; selectio.

Cic., *de Leg.*, Lib. 3.I[1]

I agree with one of your Correspondents in your 5th Journal, in hoping that you will take upon you the Office of Criticism; or, in properer Words, will place yourself at the Head of *English* Critics. Indeed, to supervise and correct these Gentlemen is more closely connected with the Political Scheme than perhaps it appears to be at first Sight. The Spirit of Criticizing, and the Spirit of Opposition, are extremely alike; and the sour ill-natured Snarler, whose Pride and Pleasure it is to revile, very seldom, I believe, excepts the Government out of his Censures.

To say the Truth, I question whether the two Characters may not often concenter in one Person. When a Man becomes infamous in the higher Circle, and is, as it were, dethroned by the Public from his Patriot Tyranny, why may he not be supposed, like the famous *Sicilian* Tyrant of Old, to condescend to exert the same Talents, and to vent the same Venom, in a lower Sphere?[2] Thus probably the Political Snarler, who hath hiss'd at the Government for many Years, when he can be no longer heard with Attention, turns the Edge of his Spleen another Way, and commences the Damner of Plays, and a Writer of Weekly Libels.[3]

Nothing indeed seems easier than to run an exact Parallel between them.

First, then, if we examine the Matter well, we shall find these Snarlers in the Republic of Letters to be composed of the same Ingredients with their Fellow Labourers in the State. These are principally Ill-nature and Envy, and, above all, Disappointment; for as bad Authors, who have been disappointed in the Pursuit of Fame, or perhaps of something more substantial, are always the severest Critics on such of their cotemporary Writers as are in Possession of what they aimed at; so discarded, rejected, disappointed Statesmen are ever the bitterest Patriots.

The Reader will pardon my using the Word Patriot as well as Critic, in a very inadequate and improper Sense. The Persons who have, without any just Pretension, assumed these Characters, must answer for the disadvantageous Light in which they have placed these Words; and while I pursue such Impostors, none but themselves will represent me as endeavouring to derogate from the great Merit of those who, with equal Talents, fill up either Character; and these, I will venture to say, are commonly, in both Instances, the very Persons who are vilified and traduced by the Pretenders to each.

And as these pretended Patriots and Critics arise from the same Source, so they act in the same manner. The Business of both is apparently, and almost professedly, to find Fault. Is this the only Office of Criticism? Did *Aristotle*, *Horace*, *Quintilian*, or even *Scaliger*,[4] the sourest of all good Critics, write with such an Intention! Again, is it the Office of a Patriot only to censure and revile? Have the greatest and truest Patriots, either antient or modern, taken this Method of expressing their Love to their Country? There is perhaps scarce a Writer extant without some Degree of Merit; nor have we had, I am sure, within our Memory, any Minister who deserved no Commendation; yet what Praise ever flows from the Pen of a modern Critic, or of a modern Patriot? How contrary is such a Spirit to the amiable Temper of *Horace*.

> *Nempe incomposito dixi pede, currere versus*
> *Lucili. Quis tam Lucili Fautor inepte est*
> *Ut non hoc fatiatur? at idem quod sale multo*
> *Urbem defricuit Charta laudatur eâdem.*[5]

What can be fairer than this? On the contrary what more barbarous than to point out the Faults of an Author, or of a Man, to the World, and at the same time, by concealing their Excellencies, to insinuate that they have none. The World wants our Assistance more to enable them to discern what is lovely than what is odious; why then should we with-hold it from them? In God's Name let us speak out honestly, and set the good against the bad, that the Public may judge which preponderates. This would be a fair Method; and this Men would pursue, if Truth, and not Spleen, Rancour, Malice and Revenge guided their Pens.

Indeed, not only Truth and Justice require this, but even Policy seems to suggest it. This would carry at least an Appearance of Impartiality, and would gain the Ear and Attention of the Public; which never pays any Regard to the Censures of a Writer, when once it is known that his Purpose is only to blame and vilify; and what can be more manifest than this Purpose in Men who have attacked the present Administration during a Course of Years, and have never touched upon a single Excellence in the bright Characters of a *Pelham* or a *Hardwick?*[6]

Another most cruel Method practised by both the above-mentioned Persons, is to condemn a Work or a Man as vicious, because they are not free from Faults or Imperfections. Whoever looks for any human Person, or any human Performance, absolutely perfect and without any Blemish, searches after

A faultless Monster which the World ne'er saw.[7]

Paradise Lost, the noblest Effort perhaps of human Genius hath its Blemishes, which Mr. *Addison* finely compares to the Spots in a Map of the Sun.[8] Neither *Socrates* nor *Brutus* were without Faults, and some of the most admired Characters, both antient and modern, have had very glaring ones.

Horace will teach us to judge of Writings,

—*Ubi plura nitent in Carmine, non ego paucis*
Offender Maculis—[9]

By the same Rule we must form our Judgment of Men. Candour, nay Humanity requires us to controll our Censures in this Manner. The snarling Critic who condemns the Works of his Cotemporaries if he can find any Faults in them, declares only that they are of human Original; and the virulent, raging, pretended Patriot, who exclaims against the Ministry because they reach not consummate Perfection, exclaims against them only because they are Men; or rather, I believe, to speak a plain honest Truth, *because they are Ministers.*[10]

I am, Sir,
Yours, &c.
CANDIDUS.

46 From *The Jacobite's Journal*, No. 10

Saturday, February 6, 1748

Proceedings at the Court of Criticism, Thursday Feb. 4

After hearing Council for and against the Managers of *Drury-Lane*, the Court came to the following Resolutions.

1. That the Part of *Tag* in *Miss in her Teens*, is a much better Part than that of Lady *Lurewell*; and that the whole Play of the *Trip to the Jubilee* is a wretched Performance, and ought to be banish'd from the Stage.[1]

2. That the true Reason why Mrs. *Clive* hath been less liked in the Characters of fine Ladies than in others, hath been, that these Characters being monstrous Pictures of Affectation, without Wit, Humour, or Nature, have given her no Opportunity of exerting her great Talents for true Comedy, or of answering the great Expectation which the Audience always entertain from her Performance: And that if ever she fails of pleasing, it is owing to the Author, and not to herself.

3. That the Business of an Actor, as well as of a Writer, is to copy Nature, and not to imitate the Excellencies of their Predecessors: That Mr. *Garrick*, Mr. *Quin*, Mrs. *Cibber*, Mrs. *Clive*, and Mrs. *Woffington*, are all, in their several Capacities, Examples of this Merit.[2]

4. That the Audience be at Liberty to carry Books to the Theatre; and that whenever an Actor presumes to add Conceits of his own to his Part, any one of the said Audience may hiss him off the Stage.

5. That by over-acting a Part, true Comedy is turned to Farce, and Tragedy into Burlesque. And that this Fault, if ever so little given way to, soon becomes incurable; and the Actor is afterwards fit only for *Bartholomew* Fair, or to give Tea.[3]

6. That an Actor of *Drury-Lane* Theatre be privately admonished of both these Imperfections; and acquainted, that if he doth not reform, he will shortly be apprehended, and publicly tried for the same at this Court.[4]

7. That Mr. *Garrick* be discharged from the Accusation brought against him; and that he do receive the Thanks of this Court for his great Improvement of our Theatrical Entertainments, not only by

his own inimitable Performance; but by his proper Regulations of the Theatre under his Direction.

It was then moved, that Mr. *Rich* might be admonished for suffering private Characters to be ridiculed by Mimickry and Buffoonry upon his Stage.

Resolved, that all such Mimickry is indecent, immoral, and even illegal; and Mr. *Rich* was admonish'd accordingly.

One *Horse piss*, alias *Horse-dung*, alias *Horse-lie*, alias THE Fool, was convicted of Scurrility, and received Sentence of CONTEMPT.[5]

The Trial of Mr. *Carte's* History was appointed for this Day Fortnight.[6] Adjourned.

47 From *The Jacobite's Journal*, No. 11

Saturday, February 13, 1748

Proceedings at the Court of Criticism, Thursday Feb. 11

The Court heard a Cause between the Corporation of *Grub-street*, Plaintiff, and the Corporation of *Billinsgate*, Defendant, concerning the Property of a late Pamphlet intitled, *A Critical Address*, &c.[1] in which it was set forth, on the Behalf of the Plaintiff, that the Corporation of *Grub-street* had, from time immemorial, a Right to claim all low, scandalous Invectives, without the least Wit, Humour, Argument, or Fact; and then they proceeded to give undeniable Proof, that the aforesaid Pamphlet contained such Invectives, and that there were only two Facts charged on the Ministry, *viz*. Attempting to take away the Liberty of the Press, and to naturalize Foreign Protestants, both which were notoriously false. It was farther urged, that the said Pamphlet was a mere Catch-penny; and in order to cheat the Public by raising it to the Price of a Shilling, the Pages were number'd to 51; whereas, in Fact, it contain'd but 42; all which were said to be certain Proofs of its belonging to *Grub-street*.

The Defendant on the contrary urged, that when these Invectives proceeded to the Use of opprobrious Terms, and to downright calling Names, such Works had always been adjudged to be the Property of *Billinsgate*. And the Court being of that Opinion, they proceeded to read in Evidence Page the 2d (in Print the 11th) unparalleled Perfidy, *pretended* Friends, Corruption, lamentable Degeneracy, Public Calamity. Page 3d. Domestic Grievances, iniquitous Schemes, dark Designs, Ambition, Corruption, Destruction of Trade, impoverishing our People, pernicious Views, destructive Practices, iniquitous Power [,] calamitous, dreadful Threats. Page 4, Ambition, Avarice, Rapaciousness, Venality, Credit decaying, Commerce destroyed, Liberties endangered, wicked Practices, shameful Misconduct, flagrant Treachery, arbitrary Wretches, motley Crew, notorious Supporters of Corruption, detestable Relicts of the old Fathers of Iniquity, shameless mercenary Band of Prostitutes. Infamous Deserters of Honour, base Betrayers of their Country, Men without Genius or Capacity, insolent

Intruders, arrogant Supporters, presumptious Power, mean Degeneracy, iniquitous Apostacy, abandoned shameless Creatures, profligate corrupt Services. Page 4. [*sic*] Imps of Power.—At which Words the Corporation of *Grubstreet* being ashamed of their Cause withdrew their Pretensions, and the Court decreed the said Pamphlet to belong justly to *Billinsgate*, and indeed to be the most *Billinsgate* Performance ever exhibited in any Language.

Porcupinus Pelagius, who was convicted of having writ a Panegyri-Satyri-Serio-Comi-nonsensi-unintelligi—Poem, called the '*Piscopade*,[2] was brought to the Bar, and his Council in Arrest of Judgment took Exception to the Indictment. 1. That the Word *Poem* was a Misnomer; for that whatever was not written in any Numbers could not be called a Poem, which being allowed to be good Critical Law, he produced several Passages, and particularly the two first Lines.

> The Cabinet summoned in Council conven'd
> Prodigious Constituents, *answering the End.*

2dly, That the Word *Satiri* or *Satirical* is improperly used on this Occasion; for that an unmannerly Abuse of a whole Body of Men, (as here on the whole Bench of Bishops) is Scandal and not Satire.

3dly, That *de minimis non curat Lex*,[3] and That such Stuff as this is too low for the Consideration of so high a Court of Critical Justice. To support this he referred to the Lines above cited. He likewise cited Line 8. *This here and that there*. Line 17. *Strangely bedumpt took his Place at his Heels*. 20. *As tho' he seem'd griev'd he went down to the Race*. 22. *He follows his Sire like a Tantony Pig*. 28. *Cheek by Jowl with his Brother* 35, 36. *His old Brother Authors look'd on him oblique. Pair'd his Coat with Don* Juan's *and thought them alike*. 45, 46. *Ready to take what Impression he'd give. So the S—f—d Petition he might but survive*. 62. *To pay the just Debt which to pay he was born*. 64. *Let us gain him, quo' he, for a Friend if we can*, &c. &c. &c. 4thly, That this unknown Scribbler, having in a former infamous Work, dared as impudently as unjustly to abuse the noble Person who at present so illustriously presides in *Westminster-Hall*, and who in his high Office doth so much Honour to his Country, all the Scandal of such a Writer for the future is to be deemed Panegyric.[4]

Tho' these Objections were all allowed to be true, the Court said they would not be bound by any other Rules but by those of Equity, and pronounced Sentence of Contempt upon the Author and all his Works.

Ordered, That the Applause of this Court be signified to Mr. *Garrick* and Mrs. *Cibber* for their inimitable Performance in the Play of *Venice preserved.*[5]

M. Cooper moved the Court against one *Thomas Snouch* of *Grub-street*, Printer; for having grubbed a Pamphlet entitled *Drury-lane Playhouse broke open*, to the great Damage of the Author, who had writ it to get a Penny which he very much wanted.[6]

Resolved, That the said Pamphlet is the lawful Property of *Grubstreet*, and that they have a Right to grub the same.

Ordered, That the Pamphlets entitled *The State of the Nation*,[7] and the *Critical Address*, together with the Poem called *The 'Piscopade*, be forthwith grubbed, at one Halfpenny each, or if possible at a less Price.

(*Adjourned.*)

48 From *The Jacobite's Journal*, No. 12

Saturday, February 20, 1748

Proceedings at the Court of Criticism, Thursday Feb. 18

Thomas Carte, *Englishman*, was indicted, for that he, not having the Love of Truth before his Eyes, nor weighing the Duty of an Historian, but being moved and seduced by the instigation of the wicked Spirit of *Jacobitism*, in the Month of —— at *Bristol* one false, foolish, ridiculous, and absurd Story, concerning one *Christopher Lovell* being cured of the King's Evil, by the Touch of a certain *then* un-anointed, eldest, lineal Descendant of a Race of Kings, *&c.* the Property of certain old Women unknown, did steal, take, and, in a vast folio Book, called *A General History of England*, did insert and publish, with a manifest Intention of imposing on weak and credulous People, in Defiance of Common Sense, to the evil Example of all bad Writers of Romances, and against the Truth of History, its Stile and Dignity.[1]

To this Indictment the Prisoner pleaded Not Guilty.

The History was then produced, and Page 291 was read, where, in a Note, this silly Story was found, attested by the Prisoner.

Then the *General Evening Post* was likewise produced and read, by which it appeared, that this ridiculous Story was false in Fact: For that the said *Christopher Lovell* was so far from being cured, that he afterwards died of that Distemper.

The Prisoner made the usual *Old-Bailey* Defence. First, said, *that he found it*; and then offered to impeach one Doctor *Lane*, and Mr. *Samuel Pye*.[2] But the Court gave but little Attention to such idle Stuff, and pronounced him Guilty of the Indictment.

Then the Court proceeded to Sentence in the following Manner: *Thomas Carte*, an *Englishman*, you are convicted of a very high Offence; no less than that of perverting the Intent of History, and applying it to the sordid and paltry Use of a Party.

This is so much the more inexcusable in you, as the Intent with which you inserted this foolish Story manifestly appears, from many Observations you have very properly made on the Credulity of the Vulgar, particularly in Page 390; where speaking of an idle Report which was current among them, you justly add: *So apt are they to swallow the absurdest Stories that can be invented, if they flatter, in any Respect, their Wishes, Passions, or Prejudices.*

Now surely no more absurd Story was ever invented than this of which you are convicted. When, pray, was this healing Power given to Kings? Or is there any Authority to suppose it was ever given? Doth the Scripture make any mention of such a Gift? If it doth not, are we not forbidden in Scripture to believe any such Power of working a Miracle?

Is this Gift bestowed on all Kings indifferently, or is it confined only to those who are Christians? If to the latter, *Charles* the Second, I am afraid, could have no Title to it, if what Bishop *Burnet* says of him, and what his Life so well confirmed, be true, that he was a Deist.[3]

For what Purpose was it given? Not as a Manifestation of Hereditary Right, as you would seem to think. For neither *Edward* the Confessor, nor *Queen Anne*, nor, indeed, one half of our Kings, who have pretended to this Power of healing the Evil, had any such Right. Nay, indeed, when we consider the numerous Offspring which must have proceeded from the many Persons who have been excluded from this Hereditary Right, it is more than possible that no such Right ever rested in the Family of *Stuart*.

At what Time do Princes come to the Possession of this Gift, if it be an Incident inseparable from that Divinity with which some think a Crown invested, and which seems the ancient Opinion, then cannot they exercise it 'till they are in Possession of the Crown; and, consequently, your Story must be, as it hath been proved to be, as false, as foolish and absurd.

Let me ask you one Question; Would you be thought to believe this Story, or to disbelieve it? If the former, what an Historian will you be thought? If the latter, what a Man must you be?

Nothing now remains but that you receive the Judgment of this Court, which is, That your History be forthwith grubbed, for the Use of those for whom it is calculated; and that you, *Thomas Carte*, an *Englishman*, be, and do remain, under the Contempt of this Court.

Other Indictments were preferred against him, for having endeavoured to prove, that a King is not bound by his Coronation Oath, *&c.* but the Court refused to hear them.

Note. He endeavoured to recommend himself to his Honour as a *Jacobite*; but his Honour said, He would always do strict Justice in this Court, without Regard to any Party or Person whatever.

The Court being informed that THE TOWN behaved in a very indecent Manner on *Saturday* last, at the Representation of the New Comedy, to the great Terror of the Actresses, and of several Ladies of the first Quality among the Audience, it was ordered, that *the said Town* be forthwith apprehended, and the Court resolved to proceed against *the said Town*, on *Thursday* next, for the said Offence.[4]

It being humbly represented to the Court, on the Behalf of several Booksellers of Credit, who are Proprietors of a certain *Grub-street* Paper called the *London Evening-Post*, that they are intirely ignorant of the scandalous Matters inserted in that Paper; with which the Writer, Printer, and Publisher are only chargeable. The Court ordered, That the said Booksellers be discharged from all Censure, on Account of every past Offence committed in that Paper; but that they do immediately relinquish their Shares in the same, or do change their said Writer, *&c.* for the future, on Pain of seeing their Names gibbeted in this Journal, together with those of the said Writer, Printer, and Publisher.[5]

(*Adjourned.*)

49 From *The Jacobite's Journal*, No. 13

Saturday, February 27, 1748

Proceedings at the Court of Criticism, Thursday Feb. 25

The Officers to whom the Warrants for apprehending THE TOWN were directed, return'd, that *the said Town* could not be found; but one of the Officers said, he had narrowly miss'd them, at an obscure Coffee house near Hounsditch; upon which the Court awarded another Process, as is usual in Cases of that Nature.

The Court were moved on Behalf of the History of *Thomas Carte*, an *Englishman*, which received Sentence of *grubbing* on *Thursday* last. It was said, that the Historian had, in the *General Evening Post* of *Tuesday* the 23d.[1] alledged in his Defence:

1. That this was inserted in a Note, *only to refute* the erroneous Notion concerning that Sanative Virtue of Touching.

2. That in Order to refute this Notion it was there inserted, *without any Design of publishing it.*

3. That this Note (tho' it hath many apparent Marks of a recent Performance, and manifestly refers to a Transaction long ago) being long since inserted, and unhappily, *without a Mark directing it should be copied*, was transcribed for the Press, and never seen by the Author 'till sent in the Proof Sheet.

4. That the Person touching not being named, what is said of him here *must be agreeable to more than one*, namely, to all the eldest Sons of the late King *James*, tho' he had never so many.

5. That tho' he hath not some Books, nor *a thousand others*, now by him, out of which he hath made Transcripts, he thinks *he may make Use of his Transcripts*; and tho' he should mistake the Name of the Author, or the Book quoted, *that is not material.*

6. That 'he passed some Days, about 26 Years ago, with Mr. *Anstis* at *Mortlake*, when a Pamphlet, wrote by a Surgeon, about the King's Evil, was advertised in the News-papers, and had a good deal of Discourse with him on that Subject; and by what was then said, the (*Carte*) was perswaded, that Mr. *Beckett's* Enquiry into the Antiquity and Efficacy of touching for the King's Evil, printed in 8vo, *A.D.* 1722,

(according to the Booksellers Stile, who begin their Year even before *Christmas*) was the Pamphlet in question;[2] tho' he never saw it, and had entirely forgot the Surgeon's Name, when having Mr. *Anstis's* Discourse abovementioned before him, and consulting a learned Gentleman, who had studied and practised Physic above 40 Years, and transcribed his (*Cart's*) [*sic*] Note for the Press, about the Name of the Surgeon referred to by Mr. *Anstis*, it was either by the Doctor's Opinion, or by his own Inadvertence, that he put down *Tucker* for the Name of the Surgeon.'

Here the Council being told by the Court, that he did not make himself understood, answered, That he could not help it; for he read Mr. *Carte's* own Words, which he could not pretend to say, he understood very well himself.

He then concluded with saying, He hoped the Court would take Pity on an old Man, who appeared to labour under the Incapacities betrayed in the said Letter, and change the Word *Contempt* in the Sentence into *Compassion*; especially as he was willing to submit to be grubbed: for that *since he had published his first Volume*, and found it did not sell, *he was willing to deliver it to such as would subscribe for it in any Manner they pleased.*

The Court having perused his Letter in the *General Evening Post*, took his Infirmities into Consideration, and ordered their Clerk to erase the Word *Contempt*, and to insert, that the said *Carte* be, and is considered by this Court *as an Object of their Compassion.*

Resolved, That it appears to this Court, that the Author of the '*Piscopade* and the Author of *Old England* are one and the same Person.[3]

Ordered, That Mrs. *Cibber* do prepare a good warm Box at her Benefit, for the Reception of Ourself and our fair *Peggy*, where we both intend to appear in our Plaids.[4]

(*Adjourned.*)

50 From *The Jacobite's Journal*, No. 14

Saturday, March 5, 1748

Proceedings at the Court of Criticism, Thursday March 3

The following Letter was read, and approved, and the Thanks of the Court were ordered to be return'd to the Writer.

To John Trott-Plaid, *Esq*; *Censor of* Great Britain.

The Observations on *Clarissa* in your 5th Journal gave me very great Pleasure, not only as being (in my Opinion) extremely just, but as giving me Hopes that something, besides Abuse of an Author, might possibly be received and relish'd by the Publick. But how was I mortified in almost every Set of Company I went into afterwards, by hear-it said with a Sneer, that *Clarissa* was finely *puff'd* in the last *Jacobite Journal*. Pray, Sir, is it fair to call all Commendation *Puffing?* As you have undertaken the Office of Censor, I wish you would endeavour to convince the World how unjust and cruel a Thing it is to give a Name of Reproach to the most deserved Praises that can be bestowed; and at the same time not only to suffer, but to encourage all Sorts of Abuse that can be thrown on the most ingenious Productions of the Age.

This, I am afraid, is a Proof of too much Ill-nature in the Human Composition; but as you have evidently shewn the very Reverse in the Proceedings at your Court, (though I declare you have not, I think, bestowed any undeserved Praise on either Book or Person) I hope by your means to see Commendation and Censure placed upon such an Equality, that neither shall be deem'd other than the Effect of an impartial Perusal; unless upon due Examination it shall be found, that one is the Effect of Malice, Envy, or Ill-nature, or that the other is (that only true Puff) the Breath of Flattery purchased by a Bribe. I promise you I am only an Advocate, and no Party concerned in this Cause; for, unless you think well enough of this short Letter to publish it, I never shall, by appearing in Print, experience the Bitterness of the present prevailing Humour of Criticism, nor the Benefit of a Reformation, should you effect one, being no Writer, but only your constant Reader, and

Humble Servant, &c.

The Pamphlet advertised as written by the Author of the *Dissertation on Parties*,[1] in order to insinuate that it was the Performance of that celebrated Hand, was read, and condemned as a meer Catch-penny, and an Imposition on the Public.

(*Adjourned.*)

51 From *The Jacobite's Journal*, No. 15

Saturday, March 12, 1748

Proceedings at the Court of Criticism, Thursday March 10

A third *non est inventus*[1] being returned upon the Warrant to apprehend THE TOWN, Process of Outlawry was issued against the *said Town*.

One *Porcupine Pillage* came into the Court, and crying out, I am the Author of the *Causidicade*, *Processionade*, *Triumvirade*, *'Piscopade*, and *Old England*,[2] threw a great Shovel-full of Dirt at his Honour, but luckily none of it hit him. He was immediately seized, and being brought to the Bar, the Court delivered themselves as follows:

I am very sorry to see, in an Age when the Liberty of the Press is pretended to be in Danger,[3] such an Abuse made of this Liberty, as must give the greatest Encouragement to its Enemies (if there were any such) to attempt a Restraint of it: For wise and good Men will, by these Means, he brought to esteem this Liberty rather as a Nusance [*sic*], than as a valuable Privilege to the Society.

Nothing ought to be, nor indeed generally is more dear to a Man than his Reputation; and if it be in the Power of every anonymous Scribbler to defame private Characters, and to publish Scandal over the Nation, without Regard either to Truth or Decency, I am apt to think every honest Man will soon wish to see this Power taken from them; and will lose all Aversion to a Law, which shall protect so valuable a Property as Reputation. For when this barbarous and wicked Practice becomes general, the Apprehension of it will reach those who have not yet been attacked, since, according to the vulgar Phrase, Men in a public Calamity know not whose Turn it will next be to suffer.— Thus *Horace*, speaking of the same abominable Custom, says:

———————Jam sævus apertam
In rabiem verti cæpit jocus & per honestas
Ire minax impune domos: doluere cruento
Dente lacessiti; fuit intactis quoque cura
Conditione super communi: Quin etiam lex,
Pænaque lata, malo quæ nollet carmine quenquam
Describi, &c.[4]

Thus translated by the Rev. Mr. *Francis*:[5]

—Cruel Wit soon turn'd to open Rage,
And dar'd the noblest Families engage.
When some who by its Tooth envenom'd, bled,
Complain'd aloud: Others were struck with dread
Tho' yet untouch'd, and in the public Cause,
Implor'd the just Protection of the Laws,
Which from injurious Libels wisely guard
Our Neighbour's Fame.*

Do not affect to misunderstand nor misrepresent me. No Man is more averse to the Destruction of the Liberty of the Press than myself; but I am likewise an Enemy to the Abuse of this Liberty: and it is from this Abuse alone it can ever be destroyed.

Now I must tell you very plainly, that, of all others, you have been the most guilty of this Abuse. In your *Causidicade*, *Processionade*, *&c.* you have attack'd the most eminent Men in the Profession of the Law, and particularly, I once more repeat it, that great and admirable Person who is at the Head of it, and whose Character soars as much above my Panegyric, as above your Slander.[6] Slander, indeed, on such a Character, is, by *Plutarch*, well compared to a Dart thrown against a solid Object, which flies back into the Face of the Darter: For, as *Seneca* well observes, *Qui talibus maledicunt sibi ipsi convicium faciunt.*[7]

In your *'Piscopade*, you have at once fallen upon the whole Privy Council, and upon the whole Bench of Bishops, whom you have traduc'd in a manner not only never permitted with Impunity, but, I believe, never attempted in any Nation.

Consider a Moment with yourself, whether you can imagine any thing more absurd, than for one in your Station of Life to pass Censure on all the greatest and most sacred Characters in the Kingdom, of whom you must be entirely ignorant, as you cannot be supposed to have had Access, even to their upper Servants.

As to your Talents as a Writer, I tell you very sincerely and very candidly too, they range you in the lowest Class. As your Ribaldry is unworthy of the Name of Wit, so your Numbers are no less undeserving of the Honour of Poetry. And if such truly contemptible Stuff should have been more propagated than it ought, do not plume

*The Law was this: If any one sing, or compose Verses injurious to the Reputation of another, let him be punished with Death. And it is remarkable, that this Law was introduced at a Time when the *Roman* Liberties were at the highest.

yourself on that Account: for, believe me, no one of any Taste will ever read you with Approbation; not will you ever be ranked even among the indifferent Poets which this Age produces. The Vulgar are eager after Scandal, from the same Curiosity that makes them flock to Executions; and in either Case their Curiosity is highest when their Superiors are the Sufferers; but the Author, like the Hangman, is so far from gaining their Admiration, that he is hardly ever considered by them. I advise you therefore for the future to lay down your Pen, or to exercise it in your own Profession, where, in the low Branch to which you was bred, you will require no Genius to enable you to succeed. For you need not apprehend having drawn on yourself the Anger of that Great Man, whose high Station must exclude you from his Notice, and whose high Mind will secure you from his Resentment.

However, your abusive Behaviour here, and your Contempt of this Court, must not go without some Punishment. It is considered therefore by this Court, that you, *Porcupine Pillage*, be committed to the Bridewell of *Billinsgate* for the Space of a Month, and that you do stand in the Pillory of our Journal on *Saturday* next, all Day long, with these Verses of *Ausonius* pasted over your Head:

Nec posthæc metues ubique dictum.
Hic est Theon Poeta falsus.*[8]

The Court then proceeded to hear Council for and against the *Foundling*,[9] and said, they would deliver Judgment on *Thursday* next.

Ordered, That Mrs. *Woffington* do prepare a good warm Box at her Benefit on *Monday* next, for the Reception of Ourself and our fair Consort *Peggy*, her Namesake.[10]

(*Adjourned.*)

*The Character which *Erasmus* gives of this *Theon* is, that he was a certain Poet of outragious Loquacity, and most petulant Scurrility, whence Persons whose Names had been scurrilously treated, were said to be bit with *Theon's* Tooth.

52 From *The Jacobite's Journal*, No. 16

Saturday, March 19, 1748

Proceedings at the Court of Criticism, Thursday March 17

The Court upon Motion delivered the following Opinion concerning the *Foundling*.[1]

The Incident upon which this Play is founded, is Mr. *Belmont* bringing into his Father's House, at Midnight, a young Woman who, tho' unknown to the Family, is there received as a Ward of his, left to his Care by a Friend. The Father makes no Objection, nor much Enquiry into the Matter, and the Sister immediately contracts an Intimacy and Friendship with her.

This is too improbable. Some better Story should have been forged by the young Gentleman, or Credulity should at least have been made the Characteristic of the Father; tho' even then the Imposition would have been almost too gross, especially in an Age which doth not greatly relish very *outres* Characters. The Conduct of the Sister is still more un-natural. A young Lady of Fashion would never have been brought even to converse with a Woman under these suspicious Circumstances; nor have been contented with so absurd a Tale, which plainly appears to be, as it really is, a trumped-up-Story: The Beauty of *Fidelia* would have been no Recommendation of her to any of her own Sex, particularly to such as *Rosetta* is described to be; nor have taken off those bad Impressions which the most candid must have received upon her first Appearance.

The Character of *Faddle* is likewise exceptionable: For tho' I do admit, that some very sorry Fellows have been admitted among their Betters, in the Light of Buffoons, who perhaps have been as great Rascals as *Faddle* himself, yet they do not thus openly and plainly appear so. Nor do I believe such a Woman as *Rosetta*, or indeed any other young Lady, ever did or wou'd make Choice of a Fellow of this kind to create Jealousy in a Lover; since she must greatly demean herself by such Conduct. Again, the Behaviour of the Colonel to *Faddle*, in the Presence of his Mistress, is altogether as improper, and foreign to the Manners of upper Life.

These I think are the principal Objections; indeed all which appear to me of any Moment.

Now, on the other Side, the Story of *Fidelia* is extremely pretty and interesting: Her Character is highly amiable, her Distress very tender and affecting, and the Incidents which occasion it are very naturally and artfully contrived. The Character of young *Belmont* is very finely drawn. The Struggles between a virtuous Disposition and vitious Habits are most nobly and usefully painted: The Redemption from evil, by the conscious Shame which results from having a base Action set before him in its true and genuine Deformity, shews great Knowledge of Human Nature in the Author; and perhaps something which is yet more to his Honour.

The Change from bad to good is, I think, more artfully brought about here, than in any other Play, and the Scene which leads to it is one of the finest upon our Stage.

The whole Play abounds with generous and worthy Sentiments, and the Diction is every where lively and full of much Wit and Spirit.

As to the malicious Insinuations of Plagiarism, they do not deserve an Answer: They are indeed made in the true Spirit of modern Criticism.

Of the same Kind is all that hath been said concerning the Confusion in the unravelling the Plot. Indeed the Art with which the Plot is conducted, the Degrees by which it opens, the Incidents which occur in the Progress, and which at last produce the final discovery, deserve great Commendation. To say Truth, the Want of Clearness is, I apprehend, not in the Author but in the Critic.

It hath been said that this is improperly called a Comedy; for that there is much to make you cry, and little to make you laugh. I would remind these Gentlemen of that famous Line in *Horace*, a Book of the highest Authority in this Court.

Interdum tamen & vocem Comœdia tollit.[2]

It is indeed true, that some good Writers, who have chosen a grave Fable for their Comedy, have intermixed inferior Characters of Mirth, as *Steele* in the *Conscious Lovers:*[3] But it must be admitted, at the same Time, that there are Precedents to the contrary, particularly in *Terence*, an Author whom we shall always mention here with the utmost Respect.

Upon the whole, we do adjudge the Comedy of the *Foundling* to be a good Play, and that it do continue to be represented and received as such—and that *the Town*, for their false Clamour, be in our Contempt, &c.

The following Paragraph out of the *London Evening Post* of *Tuesday*, was then ordered to be read.

To the AUTHOR, *&c.*

Saturday, March 12.

'SIR,—As the known pension'd Scribler for the M——try, the Author of *The Jacobite Journal*, has this Day openly thrown off the Mask, and declar'd himself an Advocate for taking away the *Liberty of the Press*, Mankind can no longer doubt of the Designs of his Patrons; and he is not only for taking it away, but for inflicting *Death* on those who make use of this truly *English* Privilege, as appears from a Note at the Bottom of the second Page.'

After which the Court recommended to the Public to revise the Passages in the last Court of Criticism here misrepresented, and then to determine what the Author of the said *London Evening Post* is, and what he deserves.

My Wife *Peggy* hath prevailed with me to go to one Benefit more, *viz*, on *Monday* next, to the *Provok'd Wife*,[4] for the Benefit of Mrs. *Clive*, where my Wife tells me, I shall be sure to see all the Ladies who have any true Taste for Wit and Humour.

(*Adjourned.*)

53 From *The Jacobite's Journal*, No. 20

Saturday, April 16, 1748

Proceedings at the Court of Criticism, Thursday April 14

The following Letter to his Honour was read, and ordered to be printed.

To the Author of the Jacobite Journal.

Sir,—I heartily agree with you, that the Cause of *Jacobitism* is become too serious an Affair, at this Time, to be treated in a ludicrous Manner; and therefore am very well pleased that you have put off the *Fool's Coat*, and re-assumed your *Orange* Colours.[1]

You very well observe—'That every Attempt, with which Malice can supply Invention, is employed to undermine and blow up the Constitution; that Popish Traytors are crept into the Seminaries of Learning, and Libels are dispersed all over the Nation.'—But among the latter, I think there is one that more particularly deserves your Attention.

There is very diligently dispersed, by the Papists, all over this Country,* a Pamphlet called *The* State *preferable to the* Church; *or, Reasons for making Sale of the whole present* Property *of the* Church *in* England *and* Ireland, *for the Use of the* State, &c.[2]—If *Ithuriel's* Spear be applied to this Piece, I fancy it will startle you,

So sudden to behold the grizly King.[3]

The Author has put on an *Orange* Dublet, and in that Guise labours, with Might and Main, to set Priests and People together by the Ears; insisting upon it as necessary, that the former part with their Glebe and Tythes to the latter: This he expects will throw the Nation into a Ferment, and raise a dreadful Outcry of the Church's Danger, which may perhaps pave the Way for his darling Point—a Restoration.

He then tries to remove those Obstacles that may at last possibly prevent his pernicious Intention.—The Church-Lands in Lay-Hands are indeed a main Hindrance, which, as it deserves his utmost Care to remove, so he has bestow'd most Pains upon it, from *p.* 22 to the End

* If needful, I can swear that I received this Book out of the Hands of a Papist.

of his Book; and has endeavoured to prove, that these Lands are more secure to Laymen under a Popish Administration, than they are, or can be, under the present Government; as being not only confirmed to them by Act of Parliament, but settled on them by the Popish Bishops and Clergy, and established to them by the unalterable Decrees of the Popes of *Rome*, by their Legate, and in their own proper Persons.

But that you may not mistake this Author's Intention, take it in his own Words, *p.* 59, *&c.*

'Before I take Leave of you, permit me to make an Observation which arises from the Subject I have been treating of: I have shewn, that if we had continued Papists, the Dispensations of *Rome* would have intirely quieted our Consciences, as to our Possession of Church-Lands; and our Minds, as to any Claim the Clergy might vainly set up, hereafter, to such Possessions: And I have endeavoured to shew likewise the moral Impossibility of an *English* Legislature's repealing that solemn Act, passed the second of *Philip* and *Mary*, to confirm the Rights of those Possessors so dispensed with by the Court of *Rome*.'

'We should have found all these Precautions necessary, if we had remained in Communion with the See of *Rome*; and should our present Infidelity ever throw us back into that mysterious Communion, we shall find these wise Precautions of our Fathers so many impenetrable Bulwarks, behind which our Possession of Church-Lands rests as firm and secure as the THRONE itself; as in *Saxony*, where, *tho' the Prince and his Family be Papists*, his *Protestant* Subjects are, and *think themselves for ever secure*,* in the Possessions of their Church-Lands.'

'The Protestant Possessors likewise of Church-Lands in the *Palatinate*, the Dutchies of *Wirtenberg*, *Baden*, and several other States of *Germany*, are no less secure in their Possession of such Lands, tho' their respective Sovereigns BE RETURN'D to the *Roman* Communion. All are tranquil, all are safe and secure in the Empire, with Regard to Church-Lands: Nor is there any, THE LEAST COLOURABLE PRETEXT FOR OUR BEING OTHERWISE HERE IN *England*, EVEN THO' OUR SOVEREIGNS SHOU'D SWERVE FROM THE ORTHODOXY OF THE REFORMATION.'

'And, Sir, the Observation I would make before I conclude is this, That as we have the Pleasure to find, and think our Possession of *Church-Lands* to be secure at all Events, UNDER ANY KING, AND OF WHAT RELIGION SOEVER HE MAY BE, so have we likewise the Satisfaction to look upon our Properties in the FUNDS to be equally solid and secure.

*Mind the Lyer; True Protestants in *Saxony* do not, nor cannot, think themselves for ever secure.

I admit that Corruption has taken deep and dangerous Root among us of late Years; but, Sir, as it was seldom known that a Man would be corrupted to his own Undoing, nay to the Undoing of his Friends and Relations, in short, of all that he holds dear; how can we suppose that an *English* Legislature will, or can, be corrupted to wipe off any of our Property in the *Funds* with a Parliamentary Sponge? And sure I am, that no Prince, ever so little versed in our Annals, and acquainted with our Tempers, will venture to lessen that Property *without Consent of Parliament.**

'As I take such a Violation to be morally impossible, I should be extremely easy as to the Disposition and RELIGION OF OUR *Future* RULERS, even if the Prospect before us had been less flattering than it is. The Royal Progeny IN VIEW,† promise all the Good we can hope for; but my Comfort shall be always this, THAT LET WHO WILL BE KING, the People will have the Power; and I am sure, they never can want the *Will* to secure their Properties in the *Funds and Church-Lands.*'

Now, Sir, who could have thought that an impudent Papist could have found a Way, in the very Face of the Court, to promote the Interest of the Pretender, and calm the Fears of his Friends? Yet this is done in the Piece before you.—Upon the Whole, it appears plain to me, that there is at this very Time A MOST DANGEROUS PLOT laid against his Majesty, his Crown, and Dignity; and that this Piece is published to prepare the Way for the Execution of it, by setting Clergy and People together by the Ears, and removing those Obstacles that have hitherto been an effectual Bar to a Popish Succession.

I therefore desire, that you'll please to bring this Libel before your next Court of *Criticism*, and there thoroughly sift and examine it, in order to your approving, or condemning it, as you in your great Wisdom shall think it deserves.

I am, SIR,
Your humble Servant,
LANCASTRENSIS

P.S. Would you plainly see a Jesuit in Disguise, look at these Expressions:

Page 59. 'The Clergy of *England* are looked upon by very many, to have sought more the Things of this World, than those Things of *Jesus Christ*; for the obtaining of WHICH (*i.e.* Things of *Jesus Christ*) *their*

*This is copied from the young Pretender's Declaration in *Scotland*.
†It would have been too plain to have said, *The Prince in View*.

Romish *Predecessors under* Philip *and* Mary, *had spontaneously released all Claim to those Things of this World that had been taken from them.'*—Here the Devil appears very plain.

Page 46. 'The Pope, PERHAPS, more tenacious of the Things of this World than he ought.'—A Jesuit durst say no more.

Page 31. 'For my own Part, *whose whole Estate is Church-Land,* I look upon myself to be signally indebted to the cautious Care of my Ancestors, *&c. &c.*'—This is plain Truth in *Jesuitical* Language.

The Court, instead of passing Sentence, recommended the Author to the Notice of higher Courts of Judicature.

(*Adjourned.*)

54 From *The Jacobite's Journal*, No. 21

Saturday, April 23, 1748

Proceedings at the Court of Criticism, Thursday April 21

That Court of Criticism in which we preside is so far from being a Court of Damnation only, that one main End of its Institution is to correct a malevolent Spirit, which at present too generally prevails, and which seems to go about *seeking what it may find Fault with.*

The Part, indeed, of the Critical Office in which we are most delighted, is that which consists in giving Praise and Recommendation to Merit; and this we shall extend to every new Scheme and Invention whatever, that anywise tends to public Utility.

After this Declaration we shall make no further Apology for printing the following Letter. We do indeed agree with the Writer, that had we suppress'd a Plan of so noble a Charity, we should have deserved his severest Censure; nor will those whom it chiefly concerns to carry it into Execution, deserve that Censure less, if they pass it over unregarded, or indeed if they omit immediately setting their Hands to so useful a Work.

The Letter which was read in Court, and ordered to be recommended, is as follows:

Most Noble 'Squire Trott-Plaid,

To penetrate into the Heart of so comical, so odd, and so unaccountable an Animal as you seem to be, is beyond all human Art, and a Task too hard for the D——l himself. Were I to judge of your Principles by what I can gather from a Paper, which has lately made its Appearance in the World under the Title of the *Jacobite Journal*, which, to your immortal Honour, they say you are the Author of, I should take you to be a downright honest Man, and a true *Briton*; one who has the Interest of your Country, and the Good of Mankind, sincerely at Heart. But I may be deceived, tho' I must confess that nothing has so much the Appearance of Honesty as that Warmth with which you recommend any Thing that has the least Shew of public Benefit. I do not know how I can try you better than by offering a Scheme to your

Consideration, which, in my Opinion, must be of great Advantage to this Nation, *viz.* For raising a Fund for maintaining the Widows and Children of inferior and distress'd Clergymen. Now if you are that generous, candid, and well-disposed Creature, that you profess yourself to be, I do not doubt but the Sequel will meet with your Approbation. But, if on the Contrary, you are a sad Dog in the Shape of Goodness, both myself and my Scheme will be the Object of your Ridicule and Contempt: So—without farther Apology here goes—*Parturiunt Montes, nascetur ridiculus Mus.*[1]

In the first Place I will tell you how this Project came into my Head. You must know, then, that some time ago I went with a Friend of mine to visit the Widow of an Officer, who, for the sake of living cheap, is settled in our Neighbourhood. She has two Children, a Boy about eight, and a Girl about ten Years old; and I think a fonder Mother, and more dutiful or lovely Children, I never saw. When we came in, the little Boy was reading to his Mamma, and Miss was working; and, as I found afterwards, they had no other Instructor. I was so charmed with the obliging Behaviour of this Lady, and the Pains that the little ones took to imitate[2] their Mamma, that I could not help saying that I thought she was quite happy in having such Children. She answer'd with a Smile, mix'd with Concern, 'Poor Things, if they had not lost their Papa, it would have been happier for them; but now they have no Friend but me. However, if it should please God to let me live till they are grown up, I hope, tho' I have nothing but my Pension to live on, that I shall be able to give them a virtuous Education; and all I desire is to see them get a Livelihood in an honest Way, tho' a mean one.'—Here I could not help reflecting how happy it was that Women, who were so often left destitute as Officers Widows were, should have such a Provision made for them, as prevented both them and their Children from falling into those Vices, to which Necessity is so irresistable a Temptation. She went on with saying, 'That if she was to begin her Life again, she would not marry an Officer; for, besides the Inconveniency of their frequent Absence from their Families, they seldom left any thing behind, except Children: But still she thought their Widows were happier than the Widows of the Generality of the Clergy, especially the inferior ones, who very often leave a numerous Issue behind them, to be maintained by the Charity of well-disposed People. A meagre Subsistence indeed!' This put me upon thinking, that if the same Thing was done in the Church as is done in the Army, Distresses of this Nature would be easily remedied. I suppose you know, that the Pensions of Officers Widows are paid out of a Fund raised by their giving one Day's Pay in the Year for that Purpose. Now if every Ecclesiastick, from the Archbishop down to the Curate, was to do the same, I'm sure it would raise a Fund large enough not only to maintain the Widows, but likewise to provide for many of their Children. I have mentioned this Scheme to every Parson that I have seen for these three Years last past, which they all to a Man approved; and as it would be a Trifle to each Individual of that Society, and of such infinite Advantage to the Whole, I cannot help thinking, if you would consider, improve, and recommend this Project, but that it would be soon carried into Execution. And what flatters me in this Opinion is, the peculiar Happiness of this Nation at present, in having an Archbishop of so public a Spirit, and so extensive a Benevolence, as Dr. *Herring* is universally acknowledg'd to be:[3] and I doubt not but his Majesty's known Goodness will incline him to give Sanction to a Thing so likely to prevent all that Misery, which at present is felt by many of the Members of this Society for want of such a Provision. I could tell you of a thousand Instances of this sort of Distress, which I have been Witness of.—But this, to a Man who has seen so much of the World as you have, would be impertinent, and only serve to shock your Humanity. And here I might likewise offer some Arguments to recommend this Scheme, as it has the Appearance of public Good, to your Patronage, did not I take you to be one who has too sincere a Pleasure in doing Good, to need any other Incitement to it than the Knowledge of any Object: And as the best of Hearts and of Heads seem to be happily united in you, I hope, as well for your own Interest as the Service of your Country, that you may continue to employ them for the excellent Uses for which they were designed by the Author of them.

With regard to the collecting or paying this Money, I would have none employ'd but either Parsons or their Children; and, to prevent Expence, it may be paid in twice a Year at the Visitations, together with their Procurations.[4] And as for the three first Years, I would have nothing paid out to any one, in order to raise a good Fund at first. Another Advantage that would accrue from this, would be an Opportunity of breeding up to the Church, now-and-then, a Boy of promising Parts, tho' he should always be the Son of a Clergyman. I took the Liberty to give you these Hints, which you may make what Use of you please; and I hope the Goodness of my Intention will excuse my Impertinence. Tho' I must tell you, that if you should bring this to bear, it would give me great Satisfaction, whose Circumstances will not admit of my doing any other Good to the Miserable than that of wishing them well. So—*Si quid novisti rectius istis—candidus imperti; si non, his utere Mecum.*[5] And now, Sir, out of pure Compassion to your Patience, I shall conclude with a Saying of an ingenious Orator, (whom it would be the highest Presumption in me to imitate in any Thing but his Modesty) who, after having made a pathetic Speech on a public Occasion, ended it with these Words, *Si quid recte dixi, hoc est quod volui; si non, hoc est quod potui.*[6]

Yours sincerely,
PHILANTHROPOS.

P.S. I assure you, on my Honour, I am not a Parson.

My Wife hath prevailed with me to go once more to the Play this Season, *viz.* on *Monday* next, to the *Provoked Wife*, for the Benefit of Mr. and Mrs. *Mills*.[7]

As Mr *Garrick* hath very kindly agreed to assist this Benefit with his own Performance, we have no Fear that the Town will do a Violence to their own Pleasure, in order to do the same Violence to their Good-nature.

Mr. *Mills*, who, from his peculiar facetious and good-humour'd Disposition, retains still the Name of *Billy Mills* among his Familiars, is a strong Example of the Fickleness and Inconstancy of Fortune. He hath, by slow Degrees, risen to the Top of Theatrical Greatness, and by as slow Degrees tumbled down again. He succeeded to the grave Parts in Comedy of *Booth*, and to the gayer Characters in which *Wilks* had shined, and maintain'd both with equal Ability.

In Tragedy he hath likewise been very considerable; where, not to dwell on every particular Excellence, he is thought of all others to have made the best Appearance through a Trap-Door: for which Reason those Characters which are in some Part of the Play to enter upon the Stage Head-foremost, generally fell to his Lot.

He was at all times a very safe Actor; and as he never shock'd you with any Absurdity, so he never raised Horror, Terror, Admiration, or any of those turbulent Sensations, to that dangerous Height to which Mr. *Garrick* (however good a Man he may otherwise be) hath been guilty of carrying them.

From the Pinnacle of Theatrical Greatness, where he was once seated, he hath by degrees fallen; not through his own Demerit, (for he is now as good as ever he was) but by the greatest Misfortune in the World, namely, successful Rivals.

This Reverse of Fortune he hath born with Heroic Constancy, and with Christian Resignation. He hath indeed continued always *Honest Billy Mills*; nor have Envy, Malice, or any other Species of Malignity, been able to taint his natural good Disposition.

Indeed his Character in private Life is so amiable, that if the Ladies will patronize one of the best and kindest of Husbands; and the World in general will encourage an honest, good-natured, inoffensive Man, he and his little Family will owe many a future happy Hour to the Public on *Monday* next, and his Benefit, tho' one of the last, will not be one of the least.

(*Adjourned.*)

55 From *The Jacobite's Journal*, No. 22

Saturday, April 30, 1748

Proceedings at the Court of Criticism, Thursday April 28

Samuel Fut,[1] of the Parish of St. *Giles's*, Labourer, was indicted, for that he being a Person of an evil Mind and Conversation, and not having the Fear of either Law or Gospel before his Eyes, but being moved and seduced by the Devil, or some of his Imps, on the 18th of *April*, and at divers other Times, at a Place called and known by the Name of the *Scandal-Shop*, in the *Haymarket*, one Justice of the Peace, one Orator, one Poet, one Lord, one Auctioneer, and divers other Persons, did steal and take off, and with a certain Instrument, called a Hatchet-Face, value Three-half-pence, which he the said *Samuel Fut*, before a certain wooden Head, then and there did wear, and hold, them the said Justice of the Peace, &c., in a certain Part called the Character, then and there wickedly, diabolically, and ridiculously, did maul and hack; and other Injuries to them did, against the Peace, &c.[2]

The Prisoner pleaded Not Guilty.

Then several Lords and Ladies were produced, and sworn, who proved the Fact beyond any Possibility of Doubt. After which the Prisoner being called upon to make his Defence, began to mimick the Court, pulling a Chew of Tobacco from his Mouth, in Imitation of his Honour, who is greatly fond of that Weed.

For this indecent Behaviour he was gently rebuked by his Honour, and advised to consider seriously of his Defence, if he had any to make. But he remaining silent, or rather contumacious, and performing many ridiculous Gestures, he was at last pronounced to be guilty of the Charge.

His Council then moved in Arrest of Judgment. 1. That the Prisoner being on many Accounts obnoxious to the Law of the Land, and having committed this Offence in open Defiance of an Act of Parliament,[3] as well as of the Government, which had refused to license this immoral Performance, was liable to the Censure of higher Courts of Justice, and consequently could not be try'd here. 2. That some of the Persons mimicked were dead, and could not be sensible of any Injury done to their Characters. That Part of the Indictment therefore was vicious, and if Part, the Whole.

To the first of these it was answered, that this Court had a concurrent Jurisdiction, to be exercised at their Discretion: And if the Government are at present too busily employed in Matters of greater Moment, to attend to such Offences, and to give them due Punishment, it becomes more necessary for this Court to exercise that concurrent Jurisdiction; and a Case lately adjudged here was cited, which was exactly in Point.[4]

To the Second; That if any of the Persons mimicked were dead, the Offence was thereby heightened rather than extenuated; since to drag Persons out of their Grave, in order to ridicule them, could be only justifiable in the Case of notorious Criminals; whereas, on the contrary, one of these was a young Nobleman of great Honour, and the other a Magistrate, to whose Care the Public were highly indebted, for having brought many notorious Rogues to Justice; many, perhaps, of the Prisoner's intimate Acquaintance; and had he been now alive, the Prisoner, through his Means, would certainly have shared the same Fate.[5]

The Objections being fully answered and overruled, his Honour proceeded to Sentence in the following Manner:

Samuel Fut, You stand convicted of a very high Crime; a Crime not only contrary to Law, but certainly *contra bonos mores.*[6]

I know not for what Reason, unless, as the Council hath said, because the Government is concerned in more weighty Matters, that you have been suffered to go on so long with Impunity; for surely the Act of Parliament, which was made to prevent Theatrical Abuse, was made on a much less Occasion than you have afforded. Persons have been formerly ridiculed under fictitious Fables and Characters; but surely since the Days of the Old Comedy, none, 'till your Time, have had the Audacity to bring real Facts and Persons upon the Stage: Nay, you have gone even beyond that Old Comedy, which was by Law banished from Athens, as an intolerable Evil; since the Representation by Mimickry is much stronger than that by Painting on a Mask.

Against this Kind of Buffoonry no Innocence can be secure. The most inoffensive Particularity may subject Men to Ridicule; nay, by Means of mixing up much Falsehood with some Truth, a very good and worthy Man may be actually exposed to Infamy.

Nor doth this Buffoonry require any Capacity, unless that of mimicking the Voice, Features, and Gestures of another Man, the meanest and vilest of all Arts. Had those Parts which form either an Author or an Actor been necessary, you know, by Experience, how unequal you must have found yourself to the Task.

And here I must take leave to mention a short Word to those who have encouraged you in this wicked Undertaking, since I find some Persons of Figure have not been ashamed, in giving their Evidence, to own they have more than once been your Spectators.

*It no more becomes a Gentleman,** says an ancient *Greek* Author, *to admit Slander willingly at his Ears, than to give it vent at his Tongue.*[7] And I am inclined to believe, that many (the Ladies especially) would not have been seen at your Slander-Shop, had they suffered themselves seriously to reflect on the Barbarity to which they became in a Manner Accessaries; and in this barbarous Light they would have presently seen your Mimickry, had they but for a Moment made the Case their own; a Circumstance which may perhaps happen to some of them, if this outragious Licentiousness continues to meet with Reward instead of Punishment: For let me tell you there are many as good Mimicks as yourself, and there are some who can supply those Mimicks with better Food than is in your Power.

As for you, happy would it have been for you, and so will the Event prove it, if you had continued to deserve the Addition of Labourer, by which you are indicted; and had endeavoured to get your Bread rather by the Labour of your Hands, than by that of your Face.

But I spend too much Time on one so despicable, and at the same time so incorrigible. I shall proceed therefore to pronounce the Judgment of the Court; which is, that you *Samuel Fut* be p—ssed upon, with Scorn and Contempt, as a low Buffoon; and I do, with the utmost Scorn and Contempt, p—ss upon you accordingly.

The Prisoner was then removed from the Bar, mimicking and pulling a Chew of Tobacco from his Mouth, while the P—ss ran plentifully down his Face.

(*Adjourned.*)

*In *Greek* a *modest Man*; by which they meant the same as the *French* do by an *honest Man*, or as we by the Compound *Gentleman*.

56 From *The Jacobite's Journal*, No. 26

Saturday, May 28, 1748

Proceedings at the Court of Criticism, Thursday May 26

Complaint was made to the Court, on behalf of several Booksellers, against the *Author of Observations* ON THE PROBABLE ISSUE OF *the Congress at Aix-la-Chapelle*, for having fraudulently taken a vast Quantity of Abuse against the Ministry, the Property of the said Booksellers, being contained in divers Pamphlets lately published by them; all which Abuse the said Author had publickly vended as his own.[1]

It was farther set forth, that the said Author, not content with this Theft, had broke open the Garrets of no less than three Gentlemen now employed by the said Booksellers at the high Rate of one Guinea per Sheet, to compose certain Essays, vulgarly called Libels, against the said Ministry; and had there taken and carried away every Thing which the aforesaid Gentlemen had to say on the Subject of the Peace, whatever it should be; the said Observations not containing a single Line, which is not the Property of the said Booksellers, save only two or three in the Title-page, which neither they nor their Authors can read, and of which consequently they do not know the Purport.[2]

Several Affidavits were then read, in Support of the Complaint, upon which it was ordered that the said Author do, on *Thursday* next, shew Cause why he should not be severely censured for these Proceedings.

It was then moved that all Persons might be forbid buying the said Book in the mean Time; but his Honour said there was no Precedent for such Prohibition, and that he believed it was as much in his Power to stop the Progress of Wild-fire.

One *Catchpenny* was indicted for publishing *Remarks on the Preliminary Articles of Peace, as they were lately transmitted to us from the Hague, &c.* by which Title he had taken in divers of his Majesty's unmeaning Subjects in the Sum of one Shilling each, the said Pamphlet in reality containing nothing at all.[3]

He was convicted on the fullest Evidence; but Judgment was arrested, the Indictment being for publishing Remarks on the Preliminary Articles, whereas there are no such Remarks in the Pamphlet.

The said *Catchpenny* was again indicted for publishing a certain execrable Collection of Stuff called *The Foundling Hospital for Wit*;[4] in which he had endeavoured to impose on the World certain Bastards of *Grubstreet*, as the true and legitimate Offspring of Wit, to the great Scandal of all such legitimate Offspring, and contrary to the Statute made against TAKING IN, *&c.*

Of this Offence he was convicted; but as he pleaded his Poverty in Excuse, and alledged that he did it only to get Bread for his Family, the Court, instead of punishing him, gave him half a Crown; but ordered his Book to be grubbed by the common Grubber attending the Court, under the true Title of *an Hospital for Nonsense.*

The Court then ordered the following Proclamation to be read and publish'd:

'Whereas the Number of those People who call themselves Authors encreases daily, to the great Scandal of Learning, and to the no less Prejudice of Trade and Husbandry, both which are thereby deprived of many useful Hands; to the great Loss of the Time, as well as Money, of several well-disposed Persons; and to the great Terror of all who are much known in the World, and have any Regard for their Reputations. And whereas it is impossible for any one Man to read all the Nonsense which is every Week published, and advertis'd in the News-papers; this Court doth earnestly recommend it to all his Majesty's Subjects, who shall happen to have been *taken in* by any of the said People calling themselves Authors, or who shall have other just Matter of Complaint against them, and shall not have Opportunity personally to appear at the said Court, to transmit an Account, by Writing, of the Name and Title of the said pretended Authors, or of their Works, in order that due Proceedings may be had against them, and that the said pretended Authors may be sent back to their respective Trades or Handicrafts, or to the Plough's-Tail, from whence they came.'

(*Adjourned.*)

57 From *The Jacobite's Journal*, No. 27

Saturday, June 4, 1748

Proceedings at the Court of Criticism, Thursday June 2

The Court delivered the following Opinion concerning the *Castle of Indolence*, lately published by Mr. *Thomson*:[1] 'This is a noble allegorical Poem, and truly breathes the Spirit of that Author which it professes to imitate.

'The Description of the Castle is truly poetical, and contains every Image which can be drawn from Nature, suitable to the Occasion. The Author hath, with wonderful Art, brought together all the Inducements to Slumber; and at the same time hath taken sufficient Care that they shall have no Effect on his Reader.

'No less Genius appears in the Wizard's Speech. The *Epicurean* System is here enforced with Arguments of such seeming Solidity, that we cannot wonder if it captivated the Hearers. Their Entrance into the Castle is finely described in the 28th Stanza, and illustrated with a beautiful Simile.

'The Inside of the Castle is described with wonderful Power of Fancy. The Subjects of the Paintings are happily chose [*sic*], and in the exact Spirit of the Antients. The Music likewise is adapted with much Knowledge and Judgment.

'Nothing can be imagined with more Propriety than the Amusements of this Place. The Crystal Globe, in which all the Inhabitants of the Earth are represented, is really a Master-piece, and would have shined in *Homer*, *Virgil*, or *Milton*; nor is the Execution here unequal to so noble a Hint.

'I shall pass over those Parts where the Author hath chosen to pay a Compliment to some of his Friends; tho' I cannot help saying that these are extremely delicate; and what is contained in the 65th and 66th Stanzas, I know to be extremely just; nor less so is, I believe, the Author's Description of himself, tho' the Character is certainly amiable.

'The Prosopopeia, with which the first Stanza concludes, is a fine Allegory, and contains an excellent Moral; and the Introduction of the

Diseases into the Castle by secret Treachery, is one of those nice Touches which, tho' they principally constitute a great Writer, pass often unobserved by the Generality of Readers.

'The Poet's Lamentation at the Beginning of the 2d Stanza; the Generation of the Knight of Arts and Industry; his Education and Accomplishments; his Introduction into *Britain*, and Establishment here; the Mischiefs wrought by Indolence; the Description of the Page; the Sally; the Conversation between the Knight and his Bard; the Attempts of the Wizard; the Bard's Song; the Destruction of the Castle, with the different Fates of those who have suffered under different Degrees of the Enchantment of Indolence; the Erection of the Hospital by the Charities descending from Heaven; and lastly, the Descriptions of Beggary and Scorn, form the principal Incidents of the 2d Stanza; nor is there one of all these which doth not deserve great Commendation.

'Upon the whole, there is much Merit in this Performance; and I do order, that the Thanks of this Court be forthwith signified to Mr. *Thomson*, the Author, for his excellent Composition.'

The Court then proceeded to hear Council on Behalf of the *Observations on the probable Issue of the Congress at Aix-la-Chapelle*. It was admitted that the Book did contain much of the Abuse which hath been already published, and which will hereafter be published against the Ministry; but it was said, that the Author did not look on this as the Property of any particular Bookseller, because it had all been already printed twenty times over by different Persons, and that he therefore imagined it to be *nullius in Boni*,[2] like every Thing else of a base Nature. The Council farther said, that when there was not a single Fact to charge on the Ministry, the only way to write against them must be by general Slander; and unless there was a Liberty granted of transcribing from one another, this would soon be totally exhausted; that such a Restraint therefore would affect the Liberty of the Press, the most valuable Privilege of which is to abuse the Government: Nor could any Injury be thus done to the Proprietors of Libels, since it was manifest by Experience, that the Public will buy the same Scurrility a hundred times over. He said it had been always held lawful to quote the Words of an Author, in order to answer or to expose them; that this was the plain and honest Intention of the Book under Consideration, as would have appeared from the Motto, had the Booksellers or their Authors understood it; for that the literal Translation of it was, 'It is natural to all Men to listen with Pleasure to Calumnies and

Accusations; but to be themselves grieved at the Praises of others.' A Disposition which, he said, greatly prevailed in this Nation at present.

The Court stopt him from proceeding farther, saying, they had perused the Book, and did recommend it to the Public as a true Piece of political Humour, well worth their Perusal; and the Complaint was dismiss'd with Contempt.

(*Adjourned.*)

58 From *The Jacobite's Journal*, No. 33

Saturday, July 16, 1748

Compare the trial of *Amelia*, No. 72.

Proceedings at the Court of Criticism, Thursday, July 14

M. Cooper, late at the *Globe* in *Pater-Noster-Row*, was indicted upon the Statute of TAKING IN, for having lately published a Poem called *The Trial of* Selim *the* Persian;[1] by which Title his Majesty's good Subjects were induced to believe, that a certain great Character was notoriously and scurrilously abused; and many of them were deceived into buying the said Poem, from the same worthy Motive, which leads them to encourage the Works of other modern Authors: But to their great Surprize, as well as Concern, they found no Satire contained in the said Poem; and so they were TAKEN IN, to their great Deceit and Prejudice, contrary to the Form of the said Statute, *&c.*

Thomas Scandal, Esq; (sworn). I bought the Poem of the Defendant, imagining it to have been a Satire against an honourable Gentleman; whereas it is one of the genteelest Panegyrics I ever read.

Prisoner's Council. You shou'd say Abuse; for no Satire can be writ on that Gentleman.

Scandal. I know what I say.

P. Council. Sir, I question whether you do or no—What is the Difference, pray, between Satire and Abuse?

Scandal. I won't answer you.

Mrs. *Grace*, (sworn). I likewise bought the Poem of the Defendant, expecting to have read some pretty Things in it, such as one reads in other Authors; something to make one laugh at some People. Upon my Word, I never was more deceived in my Life.

P. Council. So you expected Abuse too, Madam?

Mrs. *Grace*. I cannot help saying, I did.

P. Council. I am sorry a Lady should have such a Taste.

Mrs. *Grace*. Sir, I am a true *Englishman*, (here was a great Laugh)

Englishwoman, I mean; and I shall always relish Satire against any of the present Copulation of Ministers. (Here was another great Laugh, but the Lady afterwards explained her Meaning to be Coalition.)

A Point of Law now arose, whether this Fact was within the Statute; which having been very learnedly spoke to on both Sides, the Court delivered their Opinion as follows:

I am clearly of Opinion that this Case is neither within the Meaning, nor within the Words of the Statute.

Within the Meaning it cannot be: For this Statute was made to prevent a Custom which hath prevailed much of late, of TAKING IN the Reader by prefixing a pompous and promising Title Page to Books and Pamphlets which contain nothing at all; according to the Case of the Cyclic Author reported by *Horace* in his Laws of Poetry.[2]

But the Author of the Poem now under Consideration hath been so far from doing this, that he promised nothing, and hath performed very much: For what more unpromising Title could he have prefixed to his Book, than the Trial of a Gentleman, whom all the World knows to have committed nothing for which he can be liable to any Censure. A Gentleman of so unblemish'd and unstain'd a Character, that not only Justice, but even Envy and Malice must be, and have been too, obliged to acquit him.

What then cou'd any Person of Common Sense expect from a Performance, of which he must imagine the Author to have been some wretched *Grubstreet* Garreteer? For what Man who had the least Regard to Honour, could abuse such a Character? Nay, who that hath any Regard for Letters, would endeavour falsely to asperse and calumniate almost the only Patron which the Muses at present can boast among the Great?

Nothing, therefore, could be said to have been promised in such a Title; but surely much may be said to be contained in the Poem itself: Much more, indeed, of true Wit than hath lately come from the Press.

Can any Allegory be finer than the following which I will read you.

> Begin we then (as first 'tis fitting)
> With the Three CHIEFS in Judgment sitting.
> Above the rest, and in the Chair,
> Sat FACTION with dissembled Air;
> Her Tongue was skill'd in specious Lies,
> And Murmurs, whence Dissentions rise;

A smiling Mask her Features veil'd,
Her Form the Patriot's Robe conceal'd;
With study'd Blandishments she bow'd,
And drew the captivated Croud.
The next in Place, and on the Right,
Sat ENVY, hideous to the Sight;
Her snaky Locks, her hollow Eyes,
And haggard Form forbad Disguise;
Pale Discontent, and sullen Hate
Upon her wrinkled Forehead sat;
Her Left-hand, clench'd, her Cheek sustain'd,
Her Right (with many a Murder stain'd)
A Dagger clutch'd, in Act to strike,
With Starts of Rage, and Aim oblique.
Last on the Left was CLAMOUR seen,
Of Stature vast, and horrid Mien;
With bloated Cheeks, and frantic Eyes
She sent her Yellings to the Skies;
Prepar'd with Trumpet in her Hand,
To blow Sedition o'er the Land.
With these, Four more of lesser Fame,
And humbler Rank, attendant came;
HYPOCRISY with smiling Grace,
And IMPUDENCE with brazen Face,
CONTENTION bold, with Iron Lungs,
And SLANDER with her hundred Tongues.

The Walls in sculptur'd Tale were rich,
And Statues proud (in many a Nich)
Of Chiefs, who fought in FACTION's Cause,
And perish'd for Contempt of Laws.
The Roof in vary'd Light and Shade,
The Seat of ANARCHY display'd.
Triumphant o'er a falling Throne
(By emblematic Figures known)
CONFUSION rag'd, and LUST obscene,
And RIOT with distemper'd Mein,
And OUTRAGE bold, and MISCHIEF dire,
And DEVASTATION clad in Fire.
Prone on the Ground, a martial Maid

Expiring lay, and groan'd for Aid;
Her Shield with many a Stab was pierc'd,
Her Laurel torn, her Spear revers'd;
And near her, crouch'd amidst the Spoils,
A Lion panted in the Toils.[3]

But if I would read you every Beauty of it, I must go through the whole Poem.

Within the Meaning therefore of the Statute the Prisoner certainly cannot be brought; nor is the Case more within the Words, though I should not, indeed, abide by these with the Rigour of other Courts.

I admit, notwithstanding what I have said, that Satire is promised in the Title-page, and the Witnesses have sworn that they bought it from that Apprehension.

But will any Man say there is no Satire in this Poem? Surely it contains some of the finest and justest that ever was written. Satire on those who, of all others, at present, most deserve it; on the scandalous, flagitious, anonymous Writers of the Age; Wretches, who are the Scandal of the Press, and Pest of Society. Against these, here is as fine and as keen Satire, as can flow from the most spirited Pen.

Upon the whole, I order that the Prisoner be discharged, and I do most earnestly recommend the Poem to the Public, as I do the Author likewise, if ever he should be known, since I am convinced, that the Goodness of his Heart, is, at least, equal to that of his Head.

(*Adjourned.*)

PART NINE

The 'New Province' of Writing

This section contains material relating to the novel in general and to Fielding's novels in particular—the Preface and Book III, ch. 1, of *Joseph Andrews*, the Preface to the Second Edition of Sarah Fielding's *David Simple*, some of the introductory chapters of *Tom Jones* and Fielding's apology for *Amelia* in *The Covent Garden Journal*. Like the other essays and prefaces in this volume, these contain statements which relate directly to topics other than the main one, but they hang together in that they refer more particularly to Fielding's own art than the contents of other sections. Here Fielding outlines his idea of the comic epic in prose, describes the novel as the true history. Yet at the same time these passages contain important statements relating to his concept of comedy (Section VI), the principles of composition (Section V) and the function of the critic (Section III).

59 Preface to *Joseph Andrews*

1742

For details of the text, see above, No. 38.

As it is possible the mere *English* Reader may have a different Idea of Romance with the Author of these little Volumes; and may consequently expect a kind of Entertainment, not to be found, nor which was even intended, in the following Pages; it may not be improper to premise a few Words concerning this kind of Writing, which I do not remember to have seen hitherto attempted in our Language.

The EPIC as well as the DRAMA is divided into Tragedy and Comedy. HOMER, who was the Father of this Species of Poetry, gave us a Pattern of both these, tho' that of the latter kind is entirely lost; which *Aristotle* tells us, bore the same Relation to Comedy which his *Iliad* bears to Tragedy.[1] And perhaps, that we have no more Instances of it among the Writers of Antiquity, is owing to the Loss of this great Pattern, which, had it survived, would have found its Imitators equally with the other Poems of this great Original.

And farther, as this Poetry may be Tragic or Comic, I will not scruple to say it may be likewise either in Verse or Prose: for tho' it wants one particular, which the Critic enumerates in the constituent Parts of an Epic Poem, namely Metre;[2] yet, when any kind of Writing contains all its other Parts, such as Fable, Action, Characters, Sentiments, and Diction, and is deficient in Metre only; it seems, I think, reasonable to refer it to the Epic; at least, as no Critic hath thought proper to range it under any other Head, nor to assign it a particular Name to itself.

Thus the *Telemachus* of the Arch-Bishop of *Cambray*[3] appears to me of the Epic Kind, as well as the *Odyssey* of *Homer*; indeed, it is much fairer and more reasonable to give it a Name common with that Species from which it differs only in a single Instance, than to confound it with those which it resembles in no other. Such are those voluminous Works commonly called *Romances*, namely, *Clelia*,

Cleopatra, *Astræa*, *Cassandra*, the *Grand Cyrus*, and innumerable others which contain, as I apprehend, very little Instruction or Entertainment.[4]

Now a comic Romance is a comic Epic-Poem in Prose; differing from Comedy, as the serious Epic from Tragedy: its Action being more extended and comprehensive; containing a much larger Circle of Incidents, and introducing a greater variety of Characters. It differs from the serious Romance in its Fable and Action, in this; that as in the one these are grave and solemn, so in the other they are light and ridiculous: it differs in its Characters, by introducing Persons of inferiour Rank, and consequently of inferiour Manners, whereas the grave Romance sets the highest before us; lastly in its Sentiments and Diction; by preserving the Ludicrous instead of the Sublime. In the Diction I think, Burlesque itself may be sometimes admitted; of which many Instances will occur in this Work, as in the Descriptions of the Battles, and some other Places, not necessary to be pointed out to the Classical Reader; for whose Entertainment those Parodies or Burlesque Imitations are chiefly calculated.

But tho' we have sometimes admitted this in our Diction, we have carefully excluded it from our Sentiments and Characters: for there it is never properly introduced, unless in Writings of the Burlesque kind, which this is not intended to be. Indeed, no two Species of Writing can differ more widely than the Comic and the Burlesque: for as the latter is ever the Exhibition of what is monstrous and unnatural, and where our Delight, if we examine it, arises from the surprizing Absurdity, as in appropriating the Manners of the highest to the lowest, or *è converso*; so in the former, we should ever confine ourselves strictly to Nature, from the just Imitations of which, will flow all the Pleasure we can this way convey to a sensible Reader. And perhaps, there is one Reason, why a Comic Writer should of all others be the least excused for deviating from Nature, since it may not be always so easy for a serious Poet to meet with the Great and the Admirable; but Life every where furnishes an accurate Observer with the Ridiculous.

I have hinted this little, concerning Burlesque; because, I have often heard that Name given to Performances, which have been truly of the Comic kind, from the Author's having sometimes admitted it in his Diction only; which as it is the Dress of Poetry, doth like the Dress of Men establish Characters, (the one of the whole Poem, and the other of the whole Man), in vulgar Opinion, beyond any of their greater Excellencies: But surely, a certain Drollery in Style, where the Characters and Sentiments are perfectly natural, no more constitutes the

Burlesque, than an empty Pomp and Dignity of Words, where every thing else is mean and low, can entitle any Performance to the Appellation of the true Sublime.

And I apprehend, my Lord *Shaftesbury's* Opinion of mere Burlesque agrees with mine, when he asserts, 'There is no such Thing to be found in the Writings of the Antients.'[5] But perhaps, I have less Abhorrence than he professes for it: and that not because I have had some little Success on the Stage this way; but rather, as it contributes more to exquisite Mirth and Laughter than any other; and these are probably more wholesome Physic for the Mind, and conduce better to purge away Spleen, Melancholy and ill Affections, than is generally imagined Nay, I will appeal to common Observation, whether the same Companies are not found more full of Good Humour and Benevolence, after they have been sweeten'd for two or three Hours with Entertainments of this kind, than when soured by a Tragedy or a grave Lecture.

But to illustrate all this by another Science, in which, perhaps, we shall see the Distinction more clearly and plainly: Let us examine the Works of a Comic History-Painter, with those Performances which the *Italians* call *Caricatura*; where we shall find the true Excellence of the former to consist in the exactest Copy of Nature; insomuch, that a judicious Eye instantly rejects any thing *outré*; any Liberty which the Painter hath taken with the Features of that *Alma Mater*.— Whereas in the *Caricatura* we allow all Licence. Its Aim is to exhibit Monsters not Men; and all Distortions and Exaggerations whatever are within its proper Province.

Now what *Caricatura* is in Painting, Burlesque is in Writing; and in the same manner the Comic Writer and Painter correlate to each other. And here I shall observe, that as in the former, the Painter seems to have the Advantage; so it is in the latter infinitely on the side of the Writer: for the *Monstrous* is much easier to paint than describe, and the *Ridiculous* to describe than paint.

And tho' perhaps this latter Species doth not in either Science so strongly affect and agitate the Muscles as the other; yet it will be owned, I believe, that a more rational and useful Pleasure arises to us from it. He who should call the Ingenious *Hogarth* a Burlesque Painter, would, in my Opinion, do him very little Honour: for sure it is much easier, much less the Subject of Admiration, to paint a Man with a Nose, or any other Feature of a preposterous Size, or to expose him in some absurd or monstrous Attitude, than to express the Affections of

Men on Canvas. It hath been thought a vast Commendation of a Painter, to say his Figures *seem to breathe*; but surely, it is a much greater and nobler Applause, *that they appear to think*.

But to return—— The Ridiculous only, as I have before said, falls within my Province in the present Work.—Nor will some Explanation of this Word be thought impertinent by the Reader, if he considers how wonderfully it hath been mistaken, even by Writers who have profess'd it: for to what but such a Mistake, can we attribute the many Attempts to ridicule the blackest Villanies; and what is yet worse, the most dreadful Calamities? What could exceed the Absurdity of an Author, who should write *the Comedy of Nero, with the merry Incident of ripping up his Mother's Belly*; or what would give a greater Shock to Humanity, than an Attempt to expose the Miseries of Poverty and Distress to Ridicule? And yet, the Reader will not want much Learning to suggest such Instances to himself.

Besides, it may seem remarkable, that *Aristotle*, who is so fond and free of Definitions, hath not thought proper to define the Ridiculous. Indeed, where he tells us it is proper to Comedy, he hath remarked that Villany is not its Object: but he hath not, as I remember, positively asserted what is. Nor doth the *Abbé Bellegarde*, who hath writ a Treatise on this Subject, tho' he shews us many Species of it, once trace it to its Fountain.[6]

The only Source of the true Ridiculous (as it appears to me) is Affectation. But tho' it arises from one Spring only, when we consider the infinite Streams into which this one branches, we shall presently cease to admire at the copious Field it affords to an Observer. Now Affectation proceeds from one of these two Causes; Vanity, or Hypocrisy: for as Vanity puts us on affecting false Characters, in order to purchase Applause; so Hypocrisy sets us on an Endeavour to avoid censure by concealing our Vices under an Appearance of their opposite Virtues. And tho' these two Causes are often confounded, (for they require some Difficulty in distinguishing;) yet, as they proceed from very different Motives, so they are as clearly distinct in their Operations: for indeed, the Affectation which arises from Vanity is nearer to Truth than the other; as it hath not that violent Repugnancy of Nature to struggle with, which that of the Hypocrite hath. It may be likewise noted, that Affectation doth not imply an absolute Negation of those Qualities which are affected: and therefore, tho', when it proceeds from Hypocrisy, it be nearly allied to Deceit; yet when it comes from Vanity only, it partakes of the Nature of Ostentation: for instance, the Affectation of Liberality in a vain Man, differs visibly from the same Affectation in the Avaricious; for tho' the vain Man is not what he would appear, or hath not the Virtue he affects, to the degree he would be thought to have it; yet it sits less aukwardly on him than on the avaricious Man, who *is* the very Reverse of what he would *seem* to be.

From the Discovery of this Affectation arises the Ridiculous—which always strikes the Reader with Surprize and Pleasure; and that in a higher and stronger Degree when the Affectation arises from Hypocrisy, than when from Vanity: for to discover any one to be the exact Reverse of what he affects, is more surprizing, and consequently more ridiculous, than to find him a little deficient in the Quality he desires the Reputation of. I might observe that our *Ben Johnson*, who of all Men understood the *Ridiculous* the best, hath chiefly used the hypocritical Affectation.

Now from Affectation only, the Misfortunes and Calamities of Life, or the Imperfections of Nature, may become the Objects of Ridicule. Surely he hath a very ill-framed Mind, who can look on Ugliness, Infirmity, or Poverty, as ridiculous in themselves: nor do I believe any Man living who meets a dirty Fellow riding through the Streets in a Cart, is struck with an Idea of the Ridiculous from it; but if he should see the same Figure descend from his Coach and Six, or bolt from his Chair with his Hat under his Arm, he would then begin to laugh, and with justice. In the same manner, were we to enter a poor House, and behold a wretched Family shivering with Cold and languishing with Hunger, it would not incline us to Laughter, (at least we must have very diabolical Natures, if it would:) but should we discover there a Grate, instead of Coals, adorned with Flowers, empty Plate or China Dishes on the Side-board, or any other Affectation of Riches and Finery either on their Persons or in their Furniture; we might then indeed be excused, for ridiculing so fantastical an Appearance. Much less are natural Imperfections the Objects of Derision: but when Ugliness aims at the Applause of Beauty, or Lameness endeavours to display Agility; it is then that these unfortunate Circumstances, which at first moved our Compassion, tend only to raise our Mirth.

The Poet carries this very far;

> None are for being what they are in Fault,
> But for not being what they would be thought.[7]

Where if the Metre would suffer the Word *Ridiculous* to close the first Line, the Thought would be rather more proper. Great Vices are the proper Objects of our Detestation, smaller Faults of our Pity: but Affectation appears to me the only true Source of the Ridiculous.

But perhaps it may be objected to me, that I have against my own Rules introduced Vices, and of a very black Kind into this Work. To which I shall answer: First, that it is very difficult to pursue a Series of human Actions and keep clear from them. Secondly, That the Vices to be found here, are rather the accidental Consequences of some human Frailty, or Foible, than Causes habitually existing in the Mind. Thirdly, That they are never set forth as the Objects of Ridicule but Detestation. Fourthly, That they are never the principal Figure at that Time on the Scene; and lastly, they never produce the intended Evil.

Having thus distinguished *Joseph Andrews* from the Productions of Romance Writers on the one hand, and Burlesque Writers on the other, and given some few very short Hints (for I intended no more) of this Species of writing, which I have affirmed to be hitherto unattempted in our Language; I shall leave to my good-natur'd Reader to apply my Piece to my Observations, and will detain him no longer than with a Word concerning the Characters in this Work.

And here I solemnly protest, I have no Intention to vilify or asperse any one: for tho' every thing is copied from the Book of Nature, and scarce a Character or Action produced which I have not taken from my own Observations and Experience, yet I have used the utmost Care to obscure the Persons by such different Circumstances, Degrees, and Colours, that it will be impossible to guess at them with any degree of Certainty; and if it ever happens otherwise, it is only where the Failure characterized is so minute, that it is a Foible only which the Party himself may laugh at as well as any other.

As to the Character of *Adams*, as it is the most glaring in the whole, so I conceive it is not to be found in any Book now extant. It is designed a Character of perfect Simplicity; and as the Goodness of his Heart will recommend him to the Good-natur'd; so I hope it will excuse me to the Gentlemen of his Cloth; for whom, while they are worthy of their sacred Order, no Man can possibly have a greater Respect. They will therefore excuse me, notwithstanding the low Adventures in which he is engaged, that I have made him a Clergyman; since no other Office could have given him so many Opportunities of displaying his worthy Inclinations.

60 From *Joseph Andrews* (1742), Book III, ch. i

Matter prefatory in Praise of Biography

Notwithstanding the Preference which may be vulgarly given to the Authority of those Romance-Writers, who intitle their Books, the History of *England*, the History of *France*, of *Spain*, &c. it is most certain, that Truth is only to be found in the Works of those who celebrate the Lives of Great Men, and are commonly called Biographers, as the others should indeed be termed Topographers or Chorographers: Words which might well mark the Distinction between them; it being the Business of the latter chiefly to describe Countries and Cities, which, with the Assistance of Maps, they do pretty justly, and may be depended upon: But as to the Actions and Characters of Men, their Writings are not quite so authentic, of which there needs no other Proof than those eternal Contradictions, occurring between two Topographers who undertake the History of the same Country: For instance, between my Lord *Clarendon* and Mr. *Whitlock*, between Mr. *Echard* and *Rapin*, and many others;[1] where Facts being set forth in a different Light, every Reader believes as he pleases, and indeed the more judicious and suspicious very justly esteem the whole as no other than a Romance, in which the Writer hath indulged a happy and fertile Invention. But tho' these widely differ in the Narrative of Facts; some ascribing Victory to the one, and others to the other Party: Some representing the same Man as a Rogue, while others give him a great and honest Character, yet all agree in the Scene where the Fact is supposed to have happened; and where the Person, who is both a Rogue, and an honest Man, lived. Now with us Biographers the Case is different, the Facts we deliver may be relied on, tho' we often mistake the Age and Country wherein they happened: For tho' it may be worth the Examination of Critics, whether the Shepherd *Chrysostom*, who, as *Cervantes* informs us, died for Love of the fair *Marcella*, who hated him, was ever in *Spain*, will any one doubt but that such a silly Fellow hath really existed?[2] Is there in the World such a Sceptic as to disbelieve the Madness of *Cardenio*, the Perfidy of *Ferdinand*, the impertinent Curiosity of *Anselmo*, the Weakness of *Camilla*, the irresolute Friendship of *Lothario*;[3] tho' perhaps as to the Time and Place where those several Persons lived, that good Historian may be deplorably deficient: But the most known Instance of this kind is in the true History of *Gil-Blas*, where the inimitable Biographer hath made a notorious Blunder in the Country of Dr. *Sangrardo*, who used his Patients as a Vintner doth his Wine-Vessels, by letting out their Blood, and filling them up with Water.[4] Doth not every one, who is the least versed in Physical History, know that *Spain* was not the Country in which this Doctor lived? The same Writer hath likewise erred in the Country of his Archbishop, as well as that of those great Personages whose Understandings were too sublime to taste any thing but Tragedy,[5] and in many others. The same Mistakes may likewise be observed in *Scarron*, the *Arabian Nights*, the History of *Marianne* and *Le Paisan Parvenu*, and perhaps some few other Writers of this Class, whom I have not read, or do not at present recollect;[6] for I would by no means be thought to comprehend those Persons of surprizing Genius, the Authors of immense Romances, or the modern Novel and *Atalantis*[7] Writers; who without any Assistance from Nature or History, record Persons who never were, or will be, and Facts which never did nor possibly can happen: Whose Heroes are of their own Creation, and their Brains the Chaos whence all their Materials are collected. Not that such Writers deserve no Honour; so far otherwise, that perhaps they merit the highest: for what can be nobler than to be as an Example of the wonderful Extent of human Genius. One may apply to them what *Balzac* says of *Aristotle*, that they are *a second Nature*;[8] for they have no Communication with the first; by which Authors of an inferior Class, who cannot stand alone, are obliged to support themselves as with Crutches; but these of whom I am now speaking, seem to be possessed of *those Stilts*, which the excellent *Voltaire* tells us in his Letters *carry the Genius far off, but with an irregular Pace*.[9] Indeed far out of the sight of the Reader, *Beyond the Realm of Chaos and old Night*.[10]

But, to return to the former Class, who are contented to copy Nature, instead of forming Originals from the confused heap of Matter in their own Brains; is not such a Book as that which records the Atchievements of the renowned *Don Quixotte*, [*sic*] more worthy the Name of a History than even *Mariana's*:[11] for whereas the latter is confined to a particular Period of Time, and to a particular Nation; the former is the History of the World in general, at least that Part which is polished by Laws, Arts and Sciences; and of that from the time it was first polished to this day; nay and forwards, as long as it shall so remain.

I shall now proceed to apply these Observations to the Work before us; for indeed I have set them down principally to obviate some Constructions, which the Good-nature of Mankind, who are always forward to see their Friend's Virtues recorded, may put to particular parts. I question not but several of my Readers will know the Lawyer in the Stage-Coach, the Moment they hear his Voice. It is likewise odds, but the Wit and the Prude meet with some of their Acquaintance, as well as all the rest of my Characters. To prevent therefore any such malicious Applications, I declare here once for all, I describe not Men, but Manners; not an Individual, but a Species. Perhaps it will be answered, Are not the Characters then taken from Life? To which I answer in the Affirmative; nay, I believe I might aver, that I have writ little more than I have seen. The Lawyer is not only alive, but hath been so these 4000 Years, and I hope G—— will indulge his Life as many yet to come. He hath not indeed confined himself to one Profession, one Religion, or one Country; but when the first mean selfish Creature appeared on the human Stage, who made Self the Centre of the whole Creation; would give himself no Pain, incur no Danger, advance no Money to assist, or preserve his Fellow-Creatures; then was our Lawyer born; and whilst such a Person as I have described, exists on Earth, so long shall he remain upon it. It is therefore doing him little Honour, to imagine he endeavours to mimick some little obscure Fellow, because he happens to resemble him in one particular Feature, or perhaps in his Profession; whereas his Appearance in the World is calculated for much more general and noble Purposes; not to expose one pitiful Wretch, to the small and contemptible Circle of his Acquaintance; but to hold the Glass to thousands in their Closets, that they may contemplate their Deformity, and endeavour to reduce it, and thus by suffering private Mortification may avoid public Shame. This places the Boundary between, and distinguishes the Satirist from the Libeller; for the former privately corrects the Fault for the Benefit of the Person, like a Parent; the latter publickly exposes the Person himself, as an Example to others, like an Executioner.

There are besides little Circumstances to be considered, as the Drapery of a Picture which tho' Fashion varies at different Times, the Resemblance of the Countenance is not by those means diminished. Thus, I believe, we may venture to say, Mrs. *Tow-wouse* is coeval with our Lawyer, and tho' perhaps during the Changes, which so long an

Existence must have passed through, she may in her Turn have stood behind the Bar at an Inn, I will not scruple to affirm, she hath likewise in the Revolution of Ages sat on a Throne. In short where extreme Turbulency of Temper, Avarice, and an Insensibility of human Misery, with a Degree of Hypocrisy, have united in a female Composition, Mrs. *Tow-wouse* was that Woman; and where a good Inclination eclipsed by a Poverty of Spirit and Understanding, hath glimmer'd forth in a Man, that Man hath been no other than her sneaking Husband.

I shall detain my Reader no longer than to give him one Caution more of an opposite kind: For as in most of our particular Characters we mean not to lash Individuals, but all of the like sort; so in our general Descriptions, we mean not Universals, but would be understood with many Exceptions: For instance, in our Description of high People, we cannot be intended to include such, as whilst they are an Honour to their high Rank, by a well-guided Condescension, make their Superiority as easy as possible, to those whom Fortune hath chiefly placed below them. Of this number I could name a Peer no less elevated by Nature than by Fortune, who whilst he wears the noblest Ensigns of Honour on his Person, bears the truest Stamp of Dignity on his Mind, adorned with Greatness, enriched with Knowledge, and embelished [*sic*] with Genius. I have seen this Man relieve with Generosity, while he hath conversed with Freedom, and be to the same Person a Patron and a Companion. I could name a Commoner raised higher above the Multitude by superior Talents, than is in the power of his Prince to exalt him; whose Behaviour to those he hath obliged is more amiable than the Obligation itself, and who is so great a Master of Affability, that if he could divest himself of an inherent Greatness in his Manner, would often make the lowest of his Acquaintance forget who was the Master of that Palace, in which they are so courteously entertained. These are Pictures which must be, I believe, known: I declare they are taken from the Life, nor are intended to exceed it.[12] By those high People therefore whom I have described, I mean a Sett [*sic*] of Wretches, who while they are a Disgrace to their Ancestors, whose Honours and Fortunes they inherit or (perhaps a greater to their Mother, for such Degeneracy is scarce credible) have the Insolence to treat those with disregard, who have been equal to the Founders of their own Splendor. It is, I fancy, impossible to conceive a Spectacle more worthy of our Indignation, than that of a Fellow who is not only a Blot in the Escutcheon of a great Family, but a Scandal to the human

Species, maintaining a supercilious Behaviour to Men who are an Honour to their Nature, and a Disgrace to their Fortune.

And now, Reader, taking these Hints along with you, you may, if you please, proceed to the Sequel of this our true History.

61 Preface to *The Adventures of David Simple*

1744

Sarah Fielding's novel, *The Adventures of David Simple*, was first published early in 1744. The Preface reprinted below was first published in the second edition (some time after May, 1744).

As so many worthy Persons have, I am told, ascribed the Honour of this Performance to me, they will not be surprized at seeing my Name to this Preface: Nor am I very insincere, when I call it an Honour; for if the Authors of the Age are amongst the Number of those who have conferred it on me, I know very few of them to whom I shall return the Compliment of such a Suspicion.

I could indeed have been very well content with the Reputation, well knowing that some Writings may be justly laid to my charge, of a Merit greatly inferior to that of the following Work; had not the Imputation directly accused me of Falshood, in breaking a Promise, which I have solemnly made in Print, of never publishing, even a Pamphlet, without setting my Name to it: A Promise I have always hitherto faithfully kept; and, for the sake of Men's Characters, I wish all other Writers were by Law obliged to use the same Method: but, 'till they are, I shall no longer impose any such Restraint on myself.[1]

A second Reason which induces me to refute this Untruth, is, that it may have a Tendency to injure me in a Profession, to which I have applied with so arduous and intent a Diligence, that I have had no Leisure, if I had Inclination, to compose any thing of this kind.[2] Indeed I am very far from entertaining such an Inclination; I know the Value of the Reward, which Fame confers on Authors, too well, to endeavour any longer to obtain it; nor was the World ever more unwilling to bestow the glorious, envied Prize of the Laurel or Bays, than I should now be to receive any such Garland or Fool's Cap. There is not, I believe, (and it is bold to affirm) a single *Free Briton* in this Kingdom, who hates his Wife more heartily than I detest the Muses. They have indeed behaved to me like the most infamous Harlots, and have laid many a spurious, as well as deformed Production at my Door: In all which, my good Friends the Critics have, in their profound Discernment, discovered some Resemblance of the Parent; and thus I have been reputed and reported the Author of half the Scurrility, Bawdy, Treason and Blasphemy, which these few last Years have produced.

I am far from thinking every Person who hath thus aspersed me, had a determinate Design of doing me an Injury; I impute it only to an idle, childish Levity, which possesses too many Minds, and makes them report their Conjectures as Matters of Fact, without weighing the Proof, or considering the Consequence. But as to the former of these, my Readers will do well to examine their own Talents very strictly, before they are too thoroughly convinced of their Abilities to distinguish an Author's Style so accurately, as from that only to pronounce an anonymous Work to be his: And as to the latter, a little Reflection will convince them of the Cruelty they are guilty of by such Reports. For my own part, I can aver, that there are few Crimes, of which I should have been more ashamed, than of some Writings laid to my charge. I am as well assured of the Injuries I have suffered from such unjust Imputations, not only in general Character, but as they have, I conceive, frequently raised me inveterate Enemies, in Persons to whose Disadvantage I have never entertained a single Thought; nay, in Men whose Characters, and even Names have been unknown to me.

Among all the Scurrilities with which I have been accused, (tho' equally and totally innocent of every one) none ever raised my Indignation so much as the *Causidicade*:[3] this accused me not only of being a bad Writer, and a bad Man, but with downright Idiotism, in flying in the Face of the greatest Men of my Profession. I take therefore this Opportunity to protest, that I never saw that infamous, paultry Libel, till long after it had been in Print; nor can any Man hold it in greater Contempt and Abhorrence than myself.

The Reader will pardon my dwelling so long on this Subject, as I have suffered so cruelly by these Aspersions in my own Ease, in my Reputation, and in my Interest. I shall however henceforth treat such Censure with the Contempt it deserves; and do here revoke the Promise I formerly made; so that I shall now look upon myself at full Liberty to publish an anonymous Work, without any Breach of Faith. For tho' probably I shall never make any use of this Liberty, there is no reason why I should be under a Restraint, for which I have not enjoyed the purposed Recompence.

A third, and indeed the strongest Reason which hath drawn me into Print, is to do Justice to the real and sole Author of this little Book; who, notwithstanding the many excellent Observations dispersed through it, and the deep Knowledge of Human Nature it discovers, is a young Woman; one so nearly and dearly allied to me, in the highest Friendship as well as Relation, that if she had wanted any Assistance of mine, I would have been as ready to have given it her, as I would have been just to my Word in owning it: but in reality, two or three Hints which arose on the reading it, and some little Direction as to the Conduct of the second Volume, much the greater Part of which I never saw till in Print, were all the Aid she received from me. Indeed I believe there are few Books in the World so absolutely the Author's own as this.

There were some Grammatical and other Errors in Style in the first Impression, which my Absence from Town prevented my correcting, as I have endeavoured, tho' in great Haste, in this Edition: By comparing the one with the other, the Reader may see, if he thinks it worth his while, the Share I have in this Book, as it now stands, and which amounts to little more than the Correction of some small Errors, which Want of Habit in Writing chiefly occasioned, and which no Man of Learning would think worth his Censure in a Romance; nor any Gentleman, in the Writings of a young Woman.

And as the Faults of this Work want very little Excuse, so its Beauties want as little Recommendation: tho' I will not say but they may sometimes stand in need of being pointed out to the generality of Readers. For as the Merit of this Work consists in a vast Penetration into human Nature, a deep and profound Discernment of all the Mazes, Windings and Labyrinths, which perplex the Heart of Man to such a degree, that he is himself often incapable of seeing through them; and as this is the greatest, noblest, and rarest of all the Talents which constitute a Genius; so a much larger Share of this Talent is necessary, even to recognize these Discoveries, when they are laid before us, than falls to the share of a common Reader. Such Beauties therefore in an Author must be contented to pass often unobserved and untasted; whereas, on the contrary, the Imperfections of this little Book, which arise, not from want of Genius, but of Learning, lie open to the Eyes of every Fool, who has had a little *Latin* inoculated into his Tail; but had the same great Quantity of Birch been better employ'd, in scourging away his Ill-nature, he would not have exposed it in endeavouring to cavil at the first Performance of one, whose Sex and Age entitle her to the gentlest Criticism, while her Merit, of an infinitely higher kind, may defy the severest. But I believe the Warmth of my Friendship hath led me to engage a Critic of my own Imagination only: for I should be sorry to conceive such a one had any real Existence. If however any such Composition of Folly, Meanness and Malevolence should actually exist, he must be as incapable of Conviction, as unworthy of an Answer. I shall therefore proceed to the more pleasing Task of pointing out some of the Beauties of this little Work.

I have attempted in my Preface to *Joseph Andrews* to prove, that every Work of this kind is in its Nature a comic Epic Poem, of which *Homer* left us a Precedent, tho' it be unhappily lost.

The two great Originals of a serious Air, which we have derived from that mighty Genius, differ principally in the Action, which in the *Iliad* is entire and uniform; in the *Odyssey*, is rather a Series of Actions, all tending to produce one great End. *Virgil* and *Milton* are, I think, the only pure Imitators of the former; most of the other *Latin*, as well as *Italian*, *French*, and *English* Epic Poets, chusing rather the history of some War, as *Lucan* and *Silius Italicus*; or a Series of Adventures, as *Ariosto*, &c. for the Subject of their Poems.

In the same manner the Comic Writer may either fix on one Action, as the Authors of *Le Lutrin*,[4] the *Dunciad*, &c. or on a Series, as *Butler* in Verse, and *Cervantes* in Prose have done.

Of this latter kind is the Book now before us, where the Fable consists of a Series of separate Adventures detached from, and independent on each other, yet all tending to one great End; so that those who should object want of Unity of Action here, may, if they please, or if they dare, fly back with their Objection, in the Face even of the *Odyssey* itself.

This Fable hath in it these three difficult Ingredients, which will be found on Consideration to be always necessary to Works of this kind, *viz.* that the main End or Scope be at once amiable, ridiculous and natural.

If it be said, that some of the Comic Performances I have above mentioned differ in the first of these, and set before us the odious instead of the amiable; I answer, that is far from being one of their Perfections; and of this the Authors themselves seem so sensible, that they endeavour to deceive their Reader by false Glosses and Colours, and by the help of Irony at least to represent the Aim and Design of their Heroes in a favourable and agreeable Light.

I might farther observe, that as the Incidents arising from this Fable, tho' often surprising, are every where natural, (Credibility not being once shocked through the whole) so there is one Beauty very apparent, which hath been attributed by the greatest of Critics to the greatest of Poets, that every Episode bears a manifest Impression of the principal Design, and chiefly turns on the Perfection or Imperfection of Friendship; of which noble Passion, from its highest Purity to its lowest Falsehoods and Disguises, this little Book is, in my Opinion, the most exact Model.

As to the Characters here described, I shall repeat the Saying of one of the greatest Men of this Age, *That they are as wonderfully drawn by the Writer, as they were by* Nature *herself.*[5] There are many Strokes in *Orgueil*, *Spatter*, *Varnish*, *Le-vif*, the *Balancer*, and some others, which would have shined in the Pages of *Theophrastus*, *Horace*, or *La Bruyere*. Nay, there are some Touches, which I will venture to say might have done honour to the Pencil of the immortal *Shakespear* himself.

The Sentiments are in general extremely delicate; those particularly which regard Friendship, are, I think, as noble and elevated as I have any where met with: Nor can I help remarking, that the Author hath been so careful, in justly adapting them to her Characters, that a very indifferent Reader, after he is in the least acquainted with the Character of the Speaker, can seldom fail of applying every Sentiment to the Person who utters it. Of this we have the strongest Instance in *Cynthia* and *Camilla*, where the lively Spirit of the former, and the gentle Softness of the latter, breathe through every Sentence which drops from either of them.

The Diction I shall say no more of, than as it is the last, and lowest Perfection in a Writer, and one which many of great Genius seem to have little regarded; so I must allow my Author to have the least Merit on this Head: Many Errors in Style existing in the first Edition, and some, I am convinced, remaining still uncured in this; but Experience and Habit will most certainly remove this Objection; for a good Style, as well as a good Hand in Writing, is chiefly learn'd by Practice.

I shall here finish these short Remarks on this little Book, which have been drawn from me by those People, who have very falsely and impertinently called me it's Author. I declare I have spoken no more than my real Sentiments of it, nor can I see why any Relation or Attachment to Merit, should restrain me from its Commendation.

The true Reason why some have been backward in giving this Book its just Praise, and why others have sought after some more known and experienced Author for it, is, I apprehend, no other than an Astonishment how one so young, and, in appearance, so unacquainted with the World, should know so much both of the better and worse Part, as is here exemplified: But, in reality, a very little Knowledge of the World will afford an Observer, moderately accurate, sufficient Instances of Evil; and a short Communication with her own Heart, will leave the Author of this Book very little to seek abroad of all the Good which is to be found in Human Nature.

HENRY FIELDING.

62 From *The History of Tom Jones, a Foundling* (1749), Book I, ch. i

Tom Jones was probably published on April 13, 1749. The text reprinted below is reproduced from the Henley Edition (1903)

BOOK I

CONTAINING AS MUCH OF THE BIRTH OF THE FOUNDLING AS IS NECESSARY OR PROPER TO ACQUAINT THE READER WITH IN THE BEGINNING OF THIS HISTORY

*

CHAPTER 1

THE INTRODUCTION TO THE WORK, OR BILL OF FARE TO THE FEAST

An author ought to consider himself, not as a gentleman who gives a private or eleemosynary treat, but rather as one who keeps a public ordinary, at which all persons are welcome for their money. In the former case, it is well known that the entertainer provides what fare he pleases; and though this should be very indifferent, and utterly disagreeable to the taste of his company, they must not find any fault; nay, on the contrary, good breeding forces them outwardly to approve and to commend whatever is set before them. Now the contrary of this happens to the master of an ordinary. Men who pay for what they eat will insist on gratifying their palates, however nice and even whimsical these may prove; and if everything is not agreeable to their taste will challenge a right to censure, to abuse, and to d—n their dinner without control.

To prevent, therefore, giving offence to their customers by any such disappointment, it hath been usual with the honest and well-meaning host to provide a bill of fare which all persons may peruse at their first entrance into the house; and having thence acquainted themselves with the entertainment which they may expect, may either stay and regale with what is provided for them, or may depart to some other ordinary better accommodated to their taste.

As we do not disdain to borrow wit or wisdom from any man who is capable of lending us either, we have condescended to take a hint from these honest victuallers, and shall prefix not only a general bill of fare to our whole entertainment, but shall likewise give the reader particular bills to every course which is to be served up in this and the ensuing volumes.

The provision, then, which we have here made is no other than *Human Nature*. Nor do I fear that my sensible reader, though most luxurious in his taste, will start, cavil, or be offended, because I have named but one article. The tortoise—as the alderman of Bristol, well learned in eating, knows by much experience—besides the delicious calibash and calipee, contains many different kinds of food;[1] nor can the learned reader be ignorant that in human nature, though here collected under one general name, is such prodigious variety that a cook will have sooner gone through all the several species of animal and vegetable food in the world than an author will be able to exhaust so extensive a subject. An objection may perhaps be apprehended from the more delicate, that this dish is too common and vulgar; for what else is the subject of all the romances, novels, plays, and poems, with which the stalls abound? Many exquisite viands might be rejected by the epicure, if it was a sufficient cause for his contemning of them as common and vulgar, that something was to be found in the most paltry alleys under the same name. In reality, true nature is as difficult to be met with in authors as the Bayonne ham, or Bologna sausage, is to be found in the shops.

But the whole, to continue the same metaphor, consists in the cookery of the author; for, as Mr. Pope tells us,

> True wit is nature to advantage drest;
> What oft was thought, but ne'er so well exprest.[2]

The same animal which hath the honor to have some part of his flesh eaten at the table of a duke, may perhaps be degraded in another part, and some of his limbs gibbeted, as it were, in the vilest stall in town. Where, then, lies the difference between the food of the nobleman and the porter, if both are at dinner on the same ox or calf, but in the seasoning, the dressing, the garnishing, and the setting forth? Hence the one provokes and incites the most languid appetite, and the other turns and palls that which is the sharpest and keenest.

In like manner, the excellence of the mental entertainment consists less in the subject than in the author's skill in well dressing it up. How pleased, therefore, will the reader be to find that we have, in the following work, adhered closely to one of the highest principles of the best cook which the present age, or perhaps that of Heliogabalus,[3] hath produced. This great man, as is well known to all polite lovers of eating, begins at first by setting plain things before his hungry guests, rising afterwards by degrees as their stomachs may be supposed to decrease, to the very quintessence of sauce and spices. In like manner, we shall represent human nature at first to the keen appetite of our reader, in that more plain and simple manner in which it is found in the country, and shall hereafter hash and ragoo[4] it with all the high French and Italian seasoning of affectation and vice which courts and cities afford. By these means, we doubt not but our reader may be rendered desirous to read on forever, as the great person just abovementioned is supposed to have made some persons eat.

Having premised thus much, we will now detain those who like our bill of fare no longer from their diet, and shall proceed directly to serve up the first course of our history for their entertainment.

63 From *The History of Tom Jones . . .*, Book II, ch. i

BOOK II

CONTAINING SCENES OF MATRIMONIAL FELICITY IN DIFFERENT DEGREES OF LIFE; AND VARIOUS OTHER TRANSACTIONS DURING THE FIRST TWO YEARS AFTER THE MARRIAGE BETWEEN CAPTAIN BLIFIL, AND MISS BRIDGET ALLWORTHY

*

CHAPTER 1

SHOWING WHAT KIND OF A HISTORY THIS IS; WHAT IT IS LIKE, AND WHAT IT IS NOT LIKE

Though we have properly enough entitled this our work, a history, and not a life; nor an apology for a life, as is more in fashion;[1] yet we intend in it rather to pursue the method of those writers who profess to disclose the revolutions of countries, than to imitate the painful and voluminous historian who, to preserve the regularity of his series, thinks himself obliged to fill up as much paper with the detail of months and years in which nothing remarkable happened, as he employs upon those notable eras when the greatest scenes have been transacted on the human stage.

Such histories as these do, in reality, very much resemble a newspaper, which consists of just the same number of words, whether there be any news in it or not. They may likewise be compared to a stage coach, which performs constantly the same course, empty as well as full. The writer, indeed, seems to think himself obliged to keep even pace with time, whose amanuensis he is; and, like his master, travels as slowly through centuries of monkish dulness, when the world seems to have been asleep, as through that bright and busy age so nobly distinguished by the excellent Latin poet—

Ad confligendum venientibus undique pœnis,
Omnia cum belli trepido concussa tumultu

Horrida contremuere sub altis ætheris auris;
In dubioque fuit sub utrorum regna cadendum
Omnibus humanis esset, terraque marique.

Of which we wish we could give our readers a more adequate translation than that by Mr. Creech:

When dreadful Carthage frighted Rome with arms,
And all the world was shook with fierce alarms;
Whilst undecided yet which part should fall,
Which nation rise the glorious lord of all.[2]

Now it is our purpose, in the ensuing pages, to pursue a contrary method. When any extraordinary scene presents itself (as we trust will often be the case), we shall spare no pains nor paper to open it at large to our reader; but if whole years should pass without producing anything worthy his notice, we shall not be afraid of a chasm in our history; but shall hasten on to matters of consequence, and leave such periods of time totally unobserved.

These are indeed to be considered as blanks in the grand lottery of time. We, therefore, who are the registers of that lottery, shall imitate those sagacious persons who deal in that which is drawn at Guildhall, and who never trouble the public with the many blanks they dispose of; but when a great prize happens to be drawn, the newspapers are presently filled with it, and the world is sure to be informed at whose office it was sold: indeed, commonly two or three different offices lay claim to the honor of having disposed of it; by which, I suppose, the adventurers are given to understand that certain brokers are in the secrets of Fortune, and indeed of her cabinet council.[3]

My reader then is not to be surprised if, in the course of this work, he shall find some chapters very short, and others altogether as long: some that contain only the time of a single day, and others that comprise years; in a word, if my history sometimes seems to stand still, and sometimes to fly. For all which I shall not look on myself as accountable to any court of critical jurisdiction whatever: for as I am, in reality, the founder of a new province of writing, so I am at liberty to make what laws I please therein. And these laws my readers, whom I consider as my subjects, are bound to believe in and to obey; with which that they may readily and cheerfully comply, I do hereby assure them that I shall principally regard their ease and advantage in all such institutions; for I do not, like a *jure divino* tyrant,[4] imagine that they are my slaves, or my commodity. I am, indeed, set over them for their own good only, and was created for their use, and not they for mine. Nor do I doubt, while I make their interest the great rule of my writings, they will unanimously concur in supporting my dignity, and in rendering me all the honor I shall deserve or desire.

64 From *The History of Tom Jones . . .*, Book IV, ch. i

BOOK IV

CONTAINING THE TIME OF A YEAR

*

CHAPTER I

CONTAINING FIVE PAGES OF PAPER

As truth distinguishes our writings from those idle romances which are filled with monsters, the productions, not of nature, but of distempered brains, and which have been therefore recommended by an eminent critic to the sole use of the pastry-cook,[1] so, on the other hand, we would avoid any resemblance to that kind of history which a celebrated poet seems to think is no less calculated for the emolument of the brewer, as the reading it should be always attended with a tankard of good ale—

> While—history with her comrade ale,
> Soothes the sad series of her serious tale.[2]

For as this is the liquor of modern historians, nay, perhaps their muse, if we may believe the opinion of Butler, who attributes inspiration to ale,[3] it ought likewise to be the potation of their readers, since every book ought to be read with the same spirit and in the same manner as it is writ. Thus the famous author of *Hurlothrumbo* told a learned bishop that the reason his lordship could not taste the excellence of his piece was that he did not read it with a fiddle in his hand, which instrument he himself had always had in his own when he composed it.

That our work, therefore, might be in no danger of being likened to the labors of these historians, we have taken every occasion of interspersing through the whole sundry similes, descriptions, and other kind of poetical embellishments. These are, indeed, designed to supply the place of the said ale, and to refresh the mind, whenever those slumbers, which in a long work are apt to invade the reader as well as the writer, shall begin to creep upon him. Without interruptions of this kind, the best narrative of plain matter of fact must overpower every reader; for nothing but the everlasting watchfulness, which Homer hath ascribed to Jove himself,[4] can be proof against a newspaper of many volumes.

We shall leave to the reader to determine with what judgment we have chosen the several occasions for inserting these ornamental parts of our work. Surely it will be allowed that none could be more proper than the present, where we are about to introduce a considerable character on the scene; no less, indeed, than the heroine of this heroic, historical, prosaic poem. Here, therefore, we have thought proper to prepare the mind of the reader for her reception, by filling it with every pleasing image which we can draw from the face of nature. And for this method we plead many precedents. First, this is an art well known to, and much practised by, our tragic poets, who seldom fail to prepare their audience for the reception of their principal characters.

Thus the hero is always introduced with a flourish of drums and trumpets, in order to rouse a martial spirit in the audience, and to accommodate their ears to bombast and fustian, which Mr. Lock's blind man would not have grossly erred in likening to the sound of a trumpet.[5] Again, when lovers are coming forth, soft music often conducts them on the stage, either to soothe the audience with the softness of the tender passion, or to lull and prepare them for that gentle slumber in which they will most probably be composed by the ensuing scene.

And not only the poets, but the masters of these poets, the managers of playhouses, seem to be in this secret; for, besides the aforesaid kettle-drums, etc., which denote the hero's approach, he is generally ushered on the stage by a large troop of half a dozen scene-shifters; and how necessary these are imagined to his appearance, may be concluded from the following theatrical story:

King Pyrrhus was at dinner at an ale-house bordering on the theatre, when he was summoned to go on the stage. The hero, being unwilling to quit his shoulder of mutton, and as unwilling to draw on himself the indignation of Mr. Wilks (his brother-manager) for making the audience wait, had bribed these his harbingers to be out of the way. While Mr. Wilks, therefore, was thundering out, 'Where are the carpenters to walk on before King Pyrrhus?' that monarch very quietly eat his mutton, and the audience, however impatient, were obliged to entertain themselves with music in his absence.[6]

To be plain, I must question whether the politician, who hath generally a good nose, hath not scented out somewhat of the utility of this practice. I am convinced that awful magistrate my lord-mayor contracts a good deal of that reverence which attends him through the year, by the several pageants which precede his pomp. Nay, I must confess that even I myself, who am not remarkably liable to be captivated with show, have yielded not a little to the impressions of much preceding state. When I have seen a man strutting in a procession, after others whose business hath been only to walk before him, I have conceived a higher notion of his dignity than I have felt on seeing him in a common situation. But there is one instance which comes exactly up to my purpose. This is the custom of sending on a basket-woman, who is to precede the pomp at a coronation, and to strew the stage with flowers, before the great personages begin their procession. The ancients would certainly have invoked the goddess Flora for this purpose, and it would have been no difficulty for their priests or politicians to have persuaded the people of the real presence of the deity, though a plain mortal had personated her and performed her office. But we have no such design of imposing on our reader; and therefore those who object to the heathen theology may, if they please, change our goddess into the above-mentioned basket-woman. Our intention, in short, is to introduce our heroine with the utmost solemnity in our power, with an elevation of style, and all other circumstances proper to raise the veneration of our reader. Indeed we would, for certain causes, advise those of our male readers who have any hearts to read no farther, were we not well assured that how amiable soever the picture of our heroine will appear, as it is really a copy from nature, many of our fair countrywomen will be found worthy to satisfy any passion, and to answer any idea of female perfection which our pencil will be able to raise.

And now, without any further preface, we proceed to our next chapter.

65 From *The History of Tom Jones . . .*, Book V, ch. i

BOOK V

CONTAINING A PORTION OF TIME SOMEWHAT LONGER THAN HALF A YEAR

★

CHAPTER I

OF THE *serious* IN WRITING, AND FOR WHAT PURPOSE IT IS INTRODUCED

Peradventure there may be no parts in this prodigious work which will give the reader less pleasure in the perusing than those which have given the author the greatest pains in composing. Among these probably may be reckoned those initial essays which we have prefixed to the historical matter contained in every book; and which we have determined to be essentially necessary to this kind of writing, of which we have set ourselves at the head.

For this our determination we do not hold ourselves strictly bound to assign any reason, it being abundantly sufficient that we have laid it down as a rule necessary to be observed in all prosai-comi-epic writing. Whoever demanded the reasons of that nice unity of time or place which is now established to be so essential to dramatic poetry? What critic hath been ever asked, why a play may not contain two days as well as one? Or why the audience (provided they travel, like electors, without any expense)[1] may not be wafted fifty miles as well as five? Hath any commentator well accounted for the limitation which an ancient critic hath set to the drama, which he will have contain neither more nor less than five acts?[2] Or hath any one living attempted to explain what the modern judges of our theatres mean by that word *low*; by which they have happily succeeded in banishing all humor from the stage, and have made the theatre as dull as a drawing-room? Upon all these occasions the world seems to have embraced a maxim of our law, viz., *cuicunque in arte sua perito credendum est*:[3] for it seems perhaps difficult to conceive that any one should have had enough of impudence to lay down dogmatical rules in any art or science without the least foundation. In such cases, therefore, we are apt to conclude there are sound and good reasons at the bottom, though we are unfortunately not able to see so far.

Now, in reality, the world have paid too great a compliment to critics, and have imagined them men of much greater profundity than they really are. From this complacence the critics have been emboldened to assume a dictatorial power, and have so far succeeded that they are now become the masters, and have the assurance to give laws to those authors from whose predecessors they originally received them.

The critic, rightly considered, is no more than the clerk, whose office it is to transcribe the rules and laws laid down by those great judges whose vast strength of genius hath placed them in the light of legislators, in the several sciences over which they presided. This office was all which the critics of old aspired to; nor did they ever dare to advance a sentence, without supporting it by the authority of the judge from whence it was borrowed.

But in the process of time, and in ages of ignorance, the clerk began to invade the power and assume the dignity of his master. The laws of writing were no longer founded on the practice of the author, but on the dictates of the critic. The clerk became the legislator, and those very peremptorily gave laws whose business it was, first, only to transcribe them.

Hence arose an obvious and perhaps an unavoidable error; for these critics being men of shallow capacities, very easily mistook mere form for substance. They acted as a judge would, who should adhere to the lifeless letter of law, and reject the spirit. Little circumstances, which were perhaps accidental in a great author, were by these critics considered to constitute his chief merit, and transmitted as essentials to be observed by all his successors. To these encroachments time and ignorance, the two great supporters of imposture, gave authority; and thus many rules for good writing have been established which have not the least foundation in truth or nature, and which commonly serve for no other purpose than to curb and restrain genius, in the same manner as it would have restrained the dancing-master, had the many excellent treatises on that art laid it down as an essential rule that every man must dance in chains.

To avoid, therefore, all imputation of laying down a rule for posterity founded only on the authority of *ipse dixit*—for which, to say the truth, we have not the profoundest veneration—we shall here waive all the privilege above contended for, and proceed to lay before the reader the reasons which have induced us to intersperse these several digressive essays in the course of this work.

And here we shall of necessity be led to open a new vein of knowledge, which, if it hath been discovered, hath not, to our remembrance, been wrought on by any ancient or modern writer. This vein is no other than that of contrast, which runs through all the works of the creation, and may probably have a large share in constituting in us the idea of all beauty, as well natural as artificial: for what demonstrates the beauty and excellence of anything but its reverse? Thus the beauty of day, and that of summer, is set off by the horrors of night and winter. And, I believe, if it was possible for a man to have seen only the two former, he would have a very imperfect idea of their beauty.

But to avoid too serious an air: can it be doubted but that the finest woman in the world would lose all benefit of her charms in the eye of a man who had never seen one of another cast? The ladies themselves seem so sensible of this that they are all industrious to procure foils: nay, they will become foils to themselves: for I have observed (at Bath particularly) that they endeavor to appear as ugly as possible in the morning, in order to set off that beauty which they intend to show you in the evening.

Most artists have this secret in practice, though some, perhaps, have not much studied the theory. The jeweller knows that the finest brilliant requires a foil; and the painter, by the contrast of his figures, often acquires great applause. A great genius among us will illustrate this matter fully. I cannot, indeed, range him under any general head of common artists, as he hath a title to be placed among those.

Inventas qui vitam excoluere per artes.

Who by invented arts have life improved.[4]

I mean here the inventor of that most exquisite entertainment called the English Pantomime.[5]

This entertainment consisted of two parts, which the inventor distinguished by the names of the serious and the comic. The serious exhibited a certain number of heathen gods and heroes, who were certainly the worst and dullest company into which an audience was ever introduced; and (which was a secret known to few) were actually intended so to be, in order to contrast the comic part of the entertainment, and to display the tricks of harlequin to the better advantage.

This was, perhaps, no very civil use of such personages: but the contrivance was, nevertheless, ingenious enough, and had its effect. And this will now plainly appear if, instead of serious and comic, we supply the words duller and dullest; for the comic was certainly duller than anything before shown on the stage, and could be set off only by that superlative degree of dulness which composed the serious. So intolerably serious, indeed, were these gods and heroes, that harlequin (though the English gentleman of that name is not at all related to the French family, for he is of a much more serious disposition) was always welcome on the stage, as he relieved the audience from worse company.

Judicious writers have always practised this art of contrast with great success. I have been surprised that Horace should cavil at this art in Homer; but indeed he contradicts himself in the very next line:

Indignor quandoque bonus dormitat Homerus;
Verùm operi longo fas est obrepere somnum.

I grieve if e'er great Homer chance to sleep,
Yet slumbers on long works have right to creep.[6]

For we are not here to understand, as perhaps some have, that an author actually falls asleep while he is writing. It is true that readers are too apt to be so overtaken; but if the work was as long as any of Oldmixon,[7] the author himself is too well entertained to be subject to the least drowsiness. He is, as Mr. Pope observes,

Sleepless himself to give his readers sleep.[8]

To say the truth, these soporific parts are so many scenes of serious artfully interwoven, in order to contrast and set off the rest; and this is the true meaning of a late facetious writer, who told the public that whenever he was dull they might be assured there was a design in it.[9]

In this light, then, or rather in this darkness, I would have the reader to consider these initial essays. And after this warning, if he shall be of opinion that he can find enough of serious in other parts of this history, he may pass over these, in which we profess to be laboriously dull, and begin the following books at the second chapter.

66 From *The History of Tom Jones . . .*, Book VIII, ch. i

BOOK VIII

CONTAINING ABOUT TWO DAYS

★

CHAPTER I

A WONDERFUL LONG CHAPTER CONCERNING THE MARVELLOUS; BEING MUCH THE LONGEST OF ALL OUR INTRODUCTORY CHAPTERS

As we are now entering upon a book in which the course of our history will oblige us to relate some matters of a more strange and surprising kind than any which have hitherto occurred, it may not be amiss, in the prolegomenous or introductory chapter, to say something of that species of writing which is called the marvellous. To this we shall, as well for the sake of ourselves as of others, endeavor to set some certain bounds, and indeed nothing can be more necessary, as critics* of different complexions are here apt to run into very different extremes; for while some are, with M. Dacier, ready to allow that the same thing which is impossible may be yet probable,†[1] others have so little historic or poetic faith that they believe nothing to be either possible or probable, the like to which hath not occurred to their own observation.

First, then, I think it may very reasonably be required of every writer that he keeps within the bounds of possibility; and still remembers that what it is not possible for man to perform, it is scarce possible for man to believe he did perform. This conviction perhaps gave birth to many stories of the ancient heathen deities (for most of them are of poetical origin). The poet, being desirous to indulge a wanton and extravagant imagination, took refuge in that power, of the extent of

*By this word here, and in most other parts of our work, we mean every reader in the world.

†It is happy for M. Dacier that he was not an Irishman.

which his readers were no judges, or rather, which they imagined to be infinite, and consequently they could not be shocked at any prodigies related of it. This hath been strongly urged in defence of Homer's miracles; and it is, perhaps, a defence; not, as Mr. Pope would have it, because Ulysses told a set of foolish lies to the Phæacians, who were a very dull nation;[2] but because the poet himself wrote to heathens, to whom poetical fables were articles of faith. For my own part, I must confess, so compassionate is my temper, I wish Polypheme had confined himself to his milk diet, and preserved his eye; nor could Ulysses be much more concerned than myself when his companions were turned into swine by Circe, who showed, I think, afterwards, too much regard for a man's flesh to be supposed capable of converting it into bacon. I wish, likewise, with all my heart, that Homer could have known the rule prescribed by Horace, to introduce supernatural agents as seldom as possible.[3] We should not then have seen his gods coming on trivial errands, and often behaving themselves so as not only to forfeit all title to respect, but to become the objects of scorn and derision. A conduct which must have shocked the credulity of a pious and sagacious heathen; and which could never have been defended, unless by agreeing with a supposition to which I have been sometimes almost inclined, that this most glorious poet, as he certainly was, had an intent to burlesque the superstitious faith of his own age and country.

But I have rested too long on a doctrine which can be of no use to a Christian writer; for as he cannot introduce into his works any of that heavenly host which make a part of his creed, so it is horrid puerility to search the heathen theology for any of those deities who have been long since dethroned from their immortality. Lord Shaftesbury observes that nothing is more cold than the invocation of a muse by a modern;[4] he might have added that nothing can be more absurd. A modern may with much more elegance invoke a ballad, as some have thought Homer did, or a mug of ale, with the author of *Hudibras*;[5] which latter may perhaps have inspired much more poetry, as well as prose, than all the liquors of Hippocrene or Helicon.

The only supernatural agents which can in any manner be allowed to us moderns are ghosts; but of these I would advise an author to be extremely sparing. These are, indeed, like arsenic, and other dangerous drugs in physic, to be used with the utmost caution; nor would I advise the introduction of them at all in those works, or by those authors, to which, or to whom, a horse-laugh in the reader would be any great prejudice or mortification.

As for elves and fairies, and other such mummery, I purposely omit the mention of them, as I should be very unwilling to confine within any bounds those surprising imaginations, for whose vast capacity the limits of human nature are too narrow, whose works are to be considered as a new creation, and who have consequently just right to do what they will with their own.

Man, therefore, is the highest subject (unless on very extraordinary occasions indeed) which presents itself to the pen of our historian, or of our poet; and, in relating his actions, great care is to be taken that we do not exceed the capacity of the agent we describe.

Nor is possibility alone sufficient to justify us; we must keep likewise within the rules of probability. It is, I think, the opinion of Aristotle; or if not, it is the opinion of some wise man, whose authority will be as weighty when it is as old, 'That it is no excuse for a poet who relates what is incredible, that the thing related is really matter of fact.'[6] This may, perhaps, be allowed true with regard to poetry, but it may be thought impracticable to extend it to the historian; for he is obliged to record matters as he finds them, though they may be of so extraordinary a nature as will require no small degree of historical faith to swallow them. Such was the successless armament of Xerxes described by Herodotus, or the successful expedition of Alexander related by Arrian.[7] Such of later years was the victory of Agincourt obtained by Harry the Fifth, or that of Narva won by Charles the Twelfth of Sweden.[8] All which instances, the more we reflect on them, appear still the more astonishing.

Such facts, however, as they occur in the thread of the story, nay, indeed, as they constitute the essential parts of it, the historian is not only justifiable in recording as they really happened, but, indeed, would be unpardonable should he omit or alter them. But there are other facts not of such consequence nor so necessary, which, though ever so well attested, may nevertheless be sacrificed to oblivion in complacence to the skepticism of a reader. Such is that memorable story of the ghost of George Villers, which might with more propriety have been made a present of to Dr. Drelincourt, to have kept the ghost of Mrs. Veale company, at the head of his Discourse upon Death, than have been introduced into so solemn a work as the *History of the Rebellion*.[9]

To say the truth, if the historian will confine himself to what really happened, and utterly reject any circumstance, which, though never so well attested, he must be well assured is false, he will sometimes fall into the marvellous, but never into the incredible. He will often raise the wonder and surprise of his reader, but never that incredulous hatred mentioned by Horace.[10] It is by falling into fiction, therefore, that we generally offend against this rule, of deserting probability, which the historian seldom, if ever, quits till he forsakes his character and commences a writer of romance. In this, however, those historians who relate public transactions, have the advantage of us who confine ourselves to scenes of private life. The credit of the former is by common notoriety supported for a long time; and public records, with the concurrent testimony of many authors, bear evidence to their truth in future ages. Thus a Trajan and an Antoninus, a Nero and a Caligula, have all met with the belief of posterity; and no one doubts but that men so very good, and so very bad, were once the masters of mankind.[11]

But we who deal in private character, who search into the most retired recesses, and draw forth examples of virtue and vice from holes and corners of the world, are in a more dangerous situation. As we have no public notoriety, no concurrent testimony, no records to support and corroborate what we deliver, it becomes us to keep within the limits not only of possibility, but of probability too; and this more especially in painting what is greatly good and amiable. Knavery and folly, though never so exorbitant, will more easily meet with assent; for ill-nature adds great support and strength to faith.

Thus we may, perhaps, with little danger, relate the history of Fisher, who, having long owed his bread to the generosity of Mr. Derby, and having one morning received a considerable bounty from his hands, yet, in order to possess himself of what remained in his friend's scrutoire, concealed himself in a public office of the Temple, through which there was a passage into Mr. Derby's chambers. Here he overheard Mr. Derby for many hours solacing himself at an entertainment which he that evening gave his friends, and to which Fisher had been invited. During all this time, no tender, no grateful reflections arose to restrain his purpose; but when the poor gentleman had let his company out through the office, Fisher came suddenly from his lurking-place, and walking softly behind his friend into his chamber, discharged a pistol-ball into his head. This may be believed when the bones of Fisher are as rotten as his heart. Nay, perhaps it will be credited that the villain went two days afterwards with some young ladies to the play of *Hamlet*; and with an unaltered countenance heard one of the ladies, who little suspected how near she was to the person, cry out, 'Good God! if the man that murdered Mr. Derby was now present!' manifesting in this a more seared and callous conscience than even Nero himself, of whom we are told by Suetonius, 'that the consciousness of his guilt, after the death of his mother, became immediately intolerable, and so continued; nor could all the congratulations of the soldiers, of the senate, and the people, allay the horrors of his conscience.'[12]

But now, on the other hand, should I tell my reader that I had known a man whose penetrating genius had enabled him to raise a large fortune in a way where no beginning was chalked out to him; that he had done this with the most perfect preservation of his integrity, and not only without the least injustice or injury to any one individual person, but with the highest advantage to trade, and a vast increase of the public revenue; that he had expended one part of the income of this fortune in discovering a taste superior to most, by works where the highest dignity was united with the purest simplicity, and another part in displaying a degree of goodness superior to all men, by acts of charity to objects whose only recommendations were their merits, or their wants; that he was most industrious in searching after merit in distress, most eager to relieve it, and then as careful (perhaps too careful) to conceal what he had done; that his house, his furniture, his gardens, his table, his private hospitality, and his public beneficence, all denoted the mind from which they flowed, and were all intrinsically rich and noble, without tinsel, or external ostentation; that he filled every relation in life with the most adequate virtue; that he was most piously religious to his Creator, most zealously loyal to his sovereign; a most tender husband to his wife, a kind relation, a munificent patron, a warm and firm friend, a knowing and a cheerful companion, indulgent to his servants, hospitable to his neighbors, charitable to the poor, and benevolent to all mankind. Should I add to these the epithets of wise, brave, elegant, and indeed every other amiable epithet in our language, I might surely say,

> —*Quis credet? nemo Hercule! nemo;*
> *Vel duo, vel nemo;*[13]

and yet I know a man who is all I have here described.[14] But a single instance (and I really know not such another) is not sufficient to justify us while we are writing to thousands who never heard of the person, nor of anything like him. Such *raræ aves* should be remitted to the epitaph writer, or to some poet who may condescend to hitch him in a distich or to slide him into a rhyme with an air of carelessness and neglect, without giving any offence to the reader.

In the last place, the actions should be such as may not only be within the compass of human agency, and which human agents may probably be supposed to do; but they should be likely for the very actors and characters themselves to have performed; for what may be only wonderful and surprising in one man, may become improbable, or indeed impossible, when related of another.

This last requisite is what the dramatic critics call conservation of character; and it requires a very extraordinary degree of judgment, and a most exact knowledge of human nature.

It is admirably remarked by a most excellent writer that zeal can no more hurry a man to act in direct opposition to itself than a rapid stream can carry a boat against its own current.[15] I will venture to say that for a man to act in direct contradiction to the dictates of his nature is, if not impossible, as improbable and as miraculous as anything which can well be conceived. Should the best parts of the story of M. Antoninus be ascribed to Nero, or should the worst incidents of Nero's life be imputed to Antoninus, what would be more shocking to belief than either instance! whereas both these being related of their proper agent, constitute the truly marvellous.

Our modern authors of comedy have fallen almost universally into the error here hinted at; their heroes generally are notorious rogues, and their heroines abandoned jades, during the first four acts; but in the fifth, the former become very worthy gentlemen, and the latter women of virtue and discretion; nor is the writer often so kind as to give himself the least trouble to reconcile or account for this monstrous change and incongruity. There is, indeed, no other reason to be assigned for it, than because the play is drawing to a conclusion; as if it was no less natural in a rogue to repent in the last act of a play than in the last of his life; which we perceive to be generally the case at Tyburn, a place which might indeed close the scene of some comedies with much propriety, as the heroes in these are most commonly eminent for those very talents which not only bring men to the gallows, but enable them to make an heroic figure when they are there.

Within these few restrictions, I think, every writer may be permitted to deal as much in the wonderful as he pleases; nay, if he thus keeps within the rules of credibility, the more he can surprise the reader, the more he will engage his attention, and the more he will charm him. As a genius of the highest rank observes in his fifth chapter of the Bathos, 'The great art of all poetry is to mix truth with fiction, in order to join the credible with the surprising.'[16]

For though every good author will confine himself within the bounds of probability, it is by no means necessary that his characters, or his incidents, should be trite, common, or vulgar; such as happen in every street, or in every house, or which may be met with in the home articles of a newspaper. Nor must he be inhibited from showing many persons and things, which may possibly have never fallen within the knowledge of great part of his readers. If the writer strictly observes the rules above-mentioned, he hath discharged his part, and is then entitled to some faith from his reader, who is indeed guilty of critical infidelity if he disbelieves him. For want of a portion of such faith, I remember the character of a young lady of quality which was condemned on the stage for being unnatural by the unanimous voice of a very large assembly of clerks and apprentices, though it had the previous suffrages of many ladies of the first rank, one of whom, very eminent for her understanding, declared it was the picture of half the young people of her acquaintance.[17]

67 From *The History of Tom Jones . . .,* Book IX, ch. i

BOOK IX

CONTAINING TWELVE HOURS

*

CHAPTER I

OF THOSE WHO LAWFULLY MAY, AND OF THOSE WHO MAY NOT, WRITE SUCH HISTORIES AS THIS

Among other good uses for which I have thought proper to institute these several introductory chapters, I have considered them as a kind of mark or stamp, which may hereafter enable a very indifferent reader to distinguish what is true and genuine, in this historic kind of writing, from what is false and counterfeit. Indeed, it seems likely that some such mark may shortly become necessary, since the favorable reception which two or three authors have lately procured for their works of this nature from the public will probably serve as an encouragement to many others to undertake the like. Thus a swarm of foolish novels and monstrous romances will be produced, either to the great impoverishing of booksellers, or to the great loss of time and depravation of morals in the reader; nay, often to the spreading of scandal and calumny, and to the prejudice of the characters of many worthy and honest people.

I question not but the ingenious author of the *Spectator* was principally induced to prefix Greek and Latin mottoes to every paper, from the same consideration of guarding against the pursuit of those scribblers, who, having no talents of a writer but what is taught by the writing-master, are yet nowise afraid nor ashamed to assume the same titles with the greatest genius, than their good brother in the fable was of braying in the lion's skin.

By the device, therefore, of his motto, it became impracticable for any man to presume to imitate the *Spectators*, without understanding at least one sentence in the learned languages. In the same manner I have now secured myself from the imitation of those who are utterly incapable of any degree of reflection, and whose learning is not equal to an essay.

I would not be here understood to insinuate that the greatest merit of such historical productions can ever lie in these introductory chapters; but, in fact, those parts which contain mere narrative only, afford much more encouragement to the pen of an imitator than those which are composed of observation and reflection. Here I mean such imitators as Rowe was of Shakespeare, or as Horace hints some of the Romans were of Cato, by bare feet and sour faces.[1]

To invent good stories, and to tell them well, are possibly very rare talents, and yet I have observed few persons who have scrupled to aim at both; and if we examine the romances and novels with which the world abounds, I think we may fairly conclude that most of the authors would not have attempted to show their teeth (if the expression may be allowed me) in any other way of writing; nor could, indeed, have strung together a dozen sentences on any other subject whatever. *Scribimus indocti doctique passim*,*[2] may be more truly said of the historian and biographer than of any other species of writing; for all the arts and sciences (even criticism itself) require some little degree of learning and knowledge. Poetry, indeed, may perhaps be thought an exception; but then it demands numbers, or something like numbers; whereas, to the composition of novels and romances, nothing is necessary but paper, pens, and ink, with the manual capacity of using them. This, I conceive, their productions show to be the opinion of the authors themselves; and this must be the opinion of their readers, if indeed there be any such.

Hence we are to derive that universal contempt which the world, who always denominate the whole from the majority, have cast on all historical writers who do not draw their materials from records. And it is the apprehension of this contempt that hath made us so cautiously avoid the term romance, a name with which we might otherwise have been well enough contented. Though, as we have good authority for all our characters, no less indeed than the vast authentic doomsday-book of nature, as is elsewhere hinted, our labors have sufficient title to the name of history. Certainly they deserve some distinction from those works, which one of the wittiest of men regarded only as proceeding from a *pruritus*, or, indeed, rather from a looseness of the brain.[3]

*Each desperate blockhead dares to write, Verse is the trade of every living wight. FRANCIS.

But besides the dishonor which is thus cast on one of the most useful as well as entertaining of all kinds of writing, there is just reason to apprehend that by encouraging such authors we shall propagate much dishonor of another kind; I mean to the characters of many good and valuable members of society; for the dullest writers, no more than the dullest companions, are always inoffensive. They have both enough of language to be indecent and abusive. And surely if the opinion just above cited be true, we cannot wonder that works so nastily derived should be nasty themselves, or have a tendency to make others so.

To prevent, therefore, for the future, such intemperate abuses of leisure, of letters, and of the liberty of the press, especially as the world seems at present to be more than usually threatened with them, I shall here venture to mention some qualifications, every one of which are in a pretty high degree necessary to this order of historians.

The first is genius, without a full vein of which no study, says Horace, can avail us.[4] By genius I would understand that power, or rather those powers of the mind, which are capable of penetrating into all things within our reach and knowledge, and of distinguishing their essential differences. These are no other than invention and judgment; and they are both called by the collective name of genius, as they are of those gifts of nature which we bring with us into the world. Concerning each of which many seem to have fallen into very great errors; for by invention, I believe, is generally understood a creative faculty, which would indeed prove most romance writers to have the highest pretensions to it; whereas by invention is really meant no more (and so the word signifies) than discovery, or finding out; or to explain it at large, a quick and sagacious penetration into the true essence of all the objects of our contemplation. This, I think, can rarely exist without the concomitancy of judgment; for how we can be said to have discovered the true essence of two things, without discerning their difference, seems to me hard to conceive. Now this last is the undisputed province of judgment, and yet some few men of wit have agreed with all the dull fellows in the world in representing these two to have been seldom or never the property of one and the same person.

But though they should be so, they are not sufficient for our purpose without a good share of learning; for which I could again cite the authority of Horace,[5] and of many others, if any was necessary, to prove that tools are of no service to a workman when they are not sharpened by art, or when he wants rules to direct him in his work, or hath no matter to work upon. All these uses are supplied by learning;

for nature can only furnish us with capacity; or, as I have chose to illustrate it, with the tools of our profession; learning must fit them for use, must direct them in it, and, lastly, must contribute part at least of the materials. A competent knowledge of history and of the belles-lettres is here absolutely necessary; and without this share of knowledge at least, to affect the character of an historian is as vain as to endeavour at building a house without timber or mortar, or brick or stone. Homer and Milton, who, though they added the ornament of numbers to their works, were both historians of our order, were masters of all the learning of their times.

Again, there is another sort of knowledge beyond the power of learning to bestow, and this is to be had by conversation. So necessary is this to the understanding the characters of men, that none are more ignorant of them than those learned pedants whose lives have been entirely consumed in colleges and among books; for however exquisitely human nature may have been described by writers, the true practical system can be learnt only in the world. Indeed the like happens in every other kind of knowledge. Neither physic nor law are to be practically known from books. Nay, the farmer, the planter, the gardener, must perfect by experience what he hath acquired the rudiments of by reading. How accurately soever the ingenious Mr. Miller may have described the plant, he himself would advise his disciple to see it in the garden.[6] As we must perceive that after the nicest strokes of a Shakespeare or a Jonson, of a Wycherley or an Otway, some touches of nature will escape the reader, which the judicious action of a Garrick, or a Cibber, or a Clive,* can convey to him; so, on the real stage, the character shows himself in a stronger and bolder light than he can be described. And if this be the case in those fine and nervous descriptions which great authors themselves have taken from life, how much more strongly will it hold when the writer himself takes his lines not from nature, but from books? Such characters are only the faint copy of a copy, and can have neither the justness nor spirit of an original.

Now this conversation in our historian must be universal, that is, with all ranks and degrees of men; for the knowledge of what is called high life will not instruct him in low; nor, *è converso*, will his being

*There is a peculiar propriety in mentioning this great actor, and these two most justly celebrated actresses in this place; as they have all formed themselves on the study of nature only; and not on the imitation of their predecessors. Hence they have been able to excel all who have gone before them; a degree of merit which the servile herd of imitators can never possibly arrive at.

acquainted with the inferior part of mankind teach him the manners of the superior. And though it may be thought that the knowledge of either may sufficiently enable him to describe at least that in which he hath been conversant, yet he will even here fall greatly short of perfection; for the follies of either rank do in reality illustrate each other. For instance, the affectation of high life appears more glaring and ridiculous from the simplicity of the low; and again, the rudeness and barbarity of this latter strikes with much stronger ideas of absurdity, when contrasted with, and opposed to, the politeness which controls the former. Besides, to say the truth, the manners of our historian will be improved by both these conversations; for in the one he will easily find examples of plainness, honesty, and sincerity; in the other of refinement, elegance, and a liberality of spirit; which last quality I myself have scarce ever seen in men of low birth and education.

Nor will all the qualities I have hitherto given my historian avail him, unless he have what is generally meant by a good heart, and be capable of feeling. The author who will make me weep, says Horace, must first weep himself.[7] In reality, no man can paint a distress well which he doth not feel while he is painting it; nor do I doubt but that the most pathetic and affecting scenes have been writ with tears. In the same manner it is with the ridiculous. I am convinced I never make my reader laugh heartily but where I have laughed before him; unless it should happen at any time that instead of laughing with me he should be inclined to laugh at me. Perhaps this may have been the case at some passages in this chapter, from which apprehension I will here put an end to it.

68 From *The History of Tom Jones . . .*, Book X, ch. i

BOOK X

IN WHICH THE HISTORY GOES FORWARD ABOUT TWELVE HOURS

*

CHAPTER I

CONTAINING INSTRUCTIONS VERY NECESSARY TO BE PERUSED BY MODERN CRITICS

Reader, it is impossible we should know what sort of person thou wilt be; for, perhaps, thou may'st be as learned in human nature as Shakespeare himself was, and, perhaps, thou may'st be no wiser than some of his editors. Now, lest this latter should be the case, we think proper, before we go any farther together, to give thee a few wholesome admonitions; that thou may'st not as grossly misunderstand and misrepresent us, as some of the said editors have misunderstood and misrepresented their author.

First, then, we warn thee not too hastily to condemn any of the incidents in this our history as impertinent and foreign to our main design, because thou dost not immediately conceive in what manner such incident may conduce to that design. This work may, indeed, be considered as a great creation of our own; and for a little reptile of a critic to presume to find fault with any of its parts, without knowing the manner in which the whole is connected, and before he comes to the final catastrophe, is a most presumptuous absurdity. The allusion and metaphor we have here made use of, we must acknowledge to be infinitely too great for our occasion; but there is, indeed, no other, which is at all adequate to express the difference between an author of the first rate and a critic of the lowest.

Another caution we would give thee, my good reptile, is, that thou dost not find out too near a resemblance between certain characters here introduced; as, for instance, between the landlady who appears in the seventh book and her in the ninth. Thou art to know, friend, that there are certain characteristics in which most individuals of every profession and occupation agree. To be able to preserve these characteristics, and at the same time to diversify their operations, is one talent of a good writer. Again, to mark the nice distinction between two persons actuated by the same vice or folly is another; and, as this last talent is found in very few writers, so is the true discernment of it found in as few readers; though, I believe, the observation of this forms a very principal pleasure in those who are capable of the discovery; every person, for instance, can distinguish between Sir Epicure Mammon and Sir Fopling Flutter; but to note the difference between Sir Fopling Flutter and Sir Courtly Nice requires a more exquisite judgment:[1] for want of which, vulgar spectators of plays very often do great injustice in the theatre, where I have sometimes known a poet in danger of being convicted as a thief, upon much worse evidence than the resemblance of hands hath been held to be in the law. In reality, I apprehend every amorous widow on the stage would run the hazard of being condemned as a servile imitation of Dido, but that happily very few of our playhouse critics understand enough of Latin to read Virgil.

In the next place, we must admonish thee, my worthy friend (for, perhaps, thy heart may be better than thy head), not to condemn a character as a bad one because it is not perfectly a good one. If thou dost delight in these models of perfection, there are books enow written to gratify thy taste; but, as we have not, in the course of our conversation, ever happened to meet with any such person, we have not chosen to introduce any such here. To say the truth, I a little question whether mere man ever arrived at this consummate degree of excellence, as well as whether there hath ever existed a monster bad enough to verify that

——nulla virtute redemptum
A vitiis——*

in Juvenal; nor do I, indeed, conceive the good purposes served by inserting characters of such angelic perfection, or such diabolical depravity, in any work of invention; since, from contemplating either, the mind of man is more likely to be overwhelmed with sorrow and shame than to draw any good uses from such patterns; for in the former instance he may be both concerned and ashamed to see a pattern of excellence in his nature, which he may reasonably despair of ever

*Whose vices are not allayed with a single virtue.[2]

arriving at; and in contemplating the latter he may be no less affected with those uneasy sensations, at seeing the nature of which he is a partaker degraded into so odious and detestable a creature.

In fact, if there be enough of goodness in a character to engage the admiration and affection of a well-disposed mind, though there should appear some of those little blemishes, *quas humana parum cavit natura,*[3] they will raise our compassion rather than our abhorrence. Indeed, nothing can be of more moral use than the imperfections which are seen in examples of this kind, since such form a kind of surprise, more apt to affect and dwell upon our minds than the faults of very vicious and wicked persons. The foibles and vices of men, in whom there is great mixture of good, become more glaring objects from the virtues which contrast them and show their deformity; and, when we find such vices attended with their evil consequences to our favorite characters, we are not only taught to shun them for our own sake, but to hate them for the mischiefs they have already brought on those we love.

And now, my friend, having given you these few admonitions, we will, if you please, once more set forward with our history.

69 From *The History of Tom Jones . . .*, Book XI, ch. i

BOOK XI

CONTAINING ABOUT THREE DAYS

★

CHAPTER I

A CRUST FOR THE CRITICS

In our last initial chapter we may be supposed to have treated that formidable set of men who are called critics with more freedom than becomes us, since they exact, and indeed generally receive, great condescension from authors. We shall in this, therefore, give the reasons of our conduct to this august body; and here we shall, perhaps, place them in a light in which they have not hitherto been seen.

This word critic is of Greek derivation, and signifies judgment. Hence I presume some persons who have not understood the original, and have seen the English translation of the primitive, have concluded that it meant judgment in the legal sense, in which it is frequently used as equivalent to condemnation.

I am the rather inclined to be of that opinion, as the greatest number of critics hath of late years been found amongst the lawyers. Many of these gentlemen, from despair, perhaps, of ever rising to the bench in Westminster-hall, have placed themselves on the benches at the play-house, where they have exerted their judicial capacity, and have given judgment, *i.e.*, condemned without mercy.

The gentlemen would, perhaps, be well enough pleased if we were to leave them thus compared to one of the most important and honorable offices in the commonwealth, and if we intended to apply to their favor, we would do so; but as we design to deal very sincerely, and plainly too, with them, we must remind them of another officer of justice of a much lower rank, to whom, as they not only pronounce, but execute, their own judgment, they bear likewise some remote resemblance.

But in reality there is another light, in which these modern critics may, with great justice and propriety, be seen; and this is that of a common slanderer. If a person who prys into the characters of others, with no other design but to discover their faults, and to publish them to the world, deserves the title of a slanderer of the reputations of men, why should not a critic, who reads with the same malevolent view, be as properly styled the slanderer of the reputation of books?

Vice hath not, I believe, a more abject slave; society produces not a more odious vermin; nor can the devil receive a guest more worthy of him, nor possibly more welcome to him than a slanderer. The world, I am afraid, regards not this monster with half the abhorrence which he deserves; and I am more afraid to assign the reason of this criminal lenity shown towards him; yet it is certain that the thief looks innocent in the comparison; nay, the murderer himself can seldom stand in competition with his guilt: for slander is a more cruel weapon than a sword, as the wounds which the former gives are always incurable. One method, indeed, there is of killing, and that the basest and most execrable of all, which bears an exact analogy to the vice here disclaimed against, and that is poison, a means of revenge so base, and yet so horrible, that it was once wisely distinguished by our laws from all other murders, in the peculiar severity of the punishment.

Besides the dreadful mischiefs done by slander, and the baseness of the means by which they are effected, there are other circumstances that highly aggravate its atrocious quality; for it often proceeds from no provocation, and seldom promises itself any reward, unless some black and infernal mind may propose a reward in the thoughts of having procured the ruin and misery of another.

Shakespeare hath nobly touched this vice when he says,

> Who steals my purse steals trash; 'tis something, nothing;
> 'Twas mine, 'tis his, and hath been slave to thousands:
> But he that filches from me my good name
> Robs me of that WHICH NOT ENRICHES HIM,
> BUT MAKES ME POOR INDEED.[1]

With all this my good reader will doubtless agree; but much of it will probably seem too severe, when applied to the slanderer of books. But let it here be considered that both proceed from the same wicked disposition of mind, and are alike void of the excuse of temptation

Nor shall we conclude the injury done this way to be very slight, when we consider a book as the author's offspring, and indeed as the child of his brain.

The reader who hath suffered his muse to continue hitherto in a virgin state can have but a very inadequate idea of this kind of paternal fondness. To such we may parody the tender exclamation of Macduff, 'Alas! Thou hast written no book.'[2] But the author whose muse hath brought forth will feel the pathetic strain, perhaps will accompany me with tears (especially if his darling be already no more), while I mention the uneasiness with which the big muse bears about her burden, the painful labor with which she produces it, and, lastly, the care, the fondness, with which the tender father nourishes his favorite, till it be brought to maturity, and produced into the world.

Nor is there any paternal fondness which seems less to savor of absolute instinct, and which may so well be reconciled to worldly wisdom, as this. These children may most truly be called the riches of their father; and many of them have with true filial piety fed their parent in his old age: so that not only the affection, but the interest, of the author may be highly injured by these slanderers, whose poisonous breath brings his book to an untimely end.

Lastly, the slander of a book is, in truth, the slander of the author: for, as no one can call another bastard without calling the mother a whore, so neither can any one give the names of sad stuff, horrid nonsense, etc., to a book without calling the author a blockhead; which, though in a moral sense it is a preferable appellation to that of villain, is perhaps rather more injurious to his worldly interest.

Now, however ludicrous all this may appear to some, others, I doubt not, will feel and acknowledge the truth of it; nay, may, perhaps, think I have not treated the subject with decent solemnity; but surely a man may speak truth with a smiling countenance. In reality, to depreciate a book maliciously, or even wantonly, is at least a very ill-natured office; and a morose, snarling critic may, I believe, be suspected to be a bad man.

I will therefore endeavor, in the remaining part of this chapter, to explain the marks of this character, and to show what criticism I here intend to obviate: for I can never be understood, unless by the very persons here meant, to insinuate that there are no proper judges of writing, or to endeavor to exclude from the commonwealth of literature any of those noble critics to whose labors the learned world are so greatly indebted. Such were Aristotle, Horace, and Longinus, among the ancients, Dacier and Bossu among the French, and some perhaps among us, who have certainly been duly authorized to execute at least a judicial authority *in foro literario*.[3]

But without ascertaining all the proper qualifications of a critic, which I have touched on elsewhere, I think I may very boldly object to the censures of any one passed upon works which he hath not himself read. Such censurers as these, whether they speak from their own guess or suspicion, or from the report and opinion of others, may properly be said to slander the reputation of the book they condemn.

Such may likewise be suspected of deserving this character, who, without assigning any particular faults, condemn the whole in general defamatory terms; such as vile, dull, d—d stuff, etc., and particularly by the use of the monosyllable low, a word which becomes the mouth of no critic who is not RIGHT HONORABLE.

Again, though there may be some faults justly assigned in the work, yet, if those are not in the most essential parts, or if they are compensated by greater beauties, it will savor rather of the malice of a slanderer than of the judgment of a true critic to pass a severe sentence upon the whole, merely on account of some vicious part. This is directly contrary to the sentiments of Horace:

> *Verum ubi plura nitent in carmine, non ego paucis*
> *Offendor maculis, quas aut incuria fudit,*
> *Aut humana parum cavit natura*——[4]

> But where the beauties, more in number, shine,
> I am not angry, when a casual line
> (That with some trivial faults unequal flows)
> A careless hand or human frailty shows.
>
> MR. FRANCIS.

For, as Martial says, *Aliter non fit, avite, liber*.[5] No book can be otherwise composed. All beauty of character, as well as of countenance, and indeed of everything human, is to be tried in this manner. Cruel indeed would it be if such a work as this history, which hath employed some thousands of hours in the composing, should be liable to be condemned, because some particular chapter, or perhaps chapters, may be obnoxious to very just and sensible objections. And yet nothing is more common than the most rigorous sentence upon books supported by such objections, which, if they were rightly taken (and that they are not always), do by no means go to the merit of the whole. In the theatre especially, a single expression which doth not coincide with the taste of the audience, or with any individual critic of that audience, is sure to be hissed; and one scene which should be disapproved would hazard the whole piece. To write within such severe rules as these is as impossible as to live up to some splenetic opinions: and if we judge according to the sentiments of some critics, and of some Christians, no author will be saved in this world, and no man in the next.

70 From *The History of Tom Jones . . .*, Book XII, ch. i

BOOK XII

CONTAINING THE SAME INDIVIDUAL TIME WITH THE FORMER

*

CHAPTER I

SHOWING WHAT IS TO BE DEEMED PLAGIARISM IN A MODERN AUTHOR, AND WHAT IS TO BE CONSIDERED AS LAWFUL PRIZE

The learned reader must have observed that in the course of this mighty work I have often translated passages out of the best ancient authors without quoting the original, or without taking the least notice of the book from whence they were borrowed.

This conduct in writing is placed in a very proper light by the ingenious Abbé Bannier, in his preface to his Mythology, a work of great erudition and of equal judgment. 'It will be easy,' says he, 'for the reader to observe that I have frequently had greater regard to him than to my own reputation: for an author certainly pays him a considerable compliment, when, for his sake, he suppresses learned quotations that come in his way, and which would have cost him but the bare trouble of translating.'[1]

To fill up a work with these scraps may, indeed, be considered as a downright cheat on the learned world, who are by such means imposed upon to buy a second time, in fragments and by retail, what they have already in gross, if not in their memories, upon their shelves; and it is still more cruel upon the illiterate, who are drawn in to pay for what is of no manner of use to them. A writer who intermixes great quantity of Greek and Latin with his works, deals by the ladies and fine gentlemen in the same paltry manner with which they are treated by the auctioneers, who often endeavor so to confound and mix up their lots that, in order to purchase the commodity you want, you are obliged at the same time to purchase that which will do you no service.

And yet, as there is no conduct so fair and disinterested but that it may be misunderstood by ignorance, and misrepresented by malice, I have been sometimes tempted to preserve my own reputation at the expense of my reader, and to transcribe the original, or at least to quote chapter and verse, whenever I have made use either of the thought or expression of another. I am, indeed, in some doubt that I have often suffered by the contrary method; and that, by suppressing the original author's name, I have been rather suspected of plagiarism that reputed to act from the amiable motive assigned by that justly celebrated Frenchman.

Now, to obviate all such imputations for the future, I do here confess and justify the fact. The ancients may be considered as a rich common, where every person who hath the smallest tenement in Parnassus hath a free right to fatten his muse. Or, to place it in a clearer light, we moderns are to the ancients what the poor are to the rich. By the poor here I mean that large and venerable body which, in English, we call the mob. Now, whoever hath had the honor to be admitted to any degree of intimacy with this mob, must well know that it is one of their established maxims to plunder and pillage their rich neighbors without any reluctance; and that this is held to be neither sin nor crime among them. And so constantly do they abide and act by this maxim that, in every parish almost in the kingdom, there is a kind of confederacy ever carrying on against a certain person of opulence called the squire, whose property is considered as free-booty by all his poor neighbors; who, as they conclude that there is no manner of guilt in such depredations, look upon it as a point of honor and moral obligation to conceal, and to preserve each other from punishment on all such occasions.

In like manner are the ancients, such as Homer, Virgil, Horace, Cicero, and the rest, to be esteemed among us writers as so many wealthy squires, from whom we, the poor of Parnassus, claim an immemorial custom of taking whatever we can come at. This liberty I demand, and this I am as ready to allow again to my poor neighbors in their turn. All I profess, and all I require from my brethren, is to maintain the same strict honesty among ourselves which the mob show to one another. To steal from one another is indeed highly criminal and indecent; for this may be strictly styled defrauding the poor (sometimes perhaps those who are poorer than ourselves), or, to set it under the most opprobrious colors, robbing the spittal.[2]

Since, therefore, upon the strictest examination, my own conscience cannot lay any such pitiful theft to my charge, I am contented to plead guilty to the former accusation; nor shall I ever scruple to take to myself any passage which I shall find in an ancient author to my purpose, without setting down the name of the author from whence it was taken. Nay, I absolutely claim a property in all such sentiments the moment they are transcribed into my writings, and I expect all readers henceforwards to regard them as purely and entirely my own. This claim, however, I desire to be allowed me only on condition that I preserve strict honesty towards my poor brethren, from whom, if ever I borrow any of that little of which they are possessed, I shall never fail to put their mark upon it, that it may be at all times ready to be restored to the right owner.

The omission of this was highly blamable in one Mr. Moore, who, having formerly borrowed some lines of Pope and company, took the liberty to transcribe six of them into his play of the *Rival Modes*. Mr. Pope, however, very luckily found them in the said play, and, laying violent hands on his own property, transferred it back again into his own works; and, for a further punishment, imprisoned the said Moore in the loathsome dungeon of the *Dunciad*, where his unhappy memory now remains, and eternally will remain, as a proper punishment for such his unjust dealings in the poetical trade.[3]

71 From *The History of Tom Jones . . .*, Book XIV, ch. i

BOOK XIV

CONTAINING TWO DAYS

*

CHAPTER I

AN ESSAY TO PROVE THAT AN AUTHOR WILL WRITE THE BETTER FOR HAVING SOME KNOWLEDGE OF THE SUBJECT ON WHICH HE WRITES

As several gentlemen in these times, by the wonderful force of genius only, without the least assistance of learning, perhaps, without being well able to read, have made a considerable figure in the republic of letters, the modern critics, I am told, have lately begun to assert that all kind of learning is entirely useless to a writer, and, indeed, no other than a kind of fetters on the natural sprightliness and activity of the imagination, which is thus weighed down, and prevented from soaring to those high flights which otherwise it would be able to reach.

This doctrine, I am afraid, is, at present, carried much too far; for why should writing differ so much from all other arts? The nimbleness of a dancing-master is not at all prejudiced by being taught to move; nor doth any mechanic, I believe, exercise his tools the worse by having learned to use them. For my own part, I cannot conceive that Homer or Virgil would have writ with more fire if, instead of being masters of all the learning of their times, they had been as ignorant as most of the authors of the present age. Nor do I believe that all the imagination, fire, and judgment of Pitt could have produced those orations that have made the senate of England, in these our times, a rival in eloquence to Greece and Rome, if he had not been so well read in the writings of Demosthenes and Cicero as to have transferred their whole spirit into his speeches, and, with their spirit, their knowledge too.[1]

I would not here be understood to insist on the same fund of learning in any of my brethren as Cicero persuades us is necessary to the composition of an orator. On the contrary, very little reading is, I conceive, necessary to the poet, less to the critic, and the least of all to the politician. For the first, perhaps, Byshe's Art of Poetry,[2] and a few of our modern poets, may suffice; for the second, a moderate heap of plays; and, for the last, an indifferent collection of political journals.

To say the truth, I require no more than that a man should have some little knowledge of the subject on which he treats, according to the old maxim of law, *Quam quisque nôrit artem in eâ se exerceat.*[3] With this alone a writer may sometimes do tolerably well; and, indeed, without this, all the other learning in the world will stand him in little stead.

For instance, let us suppose that Homer and Virgil, Aristotle and Cicero, Thucydides and Livy, could have met all together, and have clubbed their several talents to have composed a treatise on the art of dancing: I believe it will be readily agreed they could not have equalled the excellent treatise which Mr. Essex hath given us on that subject, entitled, *The Rudiments of Genteel Education.*[4] And, indeed, should the excellent Mr. Broughton be prevailed on to set fist to paper, and to complete the above-said rudiments, by delivering down the true principles of athletics, I question whether the world will have any cause to lament that none of the great writers, either ancient or modern, have ever treated about that noble and useful art.[5]

To avoid a multiplicity of examples in so plain a case, and to come at once to my point, I am apt to conceive that one reason why many English writers have totally failed in describing the manners of upper life may possibly be that in reality they know nothing of it.

This is a knowledge unhappily not in the power of many authors to arrive at. Books will give us a very imperfect idea of it; nor will the stage a much better: the fine gentleman formed upon reading the former will almost always turn out a pedant, and he who forms himself upon the later, a coxcomb.

Nor are the characters drawn from these models better supported. Vanbrugh and Congreve copied nature; but they who copy them draw as unlike the present age as Hogarth would do if he was to paint a rout or a drum in the dresses of Titian and of Vandyke. In short, imitation here will not do the business. The picture must be after Nature herself. A true knowledge of the world is gained only by conversation, and the manners of every rank must be seen in order to be known.

Now it happens that this higher order of mortals is not to be seen, like all the rest of the human species, for nothing, in the streets, shops, and coffee-houses: nor are they shown, like the upper rank of animals, for so much apiece. In short, this is a sight to which no persons are admitted without one or other of these qualifications, viz., either birth or fortune, or, what is equivalent to both, the honorable profession of a gamester. And, very unluckily for the world, persons so qualified very seldom care to take upon themselves the bad trade of writing; which is generally entered upon by the lower and poorer sort, as it is a trade which many think requires no kind of stock to set up with.

Hence those strange monsters in lace and embroidery, in silks and brocades, with vast wigs and hoops, which, under the name of lords and ladies, strut the stage, to the great delight of attorneys and their clerks in the pit, and of the citizens and their apprentices in the galleries, and which are no more to be found in real life than the centaur, the chimera, or any other creature of mere fiction. But to let my reader into a secret, this knowledge of upper life, though very necessary for preventing mistakes, is no very great resource to a writer whose province is comedy, or that kind of novels which, like this I am writing, is of the comic class.

What Mr. Pope says of women is very applicable to most in this station, who are, indeed, so entirely made up of form and affectation, that they have no character at all, at least none which appears.[6] I will venture to say the highest life is much the dullest, and affords very little humor or entertainment. The various callings in lower spheres produce the great variety of humorous characters; whereas here, except among the few who are engaged in the pursuit of ambition, and the fewer still who have a relish for pleasure, all is vanity and servile imitation. Dressing and cards, eating and drinking, bowing and courtesying, make up the business of their lives.

Some there are, however, of this rank upon whom passion exercises its tyranny, and hurries them far beyond the bounds which decorum prescribes; of these the ladies are as much distinguished by their noble intrepidity, and a certain superior contempt of reputation, from the frail ones of meaner degree, as a virtuous woman of quality is by the elegance and delicacy of her sentiments from the honest wife of a yeoman and shopkeeper. Lady Bellaston was of this intrepid character; but let not my country readers conclude from her that this is the general conduct of women of fashion, or that we mean to represent them as such. They might as well suppose that every clergyman was represented by Thwackum, or every soldier by ensign Northerton.

There is not, indeed, a greater error than that which universally prevails among the vulgar, who, borrowing their opinion from some ignorant satirists, have affixed the character of lewdness to these times. On the contrary, I am convinced there never was less of love intrigue carried on among persons of condition than now. Our present women have been taught by their mothers to fix their thoughts only on ambition and vanity, and to despise the pleasures of love as unworthy their regard; and being afterwards, by the care of such mothers, married without having husbands, they seem pretty well confirmed in the justness of those sentiments; whence they content themselves, for the dull remainder of life, with the pursuit of more innocent but I am afraid more childish amusements, the bare mention of which would ill suit with the dignity of this history. In my humble opinion, the true characteristic of the present beau monde is rather folly than vice, and the only epithet which it deserves is that of frivolous.

72 From *The Covent Garden Journal*, No. 7

Saturday, January 25, 1752, and No 8, Tuesday, January 28, 1752

Fielding's *Amelia* was published on December 18, 1751. Its reception was very bad; critics and wits mocked the heroine for her noselessness and condemned the novel as 'low'. Before he wrote the following passages Fielding had already made an indirect reply to his critics in *The Covent Garden Journal*, No. 3; see above, No. 14.

Proceedings at the Court of Censorial Enquiry, *Etc.*
(Amelia *was set to the Bar*)

COUNSELLOR TOWN. May it please you, Mr. Censor, I am of Council in this Case, on the side of the Prosecution. The Book at the Bar is indicted upon the Statute of Dulness, a very antient Law, and too well known to need much expatiating upon. But it may be necessary to observe, *that that that* is Dulness in one Age, is not so in another, and what says that antient Sage, and Lawgiver, Horace;

Ætatis cujusque notandi sunt tibi mores.
Every Writer is to observe the Manners of the Age.[1]

I know the Word *ætatis* is, in this Place, by some Lawyers, understood in another Sense; but what I contend for, is, that it may very well be understood in that Sense that I have here given to it: and, accordingly, the same Horace lays it down as a Rule,

Et prodesse volunt, et delectare, poetæ.
Poets desire to get Money, and to please their Readers.[2]

For so I read the Law, and so I render it. A very good Law it is, and very wholesome to the Writers themselves.

Now the Humour, or Manners, of this Age are to laugh at every Thing, and the only Way to please them is to make them laugh; nor hath the Prisoner any Excuse, since it was so very easy to have done this in the present Case; what, indeed, more was necessary, than to have turned the Ridicule the other Way, and, in the Characters of Dr. Harrison, and Amelia herself, to have made a Jest of Religion, and the Clergy, of Virtue, and Innocence?

Here the Council was hastily stopt by the Censor, and desired to proceed to his Proofs.

TOWN. We shall prove then, to you, Sir, that the Book now at the Bar, is *very sad Stuff*; that Amelia herself is a *low* Character, a *Fool*, and a *Milksop*; that she is very apt to faint, and apt *to drink Water*, to prevent it. That she once *taps a Bottle of Wine, and drinks two Glasses*. That she *shews too much Kindness for her Children*, and is too apt to *forgive the Faults of her Husband*. That she exerts *no Manner of Spirit*, unless, perhaps, in supporting Afflictions. That *her concealing the* Knowledge of her Husband's Amour, when she knew he had discontinued it was *low and poor*. That *her not abusing him*, for having lost his Money at Play, when she saw his Heart was already almost broke by it, *was contemptible Meanness*. That she *dresses her Husband's Supper; dresses her Children;* and *submits* to the Thoughts of every servile Office. That she once mentions THE DEVIL, and as often swears BY HER SOUL. Lastly, That she is a Beauty WITHOUT A NOSE, I say again, WITHOUT A NOSE.[3] All this we shall prove by many Witnesses.

We shall likewise prove that Dr. Harrison is a very *low, dull, unnatural*, Character, and that his arresting Booth, *only because he had all imaginable Reason to think he was a Villain*, is unpardonable.

That Colonel Bath is a *foolish Character, very low, and ill-drawn*.

That the Scene of the Goal is *low and unmeaning*, and brought in by Head and Shoulders, without any Reason, or Design.

That the Abbé is supposed to *wear a Sword*; in short, not to descend to too many Particulars, which you will hear from the Mouths of the Witnesses, that the whole Book is a Heap of *sad Stuff, Dulness, and Nonsense*; that it contains no Wit, Humour, Knowledge of human Nature or of the World; indeed, that the Fable, moral Character, Manners, Sentiments, and Diction, are all alike bad and contemptible.

All these Matters, Sir, we doubt not to prove to your Satisfaction, and then we doubt not but that you will do exemplary Justice to such intolerable sad Stuff, and, will pass such a Sentence as may be a dreadful Example to all future Books, how they dare stand up in Opposition to the Humour of the Age.

A great Noise was now heard in the Court, and much female Vociferation; when the Censor was informed, that it was a married

Lady, one of the Witnesses against Amelia, who was scolding at her Husband for not making her Way through the Crowd.

Mr. TOWN then moved, that, as there were several Persons of great Fashion, who were to be Witnesses in this Cause, Room might be made for them by the Officers, which was ordered accordingly.

C. TOWN. Call Lady *Dilly Dally*.—(*She appeared*) Mr. Censor, we call this young Lady to the Character of Amelia, and she will give you an Account of all the low Behaviour I have opened.—Lady *Dilly*, your Ladyship knows the Prisoner at the Bar?

L. DILLY. I cannot say I ever saw the Creature before. (*At which there was a great Laugh.*)

C. TOWN. I thought your Ladyship had said that Amelia was sad Stuff from Beginning to End.

L. DILLY. I believe I might say so.—Eh! I don't always remember what I say; but if I did say so, I was told it.—Oh! yes, now I remember very well, I did say so, and Dr. Dosewell, my Physician, told me so.—The Doctor said, in a great deal of Company, that the Book, I forget the Name of it, was a sad stupid Book, and that the Author had not a Bit of Wit, or Learning, or Sense, or any Thing else.

COURT. Mr. *Town*, you know this is only Hearsay, and not Evidence.—

C. TOWN. I do not contend for it. We shall call the Doctor himself by and by.—We will give your Ladyship no further Trouble.

L. DILLY.—I am heartily glad of it.—Mr. Censor, if you are the Judge, I beg, as you have brought me into this odious Place, you will see me safe out again.

Orders were then given to clear away the Crowd, which was very great, and Lady *Dilly* got safe to her Chair.

The Residue of this Trial will be in our next.

Proceedings at the Court of Censorial Enquiry, *Etc.*

A great Number of Beaus, Rakes, fine Ladies, and several formal Persons with bushy Wigs, and Canes at their Noses, pushed forward, and offered themselves as Witnesses against poor Amelia, when a grave Man stood up and begged to be heard; which the Court granted, and he spoke as follows.

'If you, Mr. Censor, are yourself a Parent, you will view me with Compassion when I declare I am the Father of this poor Girl the Prisoner at the Bar; nay, when I go farther, and avow, that of all my Offspring she is my favourite Child. I can truly say that I bestowed a more than ordinary Pains in her Education; in which I will venture to affirm, I followed the Rules of all those who are acknowledged to have writ best on the Subject; and if her Conduct be fairly examined, she will be found to deviate very little from the strictest Observation of all those Rules; neither Homer nor Virgil pursued them with greater Care than myself, and the candid and learned Reader will see that the latter was the noble model, which I made use of on this Occasion.

'I do not think my Child is entirely free from Faults. I know nothing human that is so; but surely she doth not deserve the Rancour with which she hath been treated by the Public. However, it is not my Intention, at present, to make any Defence; but shall submit to a Compromise, which hath been always allowed in this Court in all Prosecutions for Dulness. I do, therefore, solemnly declare to you, Mr. Censor, that I will trouble the World no more with any Children of mine by the same Muse.'

This Declaration was received with a loud Huzza, by the greater Part of the Spectators; and being allowed by the Court, was presently entered of Record. Then Amelia was delivered to her Parent, and a Scene of great Tenderness passed between them, which gave much Satisfaction to many present; some of whom, however, blamed the old Gentleman for putting an End to the Cause, and several very grave and well looking Men, who knew the whole Merits, asserted, that the Lady ought to have been honourably acquitted.

Then the Court adjourned to Saturday, Feb. 1.

Appendix I: Preface to the *Miscellanies*

1743

The following Preface could hardly be included together with Fielding's other essays and Prefaces under the heading of 'Criticism', but it is of obvious relevance to his career as a writer in general and throws light on his attitude to his own writing.

The Volumes I now present the Public, consist, as their Title indicates, of various Matter; treating of Subjects which bear not the least Relation to each other; and perhaps, what *Martial* says of his Epigrams, may be applicable to these several Productions.

Sunt bona, sunt quædam mediocria, sunt mala PLURA.[1]

At least, if the *Bona* be denied me, I shall, I apprehend, be allowed the other Two.

The Poetical Pieces which compose the First Part of the First Volume, were most of them written when I was very young, and are indeed Productions of the Heart rather than of the Head. If the Good-natured Reader thinks them tolerable, it will answer my warmest Hopes. This Branch of Writing is what I very little pretend to, and will appear to have been very little my Pursuit, since I think (one or two Poems excepted) have here presented my Reader with all I could remember or procure Copies of.

My Modernization of Part of the sixth Satire of *Juvenal*, will, I hope, give no Offence to that Half of our Species, for whom I have the greatest Respect and Tenderness. It was originally sketched out before I was Twenty, and was all the Revenge taken by an injured Lover.[2] For my Part, I am much more inclined to Panegyric on that amiable Sex, which I have always thought treated with a very unjust Severity by ours, who censure them for Faults (if they are truly such) into which we allure and betray them, and of which we ourselves, with an unblamed Licence, enjoy the most delicious Fruits.

As to the *Essay on Conversation*, however it may be executed, my

Design in it will be at least allowed good; being to ridicule out of Society, one of the most pernicious Evils which attends it, *viz*. pampering the gross Appetites of Selfishness and Ill-nature, with the Shame and Disquietude of others; whereas I have endeavoured in it to shew, that true Good-Breeding consists in contributing, with our utmost Power, to the Satisfaction and Happiness of all about us.

In my Essay on *the Knowledge of the Characters of Men*, I have endeavoured to expose a second great Evil, namely, Hypocrisy; the Bane of all Virtue, Morality, and Goodness; and to arm, as well as I can, the honest, undesigning, open-hearted Man, who is generally the Prey of this Monster, against it. I believe a little Reflection will convince us, that most Mischiefs (especially those which fall on the worthiest Part of Mankind) owe their Original to this detestable Vice.

I shall pass over the remaining Part of this Volume, to the *Journey from this World to the next*, which fills the greatest Share of the second.

It would be paying a very mean Compliment to the human Understanding, to suppose I am under any Necessity of vindicating myself from designing, in an Allegory of this Kind, to oppose any present System, or to erect a new one of my own: but perhaps the Fault may lie rather in the Heart than in the Head; and I may be misrepresented, without being misunderstood. If there are any such Men, I am sorry for it; the Good-natured Reader will not, I believe, want any Assistance from me to disappoint their Malice.

Others may (and that with greater Colour) arraign my Ignorance; as I have, in the Relation which I have put into the Mouth of *Julian*, whom they call the Apostate, done many Violences to History, and mixed Truth and Falshood with much Freedom. To these I answer. I profess Fiction only; and tho' I have chosen some Facts out of History, to embellish my Work, and fix a Chronology to it, I have not, however, confined myself to nice Exactness; having often ante-dated, and sometimes post-dated the Matter I have found in the Historian, particularly in the *Spanish* History, where I take both these Liberties in one Story.[3]

The Residue of this Volume is filled with two Dramatic Pieces, both the Productions of my Youth, tho' the latter was not acted 'till this Season. It was the third Dramatic Performance I ever attempted; the Parts of *Millamour* and *Charlotte* being originally intended for Mr. *Wilks* and Mrs. *Oldfield*; but the latter died before it was finished; and a slight Pique which happened between me and the former, prevented him from ever seeing it. The Play was read to Mr. *Rich* upwards of twelve

Years since, in the Presence of a very eminent Physician of this Age, who will bear me Testimony, that I did not recommend my Performance with the usual Warmth of an Author.[4] Indeed I never thought, 'till this Season, that there existed on any one Stage, since the Death of that great Actor and Actress abovementioned, any two Persons capable of supplying their Loss in those Parts: for Characters of this Kind do, of all others, require most Support from the Actor, and lend the least Assistance to him.

From the Time of its being read to Mr. *Rich*, it lay by me neglected and unthought of, 'till this Winter, when it visited the Stage in the following Manner.

Mr. *Garrick*, whose Abilities as an Actor will, I hope, rouse up better Writers for the Stage than myself, asked me one Evening, if I had any Play by me; telling me, he was desirous of appearing in a new Part.[5] I answered him, I had one almost finished: but I conceived it so little the Manager's Interest to produce any thing new on his Stage this Season, that I should not think of offering it him, as I apprehended he would find some Excuse to refuse me, and adhere to the Theatrical Politics, of never introducing new Plays on the Stage, but when driven to it by absolute Necessity.

Mr. *Garrick's* Reply to this was so warm and friendly, that, as I was full as desirous of putting Words into his Mouth, as he could appear to be of speaking them, I mentioned the Play the very next Morning to Mr. *Fleetwood*,[6] who embraced my Proposal so heartily, that an Appointment was immediately made to read it to the Actors who were principally to be concerned in it.

When I came to revise this Play, which had likewise lain by me some Years, tho' formed on a much better Plan, and at an Age when I was much more equal to the Task, than the former; I found I had allowed myself too little Time for the perfecting it; but I was resolved to execute my Promise, and accordingly, at the appointed Day I produced five Acts, which were entitled, THE GOOD-NATURED MAN.

Besides, that this Play appeared to me, on the Reading, to be less completely finished than I thought its Plan deserved; there was another Reason which dissuaded me from bringing it on the Stage, as it then stood, and this was, that the very Actor on whose Account I had principally been inclined to have it represented, had a very inconsiderable Part in it.

Notwithstanding my private Opinion, of which I then gave no Intimation, *The Good-natured Man* was received, and ordered to be writ into Parts, Mr. *Garrick* professing himself very ready to perform his; but as I remained dissatisfied, for the Reasons abovementioned, I now recollected my other Play, in which I remembered there was a Character I had originally intended for Mr. *Wilks*.

Upon Perusal, I found this Character was preserved with some little Spirit, and (what I thought would be a great Recommendation to the Audience) would keep their so justly favourite Actor almost eternally before their Eyes. I apprehended (in which I was not deceived) that he would make so surprising a Figure in this Character, and exhibit Talents so long unknown to the Theatre, that, as hath happen'd in other Plays, the Audience might be blinded to the Faults of the Piece, for many I saw it had, and some very difficult to cure.

I accordingly sat down with a Resolution to work Night and Day, during the short Time allowed me, which was about a Week, in altering and correcting this Production of my more juvenile Years; when unfortunately, the extreme Danger of Life into which a Person, very dear to me, was reduced, rendered me incapable of executing my Task.[7]

To this Accident alone, I have the Vanity to apprehend, the Play owes most of the glaring Faults with which it appeared. However, I resolved rather to let it take its Chance, imperfect as it was, with the Assistance of Mr. *Garrick*, than to sacrifice a more favourite, and in the Opinion of others, a much more valuable Performance, and which could have had very little Assistance from him.

I then acquainted Mr. *Garrick* with my Design, and read it to him, and Mr. *Macklin*;[8] Mr. *Fleetwood* agreed to the Exchange, and thus the WEDDING DAY was destined to the Stage.

Perhaps it may be asked me, Why then did I suffer a Piece, which I myself knew was imperfect, to appear? I answer honestly and freely, that Reputation was not my Inducement; and that I hoped, faulty as it was, it might answer a much more solid, and in my unhappy Situation, a much more urgent Motive. If it will give my Enemies any Pleasure to know that they totally frustrated my Views, I will be kinder to them, and give them a Satisfaction which they denied me: for tho' it was acted six Nights, I received not 50 *l*. from the House for it.

This was indeed chiefly owing to a general Rumour spread of its Indecency; which originally arose, I believe, from some Objections of the Licenser, who had been very unjustly censured for being too remiss in his Restraints on that Head; but as every Passage which he objected to was struck out, and I sincerely think very properly so, I leave to every impartial Judge to decide, whether the Play, as it was acted, was not rather freer from such Imputation than almost any other Comedy on the Stage. However, this Opinion prevailed so fatally without Doors, during its Representation, that on the sixth Night, there were not above five Ladies present in the Boxes.

But I shall say no more of this Comedy here, as I intend to introduce it the ensuing Season, and with such Alterations as will, I hope, remove every Objection to it, and may make the Manager some Amends for what he lost by very honourably continuing its Representation, when he might have got much more by acting other Plays.

I come now to the Third and last Volume, which contains the History of *Jonathan Wild*. And here it will not, I apprehend be necessary to acquaint my Reader, that my Design is not to enter the Lists with that excellent Historian, who from authentic Papers and Records, *&c.* hath already given so satisfactory an Account of the Life and Actions of this Great Man. I have not indeed the least Intention to depreciate the Veracity and Impartiality of that History; nor do I pretend to any of those Lights, not having, to my Knowledge, ever seen a single Paper relating to my Hero, save some short Memoirs, which about the Time of his Death were published in certain Chronicles called News-Papers, the Authority of which hath been sometimes questioned, and in the Ordinary of *Newgate* his Account, which generally contains a more particular Relation of what the Heroes are to suffer in the next World, than of what they did in this.[9]

To confess the Truth, my Narrative is rather of such Actions which he might have performed, or would, or should have performed, than what he really did; and may, in Reality, as well suit any other such great Man, as the Person himself whose Name it bears.

A second Caution I would give my Reader is, that as it is not a very faithful Portrait of *Jonathan Wild* himself, so neither is it intended to represent the Features of any other Person. Roguery, and not a Rogue, is my Subject; and as I have been so far from endeavouring to particularize any Individual, that I have with my utmost Art avoided it; so will any such Application be unfair in my Reader, especially if he knows much of the Great World, since he must then be acquainted, I believe, with more than one on whom he can fix the Resemblance.[10]

In the third Place, I solemnly protest, I do by no means intend in the Character of my Hero to represent Human Nature in general. Such Insinuations must be attended with very dreadful Conclusions; nor do I see any other Tendency they can naturally have, but to encourage and soothe Men in their Villainies, and to make every well-disposed Man disclaim his own Species, and curse the Hour of his Birth into such a Society. For my Part, I understand those Writers who describe Human Nature in this depraved Character, as speaking only of such Persons as *Wild* and his Gang; and I think it may be justly inferred, that they do not find in their own Bosoms any Deviation from the general Rule. Indeed it would be an insufferable Vanity in them to conceive themselves as the only Exception to it.[11]

But without considering *Newgate* as no other than Human Nature with its Mask off, which some very shameless Writers have done, a Thought which no Price should purchase me to entertain, I think we may be excused for suspecting, that the splendid Palaces of the Great are often no other than *Newgate* with the Mask on. Nor do I know any thing which can raise an honest Man's Indignation higher than that the same Morals should be in one Place attended with all imaginable Misery and Infamy, and in the other, with the highest Luxury and Honour. Let any impartial Man in his Senses be asked, for which of these two Places a Composition of Cruelty, Lust, Avarice, Rapine, Insolence, Hypocrisy, Fraud and Treachery, was best fitted, surely his Answer must be certain and immediate; and yet I am afraid all these Ingredients glossed over with Wealth and a Title, have been treated with the highest Respect and Veneration in the one, while one or two of them have been condemned to the Gallows in the other.

If there are then any Men of such Morals who dare to call themselves Great, and are so reputed, or called at least, by the deceived Multitude, surely a little private Censure by the few is a very moderate Tax for them to pay, provided no more was to be demanded: But I fear this is not the Case. However the Glare of Riches, and Awe of Title, may dazzle and terrify the Vulgar; nay, however Hypocrisy may deceive the more Discerning, there is still a Judge in every Man's Breast, which none can cheat nor corrupt, tho' perhaps it is the only uncorrupt Thing about him. And yet, inflexible and honest as this Judge is, (however polluted the Bench be on which he sits) no Man can, in my Opinion, enjoy any Applause which is not thus adjudged to be his Due.

Nothing seems to me more preposterous than that, while the Way to true Honour lies so open and plain, Men should seek false by such perverse and rugged Paths: that while it is so easy and safe, and truly honourable, to be good, Men should wade through Difficulty and Danger, and real Infamy, to be *Great*, or, to use a synonimous Word, *Villains*.

Nor hath Goodness less Advantage in the Article of Pleasure, than of Honour over this kind of Greatness. The same righteous Judge always annexes a bitter Anxiety to the Purchases of Guilt, whilst it adds a double Sweetness to the Enjoyments of Innocence and Virtue: for Fear, which all the Wise agree is the most wretched of human Evils, is, in some Degree, always attending on the former, and never can in any manner molest the Happiness of the latter.

This is the Doctrine which I have endeavoured to inculcate in this History, confining myself at the same Time within the Rules of Probability. (For except in one Chapter, which is visibly meant as a Burlesque on the extravagant Accounts of Travellers, I believe I have not exceeded it.[12]) And though perhaps it sometimes happens, contrary to the Instances I have given, that the Villain succeeds in his Pursuit, and acquires some transitory imperfect Honour or Pleasure to himself for his Iniquity; yet I believe he oftner shares the Fate of my Hero, and suffers the Punishment, without obtaining the Reward.

As I believe it is not easy to teach a more useful Lesson than this, if I have been able to add the pleasant to it, I might flatter myself with having carried every Point.

But perhaps some Apology may be required of me, for having used the Word *Greatness*, to which the World have affixed such honourable Ideas, in so disgraceful and contemptuous a Light. Now if the Fact be, that the Greatness which is commonly worshipped is really of that Kind which I have here represented, the Fault seems rather to lie in those who have ascribed to it those Honours, to which it hath not in Reality the least Claim.

The Truth, I apprehend, is, we often confound the Ideas of Goodness and Greatness together, or rather include the former in our Idea of the latter. If this be so, it is surely a great Error, and no less than a Mistake of the Capacity for the Will. In Reality, no Qualities can be more distinct: for as it cannot be doubted but that Benevolence, Honour, Honesty, and Charity, make a good Man; and that Parts, Courage, are the efficient Qualities of a Great Man, so must it be confess'd, that the Ingredients which compose the former of these Characters, bear no Analogy to, nor Dependence on those which constitute the latter. A Man may therefore be Great without being Good, or Good without being Great.

However, tho' the one bear no necessary Dependence on the other, neither is there any absolute Repugnancy among them which may totally prevent their Union so that they may, tho' not of Necessity, assemble in the same Mind, as they actually did, and all in the highest Degree, in those of *Socrates* and *Brutus*; and perhaps in some among us. I at least know one to whom Nature could have added no one great or good Quality more than she hath bestowed on him.

Here then appear three distinct Characters; the Great, the Good, and the Great and Good.

The last of these is the *true Sublime* in Human Nature. That Elevation by which the Soul of Man, raising and extending itself above the Order of this Creation, and brighten'd with a certain Ray of Divinity, looks down on the Condition of Mortals. This is indeed a glorious Object, on which we can never gaze with too much Praise and Admiration. A perfect Work! the *Iliad* of Nature! ravishing and astonishing, and which at once fills us with Love, Wonder, and Delight.

The Second falls greatly short of this Perfection, and yet hath its Merit. Our Wonder ceases; our Delight is lessened; but our Love remains; of which Passion, Goodness hath always appeared to me the only true and proper Object. On this Head I think proper to observe, that I do not conceive my Good Man to be absolutely a Fool or a Coward; but that he often partakes too little of Parts or Courage, to have any Pretensions to Greatness.

Now as to that Greatness which is totally devoid of Goodness, it seems to me in Nature to resemble the *False Sublime* in Poetry; whose Bombast is, by the ignorant and ill-judging Vulgar, often mistaken for solid Wit and Eloquence, whilst it is in Effect the very Reverse. Thus Pride, Ostentation, Insolence, Cruelty, and every Kind of Villany, are often construed into True Greatness of Mind, in which we always include an Idea of Goodness.

This Bombast Greatness then is the Character I intend to expose; and the more this prevails in and deceives the World, taking to itself not only Riches and Power, but often Honour, or at least the Shadow of it, the more necessary is it to strip the Monster of these false Colours, and shew it in its native Deformity: for by suffering Vice to possess the Reward of Virtue, we do a double Injury to Society, by encouraging the former, and taking away the chief Incentive to the latter. Nay, tho' it is, I believe, impossible to give Vice a true Relish of Honour and Glory, or tho' we give it Riches and Power, to give it the Enjoyment of them, yet it contaminates the Food it can't taste, and sullies the Robe which neither fits nor becomes it, 'till Virtue disdains them both.

Thus have I given some short Account of these Works. I come now to return Thanks to these Friends who have with uncommon Pains forwarded this Subscription: for tho' the Number of my Subscribers be more proportioned to my Merit, than their Desire or Expectation, yet I believe I owe not a tenth Part to my own Interest. My Obligations on this Head are so many, that for Fear of offending any by Preference, I will name none. Nor is it indeed necessary, since I am convinced they served me with no Desire of a public Acknowledgment; nor can I make any to some of them, equal with the Gratitude of my Sentiments.

I cannot, however, forbear mentioning my Sense of the Friendship shewn me by a Profession of which I am a late and unworthy Member, and from whose Assistance I derive more than half the Names which appear to this Subscription.[13]

It remains that I make some Apology for the Delay in publishing these Volumes, the real Reason of which was, the dangerous Illness of one from whom I draw all the solid Comfort of my Life, during the greatest Part of this Winter. This, as it is most sacredly true, so will it, I doubt not, sufficiently excuse the Delay to all who know me.

Indeed when I look a Year or two backwards, and survey the Accidents which have befallen me, and the Distresses I have waded through whilst I have been engaged in these Works, I could almost challenge some Philosophy to myself, for having been able to finish them as I have; and however imperfectly that may be, I am convinced the Reader, was he acquainted with the whole, would want very little Good-Nature to extinguish his Disdain at any Faults he meets with.

But this hath dropt from me unawares: for I intend not to entertain my Reader with my private History: nor am I fond enough of Tragedy, to make myself the Hero of one.

However, as I have been very unjustly censured, as well on account of what I have not writ, as for what I have; I take this Opportunity to declare in the most solemn Manner I have long since (as long as from *June* 1741) desisted from writing one Syllable in the *Champion*, or any other public Paper; and that I never was, nor will be the Author of anonymous Scandal on the private History or Family of any Person whatever.[14]

Indeed there is no Man who speaks or thinks with more Detestation of the modern Custom of Libelling. I look on the Practice of stabbing a Man's Character in the Dark, to be as base and as barbarous as that of stabbing him with a Poignard in the same Manner; nor have I ever been once in my Life guilty of it.

It is not here, I suppose, necessary to distinguish between Ridicule and Scurrility; between a Jest on a public Character, and the Murther of a private one.

My Reader will pardon my having dwelt a little on this Particular, since it is so especially necessary in this Age, when almost all the Wit we have is applied this Way; and when I have already been a Martyr to such unjust Suspicion. Of which I will relate one Instance. While I was last Winter laid up in the Gout, with a favourite Child dying in one Bed, and my Wife in a condition very little better, on another, attended with other Circumstances, which served as very proper Decorations to such a Scene, I received a Letter from a Friend, desiring me to vindicate myself from two very opposite Reflections, which two opposite Parties thought fit to cast on me, *viz.* the one of writing in the *Champion*, (tho' I had not then writ in it for upwards of half a Year) the other, of writing in the *Gazeteer*, in which I never had the Honour of inserting a single Word.

To defend myself therefore as well as I can from all past, and to enter a Caveat against all future Censure of this Kind; I once more solemnly declare, that since the End of *June* 1741, I have not, besides *Joseph Andrews*, published one Word, except *The Opposition, a Vision. A Defence of the Duchess of Marlborough's Book. Miss Lucy in Town*, (in which I had a very small Share.)[15] And I do farther protest, that I will never hereafter publish any Book or Pamphlet whatever, to which I will not put my Name. A Promise, which as I shall sacredly keep, so will it, I hope, be so far believed, that I may henceforth receive no more Praise or Censure, to which I have not the least Title.

And now, my good-natured Reader, recommending my Works to your Candour, I bid you heartily farewell; and take this with you, that you may never be interrupted in the reading these Miscellanies, with that Degree of Heart-ach which hath often discomposed me in the writing them.

Appendix II: Colley Cibber's Preface to *The Provok'd Husband*

1728

This Preface may be compared with Fielding's Preface to *Tom Thumb* (No. 1), where he parodies its style. Other contemporaries found it equally ludicrous, and Cibber was later, in his *Apology*, to refer to several other attempts to ridicule it. See also No. 1, n. 5.

TO THE READER

Having taken upon me, in the Prologue to this Play, to give the Auditors some short Account of that Part of it which Sir *John Vanbrugh* left unfinished, and not thinking it advisable, in that Place, to limit their Judgment by so high a Commendation, as I thought it deserv'd; I have therefore, for the Satisfaction of the Curious, printed the whole of what he wrote, separately, under the Single Title he gave it, of *A Journey to London*, without presuming to alter a Line: which the Bookseller will sell, with, or without the *Provok'd Husband*.

Yet when I own, that in my last Conversation with him (which chiefly turn'd upon what he had done towards a Comedy) he excus'd his not shewing it me, till he had review'd it, confessing the Scenes were yet undigested, too long, and irregular particularly in the Lower Characters, I have but one Excuse for publishing, what he never design'd should come into the World, as it then was, *viz.* I had no other way of taking those many Faults to my self, which may be justly found in my presuming to finish it.

However a Judicious Reader will find in his Original Papers, that the Characters are strongly drawn, new, spirited, and natural, taken from sensible Observations on high and lower Life, and from a just Indignation of the Follies in fashion. All I cou'd gather from him of what he intended in the *Catastrophe* was, that the Conduct of his Imaginary Fine Lady had so provok'd him, that he design'd actually to have made her Husband turn her out of his Doors. But when his Performance came, after his Decease, to my Hands, I thought such violent Measures, however just they might be in real Life, were too severe for Comedy, and would want the proper Surprize, which is due to the End of a Play. Therefore with much ado (and 'twas as much as I cou'd do, with Probability) I preserv'd the Lady's Chastity, that the Sense of her Errors might make a Reconciliation not Impracticable; And I hope the Mitigation of her Sentence has been, since, justified, by its Success.

My Inclination to preserve as much as possible of Sir *John*, I soon saw had drawn the Whole into an unusual Length: the Reader will therefore find here a Scene or two of the Lower Humour, that were left out after the first Day's Presentation.

The Favour the Town has shewn to the higher Characters in this Play, is a Proof, that their Taste is not wholly vitiated, by the barbarous Entertainments that have been so expensively set off to corrupt it: But, while the Repetition of the best old Plays is apt to give Satiety, and good new Ones are so scarce a Commodity, we must not wonder, that the poor Actors are sometimes forced to trade in Trash for a Livelihood.

I cannot yet take leave of the Reader, without endeavouring to do Justice to those Principal Actors, who have so evidently contributed to the Support of this Comedy: And I wish I could separate the Praises due to them, from the secret Vanity of an Author: For all I can say will still insinuate, that they cou'd not have so highly excell'd, unless the Skill of the Writer had given them proper Occasion. However, as I had rather appear vain, than unthankful, I will venture to say of Mr. *Wilks*, that in the last Act, I never saw any Passion take so natural a Possession of an Actor, or any Actor take so tender a Possession of his Auditors.—Mr. *Mills* too, is confess'd by every Body, to have surpriz'd them, by so far excelling himself—But there is no doing Right to Mrs. *Oldfield*, without putting People in mind of what others, of great Merit, have wanted to come near her—Tis not enough to say she *Here Out-did* her usual *Out-doing*. I might therefore justly leave her to the constant Admiration of those Spectators, who have the Pleasure of living while She is an Actress. But as this is not the only Time She has been the Life of what I have given the Publick, so perhaps my saying a little more of so memorable an Actress, may give this Play a Chance to be read, when the People of this Age shall be Ancestors—May it therefore give Emulation to a Succession of our Successors of the Stage, to know, That to the ending of the Year 1727, a Co-temporary Comedian relates, that Mrs. *Oldfield* was, then, in her highest Excellence of Action, happy in all the rarely-found Requisites, that meet in one Person to compleat them for the Stage—She was in Stature just rising to that Height, where the *Graceful* can only begin to shew it self; of a Lively Aspect, and a Command in her Mein, that like the principal Figure in the finest Paintings, first seizes, and longest delights the Eye of the Spectator. Her Voice was sweet, strong, piercing, and melodious; her Pronunciation voluble, distinct, and musical; and her Emphasis always placed where the Spirit of the Sense, in her Periods, only demanded it. If She delighted more in the Higher Comick, than the Tragick Strain, 'twas because the last is too often written in a lofty Disregard of Nature. But in Characters of modern practis'd Life, she found occasions to add the particular Air and Manner which distinguish'd the different Humours she presented. Whereas in Tragedy, the Manner of Speaking varies, as little, as the Blank Verse it is written in—She had one peculiar Happiness from Nature, she look'd and maintain'd the *Agreeable* at a time, when other Fine Women only raise Admirers by their Understanding—The Spectator was always as much informed by her Eyes, as her Elocution; for the Look is the only Proof that an Actor rightly conceives what he utters, there being scarce an Instance, where the Eyes do their Part, that the Elocution is known to be faulty. The Qualities she had *acquired*, were the *Genteel* and the *Elegant*. The one in her Air, and the other in her Dress, never had her Equal on the Stage; and the Ornaments she herself provided, (particularly in this Play) seem'd in all Respects, the *Paraphonalia* of a Women of Quality. And of that Sort were the Characters she chiefly excell'd in; but her natural good Sense, and lively Turn of Conversation made her Way so easy to Ladies of the highest Rank, that it is a less Wonder, if on the Stage she sometimes *was*, what might have become the finest Woman in real Life, to have supported.

C. CIBBER

Theatre-Royal,
Jan. 27,
1728

Appendix III: (*a*) *Common Sense: or, The Englishman's Journal*, No. 31

Saturday, September 3, 1737

(*b*) *Common Sense: or, The Englishman's Journal*, No. 32

Saturday, September 10, 1737

Though usually attributed to Chesterfield, it is possible that both these essays could have been written by Fielding. Stylistic evidence is inconclusive, though the form ''em' rather weakens the case for Fielding's authorship. On the other hand, the references and opinions are often identical with his.

(*a*)

Monsieur *de la Rochefoucault* very justly observes, that People are never ridiculous from their real, but from their affected Characters; they can't help being what they are, but they can help attempting to appear what they are not. A Hump-back is by no means ridiculous, unless it be under a fine Coat; nor a weak Understanding, unless it assumes the Lustre and Ornaments of a bright one. Good Nature conceals and pities the inevitable Defects of Body or Mind, but is not oblig'd to treat acquir'd ones with the least Indulgence.——Those who would pass upon the World Talents which they have not, are as guilty in the common Course of Society, as those who in the way of Trade would put off false Money, knowing it to be such; and it is as much the Business of Ridicule to expose the former, as of the Law to punish the latter.

I don't here mean to consider the Affectation of Moral Virtues, which comes more properly under the Definition of Hypocrisy, and justly excites our Indignation and Abhorrence, as a criminal Deceit; but I shall confine myself now to the Affectation of those lesser Talents and Accomplishments, without any of which, a Man may be a very worthy valuable Man, and only becomes a very ridiculous one by pretending to 'em. Those People are the proper, and, it may be, the only proper Objects of Ridicule; for they are above Fools who are below it, and below wife Men who are above it.——They are the Coxcombs Lord *Rochester* describes as Self-created, and of whom, he says, that God never made one worth a Groat. Besides, as they are Rebels and Traitors to Common Sense, whose natural born Subjects they are, I am justified in treating 'em with the utmost Rigour.

I cannot be of the general Opinion, that these Coxcombs have first imposed upon themselves, and really think themselves what they would have others think 'em. On the contrary, I am persuaded that every Man knows himself best, and is his own severest Censor; nay, I am convinc'd, that many a Man has liv'd and died with Faults and Weaknesses, which no body but himself ever discover'd. It is true, they keep their own Secret inviolate, which makes People believe they have not found it out.——Why do we discern the Failings of our Friends sooner and better than we do other Peoples? but because we interest ourselves more in 'em; by the same Rule, we feel our own still sooner. And possibly, in this Case alone, we are kinder to our Friends than to ourselves; since, I very much question, if a Man would love his Friend so well if he were faultless, and he would certainly like himself the better for being so. If this Supposition be true, as I think it is, my Coxcombs are both the more guilty, and the more ridiculous, as they live in a constant Course of practical Lying, and in the absurd and sanguine Hopes of passing undetected.

Fatuus, the most consummate Coxcomb of this, or any other Age or Country, has Parts enough to have excell'd in almost any one Thing he would have applied himself to. But he must excel in all. He must be at once a Wit, a Lover, a Scholar, and a Statesmen; yet, conscious of the Impracticability of the Undertaking, he parcels out his Accomplishments, and compounds to have the several Branches of his Merit admir'd in separate Districts.

Hence, he talks Politicks to his Women, Wit to Ministers of State, displays his Learning to Beaux, and brags of his Success in Gallantry to his Country Neighbours. His caution is a Proof of his Guilt, and shows that he does not deceive himself, but only hopes to impose upon others. *Fatuus's* Parts have undone him, and brought him to a Bankruptcy of Common Sense and Judgment; as many have been ruin'd by great Estates, which led 'em into Expences they were not able to support.

There are few so universal Coxcombs as *Fatuus*, to whom I therefore gave the Post of Honour; but infinite are the Numbers of minor Coxcombs, who are Coxcombs *quoad hoc*, and who have singled out certain Accomplishments, which they are resolved to possess in spite of reluctant Nature. Their most general Attempts are at Wit and Women, as the two most shining and glittering Talents in the Beau Monde.

Thus *Protervus*, who has a good serious Understanding, contrives to pass almost for a Fool, because he will be a Wit. He must shine; he admires and pursues the Lustre of Wit, which, like an *Ignis-fatuus*, leads him out of his Way into all sorts of Absurdities. He is awkwardly pert, he puns, twists Words, inverts Sentences, and retails in one Company the Scraps he has pick'd up in another; but still, conscious of his own Insufficiency, he cautiously seeks to shine, where he hopes he may dazzle, and prudently declines the Encounter of the strongest Eyes. How often have I seen his unnatural Alacrity suddenly confounded, and shrinking into Silence, at the appearance of somebody of avow'd and unquestion'd Wit?

Ponderosus has a slow, laborious Understanding, a good Memory, and, with Application, might succeed in Business; but truly he must be a *fine Man*, and succeed with Women. He exposes his clumsy Figure by adorning it; makes Declaration of Love with all the Form and Solemnnity of a Proclamation; and ridiculously consumes in Revels, the Time he might usefully employ at the Desk. He can't be ignorant of his ill Success; he feels it, but endeavours to impose upon the World, by hinting, in one Set of Company, his Successes in another; and by whispering, in publick Places, with an Air of Familiarity, such indifferent Trifles, as would not justify the Woman in refusing to hear 'em. But how have I seen him skulk at the approach of the real Favourite, and betray his Consciousness of his affected Character? Be it known to *Ponderosus*, and all those of his Turn, that this Vanity, besides the Absurdity of it, leads them into a most immoral Attempt; and that this practical Defamation of a Woman, more justly deserves an Action at Law, than a coarse Word rashly uttered.

Garrulus hopes to pass for an Orator, without either Words or Matter; it's plain he knows his own Poverty, by his laborious Robbery of Authors. He passes the Nights in Book-breaking, and puts off in the Day-time the stolen Goods as his own; but so awkwardly and unskilfully, that they are always brought back to their true Owners.

Bavius, ballasted with all the Lead of a *German*, will rise into Poetry without either Ear or Invention: He recites, what he calls his Verses, to his Female Relations, and his City Acquaintance, but never mentions 'em to *Pope*.

Perplexus insists upon being a Man of Business, and though form'd, at best, for a Letter Carrier, will be a Letter Writer; but conscious that he can neither be necessary nor useful, endeavours to be tolerated by an implicit Conformity to Men and Times.

In short, there are as many Species of Coxcombs, as there are desirable Qualifications and Accomplishments in Life; and it would be endless to give Instances of every particular Vanity and Affectation by which Men either make themselves ridiculous, or, at least, depreciate the other Qualities they really possess. Every one's Observation will furnish him with Examples enough of this Kind. But I will now endeavour to point out the Means of avoiding these Errors, though, indeed, they are so obvious in themselves, that one should think it unnecessary, if one did not daily experience the contrary.

It is very certain, that no one Man is fit for every Thing; but it is almost as certain too, that there is scarce any one Man who is not fit for something; which Something Nature plainly points out to him, by giving him a Tendency and Propensity to it. I look upon Common Sense to be to the Mind, what Conscience is to the Heart, the faithful and constant Monitor of what is right or wrong. And I am convinced that no Man commits either a Crime, or a Folly, but against the manifest and sensible Representations of the one or the other. Every Man finds in himself, either from Nature or Education (for they are hard to distinguish) a peculiar Bent and Disposition to some particular Character; and his struggling against it, is the fruitless and endless Labour of *Sisyphus*. Let him follow and cultivate that Vocation, he will succeed in it, and be considerable in one Way at least; whereas, if he departs from it, he will at best be inconsiderable, probably ridiculous. Mankind, in general, have not the Indulgence and Good-nature to save a whole City for the sake of five Righteous, but are more inclined to condemn many Righteous for the sake of a few Guilty. And a Man may easily sink many Virtues by the Weight of one Folly, but will hardly be able to protect many Follies by the Force of one Virtue. The Players, who get their Parts by Heart, and are to simulate but for three Hours, have a Regard in chusing those Parts, to the natural Bent of their Genius; *Penkethman* never acted *Cato*, nor *Booth Scrub*; their invincible Unfitness for those Characters would inevitably have broke out, in the short Time of their Representation. How then shall a Man hope to act with Success all his Life long a borrow'd and illsuited Character? In my Mind, *Pinkey* got more Credit by acting *Scrub* well, than he would have got by acting *Cato* ill; and I would much rather be an excellent Shoemaker, than a ridiculous and inept Minister of State.— I greatly admire our industrious Neighbours, the *Germans*, for many Things, but for nothing more, than their steady Adherence to the Voice of Nature; they indefatigably pursue the Way she has chalk'd out to 'em, and never deviate into any Irregularities of Character. Thus many of the first Rank, if happily turn'd to Mechanicks, have employ'd their whole Lives in the Incatenation of Fleas, or the curious Sculpture of Cherry-stones; while others, whose Thirst of Knowledge leads them to investigate the Secrets of Nature, spend Years in their Elabaratory [*sic*], in pursuit of the Philosophers Stone: But none, that I have heard of, ever deviated into an Attempt at Wit. Nay, even due Care is taken in the Education of their Princes, that they may be fit for something; for they are always instructed in some other Trade besides that of Government; so that if their Genius does not lead 'em to be able Princes, it is ten to one but they are excellent Turners.

I will conclude my Remonstrance to the Coxcombs of *Great Britain* with this Admonition and Engagement, that *they disband their Affectations, and Common Sense shall be their Friend.* Otherwise I shall proceed to further Extremities, and single out, from time to time, the most daring Offenders.

I must observe, that the Word Coxcomb is of the Common Gender, both Masculine and Feminine, and that the Male Coxcombs are equall'd in Number by the Female ones, who shall be the Subject of my next Paper.

(*b*)

Having, in my former Paper, censur'd, with Freedom, the Affectations and Follies of my own Sex, I flatter myself, that I shall meet with the Indulgence of the Ladies, while I consider, with the same Impartiality, those Weaknesses and Vanities to which their Sex is as liable as ours, and, if I dare say so, rather more, as their Sphere of Action is more bounded and circumscrib'd.——Man's Province is universal, and comprehends every Thing, from the Culture of the Earth, to the Government of it; Men only become Coxcombs, by assuming particular Characters, for which they are particularly unfit, though others may shine in those very Characters. But the Case of the Fair Sex is quite different; for there are many Characters which are not of the Feminine Gender, and, consequently, there may be two Kinds of Women Coxcombs; those who affect what does not fall within their Deportment, and those who go out of their own natural Characters, tho' they keep within the Female Province.

I should be very sorry to offend, where I only mean to advise and reform; I therefore hope the Fair Sex will pardon me, when I give ours this Preference. Let 'em reflect, that each Sex has its distinguishing Characteristick, and if they can with Justice (as certainly they may) brand a Man with the Name of a Cott-Quean, if he invades a certain Female Detail, which is unquestionably their Prerogative; may not we, with equal Justice, retort upon them, when, laying aside their natural Characters, they assume those which are appropriated to us. —The Delicacy of their Texture, and the Strength of ours; the Beauty of their Form, and the Coarseness of ours, sufficiently indicate the respective Vocations.——Was *Hercules* ridiculous and contemptible with his Distaff? *Omphalé* would not have been less so at a Review, or a Council-Board.——Women are not form'd for great Cares themselves, but to sooth and soften ours; their Tenderness is the proper Reward for the Toils we undergo for their Preservation; and the Ease and Chearfulness of their Conversation, our desirable Retreat from the Labours of Study and Business. They are confined within the narrow Limits of Domestick Offices, and when they stray beyond them, they move excentrically, and consequently without Grace.

Agrippina, born with an Understanding and Dispositions which could, at best, have qualified her for the sordid Help-Mate of a Pawnbroker or Usurer, pretends to all the Accomplishments that ever adorn'd Man or Woman, without the Possession, or even the true Knowledge of anyone of 'em. She would appear Learned, and has read just enough of all Things, without comprehending any one, to make her talk absurdly upon every Thing. She looks upon the Art of Pleasing as her Master-piece, but mistakes the Means so much, that her Flattery is too gross for Self-love to swallow, and her Lies too palpable to deceive for a Moment; so that she shocks those she would gain.——Mean Tricks, shallow Cunning, and Breach of Faith, constitute her mistaken system of Politicks. She endeavours to appear Generous at the Expence of Trifles, while an indiscreet and unguarded Rapaciousness discovers her natural and insatiable Avidity.——Thus mistaking the Perfections she would seem to possess, and the Means of acquiring even them, she becomes the most ridiculous, instead of the most complete of her Sex.

Eudosia, the most frivolous Woman in the World, condemns her own Sex for being too trifling. She despises the agreeable Levity and Chearfulness of a mix'd Company; she will be serious, that she will; and emphatically intimates, that she thinks Reason and good sense very valuable Things. She never mixes in the general Conversation, but singles out some one Man, whom she thinks worthy of her good Sense, and in a half Voice, or *Sotto voce*, discusses her solid Trifles in his Ear, dwells particularly upon the most trifling Circumstances of the main Trifle, which she enforces with the proper Inclinations of Head and Body, and with the most expressive Gesticulations of the Fan, modestly confessing every now and then, by way of Parenthesis, that possibly it may be thought Presumption in a Woman to talk at all upon those Matters. ——In the mean time, her unhappy Hearer stifles a thousand Gapes, assents universally to whatever she says, in hopes of shortning the Conversation, and carefully watches the first favourable Opportunity, which any Motion in the Company gives him, of making his Escape from this excellent solid Understanding.——Thus deserted, but not discourag'd, she takes the whole Company in their Turns, and has, for every one, a Whisper of equal Importance. If *Eudosia* would content herself with her natural Talents, play at Cards, make Tea, and Visits, talk to her Dog often, and to her Company but sometimes, she would not be ridiculous, but bear a very tolerable Part in the polite World.

Sydaria had Beauty enough to have excus'd (while young) her want of common Sense. But she scorn'd the fortuitous and precarious Triumphs of Beauty. She would only conquer by the Charms of her Mind. A Union of Hearts, a Delicacy of Sentiments, a mental Adoration, or a sort of tender Quietism, were what she long sought for, and never found. Thus Nature struggled with Sentiment till she was Five and forty, but then got the better of it to such a Degree, that she made very advantageous Proposals to an *Irish* Ensign of One and twenty: Equally ridiculous in her Age and in her Youth.

Canidia, wither'd by Age, and shatter'd by Infirmities, totters under the Load of her misplac'd Ornaments; and her Dress varies according to the freshest Advices from *Paris*, instead of conforming itself (as it ought) to the Directions of her Undertaker. Her Mind, as weak as her Body, is as absurdly adorn'd; She talks Politicks and Metaphysicks, mangles the Terms of each, and, if there be Sense in either, most infallibly puzzles it; adding Intricacy to Politicks, and Darkness to Mysteries, equally ridiculous in this World and the next.

I shall not now enter into an Examination of the lesser Affectations (most of 'em are pardonable, and many of 'em are pretty, if their Owners are so) but confine my present Animadversions to the Affectation of ill-suited Characters, for I would by no Means deprive my fair

Countrywomen of their genteel little Terrors, Antipathies, and Affections. The alternate Panicks of Thieves, Spiders, Ghosts, and Thunder, are allowable to Youth and Beauty, provided they don't survive 'em. But what I mean is, to prevail with 'em to act their own natural Parts, and not other Peoples; and to convince 'em, that even their own Imperfections will become 'em better than the borrowed Perfections of others.

Should some Lady of Spirit, unjustly offended at these Restrictions, ask what Province I leave to their Sex? I answer, that I leave 'em whatever has not been peculiarly assign'd by Nature to ours. I leave 'em a mighty Empire, *Love*. There they reign absolute, and by unquestion'd Right, while Beauty supports their Throne. They have all the Talents requisite for that soft Empire, and the ablest of our Sex cannot contend with 'em in the profound Knowledge and Conduct of those *Arcana*. But then those who are deposed by Years, or Accidents, or those who by Nature were never qualified to reign, should content themselves with the private Care and Oeconomy of their Families, and the diligent Discharge of Domestick Duties.

I take the fabulous Birth of *Minerva*, the Goddess of Arms, Wisdom, Arts, and Sciences, to have been an Allegory of the Ancients, calculated to shew, that Women of natural and usual Births must not aim at those Accomplishments: She sprung arm'd out of *Jupiter's* Head, without the Co-operation of his Consort *Juno*, and, as such only, had those great Provinces assign'd her.

I confess, one has read of Ladies, such as *Semiramis*, *Thalestris*, and others, who have made very considerable Figures in the most heroick and manly Parts of Life; but considering the great Antiquity of those Histories, and how much they are mix'd up with Fables, one is at liberty to question either the Facts, or the Sex. Besides that, the most ingenious and erudite *Conrad Wolfgang Laboriosus Nugatorius*, of *Hall* in *Saxony*, has prov'd to a Demonstration, in the 14th Volume, Page 2891, of his learned Treatise *De Hermaphroditis*, That all the reputed Female Heroes of Antiquity were of this Epicene Species, though, out of Regard to the fair and modest Part of my Readers, I dare not quote the several Facts and Reasonings with which he supports this Assertion; and as for the Heroines of modern Date, we have more than Suspicions of their being at least of the Epicene Gender. The greatest Monarch that ever fill'd the *British* Throne (*till very lately*) was Queen *Elizabeth*, of whose Sex we have abundant Reason to doubt, History furnishing us with many Instances of the Manhood of that Princess, without leaving us one single Symptom or Indication of the Woman; and thus much is certain, that she thought it improper for her to marry a Man. The great *Christina*, Queen of *Sweden*, was allow'd by every body to be *above her Sex*; and the Masculine was so predominant in her Composition, that she even conform'd, at last, to its Dress, and ended her Days in *Italy*. I therefore require that those Women who insist upon going beyond the Bounds allotted to their Sex, should previously declare themselves in Form Hermaphrodites, and be register'd as such in their several Parishes; till when, I shall not suffer them to confound Politicks, perplex Metaphysicks, and darken Mysteries.

How amiable may a Woman be, what a Comfort and Delight to her Acquaintance, her Friends, her Relations, her Lover, or her Husband, in keeping strictly within her Character! She adorns all Female Virtues with native Female Softness. Women, while untainted by Affectation, have a natural Chearfulness of Mind, Tenderness and Benignity of Heart, which justly endears them to us, either to animate our Joys, or sooth our Sorrows; but how are they chang'd, and how shocking do they become, when the Rage of Ambition, or the Pride of Learning, agitates and swells those Breasts, where only Love, Friendship, and tender Care should dwell?

Let *Flavia* be their Model, who, though she could support any Character, assumes none; never misled by Fancy or Vanity, but guided singly by Reason, whatever she says or does, is the manifest Result of a happy Nature, and a good Understanding; though she knows whatever Women ought, and, it may be, more than they are requir'd to know. She conceals the Superiority she has, with as much Care, as others take to display the Superiority they have not; She conforms herself to the Turn of the Company she is in, but in a Way of rather avoiding to be distanc'd, than desiring to take the Lead: Are they merry, she is chearful; are they grave, she is serious; are they absurd, she is silent: Though she thinks and speaks as a Man would do, still it is as a Woman should do; she effeminates (if I may use the Expression) whatever she says, and gives all the Graces of her own Sex to the Strength of ours; she is well-bred without the troublesome Ceremonies, and frivolous Forms of those who only affect to be so. As her good Breeding proceeds jointly from Good-nature and good Sense, the former inclines her to oblige, and the latter shews her the easiest and best Way of doing it; Woman's Beauty, like Mens Wit, is generally fatal to the Owners, unless directed by a Judgment which seldom accompanies a great Degree of either; her Beauty seems but the proper and decent Lodging for such a Mind; she knows the true Value of it, and far from thinking that it authorizes Impertinence and Coquetry, it redoubles her Care to avoid those Errors that are its usual Attendants; thus she not only unites in herself all the Advantages of Body and Mind, but even reconciles Contradictions in others, for she is lov'd and esteem'd, though envy'd by all.

N.B. We have receiv'd a learned Dissertation sign'd *Dal-rumple*, and another sign'd *G. Cornaro*, for which we return Thanks to their respective Authors, and promise them a Place the first Vacancy.

Notes

INTRODUCTION

1 W. L. Cross, *The History of Henry Fielding* (1915, reprinted 1963), III, 274–5.

2 *The Champion*, No. 16, Saturday, December 22, 1739.

3 Fielding used this pseudonym several times: for example, *The Author's Farce* (1730), *Tom Thumb* (1730), and *The Letter-Writer's* (1731). He also signed himself Captain Lemuel Gulliver on the title page of *The Masquerade* (1728).

4 J. A. Work, 'Henry Fielding, Christian Censor', *The Age of Johnson, Essays presented to Chauncey Brewster Tinker* (1949), 148.

5 *The Covent Garden Journal*, No. 14, Thursday, February 18, 1752.

6 *The Champion*, No. 30, Thursday, January 24, 1739–40.

7 *The Covent Garden Journal*, No. 39, Saturday, May 16, 1752.

8 *The Champion*, No. 58, Thursday, March 27, 1740.

9 Ibid.

10 See below, No. 37; cf. *Miscellanies* (1743), I, 215.

11 'An Essay on Conversation', *Miscellanies* (1743), I, 215.

12 *Plutus, The God of Riches. A Comedy. Translated from the Original Greek of Aristophanes: With Large Notes Explanatory and Critical* (1742), p. 58.

13 *The Champion*, No. 58, March 27, 1740.

14 John Locke, *An Essay Concerning Human Understanding* (1690), III, ch. 11.

15 'An Essay on the Freedom of Wit and Humour' (1709); see *Characteristics* . . ., ed. J. M. Robertson (new ed., 1963), I, 44.

16 Anthony Collins, *A Discourse concerning Ridicule and Irony in Writing . . .* (1729).

17 *The True Patriot*, No. 1, Tuesday, November 5, 1745.

18 Thomas Hobbes, *Leviathan . . .* (1651), I, 6.

19 *Miscellanies* (1743), I, 192.

20 *The Champion*, No. 21, Tuesday, January 3, 1739–40.

21 Madame Dacier on Horace; see *Essay upon Satire* (1697), translated and prefixed to *Miscellany of Poems upon Several Occasions* (1692) by Charles Gildon.

1: PREFACE TO 'TOM THUMB . . .'

1 Longinus, *On the Sublime*: *A Discourse on the Profound, or the Art of Sinking in Poetry* (1728), by Martinus Scriblerus (Alexander Pope).

2 *Hurlothrumbo*, an extravagant burlesque, was by the dancing master, Samuel Johnson. It enjoyed a long run after its first appearance in 1729 and was revised the following year. Fielding refers to it several times.

3 Lucian, *Dialogues of the Dead*, 'Charon and Hermes'.

4 John Locke, *An Essay Concerning Human Understanding* (1690), III, ch. x. Fielding refers to this section of Locke's essay many times, e.g. below, No. 16, n. 7; No. 19, n. 2 ; No. 65, n. 5.

5 This is a reference to Colley Cibber's Preface to *The Provok'd Husband* (1728), in which this spelling and several of the phrases referred to below occur. The extravagant and meaningless phraseology of this Preface was often remembered

against its author: see, for example, *The Art of Sinking* . . . (1728), XVI: 'Here therefore, in the name of all our brethren, let me return our sincere and humble thanks to the most . . . undaunted Mr. Colley Cibber; of whom let it be known when the people of this age shall be ancestors, and to all the succession of our successors, that to this present day they continue to out-do even their own out-doings: and when the inevitable hand sweeping Time shall have brushed off all the works of to-day, may this testimony of a contemporary critic to their fame, be extended as far as tomorrow.' Fielding refers to the objectionable phrase several times, especially after Cibber's good-humoured attempt to recover himself in his *Apology* .... For the text of Cibber's Preface, see below, Appendix II.

6 See Appendix II.

7 Cf. *De Finibus*, II, v, where Cicero says that Plato's obscurities resulted from the difficulty of his material. I have not found a passage which corresponds more closely to Fielding's reference.

8 John Dryden, *Oedipus, King of Thebes* (1679), I, 1: 'The Curtain rises to a plaintive Tune, representing the present condition of Thebes; dead Bodies appear at a distance in the Streets; some faintly go over the Stage, others drop.'

9 Tom Tram and Tom Hickathrift were the hero's of popular chapbooks; one version of the latter's adventures has been attributed to Fielding himself (see Cross, III, 340–1).

10 Fielding's invariable spelling.

11 *Epigrammatica*, V, xvi, 1: 'That I, who could write what is serious, prefer to write what is entertaining, you are the cause.'

2: PREFACE TO 'THE TRAGEDY OF TRAGEDIES'

1 For this and the passage below I offer only hesitant renderings. 'A work of the greatest value, a Tragedy to be put before those of antiquity or those of our own day.'

2 'I would sooner have believed in the *Aeneid* of Maevius than this Tragedy to be the work of the Scriblerus of our own day, which I do not doubt to have been transmitted by Seneca the Author himself.' Fielding is referring here to Dr. Richard Bentley (1622–1742), scholar and classical editor, famous in his own time for his part in the controversy with Charles Boyle over the authorship of the *Epistles of Phalaris* (1695). Fielding elsewhere refers to his edition of Horace (1711). He was notorious as a pedantic and aggressive emendator after his edition of *Paradise Lost* (1732) and is now remembered, unjustly, for his part in the *Dunciad* (1742), IV, 201ff., *The Battle of the Books* (1697), and *The Tale of a Tub* (1704).

3 'Foremost among all heroes of Tragedy.' Petrus Burmannus (1668–1741), Dutch philologist, Professor of Greek at Leyden while Fielding attended that university (1728–9).

4 John Dennis (1657–1734), dramatist and critic, now remembered chiefly for his part in a controversy with Pope, his place in the *Essay on Criticism* (1711) and his rough handling of Shakespeare in *An Essay on the Genius and Writings of Shakespeare* (1712). Throughout this Preface Fielding is ridiculing his method of argument.

5 The piratical copy refers to the first, and perhaps also the second, editions of the play, for which, of course, Fielding was himself responsible.

6 'Most eminent Bentley.'

7 For the identification of Edward Midwinter, see J. T. Hillhouse's edition of *The Tragedy of Tragedies* (1918) and *Notes and Queries*, Series VI, vii, 442.

8 Edmund Curll or Curl (1675–1747), bookseller, was notorious in his own day as an unscrupulous publisher, Fielding refers to him again in *The Champion*; see below, No. 16.

9 Sophonisba, a daughter of Hasdrubal, was in love with Massinella, a Roman ally; Scipio feared her influence and ordered her to be brought to Rome as a captive. Massinella sent her poison, which she willingly took. The plays Fielding refers to are by Jean Mairet (1634); Nathaniel Lee (1676); Pierre Corneille (1663); and James Thomson (1730). Otway's Brutus appears in his *The History and Fall of Gaius Marius* (1680) and Voltaire's in his *Brutus* (1730).

10 The eminent author is James Thomson (1700–48), in his Preface to *Sophonisba* (1730).

11 George Farquar (1678–1707), *The Recruiting Officer* (1706), I, 1: '. . . he that has the good fortune to be born six foot high was born to be a great man'.

12 'Of Heroic Plays, An Essay' prefixed to *The Conquest of Granada* (1672); see W. P. Kerr, *Essays of John Dryden* (1900), I, 148: 'You are gone beyond it, and to continue where you are, is to lodge in the open fields, betwixt two inns.'

13 *Ars Poetica*, 96–7, with *exsul* for *exul*: 'So, too, in Tragedy Telephus and Peleus often grieve in the language of prose, when, in poverty and exile, either hero throws aside his bombast and Brobdingnagian words. . . .'

14 *Ars Poetica*, 95, with *dolere* for *dolet*.

15 *De Oratione*, I, xii, 51: '*Quid est enim tam furiosum, quam verborum, vel optimorum atque ornatissimorum, sonitus inanis, nulla subiecta sententia, nec scienta?*': 'For what so effectually proclaims the madman as the hollow thundering of words [be they ever so choice and resplendent] which have neither thought or knowledge behind them?'

16 *Tristia*, ii, 381: 'Every kind of writing is surpassed in seriousness by Tragedy.'

17 *The Unhappy Favourite: of the Earl of Essex* (1682) was by J. Banks (*c.* 1650–*c.* 1700).

18 *Tusc. Disp.* II, 7: '*quos libros non contemno equidem, quippe quos nunquam legerim*': 'Which I do not for my part despise, for I have never read them.'

3: PROLEGOMENA TO 'THE COVENT GARDEN TRAGEDY'

1 This passage, of course, was written eight years before the appearance of Samuel Richardson's *Pamela* (1740); it may serve to prepare the reader of Fielding for his parody of the introductory material to that novel in his *Shamela* (1741).

2 *Dunciad* (1728), I.

3 *The Craftsman* was an Opposition journal begun in 1726 by Nicholas Amhurst, who wrote under the name of Caleb Danvers, to which Swift, Budgell, Arbuthnot and Bolingbroke contributed from time to time. *The Grubstreet Journal* ran from 1730 to 1738 under the editorship of Richard Russell, though it was under the actual control of Pope, who wrote for it under various pseudonyms. Fielding carried on a battle with the *Journal* for some time during the 1730's, though the exact cause of the quarrel between him and Pope is not known. The *Journal* savagely attacked *The Covent Garden Tragedy* on June 8, 1732, and June 15.

Fielding replied to these and other attacks by publishing a parody of its criticisms in the *Prolegomena* and by writing to *The Daily Post* (see below, No. 4); he seems particularly to have resented the hostile treatment of *The Modern Husband* (first performed, February 14, 1732) and the criticisms of his Lady Charlotte (see below, No. 67, n. 17). For details of the whole quarrel see Cross, I, 114–41. The *History* referred to here is the translation of Voltaire's *History of Charles XII, King of Sweden . . .* (1732), by Alexander Lyon. Livonia was a theatre of war throughout the reign of Charles XII.

4 *The Grubstreet Journal* attacked *The Modern Husband* on March 30, 1732.

5 A highly fashionable Coffee-House, situated at the south-west corner of St. James St., commanding Pall Mall.

6 Obviously Pope.

7 'Either Greek or Latin.' This is the first of a number of quotations from the eighteenth-century version of William Lilly's *Grammatica Rudimenta* (1527), which, Fielding implies throughout, represents the full reach of the critic's knowledge.

8 'Let these nouns be Heterochles which do vary gender or declension and whatsoever do want or have overmuch after a new order.' The translation of this passage and others below is taken from the expanded edition of Lilly's work containing *Lilly's Rules Construed, Whereunto are added Tho. Robinson's Heteroclites . . .* (1731).

9 'The remnant which followeth is married in number or in case.'

10 *Ars Poetica*, 139, suggesting the whole phrase: 'Mountains will labour to produce a ridiculous mouse.'

11 *The Distrest Mother* (1712) was by Ambrose Philips (1675–1749); *The Covent Garden Journal* was a complete parody of the play.

12 'But why stay I in these?'

13 Mr. Leathersides was a representation of Richard Russell, Editor of *The Grubstreet Journal*.

14 *Aeneid*, I, 118: 'Here and there are seen swimmers in the vast abyss.'

15 'A kind man woes [*sic*] his love by entreaty.'

16 Cf. 'A Short Introduction of Grammar', printed with *Lilly's Rules . . .* (1731): 'A Noun Adjective . . . cannot stand by itself in Reason or Signification, but requireth to be joined with another Word.'

17 'Some nouns of one syllable are called masculines, salt, the Sun, the kidneys, or the reins of the back &c. and spleen, a Man of Caria, a man of Asia, a man, a surety.' The reference in the line above is to Pope's *Essay on Criticism* (1711), II, 347.

18 'Avoid barbarous words as very dangerous things.'

19 'Which diligent reading will teach.'

20 Cf. *Spectator*, No. 135, Saturday, August 4, 1711, where Addison complains about current tendency to shorten words 'as in *mob. rep. pos. incog.* and the like.' *Rep.* here seems to be a shortened form of *Reputation*.

21 'Never found in usage.'

22 'The termination as in the present tense formeth the preluperfect tense in *avi*.'

4: A LETTER TO 'THE DAILY POST'

1 *Sermones*, I, x, 78–80, with *crimex* for *cimex*, *crucier* for *cruciet*: 'Am I to be stung by that louse Pantilius, or tortured because Demetrius criticized me when absent, or because foolish Fannius, who sponges on Hermogenes Tigellius, attacks me?'

2 After Fielding's publication of *The Covent Garden Tragedy* further attacks followed in *The Grubstreet Journal* on June 31, July 13 and July 20, continuing until August, 1732.

3 These are pseudonyms from beneath which Fielding was attacked: Dramaticus seems to have belonged to Richard Russell.

4 *The Old Debauchees* was acted together with *The Covent Garden Tragedy* at Drury Lane on June 1, 1732. *The Covent Garden Tragedy* was later withdrawn and *The Mock Doctor* substituted for it.

5 *The Humourous Lieutenant* (1619) was by John Fletcher; the writer who approved it was Sir Richard Steele; see *Spectator*, No. 266, Friday, January 4, 1712.

6 Richard Russell was a non-juring parson.

7 That is, Jonathan Swift.

5: A LETTER TO 'COMMON SENSE'

1 *Common Sense* . . . was set up by Fielding's friends, Philip Dormer Stanhope (1694–1773), Fourth Earl of Chesterfield, and George Lyttleton (1709–73), First Baron Lyttleton, as a medium for opposition to the Walpole Administration. The first number, written by Chesterfield (February 5, 1737), refers to Fielding's dramatic labours in the cause of common sense. It is possible that this letter was not his only contribution to the journal; see Appendix III.

2 This sentence implies that Fielding was thinking at this time of establishing a periodical of his own, though *The Champion* was not begun for another two years, the first number appearing on Thursday, November 15, 1739.

3 *The Daily Gazeteer* was the official organ of the Walpole Administration, distributed free in many parts of the country. The article of May 7, supposed to have been written by Lord Hervey, warned Fielding about the danger incurred by political satire of the kind which he had been producing in *Pasquin* (1736) and *The Historical Register* (1737) and preceded the decision of the Government to bring forward the Licensing Act, which effectively ended his dramatic career.

4 That is, Robert Walpole.

5 'A Letter Concerning Enthusiasm' (1708); see *Characteristics* . . ., ed. J. M. Robertson (new ed., 1963), I, 218.

6 Bona Dea was the name given to Ops, Vesta, Cybele and Rhea among the Greeks and to Fauna among the Romans; she was the goddess of chastity, whose rites were celebrated in secret and by night.

7 Pierre Bayle (1647–1706), author of *Dictionnaire historique et critique* (1697–enlarged 1702), frequently translated. I do not know under which of the biographical headings this remark might appear.

8 First produced in 1728 with enormous success and frequently revived; this imputation was frequently made.

9 Thomas Hobbes, *Leviathan: or, The Matter, Form, and Power of A Common-*

wealth . . . (1651), I, 6; see *The English Works of Thomas Hobbes* (reprinted 1966), ed. Sir W. Molesworth, 46.

10 Cf. *Sermones*, I, x, 15–16.

11 The Opposition at this stage did indeed possess some of the most intelligent and cultured men of the day, led by John Carteret, later Earl of Granville, including Chesterfield, Lyttleton and the Duke of Argyle.

12 William Penketheman, Pinkethman or Pinkerman (d. 1725); Henry Norris (1665–1730), called Jubilee Dicky for his part in Farquar's *The Constant Couple . . .* (1700): both comic actors of great popularity and repute who often played at the booth theatres in Bartholomew Fair. It was probably there that the burlesque to which Fielding is referring was played, but I have found no reference to it. Fielding's reference to it in *The Champion*, No. 129, according to *The Champion*, No. 132, was not understood by his readers: 'And, for the Farce of *Alexander* burlesqued, not one of them could tell what to make of it.'

13 Ridiculously enough, this suggestion was actually made in the *Gazeteer* article. Fielding had been working with the company in the Little Theatre in the Haymarket as early as February, 1730, though he had transferred to Drury Lane by 1732. In February, 1736, he took over the Haymarket and remained there until the Licensing Act came in force in June, 1737. On June 24 the Haymarket was closed.

14 Joshua Ward (1685–1761) was a quack doctor who proposed to cure all ailments with the help of a drop and pill of his own invention. In February, 1753, despairing of cure by more regular methods, Fielding asked for his assistance and expressed his gratitude for Ward's help in the Introduction to the *Journal of the Voyage to Lisbon*: 'Obligations to Mr. Ward I shall always confess; for I am convinced that he omitted no care in endeavouring to serve me, without any expectation or desire of fee or reward.'

6: 'THE CHAMPION', NO. 129

1 Not Tibullus, but Ovid, *Epistulae ex Ponto*, IV, vii, 49.

2 William Milward (1702–42), a capable actor at Drury Lane.

3 Thomas Betterton (1635?–1710), a famous actor of irrepproachable character who won the approval and friendship of many of the most eminent men of his time. Robert Wilks (1665?–1732), one of the Triumvirate who ruled over Drury Lane from 1710 (see below, No. 12, n. 11), an actor most eminent in comedy, noted for his irascible temper and boundless energy.

4 James Quin (1693–1766), an actor held by many to have excelled even Booth in some tragic parts, was at Covent Garden from 1732–4 and at Drury Lane from 1734–41. Fielding was evidently under the impression that he was to take over as acting-manager from Theophilus Cibber, who had been at Drury Lane in that capacity from 1734–8, when he went to France to avoid his creditors. Cibber was at Drury Lane again from 1741–2.

5 Charles Fleetwood, a man of fortune and fashion, had taken over the patent of Drury Lane in 1734 from Mrs. Wilks and Highmore. Fielding puts the blame for his lack of success before 1740 on Theophilus Cibber, suggesting that he was responsible for the introduction of degrading farce and pantomime.

6 See above, No. 5, n. 12.

7 For Mrs. Clive, see below, No. 46, n. 2.

8 *The Devil to Pay; or the Wives Metamorphos'd. An Opera* (1732), was abridged by Theophilus Cibber from Charles Coffey's play of the same name. *Tom Thumb* and *The Lottery* (first performed January 1, 1732, at Drury Lane). *An Hospital for Fools. A dramatic Fable* (1739) was by James Miller (1706–44), dramatist and misc. writer, Rector of Upcerne in Dorset. The hobby-horses were a device of Cibber's to fill out a performance of Buckingham's *Rehearsal*; see *An Apology for the Life of Mr. T. C., Comedian* (1740), in which it is very probable that Fielding had some hand.

9 The most notorious instance of harsh treatment of French players in England occurred in October, 1738, when a company was brought over to act in the Haymarket Theatre, which had been vacated by Fielding after the Licensing Act. Soldiers with fixed bayonets, accompanied by two justices of the peace, were ineffective in preventing the riot which followed.

10 Virgil, *Georgics*, IV, 176: 'one may measure small things by great'.

11 Edward Vernon (1684–1757) created vice-admiral on July 9, 1739, took Porto Bello from the Spaniards on November 21, 1739, with six ships. Fielding refers to him frequently in *The Champion* as a popular hero whose brilliant successes disturbed the plans of an unpatriotic Walpole Government. Philip Yorke (1690–1764), Earl of Hardwicke, Whig statesmen and reforming lawyer, Lord Chancellor from February, 1737. Fielding's opinion of him suffered no diminution over the years.

7: 'THE TRUE PATRIOT', NO. 18

1 *Epigrammatica*, I, iii, 5–6; cf. Nos. 13, 14. Fielding translates in the latter: 'No town can such a gang of Critics show / Ev'n Boys turn up the Nose they cannot blow.'

2 For the opera managed in England by Handel and Buoncini see *Spectator*, No. 5, Tuesday, March 6, 1710–11, and Cibber's *Apology*, ch. xii. Fielding satirized the opera in *The Author's Farce* (1730).

3 For the Mohocs or Mohawks see *Spectator*, No. 324, Wednesday, March 12, 1711–12. 'Agreeable to their name, the avowed design of their institution is mischief. . . . An outrageous ambition of doing all possible hurt to their fellow-creatures, is the great cement of their assembly, and the only qualification required in the members . . . . They make a general sally, and attack all that are so unfortunate as to walk the streets through which they patrole. Some are knocked down, others stabbed, others cut and carbonadoed . . .' See also Swift's *Journal to Stella*, ed. H. Williams (1948), 508–9. There is some doubt as to whether or not these bands of young men, roving the streets with fiendishly casual aggression, were not the product of the public imagination.

4 William Mills (d. 1750), a son of the more famous John Mills (d. 1736). Fielding did not think highly of his talents as an actor; see No. 55. Mills played Claudius in the performance of *Hamlet* which is described in *Tom Jones*.

5 The riot mentioned here is probably one of those which took place at Drury Lane on November 17 and 19, 1744, occasioned by an increase in the prices.

6 The Upper Gallery was occupied mainly by footmen who accompanied their masters and mistresses to the play.

7 Fielding had some trouble in circulating *The True Patriot*, as he had earlier with *The Champion*. This number of the paper contained the following announcement on the title-page: 'Whereas we have been informed by several Persons, that they have not been able to procure the TRUE PATRIOT at any Rate: And we have great Reason to believe that many malicious and base Endeavours have been used to suppress the Sale of this Paper, by some who are concerned in imposing on the Public, by propagating Lies and Nonsense, which we have endeavoured to detect and expose. If any Hawkers, or others, will acquaint Mr. *A. Millar*, Bookseller, opposite *Katharine-Street* in the *Strand*, with the Name of any Person who has bribed, or offered to bribe them to refuse delivering out the TRUE PATRIOT to their Customers, they shall be well rewarded, and their Names, if they desire it, concealed.'

8 The Latin phrase is taken from Horace, *Sermones*, II, iii, 243, meaning 'a famous pair of brothers'. It is here a reference to the Lords Bath and Granville, whom Fielding attacked on account of their underhand attempt to form a Ministry before and after the resignation of Pelham and his colleagues on February 9, 1746.

8: 'THE CHAMPION', NO. 69

1 *Sermones*, II, i, 45: 'better not touch me, I shout'.

2 John Rich (1682–1761) inherited the New Theatre in Lincoln's Inn Fields from his father (also John) in 1714. He opened the new theatre in Covent Garden in 1732. He was well known in his own day as the inventor of English pantomime (for which he was satirized in *Pasquin*) and as a successful Harlequin.

3 A reference to Sir Robert Walpole; see No. 11, n. 3.

4 The passage which follows is taken from *Gaius Caligula*, XLV–XLVI.

5 Samuel Pitiscus (1637–1771), scholar and philologist, edited Suetonius (1690) and was the author of *Antiquitates Romanae* (1701).

6 The Earl of Chesterfield was widely believed to be writing his memoirs; so was Martinus Scriblerus (they appeared in 1741). I have no other suggestions to make as to whom Fielding might mean.

7 Edward Hyde (1609–74), Earl of Clarendon, author of *History of the Rebellion and Civil Wars*, published posthumously in 1702–4. The Greek phrase Fielding cites is from Thucidides, I, 22, meaning 'a work for all time'. Compare 'The Author's Preface', *The History of the Rebellion . . .* (1702), I, sections 1–3, where Clarendon shows that he is thinking of his work as directed to posterity.

8 See *Apology* (1740), 64–5. In 1740 a pamphlet appeared which contained the attack on Fielding reprinted from the *Apology*, together with Fielding's satire of Cibber from *The Champion*. Though the Preface to the pamphlet was signed by one T. Johnson and claimed that the passages were reprinted with the intention of showing both Fielding and Cibber in their true light, there are some grounds for thinking that Fielding himself may have been partly responsible for it (see No. 11, n. 3). The editor (whoever he was) comments on this passage from the *Apology*: 'This slight (as it really would any Dramatic Writer) has justly enraged Captain Hercules Vinegar to lop off the Laureate's Head, as one belonging to his *Monster Hydra*.' In view of Fielding's reaction, the comment is strange.

9 Cf. *Epodes*, I, 5: '*quibus te vita sit superstite iucunda*'—'to whom, surviving with thee, life is joyful'.

10 The title-page of the *Apology* bears the imprint, 'Printed by John Watts for the AUTHOR: And Sold by W. Lewis in *Russell-Street*, near *Covent-Garden*', John Watts (1700?–63), a high-class printer of Little Queen Street who printed many of Fielding's works, is presumably the Goody —— of this reference. William Lewis was a bookseller in Russell Street, Covent Garden.

11 Four plays of Colley Cibber: *Caesar in Egypt* (1725); *Ximena, or, The Heroic Daughter* (1712); *The Refusal, or the Ladies Philosophy* (1721); and *Love in a Riddle* (1729), this last a pastoral imitation of *The Beggar's Opera.*

12 Cibber's odes, written in performance of his duty as Laureate, were a standing joke with Fielding and his contemporaries; he also wrote at times for *The Daily Gazeteer.*

13 That is, Colley Cibber and Robert Walpole, as is made clear in *The Trial of Colley Cibber* . . ., where blanks are often filled in.

14 Presumably *The London Farthing Post.* I do not know the identity of the author.

15 Untraced.

16 Samuel Butler, *Hudibras* (1663), I, canto 1.

17 I have not traced this sentence in 'one of our poets'; but cf. Menander, *Rapizomene*, Fragment 422: 'The man that's never been flogged has never been taught.'

9: 'THE CHAMPION', NO. 72

1 *Tusc. Quaest.*, III, 6, with several words missing between *possit* and *hominis*: 'But to commit one's reflections to writing, without being able to arrange or express them clearly . . . indicates a man who makes an unpardonable misuse of learning and his pen.'

2 *Institutio Oratoria*, I, iv, 5.

3 *Ars Poetica*, 408–10 and *Epistulae*, II, i, 117.

4 *Apology* (1740), 68: 'As we have sometimes great composers of musick who cannot sing, we have as frequently great writers that cannot read. . . .'

5 Fielding's attitude to the Royal Society is one which he shared with Pope and Swift. See also his *Some Papers Proper to Read before the Royal Society* . . ., first published in *The Daily Post*, February 16, 1743, and reprinted in *Miscellanies* (1743), I, 252–77.

6 *Apology* (1740), 32. Cf. Appendix II.

7 Longinus, *On the Sublime*, I, sec. 4; 'unconquerable force'; Horace, *Ars Poetica*, 100: '*dulcia sunt / et quocumque volent animum auditoris agunto*'—'They must have charm and lead the hearer's soul where they will.'

10: 'THE CHAMPION', NO. 75

1 *Iliad*, I, 185–6; 'So that you may know how much stronger I am than you and another may shrink . . .'

2 I have not discovered who Fielding's judicious critic was, but it seems worth remarking that there is a passage very close to this (and to what follows here) in the anonymous *Apology for the Life of Mr. Theophilus Cibber* (1740), 22: 'It is not a Characteristick of Excellence to have a Stile so peculiarly singular, that in the reading half a Page you are sure of the Author? Has not the great Bentley gone

on in this Principle, in all his most erudite Castigations? Catching the Stile of the Authors, has he not said of *Horace* and *Terence,—Sic scripsit.*—Thus he wrote? . . . The same Method he has taken with *Milton.*—The amount of all this is, if a singular Stile is a Demonstration of a Genius, I will venture, without any Infringement on Modesty, to affirm that the *Cibberian* Stile is a Proof of very remarkable Talents. . . .'

3 Richard Bentley's edition of Milton (1732), attacked by Pope in *Dunciad,* IV, 201ff., offered a multitude of emendations on Milton's text, based on the argument that it was corrupt after passing through the hands of scribes and printers.

4 Lewis Theobald (1688–1744), editor, dramatist and hack, was responsible for *Shakespeare Restored, or a Specimen of the way errors are as well Committed as Unamended by Mr. Pope* . . . (1725), which earned him a prominent place in the first version of the *Dunciad* (1728). Cibber's *The Careless Husband* appeared in 1715, *Love's Last Shift,* his first play, in 1696.

5 These are the pseudonyms of certain political writers of Fielding's day. Several writers used the name of Osborne, including James Pitt, editor of the *London Journal* and contributor to *The Daily Gazeteer.* Sir Francis Walsingham was William Arnall (1715–41), editor of *The True Briton,* who boasted to have received over £10,000 in four years of writing for the Walpole Administration. Algernon Sidney may be identified either with Francis Medley or with a writer called Murray. Ralph Freeman was Ralph Courteville, from May, 1741, the chief Government writer, frequently attacked in *The Champion.* These writers were all 'BOB-tail Writers' in the sense that they followed at the heels of the Chief Minister.

6 *Hudibras,* I, canto i; 'But, when he pleas'd to show't, his speech / In loftiness of sound was rich;/A Babylonish dialect,/Which learned pedants much affect;/ It was a party-coloured dress/ Of patch'd and piebald languages:/'Twas English cut on Greek and Latin,/Like fustian heretofore on sattin.' The form 'Bobylonish', like 'Bob-tail', refers to Sir Robert Walpole.

7 That is, a miscellany or stew.

8 *Animadversions upon Dr. Sherlock's Book, Entituled A Vindication of the Holy and Ever Blessed Trinity &c. . . . By a Divine of the Church of England* (1693), 114.

9 The dashes belong to Cibber. The reference is, of course, to the proverbial saying, 'It is an ill bird that fouls his own nest.'

11: 'THE CHAMPION', NO. 80

1 Horace, *Epistulae,* II, i, 182: 'The bold poet is frightened and put to rout.'

2 That is, Alexander Pope, whose identity is made clear on the title-page of *The Trial of Colley Cibber* . . . (1740).

3 Forage, Brass and his Honour are nicknames for Sir Robert Walpole which occur frequently in *The Champion,* though one of them at least was in use long before the paper began; see *Sir Robert Brass: or, the Intrigues, serious and amorous, of the Knight of the Blazing Star* (1731), published by Andrew Millar; see also *The Champion,* No. 72, Index to the Times, where a series of lectures is advertised as to be given 'at the *Brazen Head,* a *Public House,* not far from *Downing street*', 'By *Robin Brass,* A, B, C, D, E, F, G, H, I, J, K, L, M, N, O, P, Q, R, S, T, U, V, W, X, Y, Z, & perse & . . . on *State-Lodgic* . . .' It is interesting that in the text

of this essay, which is reprinted in *The Trial . . .*, this phrase reads: 'Forage, alias Guts, alias Brass', and throughout the paper Guts is inscribed instead of Brass. Guts is used elsewhere in *The Champion* (see, e.g., No. 8, n. 3), and its insertion in the pamphlet suggests that, in spite of T. Johnson's claim to impartiality the reprinting was done in the same spirit as the original was written.

4 'Let no one touch me'; the phrase belongs to the Vulgate version of John xx. 17.

5 T. Pistol, or Theophilus Cibber, was conducting a case against a Mr. Sloper for seduction of his wife. The case was notorious because it was clearly proved during its hearing that Cibber had connived at—and in fact encouraged—his wife's adultery. Two contemporary pamphlets giving details of the case have been reprinted in *An Account of the Life of that Celebrated Actress, Mrs Susannah Maria Cibber with Interesting and Amusing Anecdotes. Also the Two Remarkable and Romantic Trials . . .* (1887).

6 Colley Cibber was left-handed.

7 Fielding is here referring to Edward Coke's famous book, *The . . . Institutes . . . A Commentary upon Lyttleton . . .* Needless to say, section 261 is not followed by 261*b*, but I do not understand the reference in Fielding's note to Bordeaux.

8 Nathan Bailey (d. 1742), *An Universal Etymological English Dictionary* (1721).

9 For Watts and Lewis, see No. 8, n. 10.

10 *Apology* (1740), 31.

11 George Cheyne, M.D. (1671–1743), author of *Essay of Health* (1724), *The English Malady* (1733), *Essay on Regimen* (1740), *The Natural Method of Curing Diseases* (1742), and *Philosophical Principles of Religion* (1705 and 1715), the last of which is the book Fielding refers to.

12 The 'certain fat Gentleman' may have been Henry Pelham, to whom the *Apology* was dedicated and who was certainly fat.

13 Chance Medley is a legal phrase referring to an accident which was not purely accidental, but of a mixed nature.

12: 'THE CHAMPION', NO. 3

1 *De Officiis*, I, xxxi, 110–11: '*Nihil decet Minerva, ut aiunt, id est adversante et repugnante natura*'. The sense of Fielding's sentence is: 'Nothing is proper that is opposed to one's genius, that is, if one's nature is against it; so you are not able to preserve decorum, if in trying to assume another's nature, you omit your own.'

2 *De Finibus*, V, 39: 'To follow the course that Nature prescribes.'

3 *Ars Poetica*, 39–40: '*quid ferre recusent,/quid valeant umeri*'—'what your shoulders refuse and what they can bear'. Lord Shaftesbury does not use this quotation, but it summarizes his advice; as, for example, in 'That their composition and vein of writing may be natural and free, they should settle matters in the first place with themselves . . .', *Characteristics . . .*, ed. J. M. Robertson (new ed., 1966), I, 180–1.

4 This seems to be the result of a conflation of two separate passages in the sermons of Dr. Robert South (1634–1716), one of Fielding's favourite authors. See *Twelve Sermons Printed upon Several Occasions* (6th ed., 1727), I, 323–4, and III, 449: 'One Man perhaps proves miserable in the Study of the Law, which

might have flourished in that of Physick, or Divinity. Another runs his Head against the Pulpit, who might have been very serviceable to his Country at the Plough.' 'Those only were accounted like St. Paul, who could *work with their Hands*, and in a literal sense, *drive the Nail home*, and be able to *make a Pulpit* before they *preached* in it.'

5 A translation of the proverbial phrase, '*poeta nascitur, non fit*'. See Florus, *De Qualitate Vitae*, fragment 8.

6 *Institutio Oratoria*, II, xix, 3: 'Without material art can do nothing, material without art does possess a certain value, while the perfection of art is better than the best material. See also II, xvii, 9.

7 René Rapin (1621–87), Jesuit and critic of distinction, whose *Réflexions sur la Poétique d'Aristote* (1674) was translated by Rymer in the year of its appearance. The work referred to here is *A Comparison between Demosthenes and Cicero* ; see *The Whole Critical Works of Mons. Rapin*, trans. Basil Kennet, D.D. (1731), I, ch. xx, 107–8.

8 William Wycherley (1640?–1716) published *Miscellany Poems* in 1704. Congreve's tragedy was *The Mourning Bride* (1697).

9 *De Augmentis Scientarum*, VIII, 2. Fielding makes this reference again in *The Champion*, No. 31, Saturday, January 26, 1739–40, and in *The Covent Garden Journal*, No. 48, Tuesday, June 16, 1752.

10 Westminster Hall, the only remaining part of the old Westminster Palace, was the principal seat of justice from the reign of Henry III through the whole of the eighteenth century.

11 The members of the famous Triumvirate which governed Drury Lane were Colley Cibber, Barton Booth (1681–1733) and Robert Wilks (1665–1731). Thomas Dogget (d. 1721) had retired before Booth was given a share of the patent in 1711.

12 See No. 5, n. 12.

13: 'THE CHAMPION', NO. 5

1 *Epigrammatica*, I, iii, 3–6; the first two lines translate as follows: 'You don't know, alas, you don't know the superciliousness of Mistress Rome; believe me, the crowd of Mars is too clever for you.' For Fielding's translation of the latter two see No. 7, n. 1.

2 Cf. Fielding's epitaph to Butler in *Miscellanies* (1743). Though apparently untrue, it was a common tradition that Butler died in poverty; see, for example, Mr. Oldham's *Satire Against Poetry* (1683), p. 173: 'Reduc'd to want, he in due time fell sick / Was fain to die/And be interr'd on tick.'

3 Horace, *Epistulae*, II, i, 181: 'denial of the palm sends me home lean, its bestowal, plump'.

4 Bentley, in his edition of Horace (1711), emended *facta* to *fata* in *Epistulae*, II, i, 6. The unamended text reads: '*post ingentia facta deorum in templa recepti*'—'after mighty deeds were received into the temples of the gods'.

5 *Amores*, I, i, 39.

6 Horace, *Epistulae*, II, i, 15: 'Upon you while you are present we bestow honours betimes.'

7 Sir William Temple, 'Of Poetry' (1690); see J. E. Spingarn, *Critical Essays*

of the Seventeenth Century (1909), III, 83: 'I know not whether . . . for one Man that is born capable of making such a Poem as Homer or Virgil, there may not be a Thousand born capable of making as great Generals of Armies or Ministers of State as any the most Renowned in Story.'

8 That is, Erostratus, who set fire to the Temple of Diana on the night that Alexander the Great was born, in order to achieve notoriety.

9 *Eclogues*, III, 90.

10 Cf. 'Of Good Nature', *Miscellanies* (1743): 'Dwells there a base malignity in men, / That 'scapes the tiger's cave, or lion's den;/Does our fear dread, or does our envy hate,/To see another happy, good, or great?/Or does the gift of fame like money seem? / Think we we lose, whene'er we give esteem?'

11 See the 'Life of Homer' prefixed to Mme. A. Dacier's translation of the *Iliad* into French (1711): 'If I durst, I would instruct those Fault-Finders, who condemn Homer, without knowing anything of him, in a way of Reasoning . . . I would have every one of those presumptuous Critics to reason after this manner . . . because I have never read *Homer* in his own Tongue, and am incapable of Reading, or of Reading him well; How then can I presume. . . .?' (trans. Mr. Ozell (1712), 29–30).

12 Fielding is referring to a phrase of Lord Chesterfield's in his speech to the House of Lords, opposing the Stage Licensing Bill of 1737: 'Wit, my Lords, is a sort of property; it is the property of those who have it, and too often the only property they have to depend on.' See Cross, I, 231.

13 For Counsellor Vinegar, see *The Champion*, No. 1, November 15, 1739. Captain Hercules Vinegar and his relations, among whom was 'some one eminent in every Science and Profession', conducted *The Champion* together. Mr. Counsellor Vinegar, the Captain's uncle, 'entered a Student in the *Middle Temple*, in the Year 1688'. This passage is a parody of legal phraseology such as one finds in Coke on Lyttleton (see No. 11, n. 7). All I can offer is a rough paraphrase: 'It is my opinion that if anyone says of J.S. that he is a Dull Poet there is a good Action, according to the Resolution in the case 1, Regina Anne 55, s. 16, whence it appears that if the Plaintiff declares that the Defendant has said of him that he is a Dunce and will get nothing by the Law, an action may be brought by an Apprentice of the Law. And it was the Opinion of the Court that there will be a good Action in the case of a Poet who is Heavy and not as pregnant as other authors, providing that he is a good Lawyer, on the grounds of the statement that he will get nothing by the Law. [This is because?] if a Poet is Heavy or Dull he will get nothing in the World [outside the Court?]'

14 *Essay on Criticism* (1711), 15–16.

15 This person remains unidentified.

14: 'THE COVENT GARDEN JOURNAL', NO. 3

1 *Epigrammatica*, I, iii, 5–6; cf. No. 7, n. 1, and No. 13, n. 1.

2 This and the preceding phrase are legal terms denoting Statutes passed in particular reigns—here the twentieth year of George II and the thirtieth of Elizabeth I.

3 Isaac Bickerstaffe, Esq., was Steele's pseudonym in *The Tatler* (April, 1709–January, 1711).

4 Dion Cassius, LXXIII, 1; Pertinax (A.D. 126–93), was murdered by his soldiers after a reign of eighty-seven days.

5 *Institutio Oratoria*, X, i, 26.

6 *Essay on Criticism* (1711), 675–6, slightly altered.

7 John Oldmixon (1673–1742), historian, author of *The Secret History of Europe* (1712–15), and of an account of the reign of George I (1735–9), also wrote an *Essay on Criticism* (1727).

8 Cf. *The Covent Garden Journal*, No. 1, Saturday, January 4, 1752, where Fielding refers to the 'great political cause between WOODALL OUT, and TAKEALL IN, Esq.; which hath been so learnedly handled in Papers, Pamphlets, and Magazines, for above thirty Years last past . . . .'

15: 'THE COVENT GARDEN JOURNAL', NO. 31

1 *Eclogues*, III, 90.

2 *Cato* (1713), V, 1, 15.

3 Cf. *Macbeth*, II, 2.

16: 'THE CHAMPION', NO. 47

1 Silius Italicus (A.D. *c.* 23–*c.* 98), called the ape of Virgil, author of a poem on the Second Punic War, IX, 636: 'Alas for our country! Alas for our people who in their wickedness bestow their favour amiss!'

2 See *The Champion*, No. 42, February 19, 1739–40: 'In the Case of Trade, this Partiality and the Pride which occasions it are more apparent. Do we not every Day confess that we give advanced Prices for the Names of particular Tradesmen who have Assurance to exact larger Prices for their Commodities than their Brethren, only because they are richer, and might consequently afford to sell cheaper.'

3 St. Dunstan's Clock, constructed in 1671, had a large gilt dial projecting into the street, and above it two lifesize statues of savages armed with clubs. I do not know whether Fielding is referring to any particular sign in Fleet Street.

4 That is, fool or gull.

5 *Epodes*, II, 1, 117.

6 *Essay on Criticism* (1711), 6.

7 *Of Human Understanding* (1690), I, ch. 1, 'Introduction'.

8 Presumably the column of advertisements.

9 An example of what Fielding is referring to is the play, *The Double Falsehood; or, the Distressed Lovers. A play . . . Written . . . by William Shakespeare; and now revised . . . by Mr. Theobald . . .* (1728).

10 Pistol was a common nickname for Theophilus Cibber. In view of this, it is possible that Fielding is suggesting that the poem Curll published was written by Cibber. *Seventeen Hundred and Thirty-nine. Or, the Modern p*[eer]*s. A satire* (1739) was inscribed to the Earl of Chesterfield.

11 Sir Richard Steel died at Carmarthen in 1729; the lodgings at Twickenham suggest an identification with Pope; *Lais's* Wash I find completely obscure.

12 Fielding is referring here to the Society for the Encouragement of Learning, an association of persons 'To assist authors in publishing and to secure them the

entire profits of their own works'. Its President was the Duke of Richmond, and it survived from 1736 to 1749. There are conflicting accounts of its state of finances at the time of its demise.

13 After this number of *The Champion* the writing was shared between Fielding and James Ralph; articles by Fielding were signed mainly with the initials C and L, those by Ralph with *** or the name Lilbourne.

17: 'THE CHAMPION', NO. 147

1 *Epigrammatica*, I, 38: 'That book you recite, O Fidentinus, is mine. But your vile recitation begins to make it your own.'

2 *Spectator*, No. 460, Friday, August 22, 1712.

3 Michel Eyquem de Montaigne (1533–92), 'Of Books', in *Essays*, II, 10: 'In the reasonings and inventions that I transplant into my soil and confound with my own . . .'.

4 *Animadversions upon Dr. Sherlock's Book, Entituled a Vindication of the Holy and Ever Blessed Trinity &c . . . By a Divine of the Church of England* (1693), 349: 'Upon which, as well as upon other occasions, I look upon this as the only sure Rule of dealing with the Author's Quotations, *viz.* To *trust them* no further than one *can see* them in their Originals.'

5 Cf. *Academica*, II, 72, 16.

6 Edward Pinchbeck (d. unknown), was an entertainments promoter who operated between 1739 and 1750 at the old tennis court in James Street and at Bartholomew Fair. His advertisements seem to have made large claims concerning the 'Machinery' he employed.

7 That is, Homer.

8 John Nourse (fl. 1730–80), at the sign of the Lamb without the Temple Bar, specialized in French literature and Scientific works and produced an edition of Horace in 1736 in collaboration with J. Brotherton. He was a friend of Fielding's, a partner in *The Champion* and evidently employed the novelist on several occasions.

9 The only candidate for admission here that I have discovered is Edmund Curll, who had a shop in Rose Street, at the sign of the Pope's Head, from 1735–1747.

18: FROM 'AMELIA', BOOK VIII, CH. V

1 *Dunciad*, I, 19–22, with *take* for *chuse* and slight changes of punctuation.

2 Walter Moyle (1672–1721), politician and student: *Dissertation on the age of Philopatris, a Dialogue commonly attributed to Lucian*, posthumously published in *Works of Walter Moyle* (1726), I. Moyle actually says 'matchless': 'But I can by no means agree with the Doctor, that Lucian was the Author of it. 'Tis so infinitely below the Wit, the Spirit, and the politeness of that matchless Writer . . .' (p. 288).

3 *The Dream, or the Cock*, a dialogue between Mycillus and Pythagoras in the form of a cock.

4 Nicholas Rowe's translation of Lucan's *Pharsalia* was published in 1718.

5 *Lucian's Works Translated by Several Hands* (1711). Dryden was general editor and author of the life which was prefixed to the translation. The other translators were Tom Brown, Walter Moyle, John Philips and Sir Henry Steens.

6 For his version of the *Iliad* Pope received £200 per volume, together with free copies for his subscribers, and he cleared £5,000. For his *Odyssey* he was paid less, receiving £600, or £100 for each book, and, having paid his collaborators £700, he cleared £4,500.

7 The conjunctive particle 'but'.

8 Mme. Anne Dacier's *Les Oeuvres d'Homère traduites en Français avec des remarques* appeared in 1711. Eustathius (fl. twelfth century A.D.) was Archbishop of Thessalonica and wrote a *Commentary on the Iliad and the Odyssey*.

9 Statius (d. A.D. *c.* 100), author of *Thebais*, *Achilleis* and *Sylvae*, poems on several subjects. Claudius Claudianus (fl. A.D. 395–404), wrote *De bello Gildonico*, *De bello Gallico*, *Epithalamium*, *Fescenna* and *De Raptu Prosepine*.

19: 'THE COVENT GARDEN JOURNAL', NO. 4

Juvenal, VIII, 32–7, with *parvam* for *pravam*: 'We call someone's dwarf "Atlas", his Ethiopian "Swan", a plain mis-shaped girl, "Europa", lazy dogs bald with mange who lick the edges of a dry lamp will be called "Leopard", "Tiger" "Lion" or after anything else that roars more fiercely.'

2 *An Essay Concerning Human Understanding* (1690), III, x.

3 *Ars Poetica*, 71–2.

4 Isaac Barrow (1630–77), one of Fielding's favourite authors, whose sermons were published after his death in 1678. His *works* were edited by John Tillotson (1630–94), Archbishop of Canterbury from 1691. Samuel Clarke (1675–1729) was author of *A Discourse concerning the being and Attributes of God . . . in Answer to Mr. Hobbes, Spinoza etc. . . .* (1705). His *Works* were published in 1738.

5 The Greek word may mean to have, hold, possess, hold fast, support, contain, keep back, hold oneself in, etc; the Latin may mean to move, drive, chase, stir up, exalt, cause, bring forth, govern, do, etc.

20: 'THE COVENT GARDEN JOURNAL', NO. 5

1 Sadler's Wells derived its name from the discovery of the wells in the garden of a house belonging to a Mr. Sadler in 1683. By Fielding's day the place had become a centre for public entertainments of a spectacular and varied kind including rope-dancing and tumbling. The price for admission was the purchase of a pint of wine or punch, after which the spectator was free to watch or to watch and drink as he pleased.

21: 'THE COVENT GARDEN JOURNAL', NO. 6

1 *Epigrammatica*, VI, lx, 7–10.

2 Cf. *Metamorphoses*, XV, 871ff.

3 Barnaby Lintott (1675–1736), bookseller, who published the work of Farquar, Fenton, Gay, Parnell, Pope, Steele, and appears in the *Dunciad*, II, 49ff. These lines were presumably written for the occasion.

4 Juvenal, XIV, 204, altered and confused. Juvenal has '*Lucri bonus est odor ex re / Qualibet.*'; 'The smell of gain is good from anything whatever.'

5 That is, damsons.

6 Cf. *Hamlet*, V, I.

7 Tibullus, *Elegies*, I, iii, 50.

8 Mrs. Ann Dodd, printer of *The Covent Garden Journal*, had her shop at the Peacock, Temple Bar; she dealt in newspapers and pamphlets of all kinds and was several times prosecuted.

9 Herodotus, VII, 45 and 46.

10 Presumably written for the occasion.

11 The piece Fielding is referring to is the fragment recording a meeting of the Robin Hood Society, published in the eighth number of *The Covent Garden Journal.*

22: 'THE COVENT GARDEN JOURNAL', NO. 15

1 *Betsy Thoughtless* (1751), a novel by Eliza Haywood (1693?–1756), whom Fielding had satirized in *The Author's Farce* (1730); she retaliated in *Betsy Thoughtless* (I, 76–7).

2 *Eclogues*, III, 90.

3 *Dunciad* (1742), IV, 1–8.

4 *Apology* (1740), 40: 'I will boldly say then, it is to the Revolution only, we owe the full Possession of what, till then, we never had more than a perpetually contested Right to . . .'

5 See *The Covent Garden Journal*, No. 3, Saturday, June 17, 1752.

23: 'THE COVENT GARDEN JOURNAL', NO. 23

1 *Iliad*, II, 204–6.

2 Presumably Monarchy, Oligarchy and Democracy.

3 That is, 'rule within rule'.

4 *Sermones*, II, i, 80.

5 That is, in a civil court.

6 Priscian (A.D. 491–518), Roman grammarian; to break his head was to break the rules of grammar.

7 Which enabled the criminal to escape from the power of the Civil Court to that of the Ecclesiastical, and, in effect, escape all but a nominal punishment by proving that he could read.

8 Henry Rolle (1589?–1656), whose *Abridgement de Plusiers Cases et Resolutions des Common Ley* was published in 1668.

9 The allegedly fundamental law of the French monarchy which excluded women from succession to the throne; see *Henry V*, I, I.

10 *The Prince* (1513), ch. xxvi.

11 Shakespeare and Beaumont died in 1616, Fletcher in 1625; Jonson thus ruled alone until his death in 1637.

12 *Essay on Criticism* (1711), II, 458–9, slightly altered.

24: 'THE COVENT GARDEN JOURNAL', NO. 46

1 Juvenal, III, 60.

2 See *The Covent Garden Journal*, No. 40, where the first letter of Misotharsus appears.

3 *Prince Arthur, an Heroic Poem in Twelve Books* (1695), by Sir Richard Blackmore (d. 1729).

4 Matthew Tindal (1657–1733), deistical writer: Henry St. John (1678–1751), Viscount Bolingbroke, a Tory politician whose friend David Mallet followed his instructions in publishing certain papers among his posthumous *Works* (1752), to which Dr. Johnson referred as a 'gun charged against Christianity'. The most important of these were the *Reflexions Concerning Innate Moral Principles* and *A Letter Occasioned by one of Archbishop Tillotson's Sermons.* When he died Fielding was preparing an answer to Bolingbroke and the part which he had finished was published with *The Journal of a Voyage to Lisbon* (1755) as *A Fragment of a Comment on L. Bolingbroke's Essays.*

5 Virgil, *Aeneid*, IX, 641.

6 That is, the pert.

7 *Carminum*, IV, iv, 33, with omission of '*sed*' after the first word: 'But care draws forth the power within'.

8 Jean Terrason (1670–1750), *Dissertation critique sur l'Iliade d'Homère* (1715).

9 Horace, *Ars Poetica*, 269: 'handle by day, handle by night'.

10 Jensen notes: 'somewhat as in Cicero's *De Republica*, II, xxx, "*Optandum magis quam sperandum*"—"Of a kind to be desired rather than hoped for." '

25: 'THE COVENT GARDEN JOURNAL', NO. 59

1 *Carminum*, IV, ix, 26–8.

2 Cf. *Thucidides*, VI, 16.

3 *Iliad*, II, 211; *Odyssey*, XVII, 381.

4 Fielding may have meant Hesiod, Arctinius, Lesches or Eumelius. On the other hand, he was probably following Quintilian and Philostratus in thinking that Hesiod came before Homer rather than after, as others have argued. Homer himself mentions Thamysis (*Iliad*, VI, 130), but he could not be referred to as a contemporary. Probably, therefore, Fielding was referring to Arctinius, supposed to have been his disciple, Lesches (*c.* 600 B.C.), and Eumelius (*c.* 750 B.C.).

5 Geradus Joannes Vossius (1577–1649), theologian and littérateur.

6 *Eclogues*, III, 90.

7 Cf. Horace, *Carminium*, I, iv, 16: '*I am te premit nox fabulaeque Manes*'—'Which now night enshrouds'.

8 A Land Tax Act was first passed in 1689; from 1692 large sums were raised by it. The rate of valuation was established in 1692, the tax rising to 4s. in the £ in time of war. The tax was collected locally and a list of the agents regularly published in the Press. Presumably it is to these names that Fielding is referring.

9 Thomas Shadwell (1640–92), Laureate from 1688, is still widely known for his part in *MacFlecknoe* (1682). George Villiers (1628–87), Second Duke of Buckingham, who attacked Dryden in his *Rehearsal* (1671) under the name of Mr. Bayes.

10 That is, Gutters.

11 That is, Erastratus.

12 The word 'Bridewell' was synonymous with a house of correction for short-term offenders against criminal and moral law. The original Bridewell was a house given to the City by Edward VI in 1553.

13 *Dunciad*, III, 123ff.

26: 'THE CHAMPION', NO. 53

1 *Pharsalia*, II, 142.

2 Terence, *Andria*, I, 1, 34: 'to much of anything is bad'. See also Cicero, *De Finibus*, III, 22, and Seneca, *Epistulae*, 94, 43.

3 That is, Ben Jonson's *Bartholomew Fayre* (1614).

4 *Spectator*, No. 266, Friday, January 4, 1712.

5 Sir Samuel Garth (1661–1719), *The Dispensary* (1699), IV, 84–5.

6 *Orator*, XXII, 73: 'Apelles said that those painters also make this error, who do not know when they have done enough.'

7 Pliny, XXXV, 10. Fielding should have said 'Timanthes' instead of 'Timai'.

8 René Rapin, *A Comparison between Homer and Virgil*, ch. xi; see *The Whole Works of Mons. Rapin*, trans. Basil Kennet, D.D. (1731), I, 174.

9 A. Pope, *Dunciad* (1742), IV, 252–3.

10 Jensen points out that Judge Gripus was the name of a member of the Robin Hood Society during its early days; on the other hand, it was also a nickname of Fielding's contemporary, Philip Yorke, Earl of Hardwicke (see No. 6, n. 11). This reference seems to be a fictional character and is untraced.

11 John Tillotson (1630–94), Archbishop from 1690.

12 *Ars Poetica*, 335–7.

13 *Sermones*, I, i, 120, with the addition of *verbosi* in place of *Crispini*; 'Not a word more will I add, or you will think I have rifled the rolls of blear-eyed Crispinus.' Fielding seems to take *Lippi* as a name.

14 Juvenal, I, 5–6, with the omission of the line '*Telephus aut summi plena iam margine libri*'. The whole passage reads: 'Shall I have no revenge on one who has consumed the day with a huge Telephus, or with an Orestes which, after filling the margin at the top of the roll and the back as well, has not even ended yet?'

27: 'THE TRUE PATRIOT', NO. 22

1 Crane Court was the home of the Royal Society from 1710–82.

2 Mirian Locke, in her edition of *The True Patriot* (1965), 189, points out that this paragraph, together with the signature of the letter ('Torricelli Junr.'), relates to the known relationship between Evangelista Torricelli (1608–47), discoverer of the principle of the barometer, and Galileo.

3 Cf. *Spectator*, No. 281, Tuesday, January 22, 1712, from which Fielding seems to have derived this idea.

4 The initials C.M.L.S. remain obscure to me.

5 If Fielding meant anything by the initials here, Lord C——, one would imagine, refers to Lord Chesterfield, and Dr. M——to Dr. Richard Meade, whom he respected, rather than to Dr. John Misaubin, as Mirian Locke suggests.

6 J. and P. Knapton in Ludgate Street, at the sign of the Crown.

28: PREFACE TO 'FAMILIAR LETTERS . . .'

1 Ovid, *Ars Amatoria*, I, 468: 'So that you seem to be speaking in her presence.'

2 A remark which one cannot but refer to Richardson's *Pamela* (1740).

3 That is, George Lyttleton, author of *Letters from a Persian in England to his Friend at Ispahan* (1735), in imitation of Montesquieu's *Lettres Persanes* (1721).

4 That is, the Court of St. James.

5 It is tempting to conjecture that this lady was Lady Mary Wortley Montague, but there is no evidence to support this or any other conjecture.

29: 'THE COVENT GARDEN JOURNAL', NO. 62

1 Horace, *Sermones*, II, iii, 271, with some alteration: 'There is a certain method in his madness.'

2 Tragicomicus is referring to *Elfride, a Dramatic Poem, Written on the Model of the Antient Greek Tragedy* (1752), by William Mason (1724–97), published with five introductory letters which argued the merits of the classical chorus.

3 George Frederick Handel (1685–1759), German composer of opera and oratorio, came to England in 1710 and took up permanent residence in 1712. His first English oratorio, *Esther*, was performed in 1720. He became Court Composer in 1727, and, in spite of several bankruptcies and vicissitudes of fortune, including persistent rivalry from Buononcini, he maintained his position in public favour until the end of his life.

30: PREFACE TO 'THE JOURNAL . . .'

1 Zachary Gray (1688–1766), antiquary and controversialist, produced his *Hudibras . . . corrected and amended; with large annotation and a preface . . .* in 1744. Richard Mead (1673–1754), physician and Vice-President of the Royal Society, possessed what was thought to be the largest contemporary private collection of books, MSS., coins and medals.

2 Gilbert Burnett (1643–1715), as well as his famous history, wrote *Some Letters containing an account of what seemed most remarkable in Switzerland, Italy . . .* (1687). Joseph Addison published *Remarks on Several Parts of Italy* (1705) and *Letters from Italy* (1701).

3 Longinus preferred the *Iliad* to the *Odyssey*, arguing that the latter showed clear evidence of being written in declining age; see *On the Sublime*, IX.

4 *Les Adventures de Télémaque* (1699), written by François de Salignac de la Mothe-Fénelon (1651–1715), Archbishop of Cambrai from 1695.

5 *Ars Poetica*, 144.

6 Gaius Plinius Secundus, the Elder (A.D. 23–79), *Historia Naturalis*.

7 This seems to refer to an incident in Aphra Behn's *The Feign'd Curtezan; or, a Night's Intrigue* (1679); the parallel is by no means exact, but I have found none closer.

8 George Anson (1697–1762), First Baron Anson. The account of his voyage round the world (1748) was written by his chaplain.

9 Gaius Sallustius Crispus (86–35 B.C.), author of *Bellum Jugurthinium* and a history covering the period 78–67 B.C.

10 E.g. *Ars Poetica*, 144: 'That then he may set forth striking and wondrous tales.'

11 Cf. Prefaces to *Pamela* (1740) and *Clarissa* (1748).

12 Untraced, but cf. *Spectator*, No. 304, Monday, February 18, 1711–12, where Steele says much the same things about letters.

13 George Villiers (1628–87) Second Duke of Buckingham, *The Rehearsal*

(1671), II, 4: 'Bayes: "There's now an odd surprise; the whole State's turned quite topsi-turvy, without any pother or stir in the whole world, I gad." Johnson: "A very silent change of Government, truly, as ever I heard of." '

31: 'THE CHAMPION', NO. 52

1 *Aeneid*, I, 179: 'they prepare to scorch'.

2 *An Inquiry Concerning Virtue or Merit* (1699), with some adaptation of the opening words and alteration of punctuation; see *Characteristics* . . ., ed. J. M. Robertson (new ed., 1963), I, 321–2.

32: PREFACE TO 'PLUTUS . . .'

1 This is not quite accurate. As Mme. Dacier pointed out, and Fielding should have known, Aristophanes says in a chorus in Act II of *Acharnians* that the Persian King inquired about him from a Spartan embassy.

2 See Olympiodorus's *Life of Plato*, 2–3, in *Diogeni Laertii . . . accedunt Olympiodori* . . ., ed. A. Westermann, Paris (1862).

3 Plato, *Phaedon*, 70b, and *Apology*, 18–19; Aelian, *Various History*, 21; and Diogenes Laertius, II, 18–46.

4 Clemens Alexandrinus, *Exhortation to the Greeks*, VI.

5 Cf. Fielding's version of the same story in *A Journey from this World to the Next*, ch. x.

6 Longinus, *On the Sublime*, XL; Horace, *Sermones*, I, iv, 1. Cf. Preface to *Le Plutus* . . . (1684). Mme. Dacier speaks of a class of readers incapable of understanding Aristophanes, who '*donneront hardiment un démenty à toute l'antiquité*'.

7 *Pharsalia*, I, 128.

8 Virgil, *Eclogues*, VIII, 63: 'We cannot do all things.'

9 Colley Cibber, *The Provok'd Husband* (1728), I, 1.

10 Lewis Theobald's translation, *Plutus, or the World's Idol, and the Clouds*, was published in 1715.

33: 'THE COVENT GARDEN JOURNAL', NO. 10

1 *Ars Poetica*, 270–2.

2 Tom D'Urfey (1653–1723), satirist, dramatist and song-writer, was very popular at the Court of Charles II. Tom Browne (1663–1704), satirist, translator and hack, was responsible for the translation of the works of Scarron (1704).

3 Cf. *Sermones*, I, x, 24–5.

4 Cf. the Preface to *Pamela* (1740) and *Clarissa* (1748); see also No. 28, n. 2.

5 I have not traced this proverb.

6 Cf. Fielding's assessment of Aristophanes in the Preface to *Plutus*; see No. 32.

7 That is, hobby-horse, a private pastime, with some suggestion of obsessive interest.

8 *Epistulae*, I, i, 11–12.

9 'The bridge of Asses'; the fifth proposition in the First Book of Euclid.

10 Untraced.

11 There is no paper in *The Covent Garden Journal* that deals explicitly with taste, though in No. 18 (see No. 34) Fielding deals with the subject indirectly.

12 I *Corinthians*, xi, 33; from Menander's *Thaïs*.

34: 'THE COVENT GARDEN JOURNAL', NO. 18

1 Juvenal, X, 1–3, with *Vina* for *Vera*.

2 In *Animadversions* . . . (1693); see No. 10, n. 8, and No. 17, n. 4.

3 Petronius Arbiter (d. A.D. *c.* 56), favourite of Nero and the author of the *Satyricon*.

4 In fact, Pope rather than Swift, *The Art of Sinking* (1728), IV.

5 Jensen presumes these are names given to different kinds of champagne.

6 *Hudibras* (1664), II, iii.

7 This is the process known at the time as disemvowelling, sometimes attributed to Tom Browne.

35: 'THE COVENT GARDEN JOURNAL', NO. 19

1 *Carminum*, III, iii, 69.

2 Bristol stones were transparent rock-crystals found in the limestone at Clifton, near Bristol.

3 I have found no other reference to a jeweller of this name.

4 *Epistulae*, II, ii, 61: 'It seems to me very like three guests who disagree.'

5 *Albumazar* (1615), was a comedy by Thomas Tomkins (fl. 1714). *The Little French Lawyer* (1619–22?), was probably by John Fletcher in collaboration with Massinger. It was played at Drury Lane on October 7, 9 and 10, 1749, and parts of it were badly hissed.

6 Joseph Michell (1684–1738) was author of *The Highland Fair*, and Fielding's story seems to refer to its performance on March 20, 1731, at Drury Lane.

7 This seems to refer to Sir E. Sherburne's translation of the *Phaedra and Hipollyta* of Seneca (1701).

8 This story is told as it appears in Lucian's *Phalaris* I and II, where the tyrant explains his actions as stemming from a humanitarian motive.

9 Compare Cicero, *Academica*, II, lxxii, 16.

36: 'THE COVENT GARDEN JOURNAL', NO. 55

1 *De Rerum Naturae*, I, 927–8.

2 This opinion was given what was generally regarded authoritative expression by Sir William Temple in his essay, 'On Poetry' (1690), published in his *Miscellanea*, IV; see J. E. Spingarn, *Critical Essays of the Seventeenth Century* (1909), III, 103ff.

3 William Congreve, 'Concerning Humour in Comedy', in *Letters on Several Occasions Written by and Between Mr. Dryden, Mr. Wycherly . . .Mr. Congreve and Mr. Dennis* (1696), published by Dennis.

4 *Everyman Out of His Humour* (1599), 'Induction'.

5 Terence, *Phormio*, 454: 'As many opinions as there are men.'

6 *Sermones*, I, ii, 24.

7 *Réflexions sur le ridicule* (1696).

8 George Lillo's *Fatal Curiosity* (1736). Fielding praised Lillo's work in the Index to the Times in *The Champion*, No. 45, Tuesday, February 26, 1739: '. . . it is evident the Author writ less from his Head, than from an Heart capable of exquisitely Feeling and Painting human Distresses, but of causing none'.

'His FATAL CURIOSITY, which is a Master-Piece in its Kind, and inferior only to *Shakespeare's* best Pieces, gives him a Title to be call'd, the best Tragic Poet of his Age; but this was the least of his Praise, he had the gentlest and honestest Manners, and, at the same Time, the most friendly and obliging.

'He had a perfect Knowledge of Human Nature, though his Contempt of all base Means of Application, which are the necessary Steps to great Acquaintance, restrained his Conversation within very narrow bounds: He had the Spirit of an old *Roman*, joined to the Innocence of a primitive Christian; he was content with his little State of Life, in which his excellent Temper of Mind, gave him an Happiness beyond the Power of Riches, and it was necessary for his Friends, to have a sharp insight into his Want of their Services, as well as good Inclinations or Abilities to serve him. In short, he was one of the best of Men, and those who knew him best, will most regret his Loss.' Molière's *L'Avare* was first produced in 1668.

9 *The Suspicious Husband* (1747) was by Dr. Benjamin Hoadly (1706–57), physician, in collaboration with his brother John.

10 For the effects of Nero's vanity see Suetonius, *Nero*, Pliny, VI, 8, and Tacitus, *Annales*. Domitian amused himself torturing flies.

11 Cf. *Essay on Conversation, Miscellanies* (1743), I.

37: 'THE COVENT GARDEN JOURNAL', NO. 56

1 *Carminum*, III, vi, 19.

2 See No. 36, n. 7; *Réflexions sur le ridicule* (1696).

38: FROM 'JOSEPH ANDREWS', BOOK V, CH. ii

1 *De Oratore*, I, 6.

2 *Poetics*, I, vi.

3 *Epistulae*, I, ii, 1.

4 *Poetics*, II, ii: 'arrangement of incidents'.

5 *Iliad*, VI, 407–39 and XXIV, 123–45.

6 *Ajax*, 485–524.

7 *Poetics*, II, iii.

39: A LETTER FROM FIELDING TO RICHARDSON

1 Volume V of *Clarissa* was published with Volumes VI and VII in December, 1748. Richardson must, therefore, have sent Fielding Volume V before publication and, as we learn from the Postscript, without the other two remaining volumes.

41: 'THE COVENT GARDEN JOURNAL', NO. 52

1 *Ars Poetica*, 323.

2 Though advertised in *The Covent Garden Journal*, No. 27, June 27, 1752, as by Fielding and Young, this translation never appeared.

3 *The Works of Lucian* . . . (1711), 43.

4 Photius, Patriarch of Constantinople in the ninth century, author of *Myrobiblion sive Biblioteca librorum*. This quotation, according to Jensen, occurs in ch. 29: 'nevertheless he is best in style'.

5 Cf. No. 32.

6 *The Works of Lucian* . . . (1711), 43–4.

7 See No. 18, n. 2.

8 *Works of Lucian* . . . (1711), 36–7.

9 Johann Georg Graefe (1632–1703), scholar and humanist; Desiderius Erasmus (1466–1536), Dutch scholar and theologian; Nicholas Perrot, Sieur D'Ablancourt (1600–4), who edited and freely translated Lucian's works (1654–1655); Jasper Mayne (1604–72), Archdeacon of Chichester, translated Lucian's *Dialogues* in 1664.

10 Marcus Aurelius appointed Lucian to the post of Registrar to the Government of Egypt.

11 *Works of Lucian* . . . (1711); a conflation of separate passages on p. 38 and p. 41. Dryden is quoting Mayne, who is quoting Ablancourt, but Dryden quotes in English. Fielding has translated Dryden's translation of Mayne's quotation of Ablancourt back into French!

12 The other translation was by F. Spence (1684–5).

42: 'THE JACOBITE'S JOURNAL', NO. 5

1 Horace, *Epodes*, II, i, 211–13: 'wrings the heart with trivialities, irritates, soothes, fills it with false terrors, like a magician'.

43: FROM 'THE JACOBITE'S JOURNAL', NO. 6

1 The Black Act, 1722, 9 Geo. I, c. 22, made it a capital offence to poach game at night; it was directed against gangs of poachers who went armed and with their faces blackened.

2 See above, No. 14, n. 3.

3 The number is dated January 9.

44: FROM 'THE JACOBITE'S JOURNAL', NO. 7

1 John Henley (1692–1756), commonly known as Orator Henley, originally a minister who left the Church and set up as a public preacher and lecturer near Newport Market in 1726. He preached a sermon on Sunday morning, delivered a discourse on Sunday night and a lecture on Wednesday, advertising the week's programme on Saturday. He was also a hack writer and on one occasion was paid £100 per annum to ridicule *The Craftsman* in *The Hyp Doctor*, in which he wrote from 1730–9. He moved to Lincoln's Inn Fields in 1729. His exaggeration and

flamboyant self-seeking earned him frequent criticism. He figures in the *Dunciad* (1729), II, 2, and III, 195–208.

2 Anon; published January, 1748.

3 For the activities of the pastry-cooks, see above, No. 21.

45: FROM 'THE JACOBITE'S JOURNAL', NO. 8

1 Cicero, *De Legibus*, III, 23: 'It is unfair in a charge against any institution to omit its advantages, enumerating its evils and selecting its special shortcomings.'

2 Fielding is referring to Dionysius II of Sicily 'who after his expulsion from Syracuse became a schoolmaster at Corinth; so complete was his inability to do without the right to rule', Cicero, *Tusc. Disp.*, V, 2.

3 Presumably Fielding has a particular 'Snarler' in mind, but I am not able to identify him.

4 Of the two Scaligers, father and son, Fielding probably means the son, Joseph Justus (1540–1609), author of *Thesaurus temporum* (1606), editor of Catullus, Tibullus and Propertius (all published in 1577), and *De emendatione temporum* (1583), one of the earliest analytical and textual critics.

5 *Sermones*, I, x, 1–4: 'Certainly I did say that the verses of Lucilius run on with halting foot. Who is a partisan of Lucilius so in and out of season as not to confess this? and on the same page the same poet is praised because he rubbed the city down with much salt.'

6 Henry Pelham (1695–1754), mediator between his brother the Duke of Newcastle and Sir Robert Walpole, was Prime Minister jointly with his brother from 1743. Hardwicke (see No. 6, n. 11) had recently been responsible for the presentation of a memorandum which urged the dismissal of Carteret (1744). He was Lord Chancellor in 1748.

7 John Sheffield, Duke of Buckingham, *Essay on Poetry* (1682), 235.

8 *Spectator*, No. 303, Saturday, February 16, 1712.

9 *Ars Poetica*, 351–2: 'But when there are more beauties in a poem, I shall not be offended by a few blots.'

10 Fielding, always a staunch Whig, had opposed authority only when it was represented by Sir Robert Walpole. During Walpole's supremacy he had supported the Opposition. When Walpole fell he did not oppose the Pelham-Carteret administration which followed, and enthusiastically supported the reconstructed Pelham Government which came into power in November, 1744, which contained several of his friends, including Lyttleton and Pitt, and successfully dealt with the Jacobite Rebellion. *The Jacobite's Journal* was largely designed to defend the Ministry against what Fielding felt to be criticism produced by mere party bitterness.

46: FROM 'THE JACOBITE'S JOURNAL', NO. 10

1 *Miss in her Teens* (1747) was by David Garrick (see Appendix I, n. 5); *The Constant Couple; or a Trip to the Jubilee* (1699) was by George Farquar. Since 1747 Garrick had been managing Drury Lane in conjunction with James Lacey.

2 Susannah Maria Cibber (1714–66), Margaret (or Peg) Woffington (1714–66) and Catherine Clive, whom Fielding had known as Miss Raftor, who had

often acted in his plays and to whom he dedicated *The Intriguing Chambermaid* (1734).

3 This is a reference to the activities of Samuel Foote (1720–77), actor and dramatist. He had been acting at the Haymarket until the theatre was closed by magistrates under the Licensing Act of 1737 and after this he practised several successful devices to evade the law. On April 25, 1747, he invited his friends for a 'dish of chocolate'—later a dish of tea—during which they were entertained by his impudent impersonations of eminent men and women. See No. 55.

4 I do not know to which actor Fielding is referring.

5 A reference to W. Horsly, who opposed the Pelham administration in *The Daily Gazeteer* under the name of The Fool; see also No. 54.

6 See Nos. 48 and 49.

47: FROM 'THE JACOBITE'S JOURNAL', NO. 11

1 *A Critical, Expatiatory and Interesting Address to a certain Right Honourable Apostate on his present unaccountable conduct at this critical juncture* (1747), published by H. Carpenter, dedicated to the Earl of Chesterfield and directed against George Lyttleton.

2 Porcupine Pelagius was the pseudonym under which a number of coarsely satyrical poems were published; they were probably written by one Macnamara Morgan, but Fielding thought that the *'Piscopade* (1748) was by the author who wrote for *Old England* under the name of Argus Centoluci. See No. 49, n. 3.

3 'The law does not care about trifles.'

4 William Murray (1705–93), afterwards Lord Mansfield, whose appointment as Solicitor-General in 1743 had been the occasion of an attack by Porcupine in his *Causidicade* (1743). See also Appendix I.

5 *Venice Preserved* (1682), by Thomas Otway.

6 Mary Cooper succeeded her husband Thomas as bookseller and printer in Paternoster Row and printed a good deal of Fielding's work. Who Thomas Snouch was, or was supposed to be, is obscure, but the pamphlet concerned is the anonymous *D——ry L——ne P——yh——se Broke Open. In a Letter to Mr. G——* (1748).

7 *The State of the Nation for the year* 1747, *and respecting* 1748; *inscribed to a member of the present Parliament* (1747) was by John Carteret, Earl of Granville.

48: FROM 'THE JACOBITE'S JOURNAL', NO. 12

1 Thomas Carte (1686–1754), historian, produced the first volume of his widely advertised and subsidized *History of England* in December, 1747. Unfortunately, he published a footnote on p. 291 in which a story was told about a supposed cure of one Christopher Lovell of the King's Evil, by the touch of the Pretender. He continued to publish his history (Vol. 2, 1750, Vol. 3, 1752, Vol. 4, 1755), but by the time that Fielding and other critics had finished with him he had become a laughing-stock.

2 Carte had written that Dr. Lane, 'an eminent physician' in Bristol, 'whom I visited on my arrival, told me of this cure, as the most wonderful thing that ever happened; and pressed me as well to see the man upon whom it was per-

formed, as to talk about his case with Mr. *Samuel Pye*, a very skilful surgeon, and I believe still living in that city'. Samuel Pye has some further claim to immortality by means of his pamphlet, *Some Observations on the Several Methods of Lithotomy. In a Letter to Dr. J. Lane* (1724).

3 Burnett does not suggest that Charles II was a Deist, but that he was devious and unreliable in his religious belief, and that he had scant respect for the Church. See *The History of My Own Times* (1724–34), III, xii, sec. 508, and III, xvii, sec. 614–15.

4 Saturday, February 13, 1748, was the date of the first performance of Edward Moore's *The Foundling* (see No. 52). The audience seems to have objected to the character of Faddle (played by Macklin).

5 *The London Evening Post*, a Jacobite newspaper appearing thrice weekly, attacked Fielding frequently, e.g. March 12–15, 29–31, April 7–9, July 28–30, September 13–15, 17–20, etc. See Cross, II, 84. No. 3165 of the paper, for Thursday February 18, 1748, included on its title-page the following: 'LONDON/ A MOTTO, to fill up the void space in the Frontispiece of the JACOBITE JOURNAL./ Ass as thou art, Thou wouldst not have to *eat*,/Did not the LONDON EV'NING *give Thee Meat*.' This is followed by a verse which closes with a slighting reference to 'WILD's Historian'. The same page contains, under the title 'From the FOOL. No. 255', a virulent attack on Fielding as a Ministerial hack.

49: FROM 'THE JACOBITE'S JOURNAL', NO. 13

1 It was in the *General Evening Post* for January 7 that public attention was first drawn to Carte's unfortunate footnote, in a letter from 'Amicus Veritatis', who wrote from Bristol.

2 William Beckett (1684–1783), a founder member of the Society of Antiquaries, author of *An Enquiry . . . with a Collection of Records* (1722), in which he was helped by John Anstis the elder (1668–1744), heraldic writer.

3 *Old England; Or, The Constitutional Journal*, later *The Broad-Bottom Journal*, was edited by William Guthrie (1708–70), who received a pension of £200 from the Pelham administration. Fielding is, however, referring here to W. Horsly. See No. 46, n. 10.

4 There does not seem to be a record of Mrs. Cibber's benefit. Peggy was presumably Dame Trottplaid, depicted with her husband in the title-page illustration to the *Journal* riding behind him on a donkey.

50: FROM 'THE JACOBITE'S JOURNAL', NO. 14

1 *A Dissertation upon Parties; in several letters to Caleb D'Anvers Esq., dedicated to the Right Honourable Sir Robert Walpole* (1735) was by Henry St. John, Viscount Bolingbroke. I have not traced the pamphlet which claimed to be by the same author.

51: FROM 'THE JACOBITE'S JOURNAL', NO. 15

1 'Not found.'

2 See No. 47, n. 2. *The Causidicade* and *The Triumvirade* were both published in 1743, *The Processionade* in 1746.

3 The Press had been asserting that the Pelham Administration was about to bring in repressive censorship and *Old England* had been in the forefront of the campaign against it; see *The Importance of the liberty of the press, reprinted from Old England*, a pamphlet published by M. Cooper in March, 1748. See also No. 52.

4 *Epistulae*, II, i, 148–54, with some alteration of word-order and *condit* for *condic*.

5 Philip Francis (1708?–73), translator and editor, produced parallel text editions of Horace in 1742 and 1746. Fielding is quoting from his verse translation (1747).

6 See No. 47, n. 4; the person referred to is William Murray.

7 Untraced; 'Who slanders, makes an outcry against himself'.

8 Ausonius, *Epistulae*, XIV, 102–3: 'No more hereafter shalt thou dread the universal cry, "This is that false poet, Theon."'

9 See No. 52.

10 On Monday, March 14, 1748, Peg Woffington played the leading role in *Jane Shore* for the first time.

52: FROM 'THE JACOBITE'S JOURNAL', NO. 16

1 Edward Moore (1712–57), author of *The Foundling*, which was badly received on its first performance on Saturday, February 13, 1748, because the audience disliked the character of Faddle. Garrick played Young Belmont; Macklin, Faddle; Barry, Sir Charles Raymond-Havard; Yates, Colonel Havard; Peg Woffington, Rossetta; Mrs. Cibber, Fidelia.

2 Horace, *Ars Poetica*, 93. 'Yet at times even Comedy raises her voice.'

3 Sir Richard Steele's *The Conscious Lovers* (1722), was based on the *Andria* of Terence.

4 Sir John Vanburgh's *The Provok'd Wife* (1697) was performed at Drury Lane on Monday, March 21, 1748. In the afterpiece Mrs. Cibber sang 'the Irish Song Ellen a Roon' by special request.

53: FROM 'THE JACOBITE'S JOURNAL', NO. 20

1 Cf. *The Jacobite's Journal*, No. 17, where Fielding declared that he would no longer maintain the Jacobite persona. 'In plain fact, I am weary of personating a character for whom I have so solemn a contempt.' '*Orange* Colours' refers to the Hanoverian cause, after William of Orange. The '*Fool's Coat*' may be a particular reference to W. Horsly, as well as a general one to Jacobitism.

2 This anonymous pamphlet was published on January 19, 1748.

3 *Paradise Lost*, IV, 821.

54: FROM 'THE JACOBITE'S JOURNAL', NO. 21

1 *Ars Poetica*, 139. 'Mountains will labour, a laughter-moving mouse will be born.'

2 This word is imperfect in the original.

3 Thomas Herring (1693–1757), showed great zeal for the Hanoverian and

Whig cause during the Jacobite Rebellion and raised £40,000 to aid the Government. He was created Archbishop in 1747.

4 Visitations refer to regular inspections of parish or diocese by ecclesiastical authorities; procurations were sums of money paid by the parish or diocese on the occasion of a visitation.

5 Seneca, *Epistulae,* I, iv, 67–8: 'If you know something better than these precepts, pass it on my good fellow. If not, join me in following these.'

6 The orator is unidentified. 'If I have said anything rightly, that is what I wanted to do, if I have not, then it was that I was unable.'

7 William Mills and his wife played Heartfree and Belinda in Sir John Vanbrugh's *The Provok'd Wife*, at Drury Lane on Monday, April 25, 1748.

55: FROM 'THE JACOBITE'S JOURNAL', NO. 22

1 That is, Samuel Foote; see No. 46, n. 3.

2 Foote's repertoire included imitations of Sir Thomas de Veil, Bow Street magistrate, Christopher Cock, a famous auctioneer and Orator Henley. I have not identified the Poet or the Lord.

3 That is, the Licensing Act of 1737.

4 See No. 54.

5 Sir Thomas de Veil is the magistrate referred to here, but I have not identified the young nobleman.

6 'against good manners'.

7 Untraced.

56: FROM 'THE JACOBITE'S JOURNAL', NO. 26

1 *Observations on the Probable Issue of the Congress at Aix la Chapelle. In a Letter to a friend* (1748), published by R. Montague and M. Cooper.

2 The title-page of the pamphlet bears an epigraph from Demosthenes.

3 Perhaps *Some Observations on the present Plan of Peace Occasion'd by two papers, published in the Gazeteer; intitled An Impartial Review of the Present State of Affairs in Europe . . .* (1736), published by H. Haines.

4 *The Foundling Hospital for Wit* appeared in several numbers from 1743, the first edited by Samuel Silence, the rest by Timothy Silence.

57: FROM 'THE JACOBITE'S JOURNAL', NO. 27

1 James Thomson (1700-48), author of *The Seasons* (1726–30) and *The Castle of Indolence: an Allegorical Poem, Written in Imitation of Spenser* (1748), which contained praise of George Lyttleton.

2 Presumably a legal tag, meaning something like 'not held to be property'.

58: FROM 'THE JACOBITE'S JOURNAL', NO. 33

1 *The Trial of Selim the Persian* was by Fielding's friend, Edward Moore. It related to George Lyttleton and contained abuse of many of the novelist's journalistic enemies, together with some well-directed praise: 'Upon this Plan, a

Champion rose, / Unrighteous Greatness to oppose, / Proving the Man *inventus non est*, / Who trades in Pow'r, and still is honest . . .'.

2 *Ars Poetica*, 136.

3 *Selim* . . ., 11–60.

59: PREFACE TO 'JOSEPH ANDREWS'

1 *Poetics*, I, vi.

2 *Poetics*, II, ii.

3 That is, Fénelon; see No. 30, n. 4.

4 *Clélie* (1654–60) and *Artamène ou le Grande Cyrus* (1649–53) were by Madeleine de Scudéry; *Astrée* (1607–27) was by Honoré D'Urfé; *Cléopatre* (1647–56) and *Cassandre* (1642–5) were by Gauthier Costes de La Calprenède. These were among the most famous of the French heroic romances.

5 *Sensus Communis; An Essay on the Freedom of Wit and Humour* (1709), I, v; see *Characteristics* . . ., ed. J. M. Robertson (new ed., 1963), 51–2.

6 *Réflexions sur le ridicule* . . . (1696). See No. 36, n. 7, and No. 37, n. 2.

7 William Congreve, 'On Pleasing, An Epistle to Sir Richard Temple', 62–4.

60: FROM JOSEPH ANDREWS, BOOK III, CH. i

1 Bulstrode Whitelock (1605–75), author of *Memorials of the English Affairs from the Beginning of the Reign of Charles I* . . . (1682); Laurence Echard (1670?–1730?), author of *The History of the Revolution and the Establishment of England in the year* 1688 (1725) and of *An Abridgement of Sir Walter Raleigh's History of the World in Five Volumes* (1700); Paul de Rapin de Thoyras (1671–1725), author of *Histoire d'Angleterre* (1724), translated by Nicholas Tindal between 1723 and 1731.

2 *Don Quixote*, I, ii, ch. 12–14.

3 Cardenio and Fernando appear throughout *Don Quixote* from I, iii, chs. 23–4. Anselmo, Camilla and Lothario are characters in the novel *The Curious Impertinent*, I, iv, chs. 33–5.

4 Alain Le Sage (1668–1747), *Gil Blas* (1715–35), II, chs. 3–4.

5 *Gil Blas*, VII, chs. 2–4; IV, ch. 8.

6 Paul Scarron (1610–60), *Le Roman Comique* (1651–7); Pierre Carlet de Chamblain de Marivaux (1688–1763), *Histoire de Marianne* (1731–41), and *Le Paysan Parvenu* (1735–6).

7 Referring to the use of the fable of Atlantis by political and philosophical writers, but particularly to works on the model of Mrs. Manley's *The New Atlantis* (1709).

8 Jean Louis Guez de Balzac (1594–1654), *Deux Discours envoyez à Rome, à monseigneur le cardinal Benevoglio* (1627), II.

9 Voltaire, *Letters Concerning the English Nation* (1734), trans. J. Lockman (by arrangement, before French publication, 1733), Letter XVIII, 'On Tragedy': 'But then it must be also confess'd that the stilts of the figurative style on which the *English* Tongue is lifted up, raises the Genius at the same time very far aloft, tho' with an irregular Pace' (p. 178).

10 *Paradise Lost*, I, 542.

11 Juan de Mariana (1536–1623), *Historia General de Espana* (1601), trans. 1699. See also Appendix I, n. 3.

12 Presumably Lord Chesterfield and Ralph Allen.

61: PREFACE TO 'DAVID SIMPLE'

1 Cf. Appendix I, n. 14.

2 That is, of course, the legal profession. Fielding had enrolled in the Middle Temple in 1737 and was called to the Bar on June 20, 1740.

3 By Porcupine Pelagius. See No. 47, n. 2.

4 *Le Lutrin* (Books 1–4, 1674, 5–6, 1683) was by Nicholas Boileaux-Despreaux (1636–1711).

5 Theophrastus (d. *c.* 287 B.C.), author of the 'Characters', which had a wide influence on early fiction-writers and were imitated by Jean de La Bruyère (1645–96), in his *Caractéres de Théophraste traduits du grec, avec les Caractères ou les Moeurs de ce siècle* (1688).

62: FROM 'TOM JONES', BOOK I, CH. i

1 Calipash and calipee, the parts near the upper and lower shell of the turtle respectively; esteemed as delicacies.

2 *Essay on Criticism* (1711), 297–8.

3 Heliogabalus (A.D. *c.* 201–22), profligate Roman Emperor from A.D. 218–22. Cross identified the cook mentioned here with a man called Lebeck; see Cross, II, 105.

4 Loosely, to add piquancy and variety.

63: FROM 'TOM JONES', BOOK II, CH. i

1 An obvious reference to Colley Cibber's *Apology*.

2 Lucretius, *De Rerum Naturae*, III, 833–7; Fielding several times refers to the translations of Thomas Creech (1659–1700).

3 For Fielding's opinion of the State Lotteries, their conduct and effect, see *The Lottery. A Farce* (1732) and Cross, I, 166–7.

4 Such as, Fielding implies, James II was and his son would be. English Jacobites often based their case on the idea of divine right.

64: FROM 'TOM JONES', BOOK IV, CH. i

1 Cf. No. 30, n. 12, where Fielding refers this statement to Addison.

2 Untraced.

3 Samuel Butler, *Hudibras* (1663), I, i: 'Thou that with ale, or viler liquors,/ Did'st inspire Withers, Pryn, and Vickers.'

4 Cf. Pope's *Iliad*, II, 4: 'the ever-watchful eye of Jove.'

5 See *An Essay Concerning Human Understanding* (1690), II, 9.

6 Fielding is describing an incident which must have taken place during the joint management of Drury Lane by Wilks, Cibber and Booth, the latter of whom played the part of King Pyrrhus in Ambrose Philips's *The Distrest Mother* (1712).

65: FROM 'TOM JONES', BOOK V, CH. i

1 Electors might be brought from a distance to attend an election, and would be entertained free by the candidate for whom they were expected to vote. The custom survived long enough to be recorded in *Pickwick Papers* (1836–7), ch. 13.

2 Horace, *Ars Poetica*, 189–90: 'Let no play be either shorter or longer than five acts. . . .'

3 'Whoever is skilled in his own art is to be trusted.'

4 Virgil, *Aeneid*, VI, 663.

5 That is, John Rich. See No. 8, n. 2.

6 *Ars Poetica*, 359–60.

7 For Oldmixon, see No. 14, n. 7.

8 *Dunciad*, 93.

9 Sir Richard Steele, *Tatler*, No. 38, Thursday, July 7, 1709.

66: FROM 'TOM JONES', BOOK VII, CH. i

1 André Dacier (1651–1722), translator and critic. Fielding is referring to a passage in the thirty-first note to ch. xxv of his translation of the *Poetics* (1692). See *Aristotle's Art of Poetry . . . with Mr. D'Acier's Notes Translated from the French* (1705), 426–7: 'There are two sorts of these Impossibilities, that are within the Bounds of Probability. . . .'

2 Cf. 'Postscript' to the *Odyssey* (1726): 'And it may be said for the credit of these fictions that they are beautiful dreams, or if you will, the dreams of Jupiter himself.' Cf., also, Preface to the *Iliad* (1715).

3 *Ars Poetica*, 191.

4 *A Letter Concerning Enthusiasm* (1707), I; see *Characteristics . . .*, ed. J. M. Robertson (new ed., 1963), 6.

5 Cf. No. 65, n. 3, and the lines which follow: 'Assist me but this once, I 'mplore,/And I shall trouble thee no more.'

6 Cf. *Poetics*, III, vi.

7 Herodotus, VII, 60–99; Flavius Arrianus (second century A.D.), *The Expedition of Alexander.*

8 Charles XII of Sweden (1682–1718) stormed the camp of Peter the Great at Narva on November 30, 1700, killing 30,000 men.

9 The ghost of Villiers appears in *The History of the Rebellion* (1702–4), I, 89–93. Daniel Defoe's pamphlet, *The True History of the Apparition of one Mrs. Veale . . . which Aparition recommended the perusal of Drelincourt's Book of Consolation against the Fears of Death*, was written in 1706. Charles Drelincourt (1595–1669) published his book in 1669. It was widely believed until recently that Defoe's account was a fabrication for the purpose of advertising Drelincourt's work. For an examination of it in this light, see *Sir Walter Scott on Novelists and Fiction* (1968), ed. I. Williams, 175–80.

10 *Ars Poetica*, 188: 'I discredit and abhor'.

11 Suetonius, VI, 34.

12 I have found no other reference to this murder.

13 Persius, *Sermones*, I, 2.

14 Presumably Ralph Allen, to whom *Tom Jones* was dedicated.

15 Untraced.

16 A. Pope, *The Art of Sinking* . . . (1728), V: 'And since the great end of all poetry is to mingle truth and fiction in order to join the credible with the surprising . . .'.

17 This is a reference to the public reception of Lady Charlotte in Fielding's *The Modern Husband* (1732); see No. 3, n. 3.

67: FROM 'TOM JONES', BOOK IX, CH. i

1 Nicholas Rowe (1674–1718), dramatist and editor of Shakespeare (1709); Fielding is referring to his play, *The Tragedy of Jane Shore. Written in imitation of Shakespeare's Style* (1714). Horace, *Epistulae*, II, i, 117.

2 *Ars Poetica*, 408–11.

3 I have not traced this reference; but Cf. Lord Shaftesbury, *Advice to an Author* (1710), III, ii. See *Characteristics* . . ., ed. J. M. Robertson (new ed., 1963), 197–212.

4 *Ars Poetica*, 408–11.

5 Ibid.

6 Philip Miller (1692–1771), author of *The Gardener's Dictionary* (1731–9).

7 *Ars Poetica*, 102–3.

68: FROM 'TOM JONES', BOOK X, CH. i

1 Sir Epicure Mammon belongs to Ben Jonson's *The Alchemist* (1610), Sir Fopling Flutter to Sir George Etherege's *The Man of Mode* (1676), and Sir Courtly Nice to the play named after him by John Crowne (1685).

2 Juvenal, IV, 2.

3 Cf. *Ars Poetica*, 353 (and No. 70, n. 4): '*quas . . . / . . . humana parum cavit natura*'—'which human frailty has failed to avert'.

69: FROM 'TOM JONES', BOOK XI, CH. i

1 Slightly misquoted from *Othello*, III, 3.

2 Cf. *Macbeth*, IV, 3.

3 'in a literary court'; Fielding may be referring to either of the Dacier's, husband or wife, though probably to the former. René Le Bossu (1631–80), author of *Traité du poème épique* (1675).

4 *Ars Poetica*, 351–4; cf. No. 69, n. 2.

5 *Epigrammatica*, I, xvi.

70: FROM 'TOM JONES', BOOK XII, CH. i

1 Antoine Banier (1673–1741), *La mythologie et les fables expliquées par l'histoire* (1738); Cross suggests (III, 336–7), that Fielding may have been involved with the translation of this work, published by Miller in 1739 and advertised in *The Jacobite's Journal*.

2 That is, hospital or other charitable institution for the relief of the poor and the sick.

3 James Moore Smythe (1702–34); the lines concerned now stand as 243–8 of *Moral Essays*, II. Pope had given permission to Moore to use them in his play, *The Rival Modes* (1727); although he later withdrew the permission, Moore insisted on using them and for this and other actions earned himself a place in the *Dunciad*. See *The Dunciad Variorum* (1729), Index.

71: FROM 'TOM JONES', BOOK XIV, CH. i

1 William Pitt the Elder (1708–78) was at Eton with Fielding, an associate of Chesterfield, Lyttleton and Pelham, and was included in the latter's Administration in November, 1746.

2 Edward Bysshe (fl. 1712), *The Art of English Poetry* (1702).

3 Cf. Cicero, *Tusc. Disp.*, I, 18: 'Whatever a man has learned, let him exercise himself in that art.'

4 John Essex, *The Young ladies conduct: or, rules for education . . .* (1722).

5 John Broughton (1705–89), known as the father of English pugilism, occupied a booth in the Tottenham Court Road until 1742, when he set up an establishment off Oxford Street. Broughton was patronized by the Duke of Cumberland until he lost his last fight on April 11, 1750, during which he lost his sight.

6 *Moral Essays*, II, 2.

72: FROM 'THE COVENT GARDEN JOURNAL', NOS. 7 AND 8

1 *Ars Poetica*, 156.

2 Ibid., 333.

3 A reference to Fielding's notorious error in forgetting to restore Amelia's damaged nose after her early accident. The mistake caused great amusement at the time and substantially damaged the success of the novel.

APPENDIX I

1 *Epigrammatica*, I, xvi, 1. 'There are good things, there are indifferent, there are more things bad.'

2 For the incident which caused Fielding to feel injured, see Cross, I, 50–5.

3 See *A Journey From This World to the Next*, ch. xvii. Fielding is referring particularly to the history of Mariana; see No. 61, n. 10.

4 The eminent physician remains unidentified.

5 Fielding's friendship with David Garrick (1717–79) seems to have begun some time before Garrick's first season at Drury Lane in 1742. After the rediscovery of *The Good Natured Man* in 1776 Garrick revised it for the stage and wrote a prologue and epilogue.

6 See No. 6, n. 5.

7 At this time, January, 1743, Fielding's daughter and his first wife were both seriously ill; the daughter, Charlotte, died the following March, aged six, and her mother never really recovered, dying at Bath in November, 1744.

8 Charles Macklin (1697?–1797), actor and manager, friend and associate of Garrick at Drury Lane until 1743.

9 Jonathan Wild had the good fortune to meet with several biographers.

Fielding may be referring to *An Authentick History . . .* (1725?); *The History of the Lives and Actions of Jonathan Wild* (1725?), by J. Blake; another *Life* (1725), by H. D., 'Late Clerk to Justice R——'; or to *The True and Genuine Account of the Life and Actions of the Late Jonathan Wild . . .* (1725), by Daniel Defoe. The second account which he is referring to is *The Ordinary of Newgate, his account of the behaviour . . . of . . . four malefactors who were executed . . . the 24th of May*, 1725.

10 In spite of this explicit denial, it was clear to all contemporaries that Jonathan Wild stood for Sir Robert Walpole. In 1753 Fielding thoroughly revised the satire in order to make it more general in its application.

11 Cf. *The Champion*, No. 12, Tuesday, December 11, 1739.

12 *Jonathan Wild*, IV, ch. 9: 'A Wonderful Chapter indeed; which, to those who have not read many Voyages, may seem incredible; and which the Reader may believe or not, as he pleases.'

13 The legal profession; see No. 62, n. 2.

14 Cf. No. 62, n. 1, where Fielding withdraws this promise.

15 *The Opposition, a Vision* (1742); *A Full Vindication of the Duchess Dowager of Marlborough's Book . . .* (1742); *Miss Lucy in Town. A Sequel to The Virgin Unmask'd* (1742). The *Miscellanies* were published on April 12, 1743, *Miss Lucy . . .* on May 31, 1742, and Fielding's *Plutus . . .* on May 6, 1742. Presumably Fielding was referring only to original works and so ignored the translation.

I. Index to works of Fielding

(Numerals in italic type refer to 'Notes'.)

II. Index of Names

III. Index of Titles